SEAPOWER IN GLOBAL POLITICS, 1494–1993

Also by George Modelski

A THEORY OF FOREIGN POLICY
LONG CYCLES IN WORLD POLITICS
TRANSNATIONAL CORPORATIONS AND WORLD
  ORDER *(editor)*
PRINCIPLES OF WORLD POLITICS

Also by William R. Thompson

CONTENDING APPROACHES TO WORLD SYSTEM
  ANALYSIS *(editor)*
RHYTHMS IN POLITICS AND ECONOMICS *(co-editor)*
THE COMPARATIVE ANALYSIS OF POLITICS *(co-author)*

Seapower in Global Politics, 1494–1993

George Modelski

Professor of Political Science
University of Washington

and

William R. Thompson

Professor of International Relations
Claremont Graduate School

University of Washington Press
Seattle

Copyright © 1988 by George Modelski and William R. Thompson

All rights reserved. No part of this publication may be reproduced or transmitted in any form or by any means, electronic or mechanical, including photocopy, recording, or any information storage or retrieval system, without permission in writing from the publisher.

Printed in Hong Kong

Library of Congress Cataloging-in-Publication Data
Modelski, George.
Seapower in global politics, 1494–1993.
Bibliography: p.
Includes index.
1. Sea-power—History 2. Sea-power—Political
aspects. 3. Warships. 4. Navies. I. Thompson,
William R. II. Title.
V25.M63 1987   359'.009'03   87–10472
ISBN 0–295–96502–9

Published simultaneously in Great Britain by
The Macmillan Press Ltd

Contents

List of Tables	vii
List of Figures	x
Preface	xi
The Long Cycle	xiii

PART 1 GLOBAL OVERVIEW

1	Seapower and Global Politics	3
2	Seapower and its Measurement Rules	27
3	Rules for counting Warships, 1494–1860	50
4	Rules for Counting Warships, 1861–1993	73
5	The Long Cycle of World Leadership	97
6	The Future of Seapower	133

PART II COUNTRY DATA

7	The World Powers: Was Portugal the First?	151
8	The World Powers: the Netherlands, Great Britain and the United States	186
9	The Other Global Powers: France, Spain, Russia/the Soviet Union, Germany and Japan	245
10	Non-global Powers	316

Appendix A: Naval Expenditures	338
Appendix B: Long cycle concentration values	351
Notes	355
References	357
Index	376

List of Tables

1.1	Long cycles and global wars	16
1.2	Precipitating causes of global wars	19
1.3	Global wars and principal sea battles	21
1.4	World powers and naval innovations	25
2.1	British naval personnel and expenditures, 1715–1900	30
2.2	Data collection outcome for the global powers' warships, 1494–1860	46
3.1	Primary sources for sixteenth-century ship estimates	55
3.2	Chaunus's description of Spanish warships employed in the Atlantic, 1522–86	58
3.3	Numerical distribution of global power warships, 1494–1654	62
3.4	Numerical distribution of global power warships, 1655–1860	67
4.1	Numerical distribution of global power battleships, 1861–1879	75
4.2	Numerical distribution of global power pre-Dreadnoughts, 1880–1913	76
4.3	Numerical distribution of global power Dreadnoughts, 1906–45	78
4.4	Global power constant naval expenditures, 1816–1938	80
4.5	Proportion of deliverable strategic nuclear warheads based at sea, 1960–80	84
4.6	Soviet nuclear ballistic submarines: Delta-class estimates	89
4.7	Primary sources for late twentieth-century naval estimates	90
4.8	The American share of global naval capability, 1946–93	91
4.9	Three indexes of contemporary military capabilities	94
5.1	The global powers	98
5.2	Years of high concentration of naval power	105
5.3	World powers and clusters of high concentration of naval power	106
5.4	Clusters of years with low concentration values	108
5.5	Global naval power concentration, 1494–1993	110
5.6	Proportional distribution of global power warships, 1494–1608	114

viii   *List of Tables*

5.7   Proportional distribution of global power warships,
      1609–1713   116
5.8   Proportional distribution of global power warships,
      1714–1815   119
5.9   Proportional distribution of global power sea power,
      1816–1945   121
6.1   Circulation of powers in the global political system,
      1494–1993   135
7.1   Portuguese galleons, 1515–80   162
7.2   Portugal's estimated annual number of *naus* and
      galleons, 1494–1580   169
7.3   Sailings in the *Carreira da India* (*Navios*)   172
7.4   Estimated distribution of Portugal's major ships, 1537   173
7.5   The 'Great Ships' of Portugal: *Naus Portuguesas*,
      1494–1580   175
8.1   Sources on Dutch warships, 1572–1815   193
8.2   The United Provinces of Netherlands' estimated annual
      number of warships, 1567–1859   194
8.3   Sources for English/British warships, 1494–1860   212
8.4   England/Great Britain's estimated annual number of
      warships, 1494–1860   213
8.5   British battleships, 1861–1945   230
8.6   The United States' estimated annual number of
      warships, 1816–60   234
8.7   United States battleships, 1861–1945   238
8.8   United States nuclear ballistic missile submarines,
      multiple class estimates (according to the type of missiles
      carried), 1960–93   239
8.9   United States nuclear ballistic missile submarines:
      warhead estimates, 1960–93   240
8.10 United States nuclear ballistic submarines: warhead
      equivalent megatonnage estimates, 1960–93   241
8.11 United States nuclear ballistic submarines: warhead
      lethality estimates, 1960–93   242
8.12 United States nuclear-attack submarines, 1954–93   244
9.1   Sources on French warships, 1494–1860   251
9.2   France's estimated annual number of warships,
      1494–1860   252
9.3   French battleships, 1861–1945   266
9.4   Sources on Spanish warships, 1494–1836   273
9.5   Spain's estimated annual number of warships, 1494–1836   274

List of Tables

ix

9.6	Sources on Russian warships, 1700–1860	287
9.7	Russia's estimated annual number of warships, 1700–1860	288
9.8	Russia's/the Soviet Union's battleships, 1861–1945	293
9.9	Soviet nuclear ballistic submarines: multiple class estimates, 1960–93	294
9.10	Soviet nuclear ballistic submarines: warhead estimates, 1960–93	296
9.11	Soviet nuclear ballistic submarines: warhead equivalent megatonnage estimates, 1960–93	298
9.12	Soviet nuclear ballistic submarines: warhead lethality estimates, 1960–93	300
9.13	Soviet nuclear attack and Cruise-missile submarines, 1958–93	302
9.14	German battleships, 1861–1945	309
9.15	Japanese battleships, 1861–1945	314
10.1	Three identifications of the most significant actors in world politics	317
10.2	Estimations of Venetian and Ottoman numbers of warships, 1423–1859	318
10.3	Estimations of Swedish and Danish numbers of warships, 1566–1859	321
10.4	Estimations of Portuguese numbers of ships-of-the line, 1640–1849	325
10.5	Estimations of Austrian numbers of ships-of-the-line, 1725–1859	326
10.6	Italian and Austro-Hungarian battleships, 1861–1945	327
10.7	Distribution of aircraft-carriers, 1917–93	331
10.8	Distribution of nuclear-attack submarines, 1954–93	333
10.9	Distribution of nuclear SLBM British and French submarines, 1960–93	334
10.10	Comparative naval strength about 1420 (China, Venice, Portugal)	336
A.1	Naval expenditures, 1816–1945	339
A.2	Price indexes for naval expenditures, 1816–1945 (1913 = 100)	343
A.3	Additional information on naval expenditures	347
B.1	Long-cycle concentration values (alternative index)	351

List of Figures

2.1	British naval personnel and expenditures, 1715–1900	29
4.1	United States shares of selected global naval capabilities, 1946–93	93
4.2	Emphasising seapower versus other indexes of strategic nuclear weapons, 1946–93	96
5.1	Two indexes of seapower concentration, 1609–1815	101
5.2	Two indexes of seapower concentration, 1946–93	104
5.3	The long cycle, 1494–1993	109
5.4	Long cycle I	125
5.5	Long cycle II	125
5.6	Long cycle III	126
5.7	Long cycle IV	126
5.8	Long cycle V	127
5.9	Capability trajectories in global war (1560–1650)	128
5.10	Capability trajectories in global war (1640–1750)	129
5.11	Capability trajectories in global war (1770–1870)	130
5.12	Capability trajectories in global war (1870–1958)	131
7.1	Portuguese relative capability share, 1494–1580	170
8.1	Netherlands relative capability share, 1579–1810	194
8.2	English/British relative capability share, 1494–1945	231
8.3	United States relative capability share, 1816–1993	237
9.1	French relative capability share, 1494–1945	267
9.2	Spanish relative capability share, 1494–1808	274
9.3	Russian/Soviet relative capability share, 1714–1993	288
9.4	German relative capability share, 1871–1945	310
9.5	Japanese relative capability share, 1875–1945	315
B–1	Two indexes of seapower concentration, 1494–1993	354

Preface

Our hope is that this book will appeal to a variety of readers. An explicit focus on seapower obviously signals something of interest to those who are drawn to military (especially naval) history. Indeed, several chapters discuss questions of geopolitics and military strategy. Moreover, in our tracing of the rise and fall of the maritime powers over the past 500 years we could not ignore the political and economic development of the modern world system and the evolution of its global leadership. It can nevertheless be said that naval affairs, military strategy and even the world's politico-economic history are not precisely what this study is about.

We see the book's contribution mainly as providing an empirical test for the validity of one perspective on international relations. Among the chief tenets of the theory of the long cycle of world politics are the following: (1) knowledge of capabilities for global reach is particularly useful in unravelling the ranking of global powers; (2) the concentration of global reach capabilities fluctuates over time non-randomly; (3) the capability concentration pattern is closely linked to periodic bouts of global warfare and struggles for systemic leadership; (4) the processes of concentration and deconcentration are critical to understanding the structure of global politics and the impacts of structural change on politico-military, economic and even cultural behaviour.

Our primary goal in the present study, then, is to develop a suitable data base, encompassing the past 500 years, in order to see how naval power (global reach capabilities) has been distributed, to what extent its possession has been concentrated in one or more states, and how the degrees of concentration have fluctuated over time. These are basic constitutional questions about the structure of politico-military power within the world system. As such, our efforts should prove relevant for all students of the world system.

In contrast to the popular practice of delegating data collection responsibilities to hired help or apprentices, almost all of the data presented in this book have been assembled by the authors. The data collection effort extended over nearly a decade and was carried out in conjunction with research and teaching activities at several institutions of higher learning. In the process, a number of libraries have helped with our sustained quest for new data. In particular, we are

xii *Preface*

grateful for access to the Library of Congress and the National Library of Portugal, and the libraries of the following universities: Florida State, George Washington, American, Arizona, Arizona State, Michigan, Washington, California (Los Angeles, Irvine and Riverside), and Claremont Graduate School. As usual, the interlibrary loan system proved invaluable. Suzanne Tappe's patient typing services were equally invaluable.

GEORGE MODELSKI
WILLIAM R. THOMPSON

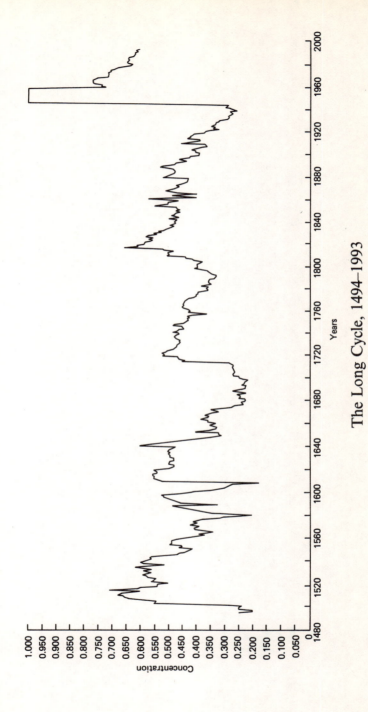

The Long Cycle, 1494–1993

Part I
Global Overview

1 Seapower and Global Politics

The purpose of this book is twofold: (i) to bring together, under one cover, the basic data on the strength of the world's major navies between 1494 and 1993, and (ii) to shed light upon the exercise of leadership in global politics in the same time-span.

These two purposes are, in the first place, independent of each other. The collection of data on the navies is a major undertaking deserving of sustained attention in its own right. Navies are functionally differentiated, continuing, and large-scale organisations of military forces operating on or about the seas. As such, they are essential components of the modern global political system. Systematic knowledge about their composition and operation constitutes essential knowledge about global politics. The gathering of the data to give us that knowledge has not so far been attempted. Apart from world population estimates there exist, in the social sciences, few continuous series of that duration and comparable coverage. The production of this volume therefore represents initially, for all those who attempt systematically to think about world affairs, a contribution to global data analysis and management.

The questions 'who exercises leadership in global politics?' and 'why?', on the other hand, constitute large questions of analysis and interpretation that cannot be resolved solely by reference to one data set. They are, by themselves, among the cardinal questions, if not in fact the cardinal questions, of world politics. But as we shall argue in this book and have argued elsewhere, data on naval strength does illuminate these questions and indeed hold one of the keys to answering it. Navies are not the only important facet of leadership and of the ups and downs that seem to be bound up with it but they form a crucial politico-strategic factor that in conjunction with other input factors, economic, social and cultural, helps to lay the foundations (or constitutes the qualifications) for operations of global reach and implementation. There can be no global system without global reach. Only those disposing of superior navies have, in the modern world, staked out a good claim to world leadership.

The concept linking these two purposes is *seapower*. In the classical definition seapower means use and control of the sea. Use and control

Global Overview

of the sea, or the denial of it to an opponent, requires naval forces and, as argued, naval forces are also essential to world leadership. In contemporary usage seapower may refer first to a *state* disposing of major naval strength, that is, forces capable of using and exercising control over the sea. All the states considered in this volume are seapowers but as we go along we shall soon draw finer distinctions among them. Second, seapower refers to the exercise of *function* in the global system by the use of naval strength. Seapower, in that conception, is a means or instrument whose use or exercise can have global (as well as national) consequences, and that is the principal meaning we shall attach to this term in the present volume.

Strictly speaking, what we really have in mind here is ocean power. For the modern world system is, characteristically and importantly, an oceanic system. Prior to about 1500 maritime activities, including naval operations, occurred principally within the confines of the narrow seas. The Mediterranean above all, but also the Arabian Sea, the Baltic, the Black Sea, the North Sea, and the South China Sea were the scenes for a variety of activities for the previous three or maybe four millenia. Even in the presence of occasional, and largely unrecorded crossings of the Atlantic and the Pacific, and the Indian Ocean traffic between India, Arabia, and East Africa, oceanic naval power was unknown and unpractised. The advent of the modern world system was at the same time also the onset of use and control of the seas on a global scale, hence the opening of an entirely new age of seapower.

The world's seas in fact constitute one interconnected system that may be referred to as the world ocean and the new age has therefore frequently been referred to as oceanic and the mode of use and control appropriate to it would arguably be ocean power. But for the sake of adhering to usage that has been conventional in this field for many decades we shall continue to use the more general term of seapower.

THE CONCEPT OF SEAPOWER

In contemporary understanding the concept of seapower is primarily associated with the writings of Alfred Mahan, and in particular with *The Influence of Sea Power upon History* (1890). It is well to recall, though, that not just the practice but also the conceptualisation of seapower have an interesting lineage of classical origins.

In ancient Greece the application of naval resources to systematic

Seapower and Global Politics

political purposes came to be known by the term *thalassocracy* whose dictionary meaning is 'maritime supremacy' or 'rule of the sea'. This term appears to have been popularised, in Athens, in the fifth century BC at about the same time that 'democracy' (rule of the many) also appeared and both seem to have a link with the career of Pericles. The term is used by Herodotus, in his *Histories*, by the Old Oligarch in the *Athenian Polity* (both written *circa* 430 BC) and forms a central part of the *History of the Peloponnesian War* by Thucydides (the war began in 431 BC).

For Thucydides, the earliest thalassocrat was Minos ruling in the Aegean some 1500 years earlier. Herodotus, too, mentions Minos but regards Polycrates as the 'first Greek we know of to plan the dominion of the sea' 'in ordinary human history' (1954, p. 253). Herodotus (1954, p. 353) also reports that Hecateus, the ethnographer and proto-historian from Miletus, when advising his fellow Ionians on the strategy to use in rising against the power of Persia, urged them to 'work for the control of the sea'. It could be, therefore, that we owe the original concept to these Ionian scholars. But the fullest exposition of seapower is the account given by Thucydides of the Periclean strategy for fighting the Peloponnesian War.

For Pericles, the fundamental fact governing Athenian strategy was the availability of the navy and the command that it allowed Athens to exercise over the sea. His formulation is classic:

> The whole world before our eyes can be divided into two parts: the land and the sea, each of which is valuable and useful to man. Of the whole of one of these parts you are in control–not only of the area at present in your power but elsewhere too, if you want to go further. With your navy as it is today there is no power on earth – not the King of Persia nor any people under the sun – which can stop you from sailing where you wish (Thucydides, 1954, p. 160)

Athens acquired the leadership of the Mediterranean system through her defeat of Persia in major naval battles. Hers was the largest navy among the Greek states and it is those conditions that entrenched in classical consciousness the concept of thalassocracy and its primary concomitant, command of the sea. But as shown by the quotation and by Thucydides' other reports the Athenians were also fully alive to the full range of functions accessible to naval forces: their potential for being the principal source of security for the city, itself *de facto* an island; their capacity for interdicting, protecting, and

Global Overview

exploiting sea communications and using trade to their advantage ('... There is no city which does not need to export or import; and these things it will not be able to do unless it accepts the bidding of the power that rules the sea') declared the Old Oligarch (*Athenian Polity*, II, 3 quoted in Meiggs, 1972, p. 266), and their ability to support and supply their allies and to deny that ability to their opponents.

The modern understanding of seapower is in part a process of practical learning handed down from the Greeks, via Byzantium, and more recently, via Venice – an earlier dependency of Byzantium and for over two centuries a virtual ruler of that city, and in part from the Arabs who controlled much of the Mediterranean in the tenth and eleventh centuries and were particularly active in the Western basin, as is shown, for example, in Ibn Khaldun's (1967, pp. 37–46) discussion of the office of admiralty in *The Muqaddimah*, written in about 1380.

An independently evolved, but not entirely unrelated, source of maritime practice has been China. For at least a millenium prior to the modern era Chinese ships have been carrying on trade on the seas to the south. The ninth to twelfth centuries (especially the Sung dynasty, 960–1127), a period that made China the most productive zone of the then world system also saw the rapid development of great, seagoing, many-masted junks. Technological innovations of this period of increased literacy aided by the spread of printing included the development of gunpowder and the introduction of the magnetic compass. In the Southern Sung era (1127–1280), China became 'as sea-minded as never before' (Needham *et al.*, 1971, p. 476). An admiralty (Imperial Commissioners' Office for the Control and Organisation of the Coastal Areas) was set up in 1132 (Lo, 1955). According to Needham (1969, p. 109) China's navy became 'assuredly the greatest in the world between 1100 and 1450'.

Both under the Yuan (1280–1368) and the early Ming dynasties, the war fleets were large, and well armed, i.e. since 1129 with trebuchets (engines designed to hurl missiles) for gunpowder bombs, as standard equipment, and somewhat later, with bombards (Needham, 1971, p. 476). For a time, then, Chinese practice was impressive indeed. But the Confucians never really took to the sea (the great expeditions of 1405–35 were led by a court eunuch of Moslem origin) and, emphasising as they did the virtues of self-sufficiency and the superfluity of foreign trade, they did not evolve a concept of seapower. 'Systematic nautical treatises did not arise in Chinese culture or at least did not get into print' (Needham *et al.*, 1971).

Seapower and Global Politics

In West European experience the first to evolve global oceanic concepts were the Portuguese. Their strategy after 1500 showed a keen appreciation of the role of seapower, as in Francisco de Almeida's advice to King Manuel in 1508: 'In so far as you are powerful on the sea, all India will be as yours' (quoted in Diffie and Winius, 1977, p. 229). Dutch policies too were seen, by Venetian diplomats *circa* 1610, as exhibiting 'a fury for dominion upon the sea' that is 'sustained with such assiduity, intelligence and interest as to show that it is the business of all, and the whole business, strength, and security of the States' (in Motley, 1895, vol. 2, p. 563).

But it was not just a matter of practice. The concept of seapower must also have survived as part of the heritage of classical learning and preserved in such texts as those of Thucydides. These served as the primary sources for the Humanist wave that animated Renaissance Europe, including Spain and Portugal, as well as the Netherlands and England where Erasmus and More (whose Utopia was an island) were particularly influential. The Greek text was familiar to Byzantine scholars but it was also apparently preserved in the West; Aeneas Silvius (later Pope Pius II) in his autobiography recalled seeing one such manuscript dating from the ninth century at St Paul's Cathedral during his visit to England in 1435 (Creighton, 1897, p. 53). Thucydides was translated into Latin by Lorenzo Valla, on commission from Pope Nicholas II, a patron of the Humanists, after 1450. The first French translation appeared in 1527, and the first English one, in 1550. Thomas Hobbes' first publication (1628) was a vigorous translation of Thucydides, possibly at the suggestion of Francis Bacon with whom he is known to have been in close contact between 1621 and 1625.

For it was Bacon, philosopher-statesman, also Lord Chancellor of England, who in one of his essays ('Of the true greatness of Kingdoms and Estates', 1625 version) brought the concept of seapower to the attention of the literate English public: 'he that commands the sea is at great liberty, and may take as much and as little of the war as he will ... and the wealth of the Indies seems in great part but an accessory of the command of the seas'. But Bacon may also have been reflecting the pungent sentiments of Sir Walter Raleigh, a famous adventurer and coloniser who died in 1618, one of whose celebrated sayings declared that 'whosoever commands the sea commands the trade; whosoever commands the trade of the world commands the riches of the world, and consequently the world itself' (quoted in Reynolds, 1974, p. 105).

8 *Global Overview*

We might note in parenthesis that in *The Sea Power of the State*, Soviet Admiral Gorshkov (1979, p. 230) describes Raleigh's saying as serving 'now as the banner of bellicose circles of English and American imperialism'; he does however cite Friedrich Engels (1865) to the effect that 'if one dominates the sea ... this is an advantage'.

Thucydides' *History* became a basic text of English classical education in which generations of future leaders and public servants were immersed at Oxford and Cambridge, until well into the twentieth century. For how could educated men miss the obvious parallels between embattled Athens, and Britain facing a hostile continent and formidable continental military powers in the Napoleonic wars and again in the twentieth century? And how could they not learn from its lessons? Understanding of seapower became part of the instinctual understructure of British policies.

Probably the clearest reviewer of British naval strategy in mid-nineteenth century Britain was John Colomb (whose brother, P. H. Colomb, also wrote on naval warfare). A Member of Parliament during the critical years of naval rearmament between 1886 and 1906, his early pamphlet, *Protection of Our Commerce and Distribution of Our Naval Forces Considered* (1867), is still notable for the analytical clarity it brings to the discussion of naval problems. Colomb saw the command of the sea as residing in Britain's capacity to confront the only challengers of that time: France, Russia, and the United States; the forces required for dealing with them would need to be deployed in home waters. In naval dispositions the other principal functions to be met were the security of the home base, and the protection of commerce, for which a number of bases would be required.

MAHAN AND HIS INFLUENCE

The achievement of Alfred Thayer Mahan (1840–1914) has been to put the concept of seapower on the active agenda of world politics. Drawing in his studies upon the history of the British experience of global warfare between the seventeenth and the nineteenth centuries, he established it as a 'cardinal principle' that the 'true end' of naval forces is 'to preponderate over the enemy's navy and so control the sea'. His vivid descriptions of naval battles vindicated the principle of command of the sea and brought out the significance of decisive battles – the confrontations between the opponents' capital ships

Seapower and Global Politics

carefully organised through elaborate instructions into powerful battle fleets. He believed that only by battle, and secondarily through blockade involving the threat of battle, could the enemy's naval forces be controlled.

By implication and by analysis Mahan deprecated the value of cruiser warfare and commerce raiding, such as had been practised by France against Britain, and which would soon be tried again by the German navy by means of submarines. He did stress the importance of communications but thought that privateering and cruiser raids against merchant shipping never proved decisive in the British case. Most importantly he documented the role of seapower in Britain's rise to world power status and laid out in some detail what he saw as the elements of seapower but what in fact amounted to qualifications for the role of world leadership. But he also foresaw the approaching end of that role for Britain and worked hard to prepare the United States to retrieve it.

Mahan's writings established command of the sea as the primary function of the navy of a world power and the denial of that command as the essential global-war task of the navies of the challengers; by implication, the ratio of the battle fleets of the major sea powers could be seen as an estimate of the way in which such a challenge would be resolved and where the command of the sea could be found. Mahan's arguments had major consequences for naval policy all over the world but most of all for Germany, Britain, and the United States (for a concise survey see Sprout, 1941, pp. 436–45).

The German Emperor, Wilhelm II, embraced Mahan's teachings with fervour and set in motion a process for creating a powerful fleet of modern battleships designed to challenge England. A basic premise laid down in the memorandum of June 1897 (for the text see Steinberg, 1965, pp. 208–21) was that 'for Germany the most dangerous naval enemy at the present time is England' and that 'the military situation against England demands battleships in as great a number as possible'. Yet the doctrine devised by Alfred von Tirpitz (the author of the memorandum) to explain and to justify that ambitious and unsettling programme was not in fact designed to attain command of the sea in case of a war with England but merely to build a force that would create, for England, no more than a risk factor. This came to be known as the 'risk-theory'.

According to Herbert Rosinski (1957, p. 54), a critic of Tirpitz:

the essence of that theory was that as the German Navy could not be made strong enough for a reasonable chance of victory against every opponent it should be made so strong that its destruction would cost even the strongest sea power such heavy losses, endangering its supremacy *vis-à-vis* third navies, that the mere thought of that risk would act as a deterrent against an attack.

In other words, the 'risk-theory' was not in fact Mahanian because it was not aimed at gaining for the new fleet a command of the sea, and in the test of global war, it failed.[1] Its expectation of indirect political leverage, a form of deterrent effect, misfired. When the German high fleet had to face the British battle fleet in 1914 it was never strong enough to win command and had to fall back on the inferior device of submarine warfare. The same doctrinal imprecision appeared in evidence in the Second World War.

In Britain, Mahan's doctrines were seen as a triumphant reaffirmation of Britain's traditional policies. Naval writers such as Julian Corbett (1911) elaborated on Mahan's ideas while later thought, such as G. S. Graham (1965), qualified it. British naval policies resolutely strove to retain command of the sea and initially continued their adherence to the two-power standard, building a fleet of major ships that was at least equal to the sum of the two next-largest fleets in the world. In the First World War the strategy of long-distance blockade of Germany was eminently successful but the rise of other major fleets could not be prevented. The Naval Act passed by the United States Congress in 1916 authorised 'a navy second to none' and in the Washington Treaties of Naval Limitation of 1922 Britain for the first time accepted a position of parity with another naval power. That naval power was the United States.

In the United States, Mahan's influence was profound, both in the navy but also most importantly in helping to create a climate of informed opinion favouring Anglo-American cooperation. In both world wars concern, and joint policies, for the safeguarding of the world's ocean highways proved to be the first avenue of that co-operation. The concept of seapower paved the way for cooperation on laying the bases of world order and finally also, for the acceptance of a leadership role in world affairs. In current American doctrine, 'sea control' is seen as being at least as important as 'power projection'.

The concept of seapower is also basic to Soviet naval policy. For Admiral Gorshkov, the post-war builder of the Soviet navy, 'the essence of sea power of the state . . . is how far it is possible to make the most effective use of the World Ocean . . . in the interests of the

Seapower and Global Politics

state'. Gorshkov condemns the Colomb–Mahan theories as an attempt to equate the attainment of 'dominance of the sea' with the 'establishment of world dominance' and therefore sees the search for 'dominance at sea' not as an end in itself but as a way of creating conditions for the fleet to solve the tasks assigned to it: 'dominance at sea is a factor ensuring the success of the actions of the forces solving the main tasks' (Gorshkov, 1979, pp. 1, 231, 233).

Gorshkov regards 'multi-purpose atomic submarines' as 'universal forces of the fleet'. His book carefully analyses the reasons for the failure of German U-boat campaigns and seems to draw lessons from these for the Soviet navy. In asserting a concept of command of the sea he is also arguing for a balanced fleet and for the view that 'the Soviet navy is more than just the submarine fleet' (Hudson, 1976, p. 107). But his view of sea dominance seems a more limited one that stresses it only for those areas that are vital to the assertion of Soviet interests. Russia remains for Gorshkov – despite his obvious interest in seapower – 'the largest continental state in the world' (Gorshkov, 1979, p. 66) and it is the implication of his arguments that the Soviet navy is not designed to contest the general command of the sea. To that extent Soviet naval policies may be evolving along the lines earlier followed by France and Germany.

CHARACTERISTICS OF SEAPOWER

To summarise our discussion so far, our conception of seapower is a condition of active participation in global politics. It is a type of resource whose absence predisposes states to a passive role as consumers of world order.

Seapower is an essential component of world order because of what navies, and navies alone, can do. In past global wars, such as those Mahan described, or in the First and Second World Wars, the navies of the winning coalition accomplished the following functions:

(1) They seized, and exercised command of the sea by neutralising and/or destroying their opponents' navies; this is the 'sea control' function of seapower. In the First World War they bottled up the powerful German fleet in the North Sea, fought one indecisive action with it and in the end saw it sink. In the Second World War they destroyed the Japanese Navy, despite its initial successes, in major battles and through steady attrition.

12 *Global Overview*

(2) They preserved their home bases from attack and invasion and subjected the home bases of their opponents to direct attack. The latter is the 'power projection' function of naval forces. In the Second World War Germany never succeeded in mounting an invasion of Britain; the Allies' amphibious invasion of Normandy was, on the other hand, a precondition of the battle for Germany. In the Napoleonic Wars the victory at Trafalgar averted Napoleon's threat to Britain; the battle of Waterloo was fought by an Anglo-Prussian army deployed on the borders of France.

(3) They safeguarded friendly communications and trade and they intercepted the lines and the commerce of their opponents. In both world wars Germany was subjected to a world-wide economic blockade enforced by naval strength; German efforts to intercept British and American shipping proved futile.

(4) They guarded and secured essential and effective links especially with core allies and proved essential in cementing coalitions. In the Second World War they protected the North Atlantic lifeline between the United States and Britain, and they expended considerable efforts to resupply the Soviet Union via Murmansk. On the other hand, because of interception, German–Japanese linkages were virtually non-existent.

In global war conditions, navies have proved decisive in winning the contest in global proportions. In other words those defeated in the naval contest could never expect to win at the global level even if they did score regional and/or continental victories. That is not to say that land forces were not required and absolutely necessary for military operations, both at the global and the regional levels because they were, both for following up naval operations and for occupying the ground and defeating the land forces of the opponent. But it was sea power and, in the Second World War, the associated air and carrier forces that created at the global level the preconditions of ultimate success in all theatres, and should therefore be regarded as the critical ingredient.

In the absence of global war, the naval strength of the world power once again plays a critical function in protecting the *status quo* established by earlier global war:

(1) The navy of the lead power, by maintaining what is in effect a strong enough and alert 'fleet-in-being' stabilises the political order and denies to a challenger the opportunity of a surprise (or first-strike) victory that could give him command of the sea. It is therefore

Seapower and Global Politics 13

in the first place a deterrent and, at the present time, in its missile and attack submarines, an essential part of the nuclear deterrent.

(2) The lead navy forms (in part through anti-submarine warfare activities) a crucial part of the defences of the home base and (in a second-strike mode) can utilise carrier forces and missile-carrying submarines to threaten retaliation against the home base of the opponent.

(3) The lead navy protects the routes of trade (such as the Straits of Hormuz) and prevents hostile attempts to close or to control them.

(4) The lead navy limits the intercontinental mobility of the military forces of the challengers (as, for example, in the Cuban missile crisis) and creates optimal conditions for moving and supporting friendly forces (as, for example, in Korea, or in the Mediterranean).

In sum, it is a fundamental postulate of this analysis that seapower (or, more precisely, ocean power) is the *sine qua non* of action in global politics because it is the necessary (though not the sufficient) condition of operations of global – that is, intercontinental – scope.

Obviously, it is not the only condition. Military forces other than naval (and naval–air) are clearly also needed for such action. What is more, requirements for global reach in the foreseeable near future may undergo extensive change and might come to include a significant component of space power. That means that seapower is not an immutable and unalterable ingredient of capacity for world-wide operations. Its relative weight could decline. But over the entire experience of the modern world since 1500 it has proved decisive in facilitating global coordination and it will remain decisive as long as it continues to do that.

A HIGHER-ORDER POWER MEDIUM

In that same vein it is the postulate of this analysis that seapower represents a higher-order medium of interaction in world politics. In terms of the analytical and conceptual framework of Talcott Parsons (1969, pp. 360 ff) in politics 'power' is a generalised symbolic medium analogous to money in the economy. If it is defined as a 'generalised capacity to secure the performance of binding obligations' it may be seen as involving both generalisation, and legitimation.

If that were so, then seapower could be regarded as a medium of higher order than land forces, that is a medium appropriate to a

14 *Global Overview*

political system of higher degree of complexity and scope. In the same way that, in the ancient world, the transition from barter, or iron money, to silver coins (and the Athenian owl) marked a move to a new level of commercial interchange, or the changeover from coins and notes to cheques and credit cards permits a higher level of financial transactions in the contemporary world, so a shift in the relative weight of military power from armies to navies, or from sea forces (galleys) to ocean forces (galleons, etc.) also signifies turning-points in the evolution of the media of power.

Seapower may be regarded as a superior medium because it offers higher generality for the following reasons:

(1) it confers greater mobility, hence access to a wider variety of resources and experiences;
(2) it employs higher-order technology, is more expensive, and generates greater innovation;
(3) it carries a larger information content, higher visibility and symbolic load;
(4) it operates world-wide and at the global level.

In as much as seapower may not be just the means of securing the performance of particular obligations, but the condition of stability for an entire system of world order it also earns greater legitimation.

In short, seapower has been effective in exploiting, in relation to systems of continental warfare, the high ground of modern politics. All military action seeks to seize, and protect, the hills, or fortresses, because they yield mobility, efficiency, information, and access. The oceans have been so far the high ground of the global system. The operation of navies has given those enterprising and resourceful enough to deploy them unrivalled access to the world system and priceless opportunities of observing how it works; a magnificent learning experience.

SEAPOWER AND LONG CYCLES

This has been, so far, a conventional analysis of seapower, showing both the provenance of the concept and some of its analytical features. But while it is already obvious that seapower is an essential part of world politics because Mahan's most crucial arguments centred on that connection, it would also be wrong to fall into the trap

Seapower and Global Politics 15

of single-factor analysis that might follow from an all-too-literal adoption of Mahanian doctrine.

That is why our second objective is to demonstrate a conceptual and a substantive bond between seapower and an approach to world politics that has come to be known as the 'long cycle' approach.

The long cycle approach, as represented by such studies as Modelski (1978, 1987) and Thompson (1983) (for a bibliography see Modelski, 1983) raises basic questions of world organisation: the conditions of world leadership and the causes and consequences of major warfare in a framework that suggests that these basic processes might be subject to regularities that are both repetitive (cyclic), and also evolutionary. Global war, for instance, may be shown to have recurred, in the experience of the modern world, with surprising regularity. World powers, too, seem to have followed each other with unexpected yet steady rhythm. And all this while the world system as a whole has also been evolving toward higher complexity at a spectacular rate. What accounts for these regularities? What are the conditions of evolution in world organisation? These questions lie at the heart of the long cycle approach.

In fact, the long cycle approach raises essentially the same questions that Mahan was attempting to answer, questions about the conditions of world leadership and global power as they affected Britain and the United States. But the long cycle approach asks these same questions in a more general fashion, and similarly attempts to answer them in a more general fashion and in a social science context.

As Mahan correctly anticipated the United States did indeed ultimately succeed to the position that Britain held in world affairs in the nineteenth century and seapower clearly had much to do with it. But seapower, even broadly conceived, was not the only factor active in that process nor was the British–American transition of power the only such case of succession in the experience of the world system. Upon inquiry we find that Britain herself arose out of an earlier competition centred upon the Netherlands, and earlier still we find the Iberian powers of Portugal and Spain as crucial global actors, all heavily involved in world-scale warfare in which seapower played extraordinarily important roles.

For students of long cycles, therefore, the interesting problems of world politics centre on world leadership and global wars, and in Table 1.1 these are schematically related to each other. The table shows the powers exercising world leadership – Portugal, the Nether-

16 *Global Overview*

Table 1.1   Long cycles and global wars

Long cycle	Global war	Participating global powers*
I	Italian and Indian Ocean Wars, 1494–1516	*Portugal* + Spain + (England) France
II	Dutch and Spanish Wars, 1580–1608	*Netherlands* + England + France: Spain
III	Wars of Louis XIV, 1688–1713	*Britain* + Netherlands: France (Spain, Russia)
IV	Napoleonic Wars, 1792–1815	*Britain* + Russia: France (Netherlands, Spain)
V	First and Second World Wars, 1914–1945	*United States* + Britain + France + Russia: Germany (Japan)

*World powers are italicised; global powers in parentheses refer to those with less than full participation.

lands, Britain, and the United States – succeeding each other at regular intervals of about one hundred years, and there is evidence of a steadily-rising capacity for leadership. It will also be noted that these powers share certain common characteristics such as insular or semi-insular position, commercial and/or industrial enterprise, capacity for coalitioning, and also, most importantly, organisation for global reach manifested most effectively through seapower. It also follows from this that the global wars in which these powers were participating were spectacular exercises in the display of seapower in world proportions. Generalising the Mahanian *problématique*, the long cycle approach therefore asserts an essential connection between long cycles and seapower. The remainder of this chapter will spell out this connection in somewhat greater detail.

WORLD POWERS AND SEAPOWER

From the vantage-point of long cycles the first proposition we should therefore like to investigate is the following:

In the modern world system, world powers have been sea (or ocean) powers, exercising command of the sea.

This will be a major hypothesis of this study, and our object will be to demonstrate that world powers – that is states exercising world

Seapower and Global Politics

leadership – have held preponderant naval strength of a kind giving them, at that time, command of the sea in the Mahanian sense. At the same time this would also give them monopoly control over global politics. The command of the sea was acquired in a global war and once acquired, laid the foundations for a new world order defined at the close of that war. This would not mean that the world power 'dominated the world' because control over the global system does not confer control over all regional and national affairs. But it does mean a good deal of influence in setting up the structure of world politics and in defining and going about solving global problems. Command of the sea substantially aided their capacity in these directions.

Carefully considered, an assertion about the connection between world leadership and seapower is not altogether surprising. Quite plainly, a power aspiring to, or exercising, world leadership requires capacity for global reach and seapower is tailor-made for that purpose. But there is also an implication that we need to consider as a second proposition:

Changes in the position of world leadership are associated with shifts in the distribution of seapower.

The process that accompanies a transition from one world power to another or that involves the possibility of such a transition is a complex one but among other things, it is also associated with changes in the command of the sea. If the distribution of seapower is indicated by the ratio or relationship of battle fleets or major naval combatants, then adverse changes in that relationship tell a great deal about changes in the world's political structure. Our purpose will be to document such changes with some precision.

Both these propositions are important, and they are also falsifiable, that is, their truth can be denied through empirical procedures. It is by no means self-evident or obvious that states prominent in world affairs should at the same time also be major seapowers or, more particularly, that changes in their standing as seapowers should be related to broader shifts in their world influence, or what is more, over the entire duration of the modern world system. Nor is it obvious that such generalisations should in particular be applicable to Portugal, or to the Netherlands – two countries that in contemporary understanding are not usually viewed as having had much capacity for leadership or global reach. Hence, a demonstration that the concept of seapower

18 *Global Overview*

is applicable here may be a significant extension of the Mahanian thesis.

But the role of seapower also extends beyond the world powers. All global powers, that is, all powers with significant involvement in, and significant capacities for acting upon, global politics, have also been seapowers. In Table 1.1 we also list, by way of illustration, the participation of global powers in the five global wars of the modern world system. All global powers participated in the global wars of their time. All such participants have also been seapowers. The only apparent exception to that rule appears to be the role of Russia in the wars of Louis XIV – wars that are commonly seen by historians as separate from the series of northern wars fought out by Russia. Yet if we look at them closely we find that these two sets of wars are closely related and that Sweden's decline coincided with Russia's rise to the status of a major power and with the building of the first Russian navy.

We thus regard all states deploying significant oceanic naval forces as global powers; among those we might also distinguish, in any given cycle, between actual or potential world powers: those holding world leadership and others having potential or aspirations for it or having held it in the past. States deploying naval forces of regional significance, for one sea only, such as the Baltic or the Mediterranean, may be referred to as regional seapowers.

SEAPOWER AND GLOBAL WARFARE

Seapower also highlights two other characteristic features of long cycles: global warfare and innovation. Let us briefly review each one of these.

Every global war has been, decisively, a naval war. Global wars have a naval and maritime complexion because the global system depends for its organisation principally upon intercontinental interactions. Since 1500, these have been, and essentially still are, maritime, hence any re-ordering of such activities, or any attempt at re-ordering them, would have to be a matter involving naval operations, hence deployment of navies in the service of national and global purposes. It could well be that the next (hypothetical) global war could have a lesser naval component than either the last one or the wars studied so carefully by Mahan. But then it also might not, considering the role which, for example, missile submarines and attack submarines might play in it.

Seapower and Global Politics 19

Global wars have been naval wars in the most general sense because global wars are contests for world leadership and world leadership requires seapower. But global wars have been naval wars in the more specific sense for at least two additional reasons: their precipitating causes have involved questions of the command of the sea or maritime communications, and in their actual conduct sea battles and sea combat have been decisive, even climactic events.

In Table 1.2 we may study the causes that made the conflict global. In each case they were actions that constituted a threat, by a continental power, to the integrity and autonomy of a centrally-situated and maritimely well-connected zone of the world system. This did not seem to be a threat to the territorial integrity of a world power, or potential world power but principally to the stability of an urban–industrial zone crucially situated in relation both to the world power and to a powerful continental state. Thus in 1494 Italy was without doubt still the most prosperous, highly urbanised, and maritimely-active part of the Mediterranean European system and a French threat to it was countered by a series of coalition wars. In the next three cases the threat concerned the Low Countries that succeeded Italy as the world's most active and strategic zone, situated across the 'narrow seas' from England. Finally in 1940 all Western

Table 1.2 Precipitating causes of global war

Global war	Triggering actions
Italian and Indian Ocean Wars	France (Charles XII) enters Italy in 1494.
	Portugal sends fleets to the Indian Ocean after 1500.
Dutch and Spanish Wars	Spain (Philip II) occupies Portugal in 1580.
	Spain seizes Antwerp: Anglo-Dutch alliance in 1585.
Wars of Louis XIV	William of Orange seizes the English throne in 1688.
	France declares war on the Netherlands in 1688.
	France attacks the Spanish Netherlands in 1701.
Napoleonic Wars	France conquers Austrian Netherlands (November, 1792).
	France declares war on Britain and the Netherlands in 1793.
First and Second World Wars	Germany invades Belgium in 1914.
	Germany attacks Western Europe in 1940.

20   *Global Overview*

Europe could be regarded as an active zone linked by active ties across the 'narrow' North Atlantic to North America. Once again the threat to its control by a single power was enough to trigger an opposing coalition.

The role of the Low Countries as the trigger of major warfare has been enshrined in English historical memory as the struggle for the control of the 'narrow seas'. It became a fixed principle of British foreign policy, known to statesmen and school children alike, that a powerful continental state should not be permitted to control the seas around the British Isles, least of all that stretch of it between Calais, Dover, the mouth of the Thames and the mouth of the Rhine. In as much as the Rhine is the central artery of Western Europe, the control of its mouth was, historically, almost as good as the control of Europe; it was in fact a proxy for it. And keeping a major power out of the Low Countries was in fact a denial of major proportions.

It was moreover a task in the accomplishment of which naval forces could, and did, play a major part and in relation to which seapower was of major consequence. In the twentieth century Western Europe as a whole could be seen to be assuming, in relation to the United States across the North Atlantic, the role that the Low Countries played in relation to Britain and its security in the previous centuries, a triggering condition of a similar kind, based on an exercise of seapower.

We see here the conditions that define the occasion on which the lead units have employed seapower so as to move the system into a global war situation. In the five known cases the triggering concept has been a denial to the continental challenger of the opportunity to dominate the active zone and the central communications of the world system. In the first place, this principle has been constitutive of the core coalitions that have determined the structure of the system. In the second place, this has also been the principle that triggered the deterrent system in the past and might do so again.

SEA BATTLES

Not only the causes but also the conduct of global wars have been significantly naval. How important have naval battles been to the fashioning of the world system? Francis Bacon asked that question in 1625 and he gave two instances: the battle of Actium in AD 31 that

Seapower and Global Politics 21

finalised Roman rule in the Mediterranean and the battle of Lepanto that defeated the Ottomans' attempt to rule that sea.

In Table 1.3 we list the major battles that mark the several global wars of the modern period. These are a dozen battles, mostly well known and famous. Suffice to say that each had a crucial role in the conflict then underway and in the order that flowed from it. The battle of Diu marked the defeat of the Egyptian–Gujerati coalition, backed by Venice and attempting to keep the Portuguese out of the Indian Ocean. In the overture to the internationalised Dutch–Spanish wars, the Battle of Zuider Zee gave the Dutch rebels – the Sea Beggars –

Table 1.3 Global wars and principal sea battles

Global war	Sea battle	Comments
Italian and Indian Ocean Wars	Diu (1509)	Portuguese squadron (Almeida) defeats Mameluk–Gujerati fleet
Dutch–Spanish Wars	Zuider Zee (1574)	Dutch (Boissot) establish local command of the sea
	Terceira (1583)	Spain (Santa Cruz) defeats French fleet in Azores
	The Armada (1588)	English and Dutch fleets defeat Spanish attempt at landing in England
Wars of Louis XIV	La Hogue (1692)	Anglo-Dutch fleet wins command of the sea
Napoleonic Wars	The Nile (1798)	Britain (Nelson) cuts off French army in Egypt
	Trafalgar (1805)	Britain (Nelson) defeats Franco-Spanish fleet
First World War/Second Word War	Jutland (1916)	Britain (Jellicoe) forces retreat of the German fleet
	Pearl Harbor (1941)	Japanese surprise attack (Nagumo) on US Pacific fleet
	Midway (1942)	US carrier forces (Nimitz) defeat Japanese attack
	Normandy (1944)	Allied amphibious landing in France
	Leyte Gulf (1944)	United States (Halsey) sinks Japanese fleet in greatest battle in naval history

final control over the local sea space and confirmed that the resupply of Spanish troops would have to be organised by the land route ('the Spanish road') from Genoa and Milan. The outcome of the Battle of Zuider Zee was also a precondition of allied victory in the Battle of the Armada fourteen years later, when a great Spanish–Portuguese fleet sailed for the English Channel in order to effect a landing in England. While the English navy harried the Armada on the seas, the Dutch fleet, which was just as strong, blockaded the Spanish army massed around Dunkirk and prevented its junction with the Armada. Similar attempts at invasion were later defeated at La Hogue and Trafalgar. The war in the Pacific (1941–5) was the last occasion for a set of spectacular naval battles.

These naval victories for the lead powers were obviously impressive but they were not necessarily conclusive especially as regards the precise outcome of the war or the settlement to be negotiated. For example, Trafalgar meant that Napoleon had to abandon plans for invading England but it took another decade of mostly land hostilities and much diplomatic, military and financial effort on Britain's part before he was finally defeated. The (air–sea) battle of Britain stopped Germany from attempting an invasion in 1940 but five more years of sustained fighting in both the East and in the West were required to procure victory for the Allied side.

Generally speaking, the naval victories and the blockades and the landing that went with them, created, at the global level, preconditions of final victory and, at best, constituted a denial to possibilities of drastic changes at the global level. But they had to be combined with much land warfare, inevitably of a coalition type, to clinch the issues at the regional and local levels. All global wars have been containment wars where one centrally-situated power was held in check by a coalition of peripherally located forces loosely strung together by mostly maritime communications. In this coalition warfare, the capacity to land forces – for instance, Britain's troops in Portugal as the basis for Wellington's famous campaign in Spain – or the capacity to keep open the trade routes, and resupply allies – for instance, with British aid and munitions in the course of the four coalition wars against Napoleon, or in the American programme of Lend-Lease during the Second World War – have been of the utmost significance. In that sense, seapower has been the infrastructure of coalition warfare and especially of the ability to organise and to lead coalitions. In turn it has been the decisive condition of victory for the world power, in a manner entirely concordant with Mahan's formulations.

Seapower and Global Politics

The core alliances of each long cycle, moreover, have also been significantly naval alliances. The primary cases are the Portuguese–Spanish working arrangement for the 'division' of the world (1494) and subsequently, for controlling access to it through coordinated naval patrol measures from the 1520s onward; the Anglo–Dutch alliance in two global wars, and finally the Anglo–American 'special relationship' of the twentieth century cemented in the Second World War by the cooperation of the two 'former naval persons', Roosevelt and Churchill.

LEARNING AND INNOVATION

We notice, finally, that throughout the modern period seapower has been closely linked to innovation, as a powerful instrument of long cycles viewed as a learning process.

If global wars punctuate long cycles and give them their major audible beat, the periods between global wars have been times of recuperation, consolidation and, above all, exploration and innovation, the silent but powerful understratum of long cycles. If world powers reach their zenith in global wars, the sources of their achievement and the true foundations of their ultimate success have usually been laid decades earlier, in those less spectacular but nonetheless crucial years of clarification and consolidation. That is when the learning process that moves the world powers, and whose major carriers they are, takes shape and gets its direction.

Students of long cycles would therefore predict that the major innovations launched by lead units, that in turn help start that unit on the world stage, come in the two phases preceding the global war. In as much as naval capacity is technology- and knowledge-intensive and subject to innovation, we would also expect it to be a field peculiarly susceptible to innovation. What is the evidence about the incidence of major innovation in respect to seapower during the rise of lead states?

At this point, we need to distinguish two levels of innovation:

(1) the major wave of innovations that transformed the global system into an oceanic one *circa* 1500;
(2) incremental innovations that, in each succeeding cycle brought major changes in global politics.

The major innovation has been the transformation of the pre-modern, semi-isolated world into the modern oceanic system. This step-level transition hinged decisively upon sea (that is, ocean) power;

24 *Global Overview*

the basic resources for the organisation of global reach had to be naval. It was Portugal that pioneered that major process with outstanding success, and with effects that have lasted to this day. Only when global reach is no longer chiefly a matter of seapower or when space-reach becomes the basic dimension of highest level political organisation, will this epochal transformation have run its course. It might do so in the next cycle, but until it does seapower deserves continuing attention.

Secondly, we notice the periodic waves of innovation associated with the major beat of the long cycle, and these too are significantly naval and maritime. Characteristically, as shown in Table 1.4, the major naval innovations, both in the matter of technological hardware, and in the question of devising the doctrinal software, have been spearheaded by those powers likely to aim at, and likely to succeed in attaining, lead power status. This is the broad generalisation and in referring to innovation we stress not the fact or moment of discovery, but rather the process of translating the idea into operational reality, deployment, and implementation. Most generally, this proposition holds for all the five cycles, and major naval innovations such as the design and employment of the caravel in Portugal (*circa* 1430), or doctrinal development of concepts of naval strategy by Mahan (1890), in each case long before attainment of a leading position, would seem to support this argument. But even naval innovation is not the complete monopoly of future lead powers, and other states (most often closely tied to the lead powers) are also shown to have made substantial contributions.

*   *   *

The aim of this chapter has been to relate the conventional and well-established concept of seapower to the concerns of students of long cycles. We have argued that knowledge of naval forces, and of changes in their relationships, is essential to understanding long-term trends in global politics, the explanation of which is central to their interests.

In what follows, we continue this argument by first discussing how the concept of seapower and command of the sea may be operationalised, that is, translated into measurable quantities so that changes over time may be determined and charted more precisely. We propose here an operationalisation that derives essentially from the Mahanian concept of command of the sea attained in battle between the principal units of the opposing powers.

Table 1.4   World powers and naval innovations

World power	Hardware	Software	Other powers
Portugal	Caravel, *circa* 1430 Nau (Great Ship), *circa* 1500 Galleon, *circa* 1515 Naval gunnery	Ocean power, 1415 Oceanic navigation (*Regimento do astrolabio*, 1480) Oceanic base network concept (*Regimento for Almeida*, 1505)	
Netherlands	Copper sheating	Mercator map, 1554	Weather gauge Racebuilt galleon (England)
Britain I	Ship-of-the-line 'Sovereign of the Seas' (1637)	Fighting instructions, 1653	
Britain II	Chronometers, 1765–73	Pitt's system	Explosive shells
United States	Armoured battleship in battle (1862) Naval aviation (1908)	Naval War College (1884) *Sea power* (1890)	Ironclads, 1850s Dreadnought, 1906 Aircraft carrier (Britain, 1916)

26 *Global Overview*

Next, we present and discuss the picture that emerges from this operation. We ask: what does it tell us about the structure of world politics? Do our data show cyclical fluctuations of a systemic kind? Do they show fluctuations at the national level, at the level of the several global powers? What does it tell us about individual powers such as Portugal, or special periods such as the sixteenth or the twentieth century?

We close the global overview section of this study with some reflections about the future. If seapower has been essential to understanding the structure of the global politics of the last half-millenium, then the question may be asked whether the same concepts and measurements might not also be extended into the future. A good case may be made for saying that in the current phase of the long cycle we are once again in a period of innovation, when the seeds need to be planted, or maybe are being planted, that will produce those major changes on which claims to future world leadership are likely to be based in the next century. It could be that in the coming cycle seapower will no longer be the preponderant condition of global reach or that global reach will have been enlarged into a new dimension. However this may be, the lessons that we derive from the past five centuries are sure to be valuable in orienting ourselves in the next one or two.

2 Seapower and its Measurement Rules

We have contended in Chapter 1 that the primary capability resource for exercising influence on a global scale – what has been termed global reach in more recent times – has been ocean-going seapower. Indeed, one partial but very important explanation for the early but gradual ascendency of a few European states over much of the rest of the world and the very development of a global system is the fact that several European states developed the sail-driven ships necessary to project European fire-power over great distances. Part of this technological revolution was inherently tactical. According to Padfield:

> Technical superiority was not simply stouter ships and more powerful guns but the fusion of these two into an altogether new system of naval warfare. For thousands of years warships in the Mediterranean system had been rather slim, light, oar-propelled craft known as galleys, which manoeuvered in a similar way to lines of infantry and fought an essentially infantry battle on the water. However, what had evolved in the west in the half-century preceding the Portuguese entry into the Indian Ocean was nothing less than the floating castle defended by all-round batteries of quick-firing guns. Fleets of galleys were as powerless against these floating castles as armies were powerless against conventional stone castles, and the traditional way of reducing castles on land by siege operations could not be attempted because the floating castles were mobile and better able to keep [to] the sea for longer periods than galleys (Padfield, 1979, p. 7).

Padfield's tactical improvements were significant but so too was the shift in reliance away from human rowers and to sails as the primary source of energy. Mediterranean galleys could not circumnavigate the globe but the sail-driven ships of Portugal, Spain, England, and the Netherlands could and did. As Cipolla has noted:

> Exchanging oarsmen for sails and warriors for guns meant essentially the exchange of human energy for inanimate power. By turning whole-heartedly to the gun-carrying sailing ship the Atlantic peoples broke down the bottleneck inherent in the use of human energy and

28 *Global Overview*

harnessed, to their advantage, far larger quantities of power. It was then that European sails appeared aggressively on the most distant seas (Cipolla, 1965, p. 81).

And since the European technological advantage was closely linked to the merger of guns and sails, Cipolla (1965, p. 140) goes on to comment that for almost three centuries, European predominance (as well as the acceleration of the globalisation process and the evolution of the global system) was confined to (and centred on) the seas.

SHIPS, EXPENDITURES, AND SAILORS

Recognition of the significance of ocean-going naval capability, however, does not indicate an obvious measurement strategy. But an appreciation of the role of seapower does imply quite strongly that many of the conventional capability attributes (i.e., economic wealth, population size, area, and non-naval military strength) need not necessarily be of direct relevance. Much the same verdict may be passed on the volume of international trade and merchant marine size. These last two variables may well be closely related to seapower in the sense that maritime trade requires maritime protection, but we have little reason to expect a perfectly linear relationship over time. This leaves us with ocean-going military strength for which the pertinent literature suggests at least four plausible indicators: (i) Mahan's number of ships in the battle fleets, (ii) naval expenditures, (iii) expenditure on naval construction, and (iv) number of seamen.

Unfortunately, little discussion of the relative advantages and disadvantages of the four is available. One exception is Cobden (1862) who expresses a preference for naval construction expenditures and the number of seamen as the two most superior indicators of naval strength. Taken in the context of Cobden's political motives (i.e., slowing an ongoing naval arms race between France and Great Britain) his argument has some merit. But, for the purposes of operationalising the role of seapower in global politics, one requirement is paramount. Not only must the selected indicators be justifiable in terms of their validity, they should also be available for a period of nearly five-hundred years. As will be demonstrated, data on naval expenditures alone is sufficiently difficult to acquire. An attempt to uncover even more specific budgetary information over time is likely to prove extremely frustrating. Even more importantly, construction expenditures reflect efforts to improve naval capabilities. Thus, by themselves, construction expenditures give us information only on capability increments and not the fundamental capability base.

A stronger case may be made for the number of seamen. For example, the Portuguese, Dutch, and the British all experienced definite shortages of seamen at critical points in history. A number of the unsuccessful aspirants to world power status (e.g. France and Spain) also experienced their share of problems in manning their fleets at various points. Ships are of little value if they have no crews. Nor can one expect maximum fighting efficiency from ships which require a crew of 400 men but which are manned by only 200. Regardless of the merits, however, reliable data on a state's number of sailors are not plentiful, especially prior to the nineteenth century.

One partial exception to this generalisation also suggests that information on the number of seamen may be somewhat redundant if one has access to relatively more available data such as naval expenditures. Figure 2.1 plots Table 2.1's 1715–1900 data on seamen

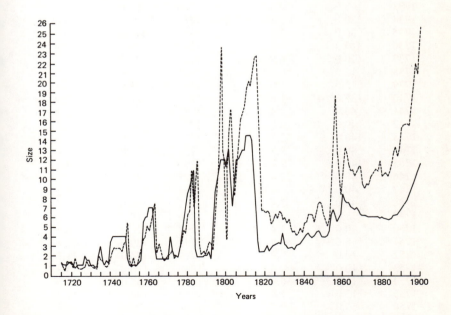

NOTES: Personnel (solid line) in ten thousands. Expenditures (broken line) in £m.

Figure 2.1 British naval personnel and expenditures, 1715–1900

30

Table 2.1   British naval personnel and expenditures, 1715–1900

Year	Naval personnel	Naval spending	Year	Naval personnel	Naval spending
1715	13.0	1.2	1762	70.0	4.9
1716	10.0	0.8	1763	30.0	7.5
1717	10.0	0.4	1764	16.0	2.2
1718	10.0	1.4	1765	16.0	3.2
1719	13.5	1.3	1766	16.0	2.5
1720	13.5	1.2	1767	16.0	1.7
1721	10.0	0.7	1768	16.0	1.4
1722	7.0	1.7	1769	16.0	1.5
1723	10.0	0.8	1770	16.0	2.1
1724	10.0	0.6	1771	40.0	2.1
1725	10.0	0.6	1772	25.0	2.7
1726	10.0	0.7	1773	20.0	1.8
1727	20.0	0.8	1774	20.0	2.0
1728	15.0	1.5	1775	18.0	1.8
1729	15.0	0.9	1776	28.0	2.7
1730	10.0	1.0	1777	45.0	3.5
1731	10.0	0.8	1778	60.0	4.6
1732	8.0	0.7	1779	70.0	4.3
1733	8.0	0.6	1780	85.0	6.3
1734	20.0	2.1	1781	90.0	6.6
1735	30.0	1.5	1782	100.0	10.8
1736	15.0	1.4	1783	110.0	7.0
1737	10.0	0.9	1784	26.0	9.4
1738	15.0	0.8	1785	18.0	11.9
1739	12.0	1.0	1786	18.0	3.1
1740	35.0	1.6	1787	18.0	2.0
1741	40.0	2.4	1788	18.0	2.3
1742	40.0	2.8	1789	20.0	2.1
1743	40.0	2.7	1790	20.0	2.5
1744	40.0	2.7	1791	24.0	3.4
1745	40.0	2.7	1792	16.0	3.3
1746	40.0	2.4	1793	45.0	2.5
1747	40.0	3.2	1794	85.0	6.1
1748	40.0	3.4	1795	100.0	9.6
1749	17.0	5.6	1796	110.0	11.5
1750	10.0	1.4	1797	120.0	23.6
1751	8.0	0.9	1798	120.0	12.8
1752	10.0	1.9	1799	120.0	11.6
1753	10.0	0.8	1800	110.0	3.8
1754	10.0	0.9	1801	135.0	14.7
1755	12.0	1.8	1802	100.0	17.3
1756	50.0	2.7	1803	70.0	12.0
1757	55.0	3.6	1804	100.0	8.1
1758	60.0	3.9	1805	120.0	11.9
1759	60.0	5.0	1806	120.0	14.3
1760	70.0	4.5	1807	125.0	16.3
1761	70.0	5.3	1808	130.0	16.9

Year	Naval personnel	Naval spending	Year	Naval personnel	Naval spending
1809	130.0	17.6	1855	67.8	13.7
1810	145.0	19.4	1856	60.7	18.9
1811	145.0	20.0	1857	54.3	12.7
1812	145.0	19.6	1858	59.4	9.6
1813	140.0	20.8	1859	62.4	8.2
1814	103.7	22.5	1860	84.1	10.8
1815	80.0	22.8	1861	77.0	13.3
1816	35.2	16.8	1862	74.9	12.6
1817	22.9	10.2	1863	75.0	11.4
1818	23.0	6.6	1864	71.0	10.8
1819	23.2	6.6	1865	69.0	10.9
1820	24.0	6.4	1866	67.9	10.3
1821	29.9	6.6	1867	69.3	10.7
1822	23.8	6.3	1868	66.8	11.2
1823	26.3	5.2	1869	63.0	11.4
1824	30.5	5.6	1870	61.0	9.4
1825	31.5	6.2	1871	61.0	9.0
1826	32.5	5.8	1872	61.0	9.5
1827	33.1	6.5	1873	60.0	9.3
1828	31.8	6.4	1874	60.0	10.0
1829	43.5	5.7	1875	60.0	10.5
1830	31.2	5.9	1876	60.0	10.8
1831	29.3	5.3	1877	60.0	11.0
1832	27.3	5.7	1878	60.0	10.8
1833	27.7	4.9	1879	58.8	11.8
1834	28.1	4.4	1880	58.8	10.2
1835	26.0	4.5	1881	58.1	10.5
1836	30.2	4.1	1882	57.5	10.6
1837	31.3	4.2	1883	57.3	10.3
1838	32.0	4.8	1884	57.0	10.7
1839	34.9	4.4	1885	58.3	11.4
1840	37.7	5.3	1886	61.4	12.7
1841	41.4	5.4	1887	62.5	13.3
1842	43.1	6.2	1888	62.4	12.3
1843	40.2	6.2	1889	65.4	13.0
1844	38.3	6.2	1890	68.8	15.3
1845	40.1	5.4	1891	71.0	15.6
1846	43.3	6.3	1892	74.1	15.6
1847	45.0	7.3	1893	76.7	15.7
1848	44.0	7.5	1894	83.4	15.5
1849	39.5	7.3	1895	88.9	17.5
1850	39.1	6.2	1896	93.8	19.7
1851	39.0	5.7	1897	100.1	22.2
1852	40.5	5.0	1898	106.4	20.9
1853	45.9	5.8	1899	110.6	24.1
1854	61.5	7.8	1900	114.9	26.0

UNITS: Naval personnel (thousands); Naval spending (millions of current British pounds). *Sources:* Naval personnel (Clowes, 1897–1903); Naval spending (Mitchell and Deane, 1962).

(Clowes, 1897–1903) and naval expenditures (Mitchell and Deane, 1962) for the case of Great Britain. A visual inspection of the parallel fluctuations in the two series provides ample support for the observation that the two variables are closely and positively correlated. Not too surprisingly, increases in the number of seamen on the British payroll tended to be accompanied by increases in the amount of naval expenditures and vice versa. It is really only towards the end of the nineteenth century that the apparent relationship begins to weaken. This, no doubt, reflects the changes in naval technology as wooden battleships gave way to a bewildering and increasingly expensive variety of pre-Dreadnought Ironclads. It does not seem unreasonable, therefore, to conclude that the number of seamen indicator falls short of providing a longitudinally reliable and independent dimension of the naval capability concept.

Naval expenditures offer a useful if patently imperfect measure of seapower. In terms of availability, data is accessible for all the conceivably relevant actors from the nineteenth century on and, for some states, information pertaining to earlier periods is available. Nevertheless, naval expenditures do suffer from several basic flaws. First, the expenditures of two different states are not always strictly comparable. Salary cost differences may be significant. For instance, at a time when British sailors were mutinying over low pay, gaps in the late eighteenth-century blockade of revolutionary France were partially and temporarily filled by Russian ships. As it turned out, Russian naval officers were being paid less than the dissident British sailors. Alternatively, the costs of building new ships are frequently less than uniform cross-nationally because of variations in labour/material costs and contracting procedures. Moreover, the budget category of naval expenditures need not mean the same thing in two different states. The accountants of one state may choose to include the costs of ordnance, veteran pensions or colonial expenditures while these same concerns may be excluded from the naval category of another state's budget.

The second major problem associated with naval expenditures involves the difficulty of ascertaining the actual expenditures for a given year. Budgets are estimated by ministries, proposed to legislatures or monarchs, authorised by the legislatures and/or executives and over- or under-spent by naval officials. Regrettably, at least from the perspective of data collectors, a different monetary figure is likely to surface at or during each of the several phases of budget determination. The problem is compounded even further by the practice of

Seapower and its Measurement 33

working with 'ordinary' (to cover normal functions) and 'extraordinary' (to cover non-normal spending needs) budget items. In effect, this adds still another phase to the annual budget cycle. Even more regrettably, both official and unofficial sources of expenditures may be reporting the figure appropriate to any one of the budgetary phases.[1] Obviously, one must exercise extreme caution in gathering budgetary data, particularly since it is clear that in some years, even governments do not have a clear idea of how much they have spent on their navies. In a few cases, they may also resort to deliberate and perpetually successful attempts to conceal their precise expenditures. Germany under Hitler and the Soviet Union after the early 1920s offer good illustrations of this phenomenon.

Other problems with naval expenditures include the necessity of employing inflation indexes and exchange rates to obtain comparable figures in a common currency. This problem is manageable only if the analyst is willing to tolerate a certain amount of arbitrariness which is inherent in utilising wholesale prices and a single exchange rate to encompass the monetary-value fluctuations of any given year. Still another source of interpretation difficulty is that naval expenditures may be utilised to pay for different types of ships. Without going into the reputed sailing and fighting quality of a nation's navy and/or the prevailing amount of corruption, relatively high naval expenditures may be spent almost exclusively on coastal defence vessels. As in the nineteenth-century American case, coastal defence resources cannot be equated with ocean-going battle capabilities.

These problems definitely restrict an analyst's ability to compare capabilities via naval expenditures. But this does not mean that they pose insurmountable problems. This is all the more true if naval expenditures are used to calculate approximate standings among a small group of global powers and if they are employed in conjunction with the fourth – and probably the single most valuable – indicator, the number of ships.

The initial image conveyed by the phrase 'number of ships' is apt to be misleading. Despite the seemingly infinite number of different types of ships built and used by navies during the past 500 years, the problems of comparison associated with counting ships, in many respects, are the least troublesome of the four indicators. Contrary to the contemporary uncertainties connected with quantifying aspects of current weapon systems (e.g., Sherwin and Laurence, 1979), naval capabilities were much easier to compare at least from the seventeenth to the first half of the nineteenth centuries. In a comparison of ship

34 *Global Overview*

lists for 1688 in England, France, and the Netherlands, Ehrman is especially reassuring on this point:

> To ourselves, whose training in such figures has been provided by our contemporary wars, lists of this type are merely a starting point for an analysis of their contents in other terms, such as those of total and individual fire-power and the performance and age of the ship. It is axiomatic to us that in naval warfare numbers in themselves mean little. But we must be careful not to read into the figures of another age more than in fact is in them. In the late seventeenth century, it was precisely and almost exclusively numbers that did matter. The quality and amount of equipment and the nature of the ship's performance were taken for granted as more or less equal within their rates; and, provided that they were in a state of repair, the date of construction was of minor importance. An examination of the lists, therefore leads us to the same simple process of addition that was practised by their original compilers (Ehrman, 1953, p. 3).

Ehrman may be guilty of slightly overstating his case for the naval simplicity of earlier times but he is not all that far off the mark. However, he is directly on target when he suggests that contemporary analysts can adopt the perspective of earlier navy capability observers who were liable simply to count the number of ships – or, more accurately, the numbers of a certain type of ship, the 'ship-of-the-line'. They were able to do this because the evolutionary interaction of naval technology and naval tactics moved in the direction of standardising the battle fleets built and maintained by the global powers and the aspirants to world-leadership. The leaders of those states who were most able both to appreciate and to adopt the changes in technology and tactics tended to be most successful at sea. Those who were either unable to appreciate, or to adopt, the technological/tactical changes by and large were forced out of the global competition or were never really in it.

Symcox aptly summarises a phase of this process in the following passage:

> About the middle of the seventeenth century, warships began to fight in line ahead – the 'line of battle' – so that the batteries mounted along their sides could be brought to bear on an enemy with maximum effect. The size of a ship now determined whether or not it could serve in the line of battle; ships below a certain tonnage were

Seapower and its Measurement

not strong enough to stand the pounding of big guns, and could not carry enough guns to reply effectively. Ships of less than about 50 guns gradually dropped out of the line; so did armed merchantmen, which could not compete with the specialized fighting ship or 'ship of the line' ... The real strength of a fleet in the later seventeenth century thus came to be reckoned by the number of ships of the line it could muster; the lesser types did not really count (Symcox, 1974, p. 36).

Symcox's point is that a more or less standard type of battleship emerged in the late seventeenth century. As a consequence, the other types of ships – the fireships, frigates, sloops, troop transports, hulks and so forth assumed a secondary importance. Rivals were not concerned with how many vessels were possessed by their competitors; what mattered was the opponent's number of ships-of-the-line, the capital battleship of the late seventeenth century through the late 1850s. Thus for at least 150–200 years of the post-1500 period, empirical comparison is simplified by developments in naval technology and tactics in the second half of the 1600s as well as by the fact that the technology and tactics associated with wooden ships-of-the-line experienced little change prior to the Crimean war and the relatively abrupt introduction of the armour-clad battleship in 1857–58.

This observation does not imply that the analytical process of counting ships-of-the-line is problem-free. This is certainly not the case but the problems are traceable in large part to the nature of the available sources as opposed to the intractability of the phenomena being compared. This is a problem area to which we will need to return later in this chapter and in Chapter 3. However, before the topic of source problems is addressed, a more substantial problem demands discussion. If the relative stability of the era characterised by the dominance of the wooden ship-of-the-line facilitates comparison, what does one do with the periods prior to the emergence of ships-of-the-line in the mid-1600s and after the wooden ship-of-the-line had clearly become obsolete in the mid-1800s? The point that needs to be stressed in answering this question is that the late-seventeenth-century development of the ship-of-the-line was neither a fluke nor a completely abrupt departure from earlier practices. On the contrary, it was the product of gradual technological and tactical changes which were intertwined with the progression and structural incentives of the global politics of the sixteenth and seventeenth centuries.

36   *Global Overview*

The Portuguese established their oceanic lead in the sixteenth century by pitting relatively well-armed sailing ships against the flimsy merchant craft and poorly gunned galleys of the Mamelukes, Indian princes, and Ottomans in the Indian Ocean. As early as 1502 (Padfield, 1973, p. 35), a small Portuguese fleet of eighteen to twenty ships was able to destroy a much larger but poorly armed 'Arab' fleet of some 170 ships through the application of superior fire-power. In the second half of the same century, the English and the Dutch sought to use a similar advantage in gunnery to defeat the 1588 Spanish Armada. In contrast, the Spanish attempted to apply traditional Mediterranean boarding tactics (to take advantage of their military edge in soldiers) and poorly-armed merchant ships against the longer guns and faster and more specialised ships of the Northern European Protestants and lost. Two generations later, the ship-of-the-line development is easily traceable to the mid-seventeenth century Anglo-Dutch Wars in which the participants learned that it was difficult to coordinate extremely large fleets in mêlée actions. Nor did these free-for-all fleet encounters take full advantage of the increasing number of guns per ships which the English were putting to use in their challenge to the Dutch maritime supremacy. As a consequence, the conventional line-abreast tactic, suitable only for relatively uncoordinated clashes at sea, gave way to the line-ahead tactic and the subsequent predominance of warships with a minimally competitive number of guns.

The relative stability (*vis-à-vis* naval technology) of the long lasting ship-of-the-line era was due initially to the natural size limitations imposed by the reliance upon trees (see Sandler, 1979, p. 17) and later to the resistance to change on the part of the naval leader. After all, the nineteenth-century British navy had little incentive to make obsolete their competitive edge in the number of wooden ships-of-the-line until their long-time antagonist, the French, perceived (incorrectly) that the switch to armour-clad battleships provided a seemingly realistic way to challenge the maritime leader. This is not meant to play down the causal significance of the early-nineteenth-century invention of explosive shells and the consequent need for the protection of armour-plating. But it is also unlikely to have been coincidence that the technological transformations were introduced first by a challenger and not by the prevailing leader. It almost goes without saying that the post-1860 period of naval competition, as manifested by increasingly larger or more lethal guns and fire-power and larger

Seapower and its Measurement

and more capable ships to carry them, was very closely connected to the global competition for world power.

In sum, the years after 1494 experienced intermittent change, subject to plateaux of relative stability, in the naval technology of ocean-going warships (especially in terms of naval artillery). It follows then that the key to creating warship series for this period involves making use of the technological changes in reasonably flexible fashion (depending on the time period). The product of this operation should be a set of explicit conventions or rules which will facilitate and indeed make possible the comparison of the global powers' warships and related patterns of capability concentration. Nevertheless, there is a large gap between the relative ease with which such an assertion can be proclaimed and the numerous decisions and judgements which are required to make the approach feasible. But even before this gap can be bridged, some attention must be devoted to the extremely important problem of information sources on the number of warships possessed by the global powers, especially for the sixteenth to the first half of the nineteenth centuries.

THE NAVAL HISTORY SOURCE PROBLEM

Perhaps the most serious dilemma which confronts an analyst who is attempting to count warships is one of having too many data sources. At first blush, this situation might appear to be an unusual one for students of world politics. The more typical situation frequently involves attempts to operationalise variables for which there are far too few sources. In this case, however, navies are and have been a fairly popular topic for a number of years. Navies have their own archives, their own lobbying groups, their own veterans, and even their own sub-field of history. Equally helpful, after an initial period of Portuguese secrecy, has been the relative openness connected with naval affairs, at least prior to the twentieth century. The result is a large amount of available information on warships. Unfortunately though, the information is widely scattered and a great proportion is of dubious value. Collecting data on warships thus quickly becomes a question of seeking 'reality' in a confusing field of information noise. In most cases, it is quite probable that much of the noise or poor information is unintentional.

A respectable proportion of the low-quality information can in fact

38 *Global Overview*

be traced to the ways in which navies have operated and to the ways in which states have maintained their war fleets. For example, in any given year, a maritime power will have X number of warships more or less at its disposal. The trick for ship-counters lies in estimating how much more or less. If the state has not been involved recently in naval warfare, it is quite likely that some fraction of the X number of ships will prove to be totally useless. For example, wooden ships tend to rot when not maintained properly. Another fraction of the X figure will require some amount of repair before they may be in a condition to put to sea. Alternatively, the state may not have the financial resources either to repair and/or to arm all its ships. Or they may simply lack access to a sufficient number of seamen to man their entire fleet. Thus, in any given year, a maritime power may have X number of warships, $X-Y$ number of warships capable of being used at sea (an often-subjective estimate characterised by disagreement), and $X-Z$ number of warships actually in commission. As a consequence, three different (and frequently more) numbers of warships may be used, quite legitimately, to summarise a maritime power's naval capabilities. The farther back one goes in history, the more treacherous even these figures become because of such early practices as temporary leasing of warships to private entrepeneurs, the reliance upon converted and armed merchantmen to augment the war-fleet and the maintenance of fleets of different size depending on the season (i.e., winter versus summer). Therefore, it is not surprising that one finds a wide range of conflicting figures per state per year.

The admission that there are structural reasons for poor information circulating throughout the many types of published materials which can be loosely termed naval history does not absolve naval historians from their appropriate share of the blame. Writing about the pre-twentieth century 'quarantining' of naval history and naval historians from the mainstream of historical knowledge, one analyst has remarked:

The 'naval historian' confined his researches to salt-water narratives, because that was the segment of war that interested him and in which not infrequently he was professionally expert. I would emphasize that his contribution was a considerable one, but without the causes of war, the financing of war, the diplomatic relationships with allies or incipient allies, and the movements and operations of armies, and you are left with naval history as formerly written. The student of sea power was 'in irons' (Graham, 1965, pp. 2–3).

The preceding indictment has considerable merit but its concerns are only partially overlapping with our present interests. Given a focus on problems in counting warships over time, the passage serves to delineate the 'salt-water narrative' character of a great deal of naval history, regardless of the century. With an emphasis on the tactics of fleet operations and sea battles, relatively little energy has been left for, or expended on, assessing a state's total number of warships. Hence, a good many of the available sources provide warship data only to the extent that it pertains to specific fleet clashes. Only rarely are we told what proportion of the navy has been assigned to a particular battle fleet.

In addition to their traditional emphasis on the details of sea battles, naval historians and their analyses, in general, are character-ised by several other and often related liabilities *vis-à-vis* warship counting:

(1) Naval historians, at best, have demonstrated a high degree of ambivalence toward numbers. It is not uncommon for a set of ship numbers to be given as a descriptive 'quick fix' on relative capabilities for a decade or several decades. Alternatively, the number of ships afloat at the beginning year of a major war is a popular occasion for recording numbers. Rarely are these initial figures followed by numbers for subsequent years even though there may be considerable fluctuations in navy sizes during – and certainly in the aftermath of – major wars.

(2) Naval historians frequently are unsystematic or relatively casual about the numbers they do choose to reveal. It is not uncom-mon for ship numbers to be treated as if they were non-controversial facts not requiring documentation. Rarely are precise sources (e.g. ship-lists versus other historians) given for estimates of ship numbers. Even more confusing is the relative lack of clarification which accompanies or should accompany the use of such figures. In some cases, readers are told whether the numbers refer to all ships on a navy's lists or only ships actually in commission or whether the cited figure refers only to capital ships (in periods when conventions prevail about what this term means) or whether every vessel (including barges, rowing-boats, and training ships) in the navy is included. More often than not, however, the reader is forced to guess. Nor is it unusual for a naval historian to change his or her terms of reference. On one page, a number may refer to all vessels while only ships-of-the-line capable of going to sea are enumerated on the next page. And

40 *Global Overview*

somewhat more surprisingly, naval historians are frequently not as careful as they might be about cross-national references in that they may use one standard of reference for counting state X's ships-of-the-line and still another for counting those of state Y. When the labels are missing, it is difficult to keep track of what is being counted.

(3) Since naval historians have tended to relish actions at sea, they tend to neglect or ignore years in which there is little or no activity. Fortunately or unfortunately, there are more years of inactivity than there are years with sea battles.

(4) Not surprisingly, naval historians are attracted to the most prominent navies. Or, put another way, states with prominent and successful navies also tend to produce more than their share of the expected distribution of naval historians. Thus, we know a great deal about the British navy (a maritime leader for several centuries) and much less about the navies of the Ottoman Empire, Austria–Hungary, or even Spain and Portugal.

(5) In a similar way, many naval historians, particularly those of earlier eras, are sometimes less than completely objective about their own navies and the navies of their country's enemies. This is of course an ancient source of distortion but in terms of ship counts, it may lead an observer to exaggerate or to underestimate the size of his country's navy as well as the size of other navies. For instance, it depends upon whose work one reads and the century in which it was written as to which side (the English or the Spanish), if either, was the naval underdog in 1588 as well as whether the defeat of the Great Armada marked the downfall of the Spanish navy or its actual birth (see Mattingly, 1959). Another example is provided by the seventeenth-century Dutch who were often credited with literally thousands more ships than they actually possessed (see Boxer, 1965, p. 114; Cipolla, 1965, p. 48). Nor is this a phenomenon which is restricted to the earlier centuries. During one of the recurring British 'naval panics' of the nineteenth century, Padfield notes that naval comparisons 'credited the potential enemies with every obsolete coast defence vessel still on the active list and every armoured vessel authorised in their future programmes' (Padfield, 1972, p. 146). Even if professional naval historians may be less likely to engage in the excesses of alarmist comparisons than other types of naval observers, the numbers produced by these patently-political exercises occasionally live on beyond the panic era and become accepted, in the absence of more reliable information, as objective representations of the relative capabilities in

Seapower and its Measurement 41

an earlier time. As such they are politicised ghosts for which collectors of naval data must be alert.

The discussion of these various problems with extracting numbers from naval history runs the risk of creating a false impression of an empirical mission impossible. The data-collection hurdles and traps are definitely there but, we will argue, it is possible to surmount and/or evade them. The remainder of this chapter will be devoted to summarising our approach to overcoming various problems associated with data on naval history in general. Specifically, rules will be established for whose naval data should be counted and how to approach the multiple sources of information available for data-creation purposes.

GLOBAL AND WORLD POWERS

The first question that requires attention involves determining which states deserve consideration as global seapowers. Since our approach to these concepts differs from earlier related concepts (e.g., great power, major power, superpower) because of the emphasis on naval capabilities as the primary criterion of status, it is not possible to rely on the customary ranks attributed to various actors in the literature of diplomatic history and of world politics. Instead, a fairly wide actor net needs to be cast to ensure against the possibility of incorrectly excluding or overlooking an appropriate component of the global system's distribution of naval capabilities. In actuality, the critical problem is not so much one of overlooking an important actor as it is a matter of making judgements about marginal candidates. All marginal candidates need to have their qualifications checked explicitly as opposed to dismissing them by analytical fiat or assumption.

Given a potentially universal set of candidates, the next requirement entails selecting minimal threshold criteria for global and world power status. Such criteria must be somewhat arbitrary for they are rarely given by theory. The task is to set a threshold which is neither too liberal (including actors that do not qualify fully) nor too conservative (excluding actors that do qualify even though only minimally).

Earlier analyses of systemic polarity (Modelski, 1974; Rapkin, Thompson and Christopherson, 1979) offer one minimal criterion for

42 *Global Overview*

naval expenditures when they suggest that a world power possesses at least 50 per cent and a great power possesses at least 5 per cent of the world's military capabilities as reflected through military expenditures. Since it is extremely difficult to estimate world expenditures in much of the post-1494 period and since the naval expenditures of the global powers are likely to constitute at least 75–80 per cent of the world's naval spending, the 50:5 per cent rule-of-thumb can be converted to read as follows: a world power must possess at least 50 per cent and a global power should possess at least 5 per cent of the total naval capabilities of the global powers as reflected through naval expenditures.

Conceivably, the same criteria could be applied to warships as well but a problem of scale interferes. Depending on the century, the combined battle fleets of the global powers in the wooden-sailing-ship era will range roughly between 180 to 400 warships. While the 50 per cent threshold for world powers can be carried over, the 5 per cent criterion for global powers will tend to be too liberal. Working with the range 180–400, the minimal threshold for global-power status would amount to approximately 9–20 warships. These numbers seem much too small to represent even a minimal competitive position when they are compared with a global power which has, say, 25 per cent of the combined fleet total and 45–100 ships. Nor is this an unfair comparison for, during the past 500 years, the typical naval-competition situation has involved at most two or three states with anything resembling equal capabilities with perhaps a few other states with distinctly inferior capabilities that are nonetheless useful for coalitional purposes. Armed with this foreknowledge, a more appropriate minimal threshold for global power status is provided by a criterion of 10 per cent.

Long cycle theory prompts us to look at the naval capabilities of global powers or those actors with global reach. But it is possible to meet or exceed the 5 per cent (naval expenditures) or the 10 per cent (warships) criteria without exhibiting truly global behaviour. This is, of course, an old problem associated with measuring 'power' in terms of capabilities. The potential influence latent to capabilities need not match the degree of influence actually manifested in behaviour.

While there is no intention of resolving this perennial problem in these pages, the capability-behaviour gap does take a special twist when the time comes to count seapower capabilities. Historically, there appears to be a local–regional–global progression in the expansion of a state's foreign policy interests. To some extent this is a function of capability restrictions; most states are restricted to local arenas by their limited capabilities. A comparatively few states have the ability to reach farther but, usually, they do not make the transition from local to global power without first fighting their way up through their own region. In the process of establishing a strong regional position in an area where a navy is useful, the minimum naval capability criterion could be met before a state had the time or the inclination to act beyond the region. England in the early sixteenth century and Russia in the early eighteenth century offer excellent examples of states with moderately stronge navies whose activities, for the most part, were restricted for some time to nearby waters.

Basically, what is needed is a third criterion that allows one to differentiate between regional and global powers other than or beyond money spent or ships built. Ideally, one might demand that a candidate for global power status should first send a battle fleet to circumnavigate the globe or that it should station powerful squadrons in all the globe's major oceans. However, such strict standards would eliminate most if not all of the candidates in too many of the years of interest to this analysis. Accordingly, some less stringent standard is necessary. A criteria which appears to meet the requirements is suggested by the distinction between ocean-going and seagoing navies. In this context, the terms 'ocean' and 'sea' are being used literally. A state which is considered to be a naval power in the Baltic, the Black Sea, the Caribbean, the Adriatic, the Red Sea, or even the Mediterranean and nowhere else is unlikely to deserve global power status. A state which can claim to be a naval power in the Atlantic, Indian, or Pacific Oceans, on the other hand, has a much better chance of deserving global power status.

An illustration of this principle is provided by the case of the Ottoman Empire. There can be little doubt that the Ottomans were a leading Mediterranean naval power in the sixteenth century (see Hess, 1970; Braudel, 1976; Shaw, 1976). They were also responsible for mounting the most serious naval opposition to the Portuguese in the Indian Ocean through naval attacks mounted principally in 1538 and 1551. But their attacks proved to be ill-fated because they attempted to transfer outdated Mediterranean tactics and undergunned galleys to fight the ocean-going fleets of the Portuguese. The limitations imposed upon the Ottomans are captured well by Godinho's conclusion:

44　　Global Overview

La seule bataille navale importante livrée par les Turcs dans l'océan Indien se soldait par une défaite définitive, et toutes ces entréprises s'achevaient misérablement. Attachés aux routines des mers étroites et au vaisseau qui leur convient – la galée – les Turcs ne pensèrent jamais en termes d'océan et leurs escadres ne s'aventurerent jamais, sauf contraite, hors de la vue des côtes (Godinho, 1969, p. 770).

In short, the Ottomans, clearly a regional naval power, did not develop a true ocean-going or blue-water capability when they needed it. Because of this they were unable to mount a serious offensive in the Indian Ocean. They were also unable to make a serious bid for global power status.

Summarising, the following criteria will be employed to identify world and global powers.[2]

1. **To qualify initially as a world power, a global power's share must equal 50 per cent of the total naval expenditures or 50 per cent of the total warships of the global powers. World powers retain their status, even though they may no longer satisfy the threshold criteria, until a new world power emerges.**
2. **A state must possess a minimum share of the world's naval capabilities to qualify as a global power. A minimum share is equal to 5 per cent of the total naval expenditures of the global powers or 10 per cent of the total warships of the global powers. Furthermore, its navy must demonstrate ocean-going activity as opposed to more circumscribed regional sea- or coastal-defence activity.**

While it is conceivable that we might be able to identify the exact year in which these criteria are satisfied, it is unlikely that most new entrants into the global-power élite have emerged as complete surprises. On the contrary, new global powers have had to develop their naval capabilities of global reach over variable periods of time. Nor is there any reason to assume that these developments go unobserved by the decision-makers of the established global powers. Consequently, it is more than a bit unrealistic to argue that a state was a global power in any given year and not one in the immediately preceding year. Thus, rather than specifying precise years of entry, we will depend on long cycle theory's emphasis on the rhythmic punctuation of global wars as our benchmarks.

3. **States that achieve global power status in the years between global wars will be treated as if they had satisfied the criteria at the**

Seapower and its Measurement

conclusion of the preceding global war. In cases in which the preceding global war predates the development of any naval capabilities or the existence of the state, the status can only be conferred after the creation of these obvious prerequisites.

These rules serve to identify the conditions for entry into the global power group. A final rule is needed to identify exits from this world élite. The predominant mode of exit from global power status is through a decisive defeat or an exhaustion of its resources in global war. Although a future return to the élite is never precluded and can be handled with the aid of the above rules, some analytical discretion is called for in cases where global powers allow their qualifications to erode below the minimum criteria prior to a global war. In absolute terms, the loss of global power status should present no conceptual problems. But, operationally, the sudden 'loss' of a global power during a relatively peaceful period may have a rather artificial and undesired impact on the enumerated capability distribution. Historically, global powers never really fade away overnight anyway, unless they suffer a devastating defeat. Even when they cross the minimal qualifying threshold peacefully, they remain an uncertain quantity in international politics. In such cases, they are also usually in a position to make an effort to recoup their losses should circumstances or opportunities encourage them to do so. For these reasons the following rule will be adopted:

4. **Once a state attains global power status, it retains that status until defeated or exhausted in global war and no longer qualifies as a global power in the post-global-war period.**

THE DILEMMA OF CONFLICTING ESTIMATES

In an ideal world, there would be no need for this section. We would invent concepts, create appropriate variables and indicators, and determine which hypotheses are supported by the data and which are not. Of course, students of world politics do not live in such a world. Instead, we struggle with elusive concepts, learn to tolerate the multiple imperfections of variables, indicators, and data, and eventually manage to get around to tests of the hypotheses. Two of the consistent sub-themes of this project are (i) the need for theoretically justified indicators, and (ii) explicit rules of data collection. Only in

46 *Global Overview*

this way can one hope to survive the struggle on the path between theory and hypothesis-testing. Unfortunately, however, the need for explicit rules does not end with decisions about what data to collect. For once the data are collected, the dilemma of conflicting estimates becomes all too apparent. For every different source consulted, different and, not infrequently, contradictory pieces of data emerge. The greater the number of sources, conceivably, the greater the ensuing dilemma.

Table 2.2 summarises the number of sources utilised and the resulting years for which seapower data are available for the global powers determined in accordance with the rules explained above and in Chapters 3 and 4. However one evaluates the ratio of sources to data yielded it is readily apparent that not only have a surprisingly large number of years been tapped for data but that it required an unusually large number of sources to accomplish the task.

Table 2.2   Data collection outcome for the global powers' warships, 1494–1860

Global power	Number of years	Number of sources
Portugal	87	1
Spain	113	51
England/Great Britain	367	85
United Provinces of the Netherlands	105	50
France	367	92
Russia/Soviet Union	75	20
United States	45	1

Some may be tempted to suggest that this is the price one should expect to pay for evading the traditionally legitimate approach of intensive archival research. By going straight to the official repositories of governmental ship lists and naval expenditures, one might expect to find the highest-quality data as well as avoiding the need to consult literally hundreds of secondary and tertiary sources.

Nevertheless, there are definite problems with this position. A genuine archival search for a project of this nature would require spending quite a few years in Washington, London, Paris, Madrid,

Seapower and its Measurement

Lisbon, Moscow, Rome, Tokyo and the Hague – to name only the more obvious places. The necessary linguistic skills and the amount of time needed would require a fairly large team of researchers. Yet there is no guarantee that the information resulting from such an ambitious undertaking would be either superior in quality or quantity to the data uncovered by this project. Archives simply do not exist for some states in certain time-periods. Nor are governmental archives free of disagreement about the number of ships afloat or the yearly amount of money spent on the navy. In many respects, the conflicting estimates found in the pertinent literature are directly related to disagreements and ambiguities easily discernible at the governmental source. In short, the conflicts about whose data to use are inevitable and unavoidable.

The reasons for conflicting estimates of ships and expenditures have been discussed earlier in this chapter. There is no need to return to a discussion of these problems. Instead, two related conclusions seem fairly obvious: (i) conflicting estimates tend to be the norm, at least for the pre-1860 years; and (ii) it is unlikely that any single source is the authoritative source for the entire global political system, for it is equally unlikely that anyone knew exactly how many ships a state possessed or precisely how much money was expended on the navy in the pre-nineteenth-century era. Thus, the solution to the problem of conflicting estimates is not simply one of discriminating between good and bad data. Rather, it involves identifying the pieces of information which seem closer to the mark without always knowing exactly what the 'mark' is. There is certainly an element of subjectivity in such a process which is only partially offset (or perhaps accentuated) by the 'intuitive feel' for the data that is developed by the data collector. Once again, the only real solution is to attempt to clarify and make explicit the rules-of-thumb developed in the effort to reduce the conflicting estimates to single series.

In accordance with these sentiments, the following decision rules have been generated for years in which sources disagree about the number of ships or the amount of money expended on naval purposes:

(1) **Preference will be given to sources that provide figures for multiple years as opposed to sources that offer figures for one or only a few years.** The operating assumption is that sources that provide a number of pieces of information over a period of time have already made some effort towards reconciling longitudinal discrepancies (i.e.,

48 *Global Overview*

a datum for year X not making much sense in the context of a datum for years $X-1$ or $X+1$). Furthermore, the more numerous the sources utilised, the greater the resulting amount of unknown bias that can be expected. Consequently, the fewer the sources needed, the fewer the sources of unknown bias.

(2) **Preference will be given to sources which are corroborated by other sources.** At the same time, one must be alert to the always-real possibility than an erroneous piece of information advanced at an early point in time may be relied upon by later sources.

(3) **Preference will be given to sources oriented explicitly toward naval administrative history as opposed to more general historical concerns or with sea battles.** The operating assumption underlying this rule is that historians of naval administration are more interested professionally in ship-expenditure numbers than are writers with broader concerns or the more narrow details of specific episodes of combat.

(4) **Caution should be exercised in cases where sources indicate a large amount of change in a brief period of time unless supporting information is available on particularly disastrous fleet battles or high-priority building and spending programmes.**

(5) **Caution should be exercised in cases where sources are internally contradictory (e.g., offer two different figures for the same year on different pages) or in cases where sources do not reveal or explain the origins of their numbers.**

(6) **Preference will be given to ship number sources which pair total warship estimates with ships actually in commission. Preference will also be given to sources which give ship numbers which are explicitly qualified according to ship type, ship rate, and/or number of cannon. Strong preference will be given to reproduced or reconstructed ship lists issued by states on an often-regular basis. Even stronger preference will be given to studies oriented toward indexing all warships either of a certain type, for a certain period, and/or for a specified state.** The simple rationale behind these related rules is that it is better to know to what the numbers are referring than to be forced to guess, particularly when the project's minimal criteria for ships are subject to change.

(7) **Preference should be given to naval expenditure series which are made available by governments or quasi-governmental sources to the extent that they stress information on closed accounts (as opposed to preliminary budget estimates) as well as information on the several parts of the typical naval budget (e.g., ordinary and extraordinary accounts)**

in the original currency of the pertinent state. Extreme caution should be exercised with annual and unofficial sources such as *Statesman's Yearbook* which rarely give reliable information on final budgets and to sources which offer currency figures that have been converted from one currency to another without disclosing the utilised exchange rates.[3]

(8) **When in doubt or when the rules outlined above do not facilitate a decision, leave the annual cell blank.** Here, the point is to resist the understandable temptation to fill holes in data series with any available data even though the accuracy of the data may be dubious. **Related to this rule is the corollary principle that it is more justified to estimate data missing between two data points in which the data collector has some confidence than it is to rely on highly suspect data or data of unknown quality.**

With these general guidelines in mind, we are now in a position to move on to the more historically specific problems associated with changes in naval technology and innovation since 1494 that will occupy the attention of Chapters 3 and 4.

3 Rules for Counting Warships, 1494–1860

Earlier mention has been made in Chapter 2 of the analytical convenience provided by the tendencies toward standardising warships which resulted in the development of the ship-of-the-line, the capital warship of the mid-seventeenth to the first half of the nineteenth centuries. Nevertheless, this period constitutes less than half and closer to a third of the five centuries in question. Clearly, the operationalisation procedures will have to go beyond simply indicating an intention to count ships-of-the-line. For that matter, there are also some comparability problems 'hidden' in the ship-of-the-line concept. The procedures will also have to be sufficiently flexible to be able to take into account changes in naval technology – predominantly in terms of gunnery.

Very broadly speaking, it is possible to divide the period 1494–1993 into four phases of warship development: (i) 1494 – *circa* 1654, the pre-ship-of-the-line warship era; (ii) *circa* 1655–1860, the ship-of-the-line era; (iii) 1861–1945, the battleship era, and (iv) 1946 on, the aircraft carrier/submarine era. While each era demarcates a reasonably distinct phase, change is experienced throughout each phase as well. This chapter will concentrate on the first two phases 1494–1654 and 1655–1860. Chapter 4 will focus on developments in the post-1860 era.

The warship era, 1494–1654, was characterised by the decline of the galley as the principal warship and the development of specialised sailing warships primarily in Atlantic Europe. Masts and sails were added. Castle-like structures for archers were phased out in favour of gunports and an increased emphasis (in comparison with the limited number and placement of cannon on galleys) was placed on naval ordnance. As the threat of piracy and general naval competition increased, specialised ships for combat came to be increasingly differentiated from the typical armed merchantmen which could still be used as circumstances required.[1]

During this period, size served as the basic unit of ranking ships but no standardised, cross-national frame of reference emerged. The English appear to have been the most explicit about the use of rating systems; however, their initial four-rate system did not appear prior to

Rules for Counting Warships, 1494–1860   51

1604 (Corbett, 1900, p. 411). Even so, it might be possible to adopt tonnage as a unit of measure for this first period were it not for three problems. First, information on the tonnage of specific ships is available in sufficient quality and quantity only for English ships. In fact, there is little available information on early Portuguese and Spanish ships on specific dimensions or attributes. Second, Portuguese ships in particular tended to be much heavier than their English, Dutch, and French counterparts because they were built for the long route to India. By and large, this was later considered a disadvantage because in the end the smaller ships of the north came to be more numerous and cheaper to build, proved to be faster and more manoeuvrable and, most importantly, better equipped with artillery. There seems to be little reason to apply a standard which rewards a state for having the more ponderous and militarily inferior ships. Third, tonnage, as previously implied, does not capture the gun factor very well. This applies internationally as well as nationally for there does not appear to be a high and consistent correlation between tonnage and number or type of guns carried.

In view of the relative lack of information and the virtual absence of recognised standards of comparison for the different types of ships utilised by the seapowers of this period, a rather conservative rule is proposed:

Between 1494 and 1654, a warship will be defined for the purposes of this analysis as any armed, sailing warship owned and maintained by a state.

Ownership and maintenance by the state is actually a more important qualification than it may seem at first, for this period was also one of a slow and gradual development of the concept of national navies. Especially during the first part of the period 1494–1654, it was not unusual for ships belonging to the state or the crown to be leased for commercial purposes in non-war times. Nor was it unusual for merchant ships of different nationalities to be seized or leased by the state during times of war. Indeed, the Spanish armadas of the late sixteenth century were composed primarily of non-Spanish ships.

It is in respect to ownership that the rule is conservative. Some ships that could be and were used for purposes of war are excluded by the rule. However, the rule's conservative nature is offset at least partially to the extent that it is applied equally to all states and that it counts any armed warship. This last qualification is intended to exclude

52 *Global Overview*

auxiliary ships used in war such as fireships or hulks (troop transports) which were not considered to be 'men-of-war' or 'ships-of-the-line' at the time. The conservative nature of the rule is somewhat offset by a 'liberalising' element in the sense that the rule gives the same weight to ships with ten guns as it does to ships with thirty guns. Nevertheless, saying that we will count state-owned warships in the first place will not suffice. Because the first phase overlaps with the emergence of the global system, the sixteenth century is characterised by a number of special measurement problems. After all, it would be unreasonable to expect the system's processes to have burst forth as fully developed and recognisable from year one. The development of seapower is no exception to this observation.

The 'sixteenth-century problems' actually consists of several different but not unrelated problems involving historical perspectives, early organisational and technological developments, and a general scarcity of data. The historical perspective problem concerns a substantial modification of the way in which the sixteenth-century world should be viewed. Conventional approaches to this period, including with some irony the world-economy viewpoint of Wallerstein (1974), are decidedly Eurocentric. The era's primary dimensions of political conflict are regarded as (i) the Hapsburg-Valois feud; (ii) the European resistance to Ottoman expansion, and (iii) the Protestant–Catholic schism in the latter half of the century. Given these dimensions of conflict, southern/south-eastern Europe and the Mediterranean emerge as the most significant theatres of combat up to the Battle of Lepanto (1571) followed by the road to Flanders and the land-oriented military operations of the Dutch revolt. The voyages of 'discovery' to, the maritime conflicts over, and the exploitation of parts of Africa, Latin America and Asia, of course, are duly noted as significant but more so for subsequent centuries than for their immediate (sixteenth-century) ramifications. In marked contrast, our perspective implies that we need to stand these priorities of historical significance on their head.

In terms of the evolution of the world system and the global political system, it is the decentralised European expansion which overshadows the partially intramural conflicts of the European and Mediterranean areas. Naturally, this need not be construed as an 'either/or' situation. European conflict patterns influenced European expansion and conflicts outside of Europe. The reverse is true as well. Nevertheless, theoretical (and operational) emphasis cannot be given equally and simultaneously to both facets of sixteenth-century history. Another way of expressing this argument is to state that in the sixteenth century one is confronted with an important choice. Either one theorises about and analyses the development of the global political system or European regional developments. The fact that this problem is due not so much to the dilemmas of choice but because so much of the available information, unfortunately, is based on a clear preference for the latter and not the former option.

The earlier reference to organisational and technological developments refers to navies and warships. The ocean-going warship, as opposed to the traditional war galley, only really emerged in some more or less standardised form well into the seventeenth century. Prior to that time, warships simply tended to be more likely to be armed and, in some cases, to be built, for the purposes of speed and manoeuvrability, along less bulky lines than the typical merchant sailing-ship. Fleet-to-fleet artillery combats did not really emerge on a premeditated scale until much later. Well into the sixteenth century, especially outside the Indian Ocean, warships retained their earlier Mediterranean purposes of troop transports/convoys and vehicles for ramming and boarding the enemy's ships.

Even more distressing from the viewpoint of the analyst, few regular navies existed. Those that did exist did so only in an embryonic fashion. Among the major European powers of the early sixteenth century, only Portugal and England maintained regular, or more accurately, royal navies. France possessed only a handful of state-owned ships before even this minuscule core disappeared in the series of internal wars of the second half of the century. Perhaps most surprisingly for readers not familiar with the period, Spain had no real navy, other than galleys, until the last quarter of the sixteenth century. Yet Spain proved capable of assembling impressively large fleets for the ill-fated and repeated attempts to invade England.

Equally inconvenient for measurement purposes are a number of naval practices of the era. Warships were rented to merchants and used as commercial carriers in peace-time. Merchant ships were rented to monarchs and states, if they were not seized first, and used as warships in wartime to such an extent that war fleets might be ten times the size of the 'regular navy'. Nor was it unknown for an entire fleet simply to be sold to pay off royal debts.[2] Moreover, much of the maritime combat of the sixteenth century was conducted by what later periods more politely referred to as privateers – armed civilian vessels and crews that operated in and out of coordination with state policies and as often as not for the purposes of private gain. If to this

54 *Global Overview*

list of empirical woes, one adds the great variety in the types of ships afloat as well as the severe paucity of information on the actual sizes of the leading navies, the enumeration of naval capabilities in the sixteenth century assumes the appearance of a genuine challenge.

A genuine challenge it may well be, but it is not, we think, an entirely insurmountable one. It is possible to calculate the annual number of ships maintained by England and France from sources designed for much different purposes. Sufficient data also exist to estimate the annual size of the Portuguese navy. The calculation of the size of the Spanish fleet is relatively straightforward once a Spanish navy actually begins to take form and enough is known about the size of the Dutch fleet to make credible estimates as well. The real question which remains is whether one is content to work with the readily-estimated data on regular navies or whether one needs to go beyond this initial base and make specific allowances for the various practices of the period. The sixteenth-century solution to be proposed here will argue that it is necessary to take certain explicit liberties with the estimated data in order to create a more valid global capability series.

A SIXTEENTH-CENTURY SOLUTION

Colledge (1969) and Le Conte (1932) provide extensive and laboriously assembled lists of the names of ships maintained as regular vessels by the English and French navies. They also provide supplementary information on ship-type, number of guns carried, status and name changes, and years in service. To make use of these sources, it is necessary to work one's way through the regrettably alphabetised lists, segregating ships into comparable categories and taking note of the time in service for each ship. This admittedly tedious accounting method permits the creation of subsequent lists of net increases and decreases in the size of each fleet which should correlate closely with governmental ship-lists assuming they had been issued on an annual basis and were available today. As a validity check, the number of ships for certain years reported by a number of historical sources, listed in Table 3.1, may be checked for rough agreement. In the English and French cases, estimates made from the Colledge (1969) and Le Conte (1932) sources do appear to provide the most consistently reliable figures and certainly offer the advantages of providing reliable longitudinal series. One nagging problem which will need

Rules for Counting Warships, 1494–1860   55

Table 3.1   Primary sources for sixteenth-century ship estimates

England	*Spain*
Archibald (1968)	Chaunu and Chaunu (1955)
Busk (1859)	Corbett (1898)
Charnock (1800–03)	Fernandez Duro (1972–3)
Clowes (1897–1903)	Graham (1972)
Colledge (1969)	Haring (1918)
Corbett (1900)	Mattingly (1959)
Cowburn (1965)	McKee (1963)
Derrick (1806)	Merriman (1934)
Marcus (1961)	Reynolds (1974)
Mattingly (1959)	Richmond (1953)
Oppenheim (1961)	Silburn (1912)
Parker (1979)	Southworth (1968)
Penn (1913)	Thompson (1976)
Richmond (1946, 1953)	
Rose (1921a)	
Stevens and Wescott (1943)	
France	*Netherlands*
Clowes (1897–1903)	Blok (1900)
Jouan (1950)	Dirks (1890)
L'Ancienne France (1888)	Edmundson (1922)
de La Roncière (1906)	Graham (1972)
Le Conte (1932)	de Jonge (1869)
	Motley (1900)
	Reynolds (1974)
	Robison and Robison (1942)
	Southworth (1968)

further attention, however, is the very small size of the French royal navy.

Scattered information is available on the size of Portuguese squadrons operating in the Indian Ocean and the Malaccan Straits as well as decennial information on the number of ships moving to and from Portugal and the Indian Ocean (see Ballard, 1927; Boxer, 1969; Charnock, 1800–03; Cipolla, 1965; Danvers, 1966; Diffie and Winius, 1977; Duffy, 1955; Guilmartin, 1974; Hess, 1970; Godinho, 1969; de Oliveira Marques, 1976; Vecchj, 1895; and Whiteway, 1967). But these data only provide very rough clues to the actual size of the Portuguese navy. To make matters worse, the royal records for this period were destroyed more than 225 years ago. In Chapter 7, the available figures and certain assumptions are utilised to reconstruct a

56 *Global Overview*

plausible estimate of annual changes in the Portuguese fleet. Fortunately, we do have one Portuguese source (da Fonseca, 1926) that can be used for an attempt to estimate a ship count for the sixteenth century.

Spain poses a different sort of problem. Despite extensive Spanish involvement in ocean-going 'trade' with its newly-acquired colonial empire in Latin America and Asia and in marked contrast to its Portuguese neighbours, no Spanish blue-water navy was developed in the first half of the sixteenth century. There are at least four reasons for this curious neglect. Whereas the Portuguese monarchy virtually monopolised the ownership of Portuguese ship construction and ownership (fewer than 10 per cent of the *naus* in our Table 7.5 are privately owned), the Spanish monarchy was content with a licensing/percentage share system. Thus, most Spanish sailing ships were not state-owned – a primary requisite for the development of a regular navy. Second, the Spanish colonial expansion met little indigenous naval opposition, again in contrast to the Portuguese who were confronted, at various and repeated times, by Mameluke, Ottoman, and Asian galley fleets and the frequent need to provide relief by sea for besieged imperial outposts. Eventually, French and English raids on the Spanish Atlantic convoys necessitated the development of small and initially *ad hoc* protective escorts, but even these escorts were not state-owned vessels until the 1570s.

Third, a great proportion of Spanish military energies were oriented towards the Mediterranean theatre where war galleys remained supreme. Hence, Spain did possess a sizeable and expensive war fleet during the first two-thirds of the sixteenth century (see Braudel, 1976), but since it was composed of galleys, it was not suited for ocean-going activities. At most, galleys were used occasionally for coastal defence purposes in the area between Cadiz and the Canary Islands as well as in the Caribbean. The beginning of a standing Spanish navy with true ocean-going capabilities had to await the seizure of Portugal (and the Portuguese navy), the problems related to suppressing the French-assisted rebellion in the Azores during the early 1580s, and the belatedly perceived need to combat the English and Dutch navies. Finally, it is often noted that there were few incentives for the Spanish nobility to go to sea. Spanish prestige, glory, and financial awards were found on land and not at sea in the sixteenth century.

Whatever the explanation, the absence of a regular navy in the first three-quarters of the century presents several options. The most simple approach would be to argue somewhat dogmatically that the

Rules for Counting Warships, 1494–1860   57

lack of a regular navy must be equated with the absence of a global naval capability. Yet Spain was fully capable of marshalling war fleets when necessary – either by leasing or seizing merchant ships. It is also rather difficult to ignore Spain as a significant actor in the emerging global political system. A more moderate approach might consist of determining the number of convoy escorts employed in the Atlantic. Table 3.2 demonstrates a good proportion of the information available for this possibility. An examination of the numbers gleaned from the presumably exhaustive Chaunu and Chaunu (1955) study of New World ship movements to and from Seville, however, yields a profile of an extremely *ad hoc* escort activity often relying on relatively small ships. While it would be inappropriate to compare *caravelles, galeazas, naves, pataches, galeazettas*, and frigates with Portuguese *naus* and galleons, the irregular character of the escort service suggests that a fair amount of caution should be exercised in using numbers such as those displayed in Table 3.2 for a base upon which to construct an estimated naval capability series.

The root of the problem is in some respects a matter of incomplete socialisation or learning processes. From a global perspective, the sixteenth century is a bit like a stage full of actors who have not quite learned their lines and who have only a foggy idea what the script is about. Spain and France, in particular, were extremely slow in acquiring an appreciation for the advantages of an ocean-going, state-owned navy. Even so, both states could and did assemble fairly sizeable fleets for short-term emergency use. In such a context, it seems most appropriate to 'bend' the ship-counting procedures in order to avoid excluding or seriously under-counting two fairly significant actors. Bending the ship-counting procedures does not mean a violation of the operationalisation rules. Rather, it is meant to suggest an explicit intervention to avoid unwarranted and distorted results.

More specifically, what is proposed is to 'award' Spain 25 per cent of the Portuguese, English, and French total number of ships. France will receive 10 per cent of this same preliminary total as an addition to its initial count. Both percentage rules are in force through 1579 and are meant to capture, albeit crudely, the ability to mobilise ships in emergency situations and, to a lesser extent, the actual maritime activities of these two states in an era in which the idea of regular navies had not yet been fully established. The assigned percentage figures are somewhat arbitrary but not completely so. They have been selected to maintain a specific hierarchy: Portugal in first place,

58

Table 3.2 Chaunus' description of Spanish 'warships' employed in the Atlantic, 1522–86

Year	Description
1522	3 caravels serve as an Andalusian coast guard
1525	no ships are available for the war fleet
1525	galleys provide a coast guard
1526	galleys provide a coast guard
1528	galleys provide a coast guard
1537	12 *navios*, 2 caravels serve as convoy escort
1538	12 *navios*, 2 caravels serve as convoy escort
1540	2 *galeazas* and 2 galleys serve as coast guard
1541	4 *navires* serve as convoy escort
1542	4 *bâtiments* serve as convoy escort
1543	4 bateaux, 5 *naos*, 1 caravels provide 3 separate escorts
1544	1 galleon, 6 *naos* serve as convoy escort
1545	1 galleon, 6 *naos* serve as convoy escort
1549	3 *navires*, 6 caravels serve as convoy escorts
1550	2 galleons, 3 *naos*, and 1 *nave* serve as convoy escorts
1552	10 *navios*, 2 *zabras* provide Atlantic convoy escort; 6 *navios* provide Indies convoy escort
1554	4 *navios*, 1 caravels, 4 *navires*, 2 *galeazas*, and 2 *pataches* or *zabras* serve as convoy escorts
1555	2 *naos*, 5 *navios*, and 2 caravels serve as convoy escorts
1557	1 *nao*, 11 *navios*, 1 caravels, 1 *galeaza*, 1 *galeazetta*, and 50 *navires* serve as convoy escort and coast guard
1558	2 large *naos*, 7 *navios*, 2 caravels, 5 *galeazas*, 3 *pataches*, and 2 *navires* provide convoy escorts
1562	8 galleys and 1 frigate serve as coast guard
1563	2 *navires* and a few brigantines serve as convoy escort
1569	4 galleons return from Florida service
1570	4 galleons added to the normal convoy escort
1571	6 galleons in Aviles armada
1572	7 galleons in Las Alas armada and 3–4 galleons serve as convoy escort
1574	4 galleons in Aviles Armada
1575	3 galleons in De Flores Armada
1576	8–12 galleons, frigates, *navios*, and *pataches* organised for Armada de la Guardia de la Carrera de las Indias (apparently 5 of the 8–12 ships are galleons)
1577	3 galleons and 2 frigates in Guardia Armada
1578	5 galleons, 4 *naos*, 8 frigates, 1 *galeaza*, and 2 galleys in Guardia Armada (for first time, denoted as royal ships)
1579	5 *naos*, 2 *galeazas*, and 5 frigates in Guardia Armada
1580	1 *galeaza*, 3 frigates in Guardia Armada
1586	9 galleons, 3 *naos*, and 3 frigates in Guardia Armada

Source: Based on annual descriptions of ships leaving and returning to Seville in Chaunu and Chaunu (1955, vols 2, 3).

followed at some distance by England and Spain as roughly equal (up to 1579), and France a trailing fourth. By keying the percentage calculations to the preliminary totals, no new source of fluctuation in capability shares or the total number of ships other than a systematic inflation of the numbers is introduced.

The percentage interventions cease in 1579. For Spain, better sources of information and changes in naval policies reduce substantially the need to rely upon the 25 per cent estimate. The conquest of Portugal, in any event, would have required a revision of Spanish naval mobilisation capabilities. It appears to be accepted that the sequence of French civil wars gradually eliminated the French state's ability to assemble any fleets for military purposes. The information given by Le Conte (1932) for example, indicates the absence of any French royal ships for the period between 1587 and 1619. Since French ships, acting in an unofficial capacity, were used to assist Portuguese rebels in the Azores (1582–3) 1579 may be slightly premature in ending the 10 per cent 'bonus' but this consideration is offset by the Dutch entry into the maritime élite in the same year. Given the large number of ships with which the United Provinces of the Netherlands entered the global ranks, a continuation of the augmentation of the French capability shares would only be misleading.

The entry of the Dutch is not without its own measurement problems. Thanks in part to the maritime provinces' early specialisation in the Baltic trade and fishing and the incentives created by their exclusion from Iberian ports, the Dutch were able to assume naval leadership early in the seventeenth century. Despite their rapid ascent from rebellion to global predominance, however, Dutch seapower suffered from a naval Achilles heel which probably contributed to their eventual loss of position. Beginning with the *ad hoc* 'Sea Beggar' fleets in the early 1570s, the Dutch had access to a relatively large number of ships by the standards of the last quarter of the sixteenth century. Even so, many of these ships had been built for purposes other than war and thus, generally, were smaller than the warships of Spain and England.

De Jonge (1869, vol. 1, pp. 747–9), for instance, notes that 84 per cent of the Dutch fleet in 1587 carried eleven or fewer guns. By way of contrast, 80 per cent of the Dutch fleet carried fourteen guns or more and about one half of the fleet had twenty guns or more in 1615. One anecdotal illustration of this Dutch naval attribute is provided by Motley (1900, vol. II, pp. 89–90). As a Dutch fleet entered the Roads of Gibraltar to attack a strong Spanish fleet at anchor in 1607, the

Global Overview

Spanish admiral summoned a Dutch prisoner and asked him what he thought the intentions of the Dutch might be. When the prisoner suggested they were preparing to attack, the admiral

> laughed loud and long. The idea that those puny vessels could be bent on such a purpose seemed to him irresistibly comic, and he promised his prisoner, with much condescension, that the *St Augustine* (the Spanish flagship) alone should sink the whole fleet (Motley, 1900, vo. II, p. 90).

As it turned out, the Dutch were able to win the battle in spectacular fashion, no doubt with some assistance from their opponent's arrogance. The point to be made is that the Dutch were able to win naval victories in spite of the small size of their ships, but that, frequently, they required superiority in the number of ships involved to be able to concentrate a sufficient amount of fire-power.

This observation supports the argument that it would be inaccurate to equate each armed Dutch warship with each armed Spanish or English warship, as would be entailed in an unqualified comparison of numerical estimates of Dutch, Spanish, and English warships. To be sure, the Dutch demonstrated repeatedly their superiority in such intangibles as sailing and naval fighting abilities well into the seventeenth century but this definite qualitative asset is also offset by the way in which the Dutch maintained their naval capabilities. Details for the sixteenth century are not abundant but, evidently and in perfect accord with the times, the Netherlands was able to rely on its ability to mobilise armed ships hastily when necessary in order to augment squadrons assigned to regular naval operations. Thus the numbers which are available pertaining to the size of the Dutch fleet through 1608 or the first phase of the Dutch war of independence appear to be swollen by ships which are neither state-owned nor engaged regularly as warships. As has been noted, this was a standard operating procedure in all fleets but in the cases of England, France and Spain, it is possible to distinguish the state's naval core from temporarily mobilised auxiliaries.

In order to maintain some form of accounting equivalency, it is necessary, therefore, to discount the data on the size of the Dutch fleet in the sixteenth century. Naturally there is no obvious or compelling formula for such a discount mechanism. Keeping in mind, however, the earlier observations on ship-size and the mobilisation bonuses granted to France and Spain prior to 1579, it does not seem unreasonable to reduce the estimates of Dutch global power for the period 1579–1608 by 50 per cent. While this may seem to be an extreme measure in the abstract, it gives the Netherlands a 23 per cent share of naval capabilities in 1579 (Portugal, 35 per cent; England, 26 per cent; Spain, 16 per cent; and France, 2 per cent) which escalates to 51 per cent in a non-linear-fashion share by 1608 (England, 31 per cent; Spain, 18 per cent; and France, 0 per cent). These results, it is argued, are not unreasonable estimates of the changes in global naval capability distribution for the period in question.

In summary, then, the following reconstructions have been made in operationalising the number of state-owned, ocean-going ships of war for the global powers of the sixteenth century:

State	Treatment
Portugal	Based on calculations derived from information given by da Fonseca (1926).
England	Based on calculations derived from ship list information in Colledge (1969)
France	Based on calculations derived from ship list information in LeConte (1932) and augmented, up to 1578, by 10 per cent of the initial Portuguese, English, and French ship totals.
Spain	Determined by an augmentation of 25 per cent of the initial Portuguese, English and French ship totals up to 1578. After 1578, based on estimates provided by a number of historical sources (see Table 3.1).
Netherlands	Based on estimates provided by a number of historical sources (see Table 3.1) and discounted by 50 per cent through 1608.

The warship counts for this period in accordance with the operational rules are listed in Table 3.3.

THE SHIP-OF-THE-LINE ERA

The second phase, 1655–1860, begins with the end of the first Anglo-Dutch war which witnessed the development of line-ahead tactics as an efficient way of organising the broadsides of large fleets. As noted earlier, this led to the emergence of the ship-of-the-line. Still, the emergence was not particularly rapid. It is not until the 1690s that a consensus began to emerge that a warship required at least fifty guns

62

Table 3.3 Numerical distribution of global power warships, 1494–1654

Year	POR	ENG	FRN A	B	SPN	NTH	Sub-total*	Total**
1494	3	6	0	1	2		9	12
1495	3	6	2	3	3		11	15
1496	3	6	2	3	3		11	15
1497	4	6	2	3	3		12	16
1498	4	6	2	3	3		12	16
1499	4	6	2	3	3		12	16
1500	5	6	4	6	4		15	21
1501	5	6	2	3	3		13	17
1502	21	6	2	5	7		29	38
1503	24	6	3	6	8		33	44
1504	26	6	3	7	9		35	48
1505	36	6	3	8	11		45	61
1506	52	6	2	8	15		60	81
1507	61	6	2	9	17		69	93
1508	69	6	2	10	19		77	104
1509	93	6	2	12	26		102	137
1510	91	7	2	12	25		100	135
1511	93	9	2	12	26		104	140
1512	112	19	4	18	34		135	183
1513	103	19	5	18	32		127	172
1514	91	17	3	14	28		111	150
1515	89	17	2	13	27		108	146
1516	80	17	2	12	25		99	134
1517	63	18	5	13	22		86	117
1518	58	18	4	12	20		80	108
1519	62	19	4	13	21		85	115
1520	50	19	5	12	19		74	100
1521	63	16	4	12	21		83	112
1522	62	15	6	14	21		83	112
1523	60	17	4	12	20		81	109
1524	64	18	5	14	22		87	118
1525	66	14	5	14	21		85	115
1526	62	12	5	13	20		79	107
1527	54	10	3	10	17		67	91
1528	51	10	4	11	16		65	88
1529	38	9	3	8	13		50	68
1530	41	9	3	8	13		53	71
1531	39	8	2	7	12		49	66
1532	38	8	4	9	13		50	68
1533	44	8	2	7	14		54	73
1534	41	7	1	6	12		49	66
1535	38	9	3	8	13		50	68
1536	36	9	1	6	12		46	63
1537	40	9	1	6	13		50	68

Table 3.3 Numerical distribution of global power warships, 1494–1654

| Year | POR | ENG | FRN | | SPN | NTH | Sub-total* | Total** |
			A	B				
1538	45	9	1	7	14		55	75
1539	41	10	1	6	13		52	70
1540	43	11	1	7	14		55	75
1541	38	11	1	6	13		50	68
1542	43	12	1	7	14		56	76
1543	42	12	1	7	14		55	75
1544	44	18	0	6	16		62	84
1545	38	22	0	6	15		60	81
1546	42	24	1	8	17		67	91
1547	38	24	2	8	16		64	86
1548	37	24	3	9	16		64	86
1549	40	25	5	12	18		70	95
1550	40	25	7	14	18		72	97
1551	50	26	4	12	20		80	108
1552	45	25	4	11	19		74	100
1553	44	24	4	11	18		70	97
1554	48	21	3	10	18		72	97
1555	42	17	5	11	16		64	86
1556	44	19	3	10	17		66	90
1557	44	19	3	10	17		66	90
1558	44	19	6	13	17		69	93
1559	36	18	3	9	14		57	77
1560	34	21	4	10	15		59	80
1561	30	22	3	9	14		55	75
1562	26	24	2	7	13		52	70
1563	28	23	2	7	13		53	71
1564	23	23	2	7	12		48	65
1565	23	23	4	9	13		50	68
1566	24	22	3	8	12		49	66
1567	32	24	2	8	15		58	79
1568	35	25	4	10	16		64	86
1569	34	25	5	11	16		64	86
1570	39	25	6	13	18		70	95
1571	39	25	4	11	17		68	92
1572	38	25	4	11	17		67	91
1573	38	28	5	12	17		71	96
1574	38	28	2	9	17		68	92
1575	37	28	3	10	18		68	93
1576	32	28	3	10	16		63	85
1577	25	30	3	9	15		58	79
1578	21	28	3	8	13		52	70
1579	21	28	2		13	25		89
1580	18	29	2		13	27		89
1581		29	2		31	29		91

64

Table 3.3   Numerical distribution of global power warships, 1494–1654

Year	POR	ENG	FRN	SPN	NTH	Total**
1582		29	2	40	32	99
1583		29	2	40	34	105
1584		29	2	45	36	112
1585		30	2	51	37	120
1586		32	2	57	39	130
1587		33	0	64	40	137
1588		33	0	70	40	143
1589		33	0	35	40	108
1590		35	0	60	39	134
1591		35	0	66	39	140
1592		35	0	69	39	143
1593		35	0	71	38	144
1594		36	0	75	38	149
1595		36	0	79	38	153
1596		39	0	81	37	157
1597		39	0	84	37	160
1598		39	0	67	37	143
1599		36	0	58	37	131
1600		34	0	51	38	124
1601		35	0	40	40	115
1602		35	0	37	41	113
1603		34	0	33	43	110
1604		31	0	31	44	106
1605		31	0	30	45	106
1606		31	0	29	46	106
1607		31	0	29	48	108
1608		30	0	17	49	96
1609		30	0	16	51	97
1610		31	0	14	53	98
1611		30	0	14	54	98
1612		30	0	15	56	101
1613		31	0	15	57	103
1614		31	0	16	59	106
1615		32	0	16	60	108
1616		34	0	17	60	111
1617		34	0	22	66	122
1618		31	0	26	72	129
1619		33	4	27	78	142
1620		34	5	46	84	169
1621		36	9	48	90	183
1622		37	16	51	96	200
1623		39	16	55	102	212
1624		36	16	55	108	215
1625		40	15	60	114	229

Table 3.3 Numerical distribution of global power warships, 1494–1654

Year	POR	ENG	FRN	SPN	NTH	Total**
1626		46	16	60	120	242
1627		53	24	60	127	264
1628		50	34	59	133	276
1629		47	39	58	134	278
1630		44	37	57	135	273
1631		44	37	57	135	273
1632		43	37	56	136	272
1633		44	37	55	137	273
1634		46	37	57	137	277
1635		43	36	58	138	275
1636		44	35	60	139	278
1637		46	36	62	139	283
1638		46	39	64	140	289
1639		46	39	70	141	296
1640		46	34	12	141	233
1641		45	32	30	142	249
1642		46	32	50	143	271
1643		55	32	48	130	265
1644		56	32	46	118	252
1645		57	34	45	104	240
1646		66	37	43	92	238
1647		69	37	41	81	228
1648		63	35	40	70	208
1649		73	35	37	66	211
1650		80	35	33	70	218
1651		91	31	30	72	224
1652		124	27	29	124	304
1653		134	27	29	106	296
1654		140	26	29	106	301

*The sub-total represents the sum of the Portuguese, English and French (A) columns.

**The total represents the sum of the Portuguese (until 1580), English, French (B up to 1578), Spanish, and Dutch columns. French (B) column entries are equal to 10 per cent of the sub-total. The Spanish column entries are equal to 25 per cent of the sub-total.

66   *Global Overview*

to deserve a place in the battle line. Hence, the period 1655–90 was characterised by the commissioning of ships with a gradually escalating number of guns. This development can be directly attributed to the three Anglo-Dutch wars of the mid-seventeenth century. Earlier in the century, the Dutch had established their leadership with small ships with few guns. The English challengers introduced heavier, more deeply-keeled ships capable of carrying more guns than the Dutch ships. The lessons of Anglo-Dutch combat forced the Dutch to respond, belatedly, with ships and tactics similar to the types employed by the English. This stimulus–response interaction through three wars is responsible in large part for the eventual primacy of the ship-of-the-line as the principal warship for fleet encounters.

It is difficult to claim that the evolution toward the minimal fifty-gun rule was completely explicit. But, it is possible to follow an incremental escalation of the minimum number of guns considered necessary to fight in the line in the evolution of the English ship-rating system. By the second half of the seventeenth century, the English rating system had switched its focus from tonnage to the number of guns carried. Of six rates, only the first four rates were considered line-of-battle material. In 1624, based on the tonnage rating system, fourth rates were likely to have between six and twenty guns. As late as 1665, new fourth rates had between thirty and fifty-nine guns. From about 1666 on, new fourth rates usually carried at least forty guns. After 1690, no new fourth rate was commissioned with fewer than forty-eight guns.

The ship-rating systems of the French and the Dutch were not identical but a rough correspondence can be established. For example, the French had five rates instead of six but they also had heavier guns than the English. In any event, the fifty-gun minimum seems to have become fairly non-controversial by the beginning of the eighteenth century. To capture the evolution towards this rule from 1655 to 1700, the following scheme, based rather loosely on the English pattern, is advanced:

Between 1655 and 1670, all warships with thirty guns or more are counted. Between 1671 and 1690, the minimum number of guns is forty. After 1691, the minimum number of guns for a ship-of-the-line is fifty guns.

This is not exactly the end of changes related to the minimum number of guns in this second phase. The French no longer con-

Rules for Counting Warships, 1494–1860

sidered their fourth rate to be worthy of ship-of-the-line status after 1730. The British also raised the conventional minimum of fifty guns to sixty guns after 1755–6, and sometime in the late 1780s or early 1790s began to restrict the line designation to their first three rates. All these changes are incorporated in this project's operationalisation procedures but the most important rules are the minimal criteria for purposes of comparison:

Years	Number of guns
1655–70	30+
1671–90	40+
1691–1756	50+
1757–1860	60+

Following these procedures produces the 1655–1860 warship array recorded in Table 3.4.

Table 3.4 Numerical distribution of global power warships, 1655–1860

Year	NTH	ENG/ GB	FRN	SPN	RUS	USA	Total
1655	81	109	25	30			245
1656	78	103	28	28			237
1657	78	99	29	27			233
1658	84	95	30	27			236
1659	79	95	30	27			231
1660	78	96	33	26			233
1661	82	95	25	25			227
1662	83	94	28	25			230
1663	87	94	29	25			235
1664	95	94	30	25			244
1665	95	103	39	24			259
1666	96	99	51	24			270
1667	95	78	61	23			257
1668	94	78	70	23			265
1669	94	80	76	23			273
1670	96	83	99	22			300
1671	80	52	81	21			234
1672	77	50	83	21			231
1673	70	54	86	21			231

68

Table 3.4 Numeral distribution of global power warships, 1655–1860

Year	NTH	ENG/ GB	FRN	SPN	RUS	USA	Total
1674	63	56	87	21			227
1675	63	60	90	20			233
1676	51	61	86	19			217
1677	51	62	84	19			216
1678	53	69	79	19			220
1679	54	80	83	19			236
1680	54	79	87	18			238
1681	54	81	84	17			236
1682	61	79	85	17			242
1683	61	81	90	17			249
1684	61	81	91	17			250
1685	65	82	89	16			252
1686	53	80	88	16			237
1687	55	79	89	17			240
1688	66	78	92	18			254
1689	71	74	96	19			260
1690	61	71	100	20			252
1691	60	68	114	21			263
1692	61	70	115	22			268
1693	65	81	122	23			291
1684	73	87	120	24			304
1695	74	97	125	24			320
1696	73	99	122	24			318
1697	73	107	119	25			324
1698	72	115	118	25			330
1699	81	117	118	26			342
1700	86	115	118	26			345
1701	86	117	118	23			344
1702	89	124	96	20			329
1703	88	117	101	17			323
1704	87	119	104	14			324
1705	86	121	106	11			324
1706	85	120	105	9			319
1707	84	114	108	6			312
1708	83	123	99	3			308
1709	82	124	96	0			302
1710	81	129	92	0			302
1711	80	129	86	0			295
1712	79	130	77	0			286
1713	78	128	68	0			274
1714	77	127	66	0	10		280
1715	73	124	60	6	17		280
1716	70	122	48	11	16		267
1717	66	122	43	17	15		263

Table 3.4 Numeral distribution of global power warships, 1655–1860

Year	NTH	ENG/ GB	FRN	SPN	RUS	USA	Total
1718	63	122	32	22	23		262
1719	59	121	23	3	26		232
1720	56	120	22	5	29		232
1721	53	122	23	7	29		234
1722	49	119	27	9	29		233
1723	45	121	30	12	30		238
1724	42	121	35	14	32		244
1725	42	120	36	17	34		249
1726	43	117	36	19	31		246
1727	43	116	38	22	28		247
1728	43	113	37	24	25		242
1729	43	113	37	25	24		242
1730	44	111	37	27	23		242
1731	44	112	40	27	23		247
1732	44	113	39	30	23		249
1733	45	113	39	31	22		250
1734	43	115	40	33	21		252
1735	40	117	41	34	21		253
1736	39	121	41	36	20		257
1737	37	123	41	41	19		261
1738	35	123	44	42	19		263
1739	33	118	47	41	18		257
1740	30	116	47	40	17		250
1741	29	119	45	38	14		245
1742	35	117	46	37	15		250
1743	35	116	46	35	17		249
1744	34	107	46	34	20		241
1745	34	110	47	32	22		245
1746	33	112	44	34	24		247
1747	33	122	37	35	24		251
1748	33	123	41	36	23		256
1749	33	114	47	37	23		254
1750	33	116	53	38	23		263
1751	33	116	55	40	22		266
1752	32	115	58	42	22		269
1753	31	117	59	43	21		271
1754	31	118	62	45	21		277
1755	29	119	63	45	21		275
1756	29	117	67	46	20		279
1757	27	95	71	46	22		261
1758	27	103	59	47	21		257
1759	25	109	49	50	20		253
1760	25	107	50	52	19		253
1761	23	111	58	49	19		260

70

Table 3.4 Numeral distribution of global power warships, 1655–1860

Year	NTH	ENG/GB	FRN	SPN	RUS	USA	Total
1762	23	116	64	47	18		268
1763	21	117	69	36	18		261
1764	20	120	71	38	17		266
1765	15	122	76	49	15		277
1766	19	120	69	43	17		268
1767	17	118	70	45	16		266
1768	16	121	74	47	15		273
1769	15	122	76	49	15		277
1770	15	121	77	51	15		279
1771	13	118	76	53	16		276
1772	12	115	80	56	16		279
1773	12	111	78	58	17		276
1774	11	110	75	60	17		273
1775	11	108	75	60	17		272
1776	11	109	75	62	18		275
1777	14	106	75	64	18		277
1778	16	104	83	66	19		288
1779	19	104	86	60	19		288
1780	22	109	85	62	19		297
1781	25	114	89	64	24		316
1782	22	126	84	65	29		326
1783	32	125	82	67	34		340
1784	33	115	76	67	39		330
1785	33	121	74	67	44		339
1786	34	127	76	67	49		353
1787	35	132	81	67	54		369
1788	36	133	82	76	48		375
1789	38	134	87	72	67		397
1790	34	137	90	74	75		410
1791	32	133	87	77	73		402
1792	38	132	87	79	71		397
1793	35	132	78	76	69		380
1794	33	133	74	74	67		380
1795	25	131	82	72	65		375
1796	16	129	79	70	62		355
1797	16	139	83	68	60		366
1798	16	147	70	66	59		358
1799	16	135	65	63	59		338
1800	15	132	61	63	58		329
1801	15	131	60	63	58		327
1802	15	129	60	63	57		324
1893	15	128	66	63	57		329
1804	15	122	69	57	56		319
1805	14	130	63	51	57		315

Table 3.4   Numerical distribution of global power warships, 1655–1860

Year	NTH	ENG/ GB	FRN	SPN	RUS	USA	Total
1806	14	129	65	42	58		308
1807	14	148	73	42	58		335
1808	14	149	72	42	59		336
1809	13	148	71		60		292
1810	13	151	81		57		302
1811		148	91		54		293
1812		154	101		51		306
1813		145	106		49		300
1814		131	77		46		254
1815		134	79		43		256
1816		130	52		40	2	224
1817		124	49		40	2	215
1818		122	34		40	2	209
1819		118	47		39	3	207
1820		118	48		39	3	208
1821		114	48		39	3	204
1822		110	46		39	3	198
1823		109	44		39	3	195
1824		107	43		39	3	192
1825		100	41		39	4	184
1826		96	39		35	4	174
1927		92	38		32	4	166
1828		91	36		32	5	164
1829		91	35		32	5	163
1830		86	33		32	5	156
1831		85	33		33	5	156
1832		82	33		34	5	154
1833		84	33		35	5	157
1834		82	33		37	5	157
1835		81	28		38	5	152
1836		79	23		39	5	146
1837		77	20		40	5	142
1838		76	20		41	6	143
1839		77	20		41	6	144
1840		78	20		41	6	145
1841		77	21		41	7	146
1842		76	21		41	7	145
1843		76	21		41	6	144
1844		75	22		42	6	145
1845		73	23		42	6	144
1846		72	23		43	6	145
1847		73	24		43	6	146
1848		73	25		43	6	147
1849		70	25		43	6	144

72

Table 3.4   Numerical distribution of global power warships, 1655–1860

Year	NTH	ENG/GB	FRN	SPN	RUS	USA	Total
1850		70	26		43	6	145
1851		71	27		43	6	147
1852		73	27		43	6	149
1853		76	30		43	6	155
1854		78	32		44	6	160
1855		80	35		30	6	151
1856		77	38		27	6	148
1857		76	41		25	5	147
1858		76	44		22	5	147
1859		78	47		19	5	149
1860		76	50		16	5	147

4 Rules for Counting Warships, 1861–1993

In the late 1850s, the wooden ship-of-the-line was quickly transformed into a naval dinosaur by the development and application of explosive shells and armour-clad battleships. But there was nothing equally rapid about the transition from the first armour-clad ships to the development of something resembling a standardised battleship. The trial-and-error experimentation of the period 1859–90 is truly a comparativist's nightmare. Wooden hulls and masts were retained even while shipbuilders raced to create thicker hulls and heavier guns. Iron plating gave way to steel ships. At one point torpedoes, mines and ramming tactics, resurrected from the galley era, seemed likely to slow down the construction race but the interlude was only temporary as ships continued to grow in terms of tonnage displacement and firepower.

As has been demonstrated, there was nothing particularly novel about the evolutionary process in naval technological developments. Yet the sliding minimum-gun criterion used in the period 1655–1860 or something akin to it does not work very well in the period 1861–90. The problem in this case has two faces. One, each navy was composed of a number of different types of battleships rendering comparison difficult and uncertain even within the navy of one state – let alone between the navies of several states. In contrast to the amazing stability of the wooden sailing-ship phase, many of the new ironclads became obsolete in very short order. Two, a number of the ironclads were simply not ocean-going battleships despite occasional claims to the contrary. Instead, they were only useful for coastal defensive purposes – a far cry from our concern with global reach. Nevertheless, it was not always clear, at least at first, to which ships this generalisation applied and to which it did not.

Two recent analysts have captured the naval spirit of the time quite aptly:

> However linear and inexorable the technological progress of the period appears in hindsight, to the contemporaries everywhere, experts and amateurs alike, things were a terrible jumble – a confused

74   *Global Overview*

jigsaw puzzle of many unknown pieces, being fitted together quite unsystematically (Buhl, 1978, p. 48).

It is unnecessary to catalogue the incredible misdirections, false starts, unsightly and unhandy steam kettles, half submerged, double elliptical, rhinoceros-skinned misfits weighted down by huge turrets swaddling one or two ponderous barrel-like pieces, which marked the fearful adolescence of the ironclad (Padfield, 1973, p. 191).

These statements do not represent rhetorical hyperbole by any stretch of the imagination. Even the strongest navy of the period has been described as being composed of twenty-five different types of battleships. Such circumstances pose nearly-overwhelming odds against quantification and comparison both then and now. Fortunately, a useful attack on this problem has recently appeared in the form of *Conway's All the World's Fighting Ships, 1860–1905* (Chesneau and Kolesnik, 1979). As the title suggests, this project represents an effort to fill in the chronological gap in the extensive cataloguing of battleships that existed prior to the late nineteenth century advent of such specialised annual volumes as Brassey's *Naval Annual* and *Jane's Fighting Ships* (1898). We will make use of Chesneau and Kolesnik's counts of capital ships, listed in Table 4.1, for the muddled period between 1861 and 1879.

Buhl's 'terrible jumble' appears to have become stabilised in the 1880s and 1890s. In these decades some level of consensus was reached about how ocean-going battleships should be built and, as a consequence, the principal naval competitors increasingly are found building similar, if not identical, kinds of battleships. In particular, a return to internationally comparable ratings (i.e. first class, second class, third class) for battleships re-emerged in the 1880s even though the precise criteria which were used are not entirely clear. Brassey's *Naval Annual* which began publication in the late 1880s provides a convenient source of battleship classifications for the major maritime powers after 1895. Focusing on the 'first-class battleship', it is possible to use the Brassey ship lists to trace the introduction of these capital ships back to about 1880 and forward to 1913. The lists are particularly useful in that they provide appropriate adjustments for vessels built earlier which became obsolete and/or were reduced to second- and third- (coastal defence) class status.

It is at this juncture that there is a need for a new criterion for global power status. The abandonment of the wooden ship-of-the-line

Rules for Counting Warships, 1861–1993

Table 4.1   Numerical distribution of global power battleships, 1861–79

Year	GB	FRN	RUS	GER	JAP	Total
1861	2	1				3
1862	5	6				11
1863	7	6				13
1864	12	6	1			19
1865	16	11	5			32
1866	22	12	6			40
1867	25	16	6			47
1868	29	16	8			53
1869	30	16	9			55
1870	37	18	13			68
1871	38	17	13	5		73
1872	40	16	13	5		74
1873	42	16	13	5		76
1874	43	16	14	5		78
1875	40	16	14	8	2	80
1876	40	18	15	9	2	84
1877	45	19	16	10	2	92
1878	45	21	17	9	5	97
1879	44	20	17	9	5	95

renders the ten per cent rule awkward. The 'back-dating' approach to Brassey's ship lists and classifications forces some degree of caution in using a percentage approach because the technique singles out certain battleships and excludes others afloat in the 1880s and early 1890s.

In addition to the 5 per cent rule for naval expenditures which remains in force, the new minimal criterion is the possession of at least three battleships rated as first class in 1895.

The number 'three' is only partially arbitrary. The number corresponds to the minimum size of a squadron in the days of sail and it is approximately 5 per cent of the global powers' total first-class battleships throughout the 1890s. Since there were no global wars between 1816 and 1913 (and therefore, according to an earlier rule, no opportunity for exit from global power status) this new criterion applies only to new candidates for global power status.

Our treatment of the new battleships of the late nineteenth century is complicated by the introduction of an even more advanced battleship type – the Dreadnought – in 1906. This development created two basic classes of battleships: pre-Dreadnoughts (Table 4.2) and Dread-

76 *Global Overview*

Table 4.2 Numerical distribution of global power pre-Dreadnoughts, 1880–1913

Year	GB	FRN	RUS	GER	USA	JAP	Total
1880	7	3	1				11
1881	8	4	1				13
1882	8	4	1				13
1883	10	5	1				16
1884	10	5	1				16
1885	10	6	1				17
1886	13	7	3				23
1887	16	9	4				29
1888	17	9	4				30
1889	21	9	4				34
1890	22	10	4				36
1891	22	10	4	3			39
1892	23	10	4	4			41
1893	24	10	5	4	3		46
1894	19	10	5	4	3		41
1895	19	9	5	4	3		40
1896	21	10	5	4	3	1	44
1897	24	13	6	4	3	2	52
1898	29	14	6	4	4	3	60
1899	18	8	4	5	4	3	42
1900	22	9	6	5	8	4	54
1901	24	10	6	7	9	5	61
1902	29	10	7	9	9	6	70
1903	32	11	8	12	10	6	79
1904	38	11	10	14	11	6	90
1905	43	11	8	16	12	4	94
1906	45	11	4	18	15	10	103
1907	50	13	4	20	22	11	120
1908	41	9	3	18	20	11	102
1909	43	9	3	20	21	10	106
1910	32	7	3	17	20	8	87
1911	37	7	4	20	20	9	97
1912	41	12	7	19	22	9	110
1913	25	6	2	13	8	4	58

noughts. By the advent of war in 1914, it had become clear that the pre-Dreadnoughts' combat capabilities were decidedly inferior to the modern Dreadnoughts. The gap was so great that the British expected a German pre-Dreadnought to last no more than five minutes in a fight with a British Dreadnought. For reasons such as these (i.e., ordnance, armour, speed), Brassey's comparative naval tables count

Rules for Counting Warships, 1861–1993

only Dreadnoughts as 'modern' battleships after 1913. Following this lead and making use of detailed Dreadnought information available in such studies as Breyer (1973) and McMahon (1978) in conjunction with the Brassey *Naval Annual* material, it is possible to construct a complete Dreadnought series from 1906 to 1945 (Table 4.3) which partially overlaps with the earlier first-class battleship series (1880–1913). We will use 1910 as the year in which we switch from one series to the next.

The Dreadnoughts were usually treated as a relatively homogeneous class of fighting ship despite their comparatively long reign (1906–45) and despite trends toward more powerful ordnance and general combat capabilities within this same time-span. While it is quite possible that the simple numerical approach (subject to various qualifications and caveats) used in the earlier centuries will suffice until 1945, it may be that more sophisticated indexes could prove worthwhile. For example, Brassey's *Naval Annual* distinguishes between ships with 14-inch guns and those with less fire-power. Lambelet (1974, 1975, 1976) has explored such 1905–16 battleship attributes as displacement, cost, broadside weight, thickness of armour, and speed in a series of naval arms race models. Nevertheless, it remains an empirical question whether more precise information will have much impact on the distribution of seapower capability patterns which continue to constitute the primary concern of this project.

More critical to the longitudinal utility of our battleship series, however, are the discontinuities in the nineteenth-century evolution of capital ships. In contrast to the smoother escalation of the minimal number of guns that needed to be carried for front-line duties in earlier centuries, the changes in naval technology in the late 1850s, the early 1880s and 1906 practically forced the maritime powers of the time to start again from scratch. The British maintained a fairly consistent lead throughout these various design departures but, in certain years, the extent of their lead is exaggerated by the British ability to retool somewhat faster than their rivals. For example, in the years 1906 and 1907, Great Britain had commissioned one Dreadnought while no other state had yet done so. It hardly makes sense to grant the British a perfect monopoly in those two years on the basis of one ship. We can, in this case, smooth the abrupt changes by postponing the Dreadnought-counting shift to 1910, as opposed to 1906. But postponement is only a partial remedy and one that is not very helpful in the two earlier periods of abrupt changes.

A more general solution to this era's discontinuity problem consists

Table 4.3 Numerical distribution of global power Dreadnoughts, 1906–45

Year	GB	FRN	RUS/ USSR	GER	USA	JAP	Total
1906	1	0	0	0	0	0	1
1907	1	0	0	0	0	0	1
1908	4	0	0	0	0	0	4
1909	8	0	0	2	0	0	10
1910	10	0	0	5	4	0	19
1911	14	0	0	9	6	0	29
1912	21	0	0	14	8	3	46
1913	27	2	0	17	8	4	58
1914	34	4	4	22	10	4	78
1915	38	6	6	23	10	7	90
1916	42	7	5	24	14	7	99
1917	44	7	6	25	15	9	106
1918	44	7	5	0	17	9	107
1919	44	7	5	0	17	9	82
1920	39	7	4	0	18	10	78
1921	37	7	4	0	20	10	78
1922	24	6	3	0	19	10	62
1923	24	6	3	0	21	10	64
1924	21	6	3	0	18	10	58
1925	21	6	3	0	18	10	58
1926	18	6	3	0	18	10	55
1927	20	6	3	0	18	10	57
1928	20	6	3	0	17	10	57
1929	20	6	3	0	15	9	56
1930	20	6	3	0	15	9	56
1931	15	5	3	0	15	9	49
1932	15	5	3	0	15	9	47
1933	15	5	3	1	15	9	48
1934	15	5	3	2	15	9	49
1935	15	5	3	2	15	9	49
1936	15	5	3	3	15	9	50
1937	15	5	3	3	15	9	50
1938	15	7	3	4	15	9	53
1939	14	7	3	5	15	9	54
1940	15	7	3	5	15	10	55
1941	13		2	5	15	11	46
1942	15		2	4	19	10	50
1943	15		2	4	21	9	51
1944	14		3	2	25	5	49
1945	14	2	3	0	20	1	40

Rules for Counting Warships, 1861–1993

79

of merging ship counts and the more stable (in the comparative sense) indicator of naval expenditures. Although the naval expenditures have the advantage of greater continuity, they possess too many limitations of comparability to rely upon them as an exclusive indicator of seapower in the nineteenth and early twentieth centuries. Consequently, we will construct a composite scoring system for measuring seapower by adding relative (percentage) ship and naval expenditure shares and then dividing by two. While we are proposing these smoothing procedures to apply primarily to problems in the period 1860–1913, our interest in measuring the long cycle suggests that we need to be as consistent as possible between periods of global war. Accordingly, the composite scoring system will be utilised to encompass the entire period 1816–1945. The naval expenditure data for 1816–1945, expressed in 1913 British £s after correcting for each country's inflation history, are reported in Table 4.4.[1]

THE LATE TWENTIETH CENTURY PROBLEMS

The round sailing-tubs of the fourteenth century gave way to the sleeker galleons of north-west Europe and the more ponderous versions of south-west Europe in the sixteenth century. The ship-of-the-line evolved from the north-western variety toward the end of the seventeenth century creating a global naval standard which endured through the middle of the nineteenth century – although certainly not without improvements from time to time. Eventually and not without resistance, the industrial revolution penetrated even naval technology. Explosive shells – first used at Sinope in 1853 – made wooden hulls obsolete for military purposes: steam engines made sailors less dependent on the wind. Between 1860 and 1880 a new global standard for capital ships emerged – the first-class battleship – once again capable of assuming a front-rank position in the fleet battle-line. The minimal threshold was no longer measured primarily in terms of the number of guns carried but rather in the range of the guns.

Despite the undeniable increase in naval lethality, the reign of the battleship as the undisputed capital ship was relatively short-lived. Fleets fought fleets only rarely in the First World War, thanks in part to the naval asymmetries of the conflict. The First World War, however, did facilitate the emergence of two types of naval vessels which gradually rendered the battleship obsolete – at least as a capital ship. One of the innovations was the submarine which, while actually

80

Table 4.4   Global power constant naval expenditures, 1816–1938
(British £m [1913])

Year	GB	FRN	RUS*	USA	GER	JAP**	Total
1816	7.50	1.19	0.82	0.54			10.15
1817	4.36	1.02	0.97	0.45			6.80
1818	4.40	1.03	0.96	0.42			6.81
1819	4.60	1.27	1.09	0.64			7.57
1820	5.32	1.49	1.08	0.86			8.75
1821	5.50	1.67	1.14	0.67			8.98
1822	4.76	2.01	1.05	0.43			8.25
1823	4.96	2.35	1.11	0.50			8.92
1824	5.36	2.17	0.96	0.61			9.10
1825	4.68	1.98	1.01	0.61			8.28
1826	5.95	1.98	0.91	0.88			9.72
1827	5.84	2.11	1.00	0.90			9.85
1828	5.35	2.87	1.15	0.84			10.21
1829	5.67	2.58	1.30	0.86			10.41
1830	5.16	3.17	1.32	0.74			10.39
1831	5.37	2.62	1.29	0.85			10.13
1832	4.74	2.33	1.28	1.08			9.43
1833	4.32	2.30	1.27	0.93			8.82
1834	4.25	2.21	1.26	1.06			8.78
1835	3.87	2.16	1.56	0.87			8.46
1836	3.63	2.32	1.50	1.13			8.58
1837	4.28	2.39	1.52	1.19			9.38
1838	4.04	2.50	1.48	1.15			9.17
1839	4.46	2.79	1.57	1.14			10.72
1840	4.63	3.36	1.57	1.33			10.89
1841	5.69	4.23	1.84	1.35			13.11
1842	6.32	4.63	1.95	2.13			15.03
1843	6.68	4.52	1.75	1.04			13.99
1844	5.75	4.70	1.70	1.76			13.91
1845	6.55	4.53	2.30	1.58			14.96
1846	7.57	4.81	1.70	1.62			15.70
1847	7.42	5.14	1.79	1.82			16.17
1848	8.43	6.03	1.80	2.39			18.65
1849	7.71	5.11	2.33	2.48			17.63
1850	7.16	4.29	1.91	1.95			15.31
1851	6.80	4.18	2.26	2.22			15.46
1852	7.45	4.12	2.74	2.10			16.41
1853	8.16	3.97	3.32	2.36			17.81
1854	12.28	6.21	2.27	2.06			22.82
1855	16.66	7.13	2.82	2.50			29.11
1856	11.50	6.62	2.65	2.77			23.54
1857	8.83	3.83	2.96	2.36			17.98
1858	8.78	4.44	2.69	3.13			19.04
1859	10.95	9.76	2.74	3.21			26.65

Table 4.4   Global power constant naval expenditures, 1816–1938
(British £m [1913])

Year	GB	FRN	RUS*	USA	GER	JAP**	Total
1860	11.80	7.67	3.11	2.57			25.15
1861	11.67	6.66	3.06	2.89			24.28
1862	10.06	7.05	2.65	8.48			28.24
1863	9.49	4.40	2.66	9.87			26.42
1864	9.73	6.22	2.81	9.20			27.96
1865	9.93	6.62	2.61	13.75			32.91
1866	9.45	6.07	3.02	5.14			23.68
1867	9.77	5.55	2.23	3.96			21.51
1868	10.31	5.36	2.41	3.37			21.45
1869	9.34	5.74	2.49	2.74			20.30
1870	8.63	6.70	2.42	3.35			21.10
1871	8.76	5.52	2.63	3.10	1.19		21.20
1872	7.67	4.55	2.98	3.24	1.31		19.75
1873	8.38	4.80	3.00	3.67	1.04		20.89
1874	9.18	5.26	3.36	5.10	1.66		24.56
1875	9.82	5.51	3.45	3.76	2.37	0.59	25.50
1876	10.19	5.97	3.48	3.56	2.08	0.71	25.99
1877	10.38	6.70	3.86	2.92	3.19	0.66	27.71
1878	12.41	8.53	3.16	3.96	3.58	0.59	31.23
1879	11.12	7.56	2.90	3.49	2.60	0.56	28.23
1880	10.95	7.39	3.00	2.80	2.20	0.51	26.85
1881	11.35	8.06	3.13	3.15	2.15	0.44	28.28
1882	10.80	8.90	3.13	2.88	2.16	0.51	28.38
1883	11.29	10.72	3.24	3.13	2.40	1.91	31.97
1884	12.70	13.48	3.26	3.85	2.99	1.45	37.73
1885	15.25	14.30	3.91	3.87	3.34	1.16	41.83
1886	17.01	13.04	4.32	3.53	3.38	2.12	43.40
1887	16.22	9.94	3.70	3.45	2.28	2.28	39.29
1888	16.46	8.57	3.46	4.09	3.28	2.29	38.14
1889	19.33	9.09	4.16	5.49	3.22	1.99	43.28
1890	18.96	9.20	4.36	5.58	3.99	1.86	43.95
1891	19.23	10.76	5.20	6.62	4.78	1.88	48.47
1892	20.43	12.07	4.61	7.89	5.44	1.78	52.22
1893	20.10	12.29	4.95	8.05	5.08	1.69	52.16
1894	25.07	14.37	5.35	9.32	5.18	2.05	61.34
1895	29.00	14.43	5.78	8.35	5.74	2.50	65.80
1896	32.13	14.66	6.01	8.35	6.16	3.15	70.46
1897	29.79	14.23	6.24	10.46	7.25	7.62	75.59
1898	32.53	15.38	7.01	17.30	8.00	8.48	88.70
1899	32.91	15.84	8.61	17.30	8.93	8.91	92.50
1900	34.33	17.24	8.89	14.19	8.94	7.79	91.38
1901	38.32	16.50	9.90	15.54	11.93	6.15	98.34
1902	38.49	14.48	10.21	16.37	12.92	5.03	97.50
1903	43.80	14.42	12.35	19.72	13.21	4.71	108.21

82

Table 4.4   Global power constant naval expenditures, 1816–1938
(British £m [1913])

Year	GB	FRN	RUS*	USA	GER	JAP**	Total
1904	47.22	14.21	11.95	24.29	13.42	2.61	113.70
1905	41.11	14.78	12.39	27.73	13.89	2.67	112.57
1906	35.72	13.36	12.49	25.18	9.18	6.95	102.88
1907	33.85	13.20	18.85	21.19	15.05	7.50	109.64
1908	39.26	14.94	10.22	26.61	18.59	7.82	117.44
1909	40.91	15.70	9.65	24.17	22.22	8.05	120.70
1910	43.89	12.83	9.72	24.74	22.49	9.42	123.09
1911	44.65	21.02	11.69	26.17	23.14	10.86	137.53
1912	45.28	19.13	17.68	27.79	21.85	9.70	141.43
1913	48.83	21.73	24.48	27.04	23.12	9.80	155.00
1919	62.85	16.64		205.17		13.44	298.1
1920	28.79	6.95		67.57		15.88	119.2
1921	41.02	12.42		94.25		24.70	172.4
1922	35.35	14.78		70.09		19.48	139.7
1923	33.08	10.36		46.94		14.11	104.5
1924	33.49	11.89		47.81	3.54	12.29	109.0
1925	37.55	9.37		47.45	5.26	11.57	111.2
1926	38.92	9.00		44.37	7.30	13.52	113.1
1927	40.92	15.28		47.23	7.79	16.45	127.7
1928	40.64	16.32		48.36	7.38	16.00	128.7
1929	40.73	21.97		54.38	7.05	16.48	140.6
1930	43.83	22.61		61.22	7.63	18.03	153.3
1931	48.67	28.79		69.01	8.32	19.98	174.8
1932	49.02	22.27		77.99	9.40	26.19	184.9
1933	52.45	28.70		75.40	16.14	30.77	203.5
1934	53.90	29.82		56.30	24.15	36.52	200.7
1935	61.13	32.41		76.97	33.14	39.08	242.7
1936	71.77	35.35		92.50	53.73	38.59	291.9
1937	78.46	32.86		91.08	67.16	36.38	305.9
1938	105.21	38.49		107.03	79.77	36.48	367.0

*In the absence of a continuous Russian price index, we first converted the
Russian rouble figures, on an annual basis, to British £ (using 1816–1913
exchange rates supplied through the courtesy of J. David Singer's Correlates of War project at the University of Michigan) and then applied the
British price index to the converted Russian series. Post-First World War
Soviet naval expenditures are simply unavailable for most years. Accordingly, after 1913, only the proportional number of battleships is utilised in
calculating the Russian/Soviet global capability share.

**We suspect that Japan's twentieth-century naval expenditures are under-
stated but by what factor is unclear.

introduced into naval service well before the war, gained prominence during the war as an instrument that could be used by the weaker naval side to carry out a traditional *guerre de course* strategy. As the French attempted to demonstrate in the global wars of the late seventeenth/early eighteenth centuries, if one's regular navy was too weak to confront the opponent's navy openly, emphasis could be shifted to a form of naval guerrilla warfare conducted against commercial shipping. Twentieth-century submarines proved to be more effective than the French privateers of the earlier era at this type of warfare even though their ultimate success in the Atlantic theatre was eventually checked in both world wars. The development of a new form of propulsion which would permit submarines to remain submerged for lengthy periods, however, was necessary before the submarine could replace the battleship as a capital fighting ship.

Instead, the battleship surrendered its capital position to the aircraft-carrier. As range of fire had grown in significance, the aeroplane, capable of taking off and landing on a floating platform, certainly lengthened the range at which naval power could be projected. Even so, it was not until the Second World War that the transition was fully recognised. Only when fleets engaged in combat with other fleets without even sighting one another, except through the eyes of their fighter aircraft, did it become clear that the battleship was in fact as vulnerable as Billy Mitchell had demonstrated in the early 1920s.

The reign of the flat-top as the undisputed capital ship after 1945 was even shorter-lived than that of its battleship predecessors. The development of the atomic bomb and the capability to project armed missiles on an intercontinental scale seemed to displace or subordinate the role of seapower as the primary medium of global power projection. Navies appeared to be restricted primarily to conventional weaponry. Sea-lane protection, amphibious landings, shore bombardments, and 'showing the flag' throughout the globe remained important politico-military functions but they no longer represented a global power's first line of offence and defence against other global powers. This too changed, however, as nuclear missiles began to be sent to sea in the late 1950s and early 1960s. As advance bases for nuclear bombers became increasingly difficult to obtain or keep and as land-based missile-sites became more vulnerable, the flexibility and mobility offered by utilising submarines as nuclear-missile platforms became increasingly attractive. As indicated in Table 4.5, between 1960 and 1980, the proportion of American and Soviet nuclear

84 *Global Overview*

Table 4.5   Proportion of deliverable strategic nuclear warheads based at sea, 1960–80

Year	United States	Soviet Union	United States and Soviet Union
1960	0.9		0.7
1961	2.8		2.0
1962	3.7		2.7
1963	5.5	1.7	4.4
1964	9.6	1.6	7.4
1965	18.6	1.8	14.4
1966	26.5	1.8	20.4
1967	30.9	1.6	23.5
1968	31.2	2.9	23.1
1969	33.1	6.5	24.1
1970	37.4	9.0	27.1
1971	44.4	12.6	33.6
1972	47.7	15.8	37.5
1973	49.3	18.4	40.6
1974	46.9	20.1	39.7
1975	47.9	21.2	41.0
1976	50.6	21.1	42.7
1977	51.4	19.6	41.9
1978	53.1	17.9	41.1
1979	54.4	16.5	39.6
1980	51.1	17.3	36.6

Source: Calculated from data in Ha (1983, pp. 25–7).

warheads at sea increased from less than 1 per cent to almost 37 per cent, nor is there little current reason to anticipate that the trend initiated in 1960 is likely to alter its direction of change substantially.

The uncertainties underlying the way(s) in which future global wars will be fought make it difficult to state unequivocally that the ballistic-missile submarine has replaced the aircraft-carrier as *the* current capital ship. One could agree that the very use of sea-based nuclear missiles will have negated their fundamental purpose of deterrence. Certainly, if the missiles are ever fired, the submarine-launchers will have lost a significant proportion of their fighting capability. But even if the ultimate significance of ballistic missiles is put aside for the moment, a case can be made for a third candidate for the contemporary capital-ship title. Harnessing nuclear propulsion to the submarine overcame that vessel's previous chief liability – namely,

Rules for Counting Warships, 1861–1993

its inability to avoid spending a relatively excessive amount of time on the surface. The Soviet admiral Gorshkov makes a strong case for considering nuclear attack submarines in general as capital ships:

> The ability to stay under water practically throughout the period of independent action, the great depth of submergence and sailing on low-noise course give atomic submarines high concealment, ability to conduct combat actions on a global scale to destroy important land objectives, submarines and surface ships of the enemy (Gorshkov, 1979, p. 192).

Similar claims are made for the ship-killing potential (especially in reference to carriers) and capital-ship status of nuclear-attack submarines in such treatments as Whitestone (1973) and Wilmott and Pimlott (1979).

Thus, the late twentieth century's operationalisation problem *vis-à-vis* capability concentration is again a matter of which precise capabilities should be examined. But can one restrict the post-1945 examination to naval weaponry? And if so, which one(s)? Even when these questions are answered the usual problem of how to enumerate the selected capabilities will also require some discussion.

A LATE-TWENTIETH-CENTURY SOLUTION

There is no denying the increased military importance of air power after 1945, nor is it reasonable to contend that air power does not represent a significant component in a global power's ability to project its resources on a global scale. A parallel observation could be made about economic capabilities which were significant both before and after 1945 but which have been advanced, more recently, as the pre-eminent 'capability' of the late twentieth century. But, one need not take issue with these positions in suggesting that naval power has retained much of its politico-military significance in the global political system by becoming more aerospace-oriented. Nor has it ever been suggested that naval power is or ever was the only appropriate indicator of global reach in the modern world system. Rather, our perspective suggests only that naval power has been a leading indicator of global capability since about 1500. In that sense, it appears to be justifiable to extend the capital ship analysis beyond 1945.

Global Overview

As for identifying the contemporary capital ship, a case can be made for all three candidates although admittedly the case for aircraft-carriers was stronger prior to the development of nuclear submarines. Thus, instead of focusing exclusively on one type of ship, the solution proposed here advocates a fairly simple combination of the three different types of naval capability – aircraft-carriers, nuclear-attack submarines, and ballistic-missile systems based at sea. Of the three types, the first two are the least difficult to enumerate.

It is always possible to attempt extremely complex analyses of twentieth-century weapon systems. When one is dealing with the Soviet Union's naval capability, however, specific performance indicators are frequently based on little more than educated guesses. Therefore, more simple indicators are definitely preferable. In addition, a consistent theme in analysing sea power is that numbers of ships within roughly equivalent classes will usually suffice for our more general purposes. Accordingly, the number of light- and heavy-attack carriers and nuclear-attack submarines will be treated and enumerated as if each respective vessel shared membership within a roughly homogeneous class. Obviously, this is rarely the case. Ships launched, say, twenty years apart tend to be qualitatively different in terms of weight, speed, noise, and such factors as armament, propulsion systems, and life expectancy. But the same observation may be applied as well to ships-of-the-line or battleships. The argument made here is that it is possible to ignore short-term qualitative improvement for long-term analysis purposes until the qualitative improvements represent a recognisable technological breakthrough as in the distinction between pre-Dreadnought and Dreadnought battleships or diesel and nuclear submarines.

In the case of aircraft-carriers and attack submarines (including Soviet nuclear submarines armed with Cruise missiles), the nuclear submarines present few enumeration problems. Fairly reliable estimates of the number of American and Soviet nuclear submarines can be made using the sources to be discussed for sea-based ballistic missiles. Aircraft-carriers, however, do represent a unique problem. No Soviet aircraft-carriers, other than the non-qualifying helicopter/anti-submarine-warfare variety, are likely to be commissioned prior to the 1990s. The measurement question, consequently, is whether it is realistic to allocate a 100 per cent capability score for the American monopoly – even though the absolute number of American carriers has declined by about two-thirds in the period since 1946. There is

Rules for Counting Warships, 1861–1993　　87

also some question as to the aircraft-carrier's continued claim to capital-ship status after the introduction of nuclear submarines.

The major exception to the preference for disregarding differences within general classes of naval vessels is found in the sea-based ballistic-missile category. In the Soviet case, eight types of nuclear ballistic missiles (SS-N-4, SS-N-5, SS-N-6, SS-N-8, SS-N-17, SS-N-18, SS-N-20, SS-N-23) have been or will be installed on fifteen classes of diesel and nuclear submarines (Zulu-V, Golf I–IV, Hotel I–III, Yankee I–II, Delta I–IV, and Typhoon). The Americans have relied upon six types of nuclear missiles (Polaris A-1, Polaris A-2, Polaris A-3, Poseidon, Trident C-4/D-5) placed on six classes of nuclear submarines (George Washington, Ethan Allen, Lafayette, James Madison, Benjamin Franklin, Ohio). Each missile type has different performance and lethality characteristics. Moreover, the missile systems developed early in the competition have been gradually phased out and replaced by more sophisticated systems. The number of warheads carried by American missiles has also increased in recent years. To make matters even more confusing, there is very little exact agreement on the actual number of Soviet submarines and/or missiles ready for sea duty in any given year.

The preceding observations suggest two things. First, it is inappropriate or misleading to count merely the number of ballistic-missile submarines, the number of sea-based missile-launchers, or the number of warheads at sea. None of these three indicators lend themselves readily to straightforward aggregation. Second, to determine the static force levels available to each side, some other unit or units of measurement are necessary. Unfortunately, no single standard unit of measurement enjoys consensus approval at the present time. The three main attributes of relevance to missile performance are range, accuracy, and warhead yield. However, the main reason analysts disagree over their relative importance is that their ultimate significance depends on the intended target and the geographical obstacles involved in reaching the target. For example, hardened-missile silo targets require more accurate hits of certain yields than do 'soft' city targets. Alternatively, population centres are more concentrated and closer to the sea in the United States than they are in the Soviet Union. Consequently, it is very conceivable that different targeting priorities and opportunities favour different combinations of attributes of missile-performance.

Long cycle theory or the analysis of seapower cannot be expected to

88 *Global Overview*

resolve these continuing policy debates about strategic target priorities and their measurement. In the spirit of global capability analyses of earlier periods, however, the empirical focus needs to be placed on relatively simple and accessible indicators of the capability to project force. Two indicators of missile destructiveness seem most pertinent in this light. The first is described as 'equivalent megatonnage' (*EMT*) which adjusts warhead yield for the fact that increases in yield cannot be equated with proportional increases in destructiveness. In the context of sea-based missiles, $EMT = Y^{2/3}$, where Y is warhead yield.

The main drawback of the *EMT* indicator is that it only assesses the amount of damage that may be done to unprotected targets. For protected targets, a calculation of missile accuracy must be considered. This is accomplished in the 'counter military potential' (*CMP*) indicator which corrects the equivalent megatonnage by the square of an accuracy indicator – *CEP* or circular error probable. Thus,

$$CMP = \frac{Y^{2/3}}{CEP}$$

Of course, *CMP* does not involve any calculation of the degree of protection available to specific targets. While this is a drawback, an analyst would require access to a great deal of classified information on target characteristics which is simply unavailable and presumably subject to some amount of change as well.

The approach proposed here entails using both *EMT* and *CMP* as two separate indicators of sea-based missile destructive capability. Using both indicators, as opposed to one or the other, does not restrict the interpretation of the resulting scores to a single targeting strategy when, in fact, the current global powers may be operating on different strategic priority premises. The reader will note that both accuracy and yield attributes are encompassed by the indicators. Some thought was given to including an indicator component for range as well but as there seems to be some imperfect relationship between improvements in *CEP* and range, the additional component appeared to be somewhat redundant.

To calculate aggregate *EMT* and *CMP*, several preliminary steps are necessary. As is so often the case in long cycle analyses no annual series is currently available which is capable of being expressed in *EMT* and *CMP* terms. Thus, to construct the appropriate series, it is first necessary to calculate the number of missile-launching submar-

Rules for Counting Warships, 1861–1993

ines by class that were available to the late twentieth century's two global powers. Most sources disagree on these numbers but not necessarily by a wide margin. Table 4.6 provides an illustration using information on Soviet Delta-class ballistic submarines. The sources will tend to converge over time on their estimates but will tend to disagree on the annual rate of introduction of new submarines. In such cases where longitudinal series are made available by several

Table 4.6   Soviet nuclear ballistic submarines: Delta-class estimates

| | *Jane's* | | | | *IISS** | | | |
Year	DI	DII	DIII	D	DI	DII	DIII	D
1973	4	0	0	4	3	0	0	3
1974	5	1	0	6	9	0	0	9
1975	6	1	0	7	13	0	0	13
1976	10	2	0	12	13	4	0	17
1977	15	4	0	19	13	8	0	21
1978	15	5	6	26	15	13	0	28
1979	19	5	7	31	15	5	9	29
1980	18	4	10	32	19	4	10	33

| | *SIPRI*** | | | | *Collins (1980)* | | | |
Year	DI	DII	DIII	D	DI	DII	DIII	D
1973	1	0	0	1	1	0	0	1
1974	7	0	0	7	5	0	0	5
1975	12	0	0	12	11	0	0	11
1976	12	6	0	18	17	0	0	17
1977	12	11	0	23	17	4	5	26
1978	12	11	2	25	18	4	8	30
1979	12	11	4	27	18	4	10	32
1980	12	11	9	32	—	—	—	—

| | *Combined Estimate* | | | |
Year	DI	DII	DIII	D
1973	2			2
1974	7			7
1975	11			11
1976	13	4		17
1977	14	7	1	22
1978	15	8	4	27
1979	16	6	8	30
1980	16	6	10	32

*International Institute for Strategic Studies
**Stockholm International Peace Research Institute

90 *Global Overview*

sources, it seems reasonable simply to compute the annual average. This rule is most applicable to the more detailed source coverage of Soviet submarines in the 1970s. The information available for Soviet submarines in the 1960s is much less precise and requires occasionally the type of estimation and extrapolation techniques sometimes used in estimating ships-of-the-line.

In contrast, sufficient information is available for American ballistic-missile submarines to avoid the need for estimation. Indeed, it is the clarity of the available United States fleet information which enables us to project our series forward to encompass the last decade of the half-millenium 1494–1993. While the assumptions that need to be made pertaining to United States building plans for the immediate future are relatively few (see Chapter 8), Soviet plans admittedly can only be guesstimated (as described in Chapter 9).

Once the submarine-by-class series are constructed, using the sources indicated in Table 4.7, it is then possible to translate the

Table 4.7   Primary sources for late-twentieth-century naval estimates

Aircraft-carriers	*Submarines*
Bauer (1969)	Bauer (1969)
Collins (1980)	Blechman (1975)
International Institute for Strategic Studies (IISS) (multiple volumes)	Breyer and Polmar (1977)
	Brodeur (1975)
	Collins (1980, 1985)
Jane's Fighting Ships (multiple volumes)	*Congressional Record* (1977)
	Gatland (1977)
Polmar (1969, 1978)	Gunston (1977)
	Hoeber (1977)
	International Institute for Strategic Studies (IISS) (multiple volumes)
	Jane's Fighting Ships (multiple volumes)
	MccGwire (1973a, 1973b, 1973c, 1973d, 1975a, 1975b, 1975c, 1980)
	Moore (1977)
	Morris (1977)
	Perry (1974)
	Polmar (1969, 1974, 1978, 1984)
	Rohwer (1975)
	Scherer (1977, 1978)
	Stockholm International Peace Research Institute (SIPRI) (multiple volumes)

number of submarines within their respective classes into the number and types of missile-launchers and warheads believed to be associated with each type of vessel. Taking into consideration programmes to convert old-generation missiles for new models, ship-losses through accidents, the introduction of multiple warheads, and retirements of ships from first-line duty, one can thus calculate the annual number of sea-based warheads by type. Since each type of missile/warhead series, is believed to be characterised by specific if approximate yield and *CEP* attributes, the warhead series, in turn, can then be converted through the respective formulas into aggregate *EMT* and *CMP* series for the United States and the Soviet Union.[2]

The procedures discussed in the past few pages produce four separate post-1945 series: one each for aircraft-carriers and nuclear-attack submarines and two for sea-based ballistic-missile systems. The annual indicators are reported in Table 4.8 as the proportion controlled by the late twentieth century's maritime leader, the United States. Figure 4.1 illustrates in a more graphic way the observation that each indicator presents a different image of American (and Soviet) relative naval strengths or capabilities. For instance, *CMP* clearly favours the American navy while the reverse is true of *EMT*. The proportional number of attack nuclear submarines indicates a Soviet lead that appears to be relatively stable while the aircraft-carrier scores signal obvious American predominance.

Table 4.8   The American share of global naval capability, 1946–93

Year	Aircraft-carriers	Nuclear attack submarines	Nuclear ballistic missiles at sea		Average score
			CMP	*EMT*	
1946	1.000				1.000
1947	1.000				1.000
1948	1.000				1.000
1949	1.000				1.000
1950	1.000				1.000
1951	1.000				1.000
1952	1.000				1.000
1953	1.000				1.000
1954	1.000				1.000
1955	1.000				1.000
1956	1.000				1.000
1957	1.000				1.000
1958	1.000				1.000

92   *Global Overview*

Table 4.8   The American share of global naval capability, 1946–93

Year	Aircraft-carriers	Nuclear attack submarines	Nuclear ballistic missiles at sea CMP	EMT	Average score
1959	1.000				1.000
1960	1.000	0.348	0.935	0.614	0.724
1961	1.000	0.438	0.929	0.592	0.740
1962	1.000	0.486	0.915	0.544	0.736
1963	1.000	0.425	0.949	0.673	0.762
1964	1.000	0.438	0.952	0.688	0.770
1965	1.000	0.440	0.952	0.689	0.770
1966	1.000	0.431	0.954	0.698	0.771
1967	1.000	0.443	0.936	0.680	0.765
1968	1.000	0.462	0.917	0.654	0.758
1969	1.000	0.473	0.826	0.569	0.717
1970	1.000	0.455	0.857	0.544	0.714
1971	1.000	0.457	0.870	0.528	0.714
1972	1.000	0.460	0.878	0.515	0.713
1973	1.000	0.465	0.881	0.514	0.715
1974	1.000	0.459	0.877	0.484	0.705
1975	1.000	0.457	0.886	0.484	0.707
1976	1.000	0.441	0.874	0.448	0.691
1977	1.000	0.447	0.862	0.431	0.685
1978	1.000	0.447	0.815	0.388	0.663
1979	1.000	0.438	0.766	0.352	0.639
1980	1.000	0.435	0.742	0.329	0.627
1981	1.000	0.451	0.766	0.362	0.645
1982	1.000	0.449	0.769	0.373	0.648
1983	1.000	0.445	0.752	0.373	0.643
1984	1.000	0.430	0.747	0.384	0.640
1985	1.000	0.429	0.750	0.402	0.645
1986	1.000	0.422	0.749	0.402	0.643
1987	1.000	0.433	0.683	0.388	0.626
1988	1.000	0.449	0.665	0.368	0.620
1989	1.000	0.445	0.674	0.364	0.621
1990	1.000	0.456	0.678	0.356	0.622
1991	0.933	0.461	0.687	0.356	0.609
1992	0.938	0.466	0.707	0.352	0.616
1993	0.875	0.484	0.712	0.351	0.605

It might seem attractive to be in a position to weight the different scores according to their relative contribution to global capability. However, the justification for a complicated weighing scheme is not intuitively obvious. In its absence, the more prudent course entails adding across the separate indicators to arrive at an annual average score, as provided in Table 4.8.

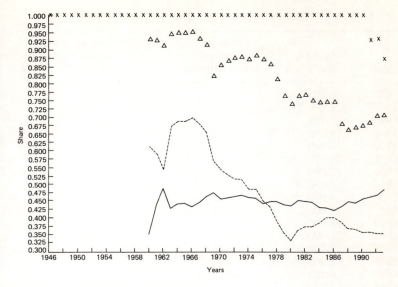

Notes: Aircraft-carriers (XXXXX)
Nuclear-attack submarines (solid line)
Counter military potential (triangles)
Equivalent megatonnage (broken line)

Figure 4.1 United States share of selected global naval capabilities, 1946–93

Finally, it is instructive to compare the outcome of the averaging procedure performed in Table 4.8 with two broader-based indexes presented in Table 4.9. We have noted earlier that an index focusing on such weapons as aircraft-carriers and sea-based ballistic missiles is no longer a strictly traditional seapower measure. A substantial element of aerospace power has been incorporated to the extent that contemporary weapon systems afloat also tend to merge aerospace and seapower. We have also insisted throughout our presentation that long cycle theory's focus on sea- or ocean-power does not imply that other types of capabilities, either military or non-military, have no relevance for global reach. Our argument is only that sea power represents an important leading indicator of global reach. Moreover, in constructing a lengthy time-series, there is always a possibility that the phenomena being measured will undergo radical changes necessitating equally radical shifts in analysis procedures. While our 500-year series has required periodic shifts in measurement objectives, it would be difficult to characterise these shifts as all that radical in nature.

94

Table 4.9   Three indexes of contemporary military capabilities

Year	Long cycle index	Ha index of strategic nuclear weapons	Proportionalised index of Ward military stockpile data
1946	1.000	1.000	—
1947	1.000	1.000	—
1948	1.000	1.000	—
1949	1.000	1.000	—
1950	1.000	1.000	—
1951	1.000	1.000	0.959
1952	1.000	1.000	0.970
1953	1.000	1.000	0.974
1954	1.000	0.992	0.976
1955	1.000	0.903	0.877
1956	1.000	0.850	0.847
1957	1.000	0.792	0.867
1958	1.000	0.763	0.877
1959	1.000	0.737	0.882
1960	0.724	0.717	0.860
1961	0.740	0.679	0.881
1962	0.736	0.697	0.900
1963	0.762	0.704	0.902
1964	0.770	0.700	0.902
1965	0.770	0.728	0.863
1966	0.771	0.739	0.864
1967	0.765	0.734	0.818
1968	0.758	0.691	0.801
1969	0.717	0.642	0.771
1970	0.714	0.620	0.713
1971	0.714	0.641	0.679
1972	0.713	0.662	0.681
1973	0.715	0.697	0.704
1974	0.705	0.711	0.707
1975	0.707	0.726	0.674
1976	0.691	0.705	0.627
1977	0.685	0.692	0.589
1978	0.663	0.644	0.531
1979	0.639	0.611	0.531
1980	0.627	0.607	—
1981	0.645	—	—
1982	0.648	—	—
1983	0.643	—	—

Note: Ha's index (Ha, 1983, p. 35) represents the United States' proportion of strategic nuclear warheads deliverable by bombers, land-based missiles and sea-based missiles. The US share is based on an N encompassing the Soviet Union, United Kingdom, France, China,

Rules for Counting Warships, 1861–1993

Along these lines, we are particularly sensitive to the fact that a good many students and observers of world politics are convinced that the nature of military power underwent a particularly radical change in 1945. Indeed, it is likely that while our seapower arguments may hold some appeal for the pre-nuclear, pre-1945 world, there will undoubtedly be a certain amount of resistance to applying similar arguments to the post-1945 world. We have addressed this problem earlier in this chapter and in Chapter 1, as well as elsewhere. There is probably little to be gained by dwelling further on this topic. Nevertheless, it is intriguing that the post-1945 long cycle series bears a close resemblance to recently developed indexes of post-1945 military power concentration – those that give equal weight to various types of nuclear warheads and weapon systems – regardless of the medium through which they are meant to be delivered.

In addition to giving equal weight to data on the full triad of delivery systems, Ha's index of 1983, listed in Table 4.9, also incorporates the small nuclear inventories of France, the United Kingdom, and China – all of which are excluded from the long cycle index. Ward's focus on a central European confrontation combines information on strategic and conventional weapons possessed by the United States, the Soviet Union, as well as the two Germanys. Despite these differences in index-construction principles, the outcomes of the power-concentration measurement are remarkably similar – a point that is graphically illustrated in Figure 4.2.

There are of course a number of ways to measure nuclear arsenals just as there are plausible arguments to be entertained for regarding such measurements, or any measurement, as the statistical analogue of weaponry overkill. Be that as it may, Table 4.9 and Figure 4.2 suggest, at the very least, that a seapower approach to global-power concentration may be no less tenable as a measurement strategy for the late twentieth century than it was for the seventeenth or eighteenth centuries.

---

and the United States. Ward's military stockpile data (Ward, 1984, p. 312) combine two indexes. One measures the conventional forces (manpower × fire-power × mobility) of the Soviet Union, East Germany, West Germany, and the United States. The second series focuses on US and USSR strategic forces (total number of weapons weighted by lethality). The two indexes are added and then divided by 1000. The series in this table is the United States (and the West German contribution to the conventional index) share of the total stockpile data.

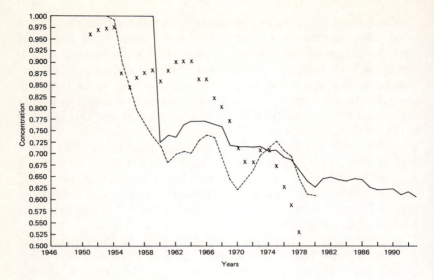

Notes: Long-cycle index (solid line)
Ha index (broken line)
Ward index (XXXX)

Figure 4.2 Emphasising seapower versus other indexes of strategic nuclear weapons, 1946–93

5 The Long Cycle of World Leadership

The long cycle of global politics refers to the process of fluctuations in the concentration of global reach capabilities which provide one foundation for world leadership. Given the basic geographical nature of the world – great masses of land separated by large bodies of water – and the technological history of the modern, post-1500 era, a primary capability for global reach has been and continues to be seapower. Previous chapters have discussed why we believe this to be the case, how we propose to measure seapower, and what principles have guided the data collection of the predominantly capital-ship index of naval power. The subsequently collected information is reported in some detail in Chapters 7–9. With this information, guided by the insights of long cycle theory and the measurement rules reviewed earlier, we are now in a position to answer two questions. First, which states qualify as global and world powers and when do they qualify? Second, is there a long cycle of fluctuations in the extent to which naval power is concentrated that follows essentially a sequential pattern of global war, relatively high concentration, deconcentration, and then a return to global war?

The answers to both these questions, in turn, will hinge on long cycle theory's identification of the phases of global war (1494–1516, 1580–1608, 1688–1713, 1792–1815, and 1914–45) for it is these system-transforming bouts of warfare that constitute the watershed phases of the hypothesised long cycle process. Global and world powers enter into and may lose membership in the global political system within the intervals of time demarcated by two successive global wars. Moreover, it is during the global war phase that the system's tendency toward concentration–deconcentration essentially switches from deconcentration to a fairly high level of concentration for some finite post-war period of time.

THE GLOBAL POWERS

Global powers must satisfy minimal criteria pertaining to the possession of a number of capital ships and the geographical scope of

98 *Global Overview*

capital-ship deployments. As outlined in Table 5.1, throughout the period 1494–1993 only nine states qualify and the number of states qualifying at any point in time ranges from two to six. The crude emergence of a global political system is dated from 1494 with a 'charter' membership of Portugal, Spain, England, and France. The precise entry date of the United Provinces of the Netherlands is somewhat arbitrary but 1579 is useful as the year in which the new state formally constituted itself as an effective political unit. Two years later, in 1581, the newly-formed Union of Utrecht renounced allegiance to Philip II.

Table 5.1   The global powers

Global powers	Years as global powers
Portugal	1494–1580
Spain	1494–1808
England (Great Britain)	1494–1945
France	1494–1945
United Provinces of the Netherlands	1579–1810
Russia (Soviet Union)	1714–
United States	1816–
Germany	1871–1945
Japan	1875–1945

The identity of the élite subset of global powers changed very little for the first two to three hundred years. Portugal was absorbed by Spain in 1580 and failed to regain global-power status after its successful revolt in 1640. The one new member prior to the Napoleonic Wars was Russia (1714). Only in the nineteenth century is the membership list substantially altered. Spain and the Netherlands finally lost their global power status in the waning years of the Napoleonic Wars. The United States is credited with global power status from 1816 on. This date may seem premature but it follows from our rule that global power membership is backdated whenever possible to the beginning of a new post-global war period regardless of the precise year in which the capital ship and extra-regional activity requirements are viewed as fully satisfied.

Germany and Japan must be treated a bit differently from the

United States. Although the small Prussian navy became the core of the German navy, Germany did not exist as a unified state prior to 1871. Japan, on the other hand, remained isolated from the rest of the world until the 1850s. More to the point and in contrast to the US case, a naval department was not established until 1872. Nevertheless, defeat in the Second World War terminated the global power status of both Germany and Japan. The last two charter members, Great Britain and France, finally lost their capability to compete on a global scale during the Second World War as well.[1] From 1946 on, only the United States and the Soviet Union have demonstrated the capabilities regarded as necessary for membership in the global power élite sub-system.

CONCENTRATION IN SEAPOWER

To answer the question of whether or not a long cycle of naval power concentration exists, we must first address one last preliminary question. Earlier chapters have provided details about what is to be counted (primarily capital ships) and whose capability units (the global power) are to be counted. The final preliminary question to be tackled is how concentration is to be measured. A variety of indexes are available ranging from the most simple to more complex formulations. Choosing one from among several alternative computation methods need not – nor should it – be an arbitrary process. Different indexes have known advantages and liabilities. More importantly, different indexes supply different types of information. The choice should therefore be guided by the specific question or questions being addressed.

Long cycle theory emphasises the significance of periods of single-state or world power naval preponderance. It is doubtful therefore whether changes in the relative positions of say the third- or fourth-ranked states that did not affect the leader's position would be very critical to measuring the long cycle. If we are able to identify periods when one state possesses a decisive lead over its global power rivals and allies (as in the post-global-war '50 per cent' criterion for world power status) then we should be able to opt for one of the most simple indexes: the proportion of total global power capabilities controlled by the world power.

The adoption of the simple proportional index has at least three implications that deserve some attention. First, as suggested above,

Global Overview

some of the variance in systemic concentration is 'lost' or ignored in exchange for the simplicity of calculation and interpretation. It is quite conceivable, for example, that systemic capability concentration could increase or decrease while the leader's relative position remained unchanged. Consider the following three-actor scenario. At time t leader A possesses 100 ships, B has 50 and C controls 50 as well. By time $t+1$, leader A still has 100 ships, B now has 20 and C has 80. Between T and $T+1$, the system's capability distribution has become more concentrated but the leader's proportional capability control has remained unchanged. In this instance, the positional changes of actors B and C technically do not affect A's position, but in reality the changes would most certainly have some clear implications for changes in behaviour. An actor with 50 per cent of the system's capabilities should be able to be more successful in influencing B's and C's behaviour when B and C possess 25 per cent shares than when B has 40 per cent and C has 10 per cent.

Still, the scenario outlined above seems likely to represent an extreme case. What is more likely are situations involving minor positional shifts between B and C and/or more major growth in the capability position of B or C being reacted to by A. But rather than simply ruling out cases that would threaten the validity of the chosen index as less than probable, it should be more convincing to treat the issue as an empirical question. How much information about systemic concentration is lost by focusing only on the leader's proportional position?

To investigate this question empirically, it is necessary to calculate an index designed to capture changes in the overall level of concentration and to compare the results with the information supplied by inspecting the leader's share index. One appropriate alternative index is the computation constructed by Ray and Singer (1973) to measure the extent to which a system's power is concentrated:

$$\text{Systemic concentration} = \sqrt{(\sum s_i^2 - 1/N)/(1 - 1/N)}$$

where s = each actor's percentage share and N = the number of actors in the system.

Figure 5.1 plots the series that emerges from this calculation along with the simpler leader's share series for the representative period 1609–1815. It is readily apparent that both series are capturing very similar changes in the system's concentration property. To be sure, there are some changes in one series that are not mirrored exactly in

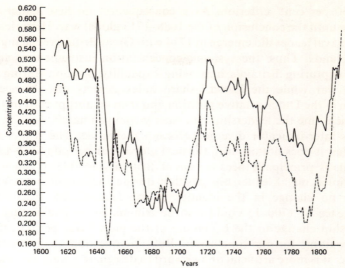

Notes: World power's proportional index (solid line)
Systemic-concentration index (broken line)

Figure 5.1 Two indexes of seapower concentration, 1609–1815

the second series but, for the most part, these cases of divergence are very minor indeed.

The one exception to the rule of minor divergences introduces the second implication of adopting the leader's share-index approach. The only divergence of the two series in Figure 5.1 that seems noteworthy is located in the interval roughly between 1700 and 1715. The systemic-concentration index depicts a gradually rising level of concentration while the leader's share-index suggests no change until about 1711, followed by an abrupt increase in 1714. One would think that if one of the series is relatively accurate, the other one must be in error. A system's capability distribution cannot be rising at the same time that it is remaining unchanged. Yet there is really no mystery here and, depending upon how one views the 1700–15 developments, neither series is demonstrating a genuine lack of reliability.

One major difference between the two series is that in order to calculate the leader's share index, one must already have decided who the leader is, and how to deal with the leader's term or tenure. In long cycle analysis, this identification is made by applying the post-global-

102 *Global Overview*

war '50 per cent' criterion. As a consequence, no new leader can emerge until the conclusion of the 1688–1713 global war. Historically, a new naval leader did emerge in 1714 with Great Britain replacing the Netherlands. Thus, the systemic-concentration instrument is accurately capturing Britain's improving capability position during the global war while the leader's-share index depicts the absence of change in the Dutch relative position and then an abrupt shift in 1714 by which time the leadership had clearly changed hands.

This inter-indicator divergence is not inevitable. The reader will note that it does not occur in the next global war period (1792–1815) but this is principally because Great Britain was able to renew its exceptional naval leadership position during the Napoleonic Wars. Hence no change in the identity of the leader took place. The divergence of 1700–15 could also be eliminated by backdating the leadership change to the beginning of the global war period rather than waiting for its conclusion. But the question then becomes whether it is more artificial or awkward to designate a state as a leader before it satisfies the leadership criteria or to continue to focus on the old leader's share while the issue of leadership is being bitterly contested. Since it would become more difficult to test long cycle theory's assertions about the relationship between capability concentration and conflict if the backdating procedure was pursued, the latter focus ultimately seems less awkward. There is also the question of adhering to our convention on leadership identification to be considered.

The main point is that the leader's-share approach requires intermittent analytical intervention and a shift in computational focus whenever the leadership criteria are met. Other indexes of concentration, such as the systemic-concentration calculation do not. While one might wish to minimise analytical intervention in order to avoid injecting unnecessary bias, the identification of world leadership is simply too crucial to long cycle theory to insist on a pure non-interventionist approach. Once the interventions have been made, it is also important to realise that the leader's-share approach is apt to have a blind side to the rise of challengers or successors. To pursue these phenomena, an analyst must examine more specific information (i.e. the capability shares of the other actors) but then the same observations can be applied to the more neutral concentration indexes as well. If we only know that the system's capability concentration is rising, we still do not know who is benefiting from the rise until more specific information is examined.

The Long Cycle of World Leadership

The third and final implication of adopting the leader's-proportional-share index is linked to an element of non-comparability in the interpretation of proportional shares. We have already hinted at this problem in the scenario that compared a 50 per cent leadership position in two cases: one where no other actor possessed more than 25 per cent and one where one other actor possessed 40 per cent. The two situations are not structurally identical even though the leader's proportional position is identical. This scenario was labelled extreme because, in part, movement from one situation to the other is not all that probable within a reasonably finite period of time. Nevertheless the problem can be translated into more generalised terms. As we have noted, the number of significant actors in the global political system has ranged from a low of two (after 1945) to a high of six. Unfortunately, a 50 per cent leadership position in a six-actor system does not mean the same thing in a two-actor system. A 50 per cent share in a six-actor system could provide an impressive capability foundation for exercising leadership. However, the same 50 per cent share in a two-actor system suggests that the two actors that count must have identically equal capability bases.

The upshot of this discussion is that we need to exercise caution in comparing percentage shares across time and different actor configurations. Figure 5.2, for example, compares the same two series contrasted in Figure 5.1, but this time for the two-actor, post-1945 era. According to the leader's-percentage-share index, the concentration values have remained unusually high, particularly in comparison with the highest values plotted in Figure 5.1. The systemic-concentration index also records unusually high values up to 1959. After 1959, however, the level of concentration falls off markedly – reaching a low of 0.261 in 1981. For the sake of comparison, post-global-war, systemic-concentration values as low as this were not reached in the period 1609–1815, until 1644 (temporarily) and 1778 respectively. Thus, even though the direction of movement of the two series remains similar, the concentration interpretation of the numbers differs substantially by index.

This might appear to be an indictment of the leader-share index in that it performs least well in two-actor systems (in comparison with systems with more than two actors). That this is a weakness of the indicator system for purposes of comparison across time cannot be denied but it is worth pointing out that it is not clear that the systemic-concentration index or other such indexes are any more comparable across time- and actor-configurations. The problem reduces to the

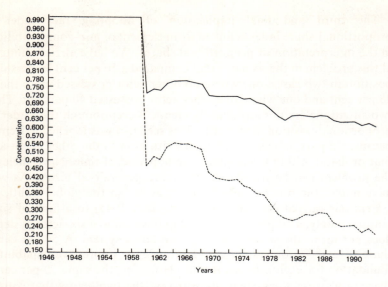

Notes: World power's proportional index (solid line)
Systemic-concentration index (broken line)

Figure 5.2 Two indexes of seapower concentration, 1946–93

question of whether a given level of concentration means the same thing regardless of the number of actors involved. Does bipolar parity mean the same thing as parity between the two leading actors in a multipolar setting? Fortunately or unfortunately, this question has not yet been resolved theoretically or empirically. In the interim, we choose to continue our reliance on the leader-share index. But we also recognise that it may be less appropriate for some types of questions. As an alternative, a concentration series for 1494–1993, based on the systemic-concentration formula, can be found in Appendix B.

THE CYCLICAL FLUCTUATION OF SEAPOWER CONCENTRATION

The identification, and the measurement of their capability shares, of the world powers is closely intertwined with ascertaining whether there is a cyclical fluctuation of sea power capability concentration. If one state does satisfy the definitional attribute of the world power

The Long Cycle of World Leadership 105

status (controlling 50 per cent or more of global naval-power capabilities at the end of a global war phase), we will also have a partial answer to the question of whether capability concentration is cyclical.

Table 5.2 isolates those years between 1494 and 1993 in which naval power concentration equalled or exceeded the 50 per cent threshold and the identity of the global power that controlled half or more of the system's naval power. Some 156 years are enumerated and few surprises emerge in the identities of the states listed. If we remove but

Table 5.2   Years of high concentration of naval power

Years in which 50% concentration levels were attained or exceeded	*State controlling 50% or more of naval-power capabilities*
1494	England
1502–1544	Portugal
1594–1597	Spain
1608–1619	Netherlands
1624	Netherlands
1632–1633	Netherlands
1635–1636	Netherlands
1640–1642	Netherlands
1719–1723	Great Britain
1809–1812	Great Britain
1814–1834	Great Britain
1843	Great Britain
1854–1857	Great Britain
1861	Great Britain
1868–1869	Great Britain
1880–1881	Great Britain
1889–1890	Great Britain
1944–	United States

two of the entries in Table 5.2 (1494 and 1594–7) all the remaining years are readily aligned with the phases of global war and the years that follow, as demonstrated in Table 5.3. In fact, with the exception of eleven points in the second half of the nineteenth century (1854–7, 1861, 1868–9, 1880–1, 1889–90) the other 145 years all fall within a global war phase or within the immediate 35 post-global war years.

The sequential pattern, of course, is less than perfect but the deviations can be accounted for quite readily. The initial deviation, 1494, is the first year in the series and reflects the rather small number

106   *Global Overview*

Table 5.3   World powers and clusters of high concentration of naval power

Global-war phase	Clusters of years with concentration values greater than or equal to 0.500	World power
1494–1517	1502–44	Portugal
1580–1608	1608–19, 1624, 1632–3 1635–6, 1640–2	Netherlands
1688–1713	1719–23*	Great Britain
1792–1815	1809–12, 1814–34, 1843, 1854–7, 1861, 1868–9, 1880–1, 1889–90	Great Britain
1914–45	1944–present	United States

*The average concentration value for 1714–50 is 0.472.

of warships maintained by states at the end of the fifteenth century. The second departure, 1594–7, captures the belated and unsuccessful attempt on the part of Spain to become the system's leading seapower during the global war of 1580–1608. By the next decade, Spain's capability share had fallen as quickly as it had risen.

The Portuguese and Dutch periods of high capability follow the anticipated pattern. Portugal gained an early lead almost at the beginning of the sixteenth century although, to some extent, its lead was achieved by default. The other potential seapower states were still preoccupied with more local issues and/or had not yet seriously begun to cultivate their state navies. Approximately a century later, the Dutch emerged from the first half of their war of independence with an impressive lead in seapower and retained this lead well into the middle of the seventeenth century – much as the Portuguese had done earlier. Unlike the Portuguese, however, the United Provinces of the Netherlands never enjoyed the relative absence of naval competition. Shortly after the lingering Spanish threat had been dealt with at sea (1639), serious challenges arose first from the English and later from the French.

The brevity of the first period of British naval predominance may seem odd. The level of concentration in the post-global war period equals or exceeds 0.500 in only five years (1719–23 inclusive). But this apparent brevity is misleading for the average concentration level between 1714 and 1750 is a high 0.472. The variation in concentration

The Long Cycle of World Leadership

during the period 1714–50 ranges between 0.441 and 0.522. Thus what may seem to be a weak case for high concentration at first glance is actually not quite as marginal as it appears. Rather than stressing the 'weakness' of the first British naval lead, it may be more useful to contrast it with the much stronger second British period of naval leadership. In the first third or so of the second British period, the level of concentration values are not only higher than in the first period, but the British relative decline in naval power is reversed repeatedly by changes in naval technology which the British were able to channel to their own advantage. These technological changes were also responsible for the unusually high concentration level reported in the second half of the nineteenth century (e.g. 1861, 1880–1, 1889–90). Whether this consequence of industrialisation is a harbinger for the course of the long cycle in the US era of naval leadership – an era which has conformed closely to the expected post-global war concentration pattern – remains to be seen.

So far we have found evidence of relatively high concentration levels (greater than or around 0.500) primarily in the five periods immediately following the phases of global war. This information enables us to identify the world power naval leaders. Yet while these periods of high concentration values recur with convincing regularity, we still lack some of the information needed to be able to refer to these fluctuations in capability concentration as cyclical in nature. If, for example, what we are describing as relatively high concentration values are maintained throughout the periods between global wars, it would be more appropriate to refer to the process as simply a straightforward circulation of naval power élites. What we need is a better sense of the extent of fluctuation in naval-power concentration levels. Table 5.3 informs us about the location of the highest points in the process. Where are the low points and how low have they tended to be?

Both long cycle theory and the very notion of a cycle predicts movement away (decline or decay) from the high concentration values in the post-war era toward progressively lower values until and into the next phase of global war. Accordingly, we should expect to find the lowest values in the concentration series clustered roughly in the second halves of the periods between global wars, and especially in the years immediately preceding the renewed onset of global war.

Table 5.4 identifies those years in the concentration series which have values less than 0.400 and 0.300. The outcome follows the predictions quite closely. Concentration values equal to or greater

108 *Global Overview*

Table 5.4 Clusters of years with low concentration values

Global war phases	Naval power concentration values less than	
	0.400	*0.300*
1494–1517		
	1562–5	
	1569–1570	
	1570	
1580–1608	1575–83	1579–80
	1589	
	1601–8	1604–8
	1646–51	
1688–1713	1653–1713	1674–1713
	1757	
1792–1815	1775–97	
	1799	
	1802–4	
	1899–1901	
	1906–9	
	1912–13	
1914–45	1919–45	1931–41
		1942–3

than 0.400 tend to be found in the periods following global war through about the first half of the inter-war interval. The one exception is the second British leadership period in which values of 0.400 or greater were maintained through 1898. Concentration values of less than 0.400 characterise the second halves of the inter-war periods as well as most of the years during the global war phases. Even lower values (less than 0.300) are found primarily within the global-war years. The exceptions here are the low values immediately preceding the global war of 1688–1713. However, it is interesting to note that no value less than 0.300 can be found at any time in the first British leadership period – the one that was supplanted by a second era of British naval predominance.

REGULARITIES AND IRREGULARITIES IN THE LONG CYCLE

The general pattern is thus one of clusters of high concentration values following, and clusters of lower concentration values preceding, periods of global war. What appearance should this pattern take if plotted over time? Ideally, it might resemble the prototypical cyclical image – the smooth undulations of a sine wave. Of course, real behavioural cycles rarely do more than approximate the prototypical image. And given our intermittently discontinuous approach to operationalisation (new leaders bring about a shift in the leader's-share-measurement focus) the smooth undulations are more likely to resemble spiky waves cresting immediately after a global war and gradually subsiding into a trough that precedes the next spiked crest. This expectation is very roughly realised in the 500-year fluctuation of the concentration–deconcentration process that is recorded in Table 5.5 and plotted in Figure 5.3 (see also the same diagram in the prelims, enlarged for clarity).

Figure 5.3 portrays a process characterised by an intriguing mixture of regularities and irregularities. For instance, each of the post-global war peaks has a different shape and height. If each of these peaks were to be connected, the resulting pattern would resemble an asymmetrical 'U' with the first three crests (post-1516, post-1608, and post-1713) declining in height, reflecting perhaps the increasing naval

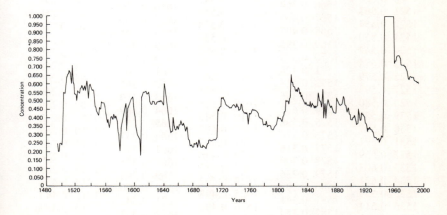

Figure 5.3   The long cycle, 1494–1993

Table 5.5 Global naval power concentration, 1494–1993

Year		Year		Year		Year		Year	
1494	0.250	1539	0.586	1584	0.402	1629	0.482	1674	0.278
1495	0.200	1540	0.573	1585	0.425	1630	0.495	1675	0.270
1496	0.200	1541	0.559	1586	0.438	1631	0.495	1676	0.235
1497	0.250	1542	0.566	1587	0.467	1632	0.500	1677	0.236
1498	0.250	1543	0.560	1588	0.490	1633	0.502	1678	0.241
1499	0.250	1544	0.524	1589	0.324	1634	0.495	1679	0.229
1500	0.238	1545	0.469	1590	0.448	1635	0.502	1680	0.227
1501	0.294	1546	0.462	1591	0.471	1636	0.500	1681	0.229
1502	0.553	1547	0.442	1592	0.483	1637	0.491	1682	0.252
1503	0.545	1548	0.430	1593	0.493	1638	0.484	1683	0.245
1504	0.542	1549	0.421	1594	0.503	1639	0.476	1684	0.244
1505	0.590	1550	0.412	1595	0.516	1640	0.605	1685	0.258
1506	0.642	1551	0.463	1596	0.516	1641	0.571	1686	0.224
1507	0.656	1552	0.450	1597	0.525	1642	0.528	1687	0.229
1508	0.663	1553	0.454	1598	0.469	1643	0.491	1688	0.260
1509	0.679	1554	0.495	1599	0.443	1644	0.468	1689	0.273
1510	0.674	1555	0.488	1600	0.411	1645	0.433	1690	0.242
1511	0.664	1556	0.489	1601	0.348	1646	0.387	1691	0.228
1512	0.612	1557	0.489	1602	0.327	1647	0.355	1692	0.228
1513	0.599	1558	0.473	1603	0.300	1648	0.337	1693	0.223
1514	0.707	1559	0.468	1604	0.292	1649	0.313	1694	0.240
1515	0.610	1560	0.425	1605	0.283	1650	0.321	1695	0.231
1516	0.597	1561	0.400	1606	0.274	1651	0.321	1696	0.230
1517	0.538	1562	0.371	1607	0.269	1652	0.408	1697	0.225
1518	0.537	1563	0.394	1608	0.177	1653	0.358	1698	0.218
1519	0.539	1564	0.354	1609	0.526	1654	0.352	1699	0.237
1520	0.500	1565	0.338	1610	0.541	1655	0.331	1700	0.249
1521	0.563	1566	0.364	1611	0.551	1656	0.329	1701	0.250
1522	0.554	1567	0.405	1612	0.554	1657	0.335	1702	0.271
1523	0.550	1568	0.407	1613	0.553	1658	0.356	1703	0.272
1524	0.542	1569	0.395	1614	0.557	1659	0.342	1704	0.269
1525	0.574	1570	0.389	1615	0.556	1660	0.335	1705	0.265
1526	0.579	1571	0.424	1616	0.541	1661	0.361	1706	0.266
1527	0.593	1572	0.418	1617	0.541	1662	0.361	1707	0.269
1528	0.580	1573	0.396	1618	0.558	1663	0.370	1708	0.269
1529	0.559	1574	0.413	1619	0.549	1664	0.389	1709	0.272
1530	0.577	1575	0.398	1620	0.497	1665	0.359	1710	0.268
1531	0.591	1576	0.376	1621	0.492	1666	0.357	1711	0.271
1532	0.559	1577	0.316	1622	0.480	1667	0.370	1712	0.276
1533	0.603	1578	0.300	1623	0.481	1668	0.355	1713	0.285
1534	0.621	1579	0.236	1624	0.502	1669	0.344	1714	0.454
1535	0.559	1580	0.202	1625	0.498	1670	0.320	1715	0.443
1536	0.511	1581	0.341	1626	0.496	1671	0.342	1716	0.457
1537	0.588	1582	0.354	1627	0.481	1672	0.333	1717	0.464
1538	0.600	1583	0.381	1628	0.482	1673	0.303	1718	0.466

Table 5.5 Global naval power concentration, 1494–1993

Year		Year		Year		Year		Year	
1719	0.522	1764	0.451	1809	0.507	1854	0.513	1899	0.393
1720	0.517	1765	0.446	1810	0.500	1855	0.551	1900	0.392
1721	0.521	1766	0.448	1811	0.505	1856	0.505	1901	0.392
1722	0.511	1767	0.444	1812	0.503	1857	0.504	1902	0.405
1723	0.508	1768	0.443	1813	0.483	1858	0.489	1903	0.405
1724	0.496	1769	0.440	1814	0.516	1859	0.467	1904	0.419
1725	0.482	1770	0.434	1815	0.523	1860	0.493	1905	0.411
1726	0.476	1771	0.428	1816	0.660	1861	0.574	1906	0.392
1727	0.470	1772	0.412	1817	0.609	1862	0.401	1907	0.363
1728	0.467	1773	0.402	1818	0.615	1863	0.449	1908	0.368
1729	0.467	1774	0.403	1819	0.589	1864	0.490	1909	0.373
1730	0.461	1775	0.397	1820	0.588	1865	0.401	1910	0.442
1731	0.457	1776	0.396	1821	0.586	1866	0.475	1911	0.404
1732	0.461	1777	0.383	1822	0.567	1867	0.483	1912	0.389
1733	0.459	1778	0.361	1823	0.558	1868	0.514	1913	0.391
1734	0.466	1779	0.361	1824	0.573	1869	0.523	1914	0.436
1735	0.474	1780	0.367	1825	0.554	1870	0.477	1915	0.422
1736	0.480	1781	0.361	1826	0.582	1871	0.467	1916	0.424
1737	0.477	1782	0.387	1827	0.574	1872	0.465	1917	0.415
1738	0.473	1783	0.368	1828	0.540	1873	0.477	1918	0.411
1739	0.461	1784	0.348	1829	0.552	1874	0.463	1919	0.374
1740	0.464	1785	0.357	1830	0.524	1875	0.443	1920	0.371
1741	0.486	1786	0.360	1831	0.538	1876	0.434	1921	0.356
1742	0.468	1787	0.358	1832	0.518	1877	0.432	1922	0.320
1743	0.466	1788	0.355	1833	0.513	1878	0.431	1923	0.346
1744	0.444	1789	0.338	1834	0.503	1879	0.429	1924	0.335
1745	0.449	1790	0.334	1835	0.495	1880	0.522	1925	0.350
1746	0.453	1791	0.331	1836	0.482	1881	0.508	1926	0.336
1747	0.486	1792	0.332	1837	0.499	1882	0.498	1927	0.336
1748	0.480	1793	0.347	1838	0.486	1883	0.489	1928	0.334
1749	0.449	1794	0.340	1839	0.476	1884	0.481	1929	0.324
1750	0.441	1795	0.355	1840	0.482	1885	0.477	1930	0.322
1751	0.436	1796	0.363	1841	0.481	1886	0.479	1931	0.292
1752	0.428	1797	0.380	1842	0.472	1887	0.483	1932	0.292
1753	0.432	1798	0.411	1843	0.503	1888	0.499	1933	0.286
1754	0.426	1799	0.399	1844	0.465	1889	0.533	1934	0.288
1755	0.433			1845	0.473	1890	0.521	1935	0.279
1756	0.419	1800	0.401	1846	0.493	1891	0.481	1936	0.273
1757	0.364	1801	0.401	1847	0.480	1892	0.476	1937	0.278
1758	0.401	1802	0.398	1848	0.475	1893	0.454	1938	0.285
1759	0.431	1803	0.389	1849	0.462	1894	0.436	1939	0.259
1760	0.423	1804	0.382	1850	0.476	1895	0.458	1940	0.273
1761	0.427	1805	0.413	1851	0.462	1896	0.467	1941	0.283
1762	0.433	1806	0.419	1852	0.472	1897	0.428	1942	0.300
1763	0.448	1807	0.442	1853	0.474	1898	0.425	1943	0.294
		1808	0.443						

112 *Global Overview*

Table 5.5   Global naval power concentration, 1494–1993

Year		Year		Year		Year		Year	
1944	0.286	1954	1.000	1964	0.770	1974	0.705	1984	0.640
1945	0.350	1955	1.000	1965	0.770	1975	0.707	1985	0.645
1946	1.000	1956	1.000	1966	0.771	1976	0.691	1986	0.643
1947	1.000	1957	1.000	1967	0.765	1977	0.685	1987	0.626
1948	1.000	1958	1.000	1968	0.758	1978	0.663	1988	0.620
1949	1.000	1959	1.000	1969	0.717	1979	0.639	1989	0.621
1950	1.000	1960	0.724	1970	0.714	1980	0.627	1990	0.622
1951	1.000	1961	0.740	1971	0.714	1981	0.645	1991	0.609
1952	1.000	1962	0.736	1972	0.713	1982	0.648	1992	0.616
1953	1.000	1963	0.762	1973	0.715	1983	0.643	1993	0.605

competition in the global political system. The other side of the 'U' of course demonstrates the reverse pattern of ascending crests no doubt hinting at the underlying impact of the industrial revolution on the ability to concentrate capabilities and the increasing severity of global war's impact on the participants.

Yet none of these irregularities should detract from the patterned repetition or cyclicality of post-global war concentration peaks and pre-global war deconcentration troughs. The recurrence of these phenomena are all that is required to earn the label of 'cycle'.

Despite the obvious irregularities and the variety of ways to measure cyclical time, the length of time involved in moving from one cycle to the next is remarkably consistent. The five periods of global war are 23 to 32 years in length and average 26.8 years. The four completed intervals between global wars range from 63 to 97 years in length and average 79.3 years. If we add the average length of a period of global war to the average length of a period between global wars, the outcome is 106.1 years. If instead, the length of time from the beginning of one global war to the beginning of the next one is averaged, the typical span encompasses 104.8 years. More in tune with our emphasis on world leadership, measuring from the end of one global war to the end of the next transitional struggle, however, yields an average length of 107 years.

Regardless of how the length is determined, the life of the long cycle approximates roughly four generations in sociological time. Whether coincidental or not, for this statement to be wholly valid the historical changes in child-bearing ages and life expectancies would probably

The Long Cycle of World Leadership · 113

require that the long cycles have been somewhat longer in each successive cycle. The data, limited of course to the four completed cycles, are suggestively supportive in this regard. The historical deviations from the mean have not been all that great but they could be interpreted as moving toward longer cycles. The first long cycle (92 years, from 1517–1608) was also the shortest – to be precise, 15 years short of the mean length. The fourth and longest long cycle (129 years, from 1816 to 1945) exceeds the average length by 22 years. The second (1609–1713) and third (1714–1815) long cycles are nearly identical in terms of length (105 and 102 years respectively) and deviate the least from the 107-year standard. Nevertheless, it is doubtful that these observations can permit us to make any predictions about the possible length of the fifth long cycle. The N size is far too restrictive and our understanding of the dynamics governing the long cycle process is still much too underdeveloped. If, for example, the fourth long cycle had ended in 1918 as it might have done if the First World War's impact on global politics had been more conclusive, the 129-year long cycle would have lasted only 102 years. The long cycle mean length would then have been 101.8 year and the consistency in the length of the long cycle would have been even more remarkable and far less supportive of any trending tendencies.

By focusing on each long cycle separately, Tables 5.6–5.9 and Figures 5.4–5.8 facilitate our search for descriptive regularities and irregularities. It has already been established that each long cycle begins with a world power enjoying a near monopoly of naval power. Once gained, this position is not lost quickly. Using the 50 per cent threshold as a benchmark once again, we find that Portugal maintained its naval supremacy through the early 1540s and regained the 45–50 per cent level in the 1550s. A century later, the Netherlands remained near or above the threshold through the early 1640s. As remarked earlier, the proportional lead of the British in the third long cycle was not as large as in others but, even so, Great Britain managed to remain within the 45–50 per cent band throughout most of the 1740s. In the fourth long cycle, however, Britain dropped below the 50 per cent line in the mid-1830s but managed to hover in the 45–50 per cent band for all but a few years between 1836 and 1896. From the perspective of our selected indicators, the United States lead remained substantial through the 1970s although the number of global rivals has been dramatically reduced.

The decay of the world power's naval leadership position then is more gradual than sudden. Nor is the decay inexorably linear. Each

114

Table 5.6   Proportional distribution of global power warships, 1494–1608

Year	Portugal	England	France	Spain	Netherlands
1494	0.250	0.500	0.083	0.167	
1495	0.200	0.400	0.200	0.200	
1496	0.200	0.400	0.200	0.200	
1497	0.250	0.375	0.188	0.188	
1498	0.250	0.375	0.188	0.188	
1499	0.250	0.375	0.188	0.188	
1500	0.238	0.286	0.286	0.190	
1501	0.294	0.353	0.176	0.176	
1502	0.553	0.158	0.132	0.184	
1503	0.545	0.136	0.136	0.182	
1504	0.542	0.125	0.146	0.188	
1505	0.590	0.098	0.131	0.180	
1506	0.642	0.074	0.099	0.185	
1507	0.656	0.065	0.097	0.183	
1508	0.663	0.058	0.096	0.183	
1509	0.679	0.044	0.088	0.190	
1510	0.674	0.052	0.089	0.185	
1511	0.664	0.064	0.086	0.186	
1512	0.612	0.104	0.098	0.186	
1513	0.599	0.110	0.105	0.186	
1514	0.607	0.113	0.093	0.187	
1515	0.610	0.116	0.089	0.185	
1516	0.597	0.127	0.090	0.187	
1517	0.538	0.154	0.120	0.188	
1518	0.537	0.167	0.111	0.185	
1519	0.539	0.165	0.113	0.183	
1520	0.500	0.190	0.120	0.190	
1521	0.563	0.143	0.107	0.188	
1522	0.554	0.134	0.125	0.188	
1523	0.550	0.156	0.110	0.183	
1524	0.542	0.153	0.119	0.186	
1525	0.574	0.122	0.122	0.183	
1526	0.579	0.112	0.121	0.187	
1527	0.593	0.110	0.110	0.187	
1528	0.580	0.114	0.125	0.182	
1529	0.559	0.132	0.118	0.191	
1530	0.577	0.127	0.113	0.183	
1531	0.591	0.121	0.106	0.182	
1532	0.559	0.118	0.132	0.191	
1533	0.603	0.110	0.096	0.192	
1534	0.621	0.106	0.191	0.182	
1535	0.559	0.132	0.118	0.191	
1536	0.511	0.143	0.095	0.190	
1537	0.588	0.132	0.088	0.191	
1538	0.600	0.120	0.093	0.187	

Table 5.6   Proportional distribution of global power warships, 1494–1608

Year	Portugal	England	France	Spain	Netherlands
1539	0.586	0.143	0.086	0.186	
1540	0.573	0.147	0.093	0.187	
1541	0.559	0.162	0.088	0.191	
1542	0.566	0.158	0.092	0.184	
1543	0.560	0.160	0.093	0.187	
1544	0.524	0.214	0.071	0.190	
1545	0.469	0.272	0.074	0.185	
1546	0.462	0.264	0.088	0.187	
1547	0.442	0.279	0.088	0.186	
1548	0.430	0.279	0.105	0.186	
1549	0.421	0.263	0.126	0.189	
1550	0.412	0.258	0.144	0.186	
1551	0.463	0.241	0.111	0.185	
1552	0.450	0.250	0.110	0.190	
1553	0.454	0.247	0.113	0.186	
1554	0.495	0.216	0.103	0.186	
1555	0.488	0.198	0.128	0.186	
1556	0.489	0.211	0.111	0.189	
1557	0.489	0.211	0.111	0.189	
1558	0.473	0.204	0.140	0.183	
1559	0.468	0.234	0.117	0.182	
1560	0.425	0.263	0.125	0.188	
1561	0.400	0.293	0.120	0.187	
1562	0.371	0.343	0.100	0.186	
1563	0.394	0.324	0.099	0.183	
1564	0.354	0.354	0.108	0.185	
1565	0.338	0.338	0.132	0.191	
1566	0.364	0.333	0.121	0.182	
1567	0.405	0.304	0.101	0.190	
1568	0.407	0.291	0.116	0.186	
1569	0.395	0.291	0.128	0.186	
1570	0.389	0.263	0.137	0.189	
1571	0.424	0.272	0.120	0.185	
1572	0.418	0.275	0.121	0.187	
1573	0.396	0.292	0.125	0.188	
1574	0.413	0.304	0.098	0.185	
1575	0.398	0.301	0.108	0.194	
1576	0.376	0.329	0.106	0.188	
1577	0.316	0.380	0.114	0.190	
1578	0.300	0.400	0.114	0.186	
1579	0.236	0.315	0.022	0.146	0.281
1580	0.202	0.326	0.022	0.146	0.303
1581		0.319	0.022	0.341	0.319
1582		0.293	0.030	0.354	0.323
1583		0.276	0.019	0.381	0.324

116

Table 5.6 Proportional distribution of global power warships, 1494–1608

Year	Portugal	England	France	Spain	Netherlands
1584		0.259	0.018	0.402	0.321
1585		0.250	0.017	0.425	0.308
1586		0.246	0.015	0.438	0.300
1587		0.241		0.467	0.292
1588		0.231		0.490	0.280
1589		0.306		0.324	0.370
1590		0.261		0.448	0.279
1591		0.250		0.471	0.279
1592		0.245		0.483	0.273
1593		0.243		0.493	0.264
1594		0.242		0.503	0.255
1595		0.235		0.516	0.248
1596		0.248		0.516	0.236
1597		0.244		0.525	0.231
1598		0.273		0.469	0.259
1599		0.275		0.443	0.282
1600		0.282		0.411	0.306
1601		0.282		0.348	0.348
1602		0.310		0.327	0.363
1603		0.309		0.300	0.391
1604		0.292		0.292	0.415
1605		0.292		0.283	0.425
1606		0.292		0.274	0.434
1607		0.287		0.269	0.444
1608		0.313		0.177	0.510

Table 5.7 Proportional distribution of global power warships, 1609–1713

Year	Netherlands	England	France	Spain
1609	0.526	0.309	0.000	0.165
1610	0.541	0.316	0.000	0.143
1611	0.551	0.306	0.000	0.143
1612	0.554	0.297	0.000	0.149
1613	0.553	0.301	0.000	0.146
1614	0.557	0.292	0.000	0.151
1615	0.556	0.296	0.000	0.148
1616	0.541	0.306	0.000	0.153
1617	0.541	0.279	0.000	0.180
1618	0.558	0.240	0.000	0.202
1619	0.549	0.232	0.028	0.190
1620	0.497	0.201	0.030	0.272

117

Table 5.7 Proportional distribution of global power warships, 1609–1713

Year	Netherlands	England	France	Spain
1621	0.492	0.197	0.049	0.262
1622	0.480	0.185	0.080	0.255
1623	0.481	0.184	0.075	0.259
1624	0.502	0.167	0.074	0.256
1625	0.498	0.175	0.066	0.262
1626	0.496	0.190	0.066	0.248
1627	0.481	0.201	0.091	0.227
1628	0.482	0.181	0.123	0.214
1629	0.482	0.169	0.140	0.209
1630	0.495	0.161	0.136	0.209
1631	0.495	0.161	0.136	0.209
1632	0.500	0.158	0.136	0.206
1633	0.502	0.161	0.136	0.201
1634	0.495	0.166	0.134	0.206
1635	0.502	0.156	0.131	0.211
1636	0.500	0.158	0.126	0.216
1637	0.491	0.163	0.127	0.219
1638	0.484	0.159	0.135	0.221
1639	0.476	0.155	0.132	0.236
1640	0.605	0.197	0.146	0.052
1641	0.571	0.181	0.129	0.120
1642	0.528	0.170	0.118	0.185
1643	0.491	0.208	0.121	0.181
1644	0.468	0.222	0.127	0.183
1645	0.433	0.238	0.142	0.188
1646	0.387	0.277	0.155	0.181
1647	0.355	0.303	0.162	0.180
1648	0.337	0.303	0.168	0.192
1649	0.313	0.346	0.166	0.175
1650	0.321	0.367	0.161	0.151
1651	0.321	0.406	0.138	0.134
1652	0.408	0.408	0.089	0.095
1653	0.358	0.453	0.091	0.098
1654	0.352	0.465	0.086	0.096
1655	0.331	0.445	0.102	0.122
1656	0.329	0.435	0.118	0.118
1657	0.335	0.425	0.124	0.116
1658	0.356	0.403	0.127	0.114
1659	0.342	0.411	0.130	0.117
1660	0.335	0.412	0.142	0.112
1661	0.361	0.419	0.110	0.110
1662	0.361	0.409	0.122	0.109
1663	0.370	0.400	0.123	0.106
1664	0.389	0.385	0.123	0.102
1665	0.359	0.398	0.151	0.093

Table 5.7 Proportional distribution of global power warships, 1609–1713

Year	Netherlands	England	France	Spain
1666	0.356	0.367	0.189	0.089
1667	0.370	0.304	0.237	0.089
1668	0.355	0.294	0.264	0.087
1669	0.344	0.293	0.278	0.084
1670	0.320	0.277	0.330	0.073
1671	0.342	0.222	0.346	0.090
1672	0.333	0.216	0.359	0.091
1673	0.303	0.234	0.372	0.091
1674	0.278	0.247	0.383	0.093
1675	0.270	0.258	0.386	0.086
1676	0.235	0.281	0.396	0.088
1677	0.236	0.287	0.389	0.088
1678	0.241	0.314	0.359	0.086
1679	0.229	0.339	0.352	0.081
1680	0.227	0.332	0.366	0.076
1681	0.229	0.343	0.356	0.072
1682	0.252	0.326	0.351	0.070
1683	0.245	0.325	0.361	0.068
1684	0.244	0.324	0.364	0.068
1685	0.258	0.325	0.353	0.063
1686	0.224	0.337	0.371	0.068
1687	0.229	0.329	0.371	0.071
1688	0.260	0.307	0.362	0.071
1689	0.273	0.285	0.369	0.073
1690	0.242	0.282	0.397	0.079
1691	0.228	0.259	0.433	0.080
1692	0.228	0.261	0.429	0.082
1693	0.223	0.278	0.419	0.079
1694	0.240	0.286	0.395	0.079
1695	0.231	0.303	0.391	0.075
1696	0.230	0.311	0.384	0.075
1697	0.225	0.330	0.367	0.077
1698	0.218	0.348	0.358	0.076
1699	0.237	0.342	0.345	0.076
1700	0.249	0.333	0.342	0.075
1701	0.250	0.340	0.343	0.067
1702	0.271	0.377	0.292	0.061
1703	0.272	0.362	0.313	0.053
1704	0.269	0.367	0.321	0.043
1705	0.265	0.373	0.327	0.034
1706	0.266	0.376	0.329	0.028
1707	0.269	0.365	0.346	0.019
1708	0.269	0.399	0.321	0.010
1709	0.272	0.411	0.318	0.000

119

Table 5.7 Proportional distribution of global power warships, 1609–1713

Year	Netherlands	England	France	Spain
1710	0.268	0.427	0.305	0.000
1711	0.271	0.437	0.292	0.000
1712	0.276	0.455	0.269	0.000
1713	0.285	0.467	0.248	0.000

Table 5.8 Proportional distribution of global power warships, 1714–1815

Year	Great Britain	Netherlands	France	Spain	Russia
1714	0.454	0.275	0.236	0.000	0.036
1715	0.443	0.261	0.214	0.021	0.061
1716	0.457	0.262	0.180	0.041	0.060
1717	0.464	0.251	0.163	0.065	0.057
1718	0.466	0.240	0.122	0.084	0.088
1719	0.522	0.254	0.099	0.013	0.112
1720	0.517	0.241	0.095	0.022	0.125
1721	0.521	0.226	0.098	0.030	0.124
1722	0.511	0.210	0.116	0.039	0.124
1723	0.508	0.189	0.126	0.050	0.126
1724	0.496	0.172	0.143	0.057	0.131
1725	0.482	0.169	0.145	0.068	0.137
1726	0.476	0.175	0.146	0.077	0.126
1727	0.470	0.174	0.154	0.089	0.113
1728	0.467	0.178	0.153	0.099	0.103
1729	0.467	0.178	0.153	0.103	0.099
1730	0.461	0.183	0.154	0.112	0.091
1731	0.457	0.180	0.163	0.114	0.086
1732	0.461	0.180	0.159	0.122	0.078
1733	0.459	0.183	0.159	0.126	0.073
1734	0.466	0.174	0.162	0.134	0.069
1735	0.474	0.162	0.166	0.138	0.061
1736	0.480	0.155	0.163	0.143	0.060
1737	0.477	0.143	0.159	0.159	0.062
1738	0.473	0.135	0.169	0.162	0.062
1739	0.461	0.129	0.184	0.160	0.066
1740	0.464	0.120	0.188	0.160	0.068
1741	0.486	0.118	0.184	0.155	0.057
1742	0.468	0.140	0.184	0.148	0.060
1743	0.466	0.141	0.185	0.141	0.068
1744	0.444	0.141	0.191	0.141	0.083
1745	0.449	0.139	0.192	0.131	0.090

120

Table 5.8   Proportional distribution of global power warships, 1714–1815

Year	Great Britain	Netherlands	France	Spain	Rusia
1746	0.453	0.134	0.178	0.138	0.097
1747	0.486	0.131	0.147	0.139	0.096
1748	0.480	0.129	0.160	0.141	0.090
1749	0.449	0.130	0.185	0.146	0.091
1750	0.441	0.125	0.202	0.144	0.087
1751	0.436	0.124	0.207	0.150	0.083
1752	0.428	0.119	0.216	0.156	0.082
1753	0.432	0.114	0.218	0.159	0.077
1754	0.426	0.112	0.224	0.162	0.076
1755	0.433	0.105	0.229	0.164	0.076
1756	0.419	0.104	0.240	0.165	0.072
1757	0.364	0.103	0.272	0.176	0.084
1758	0.401	0.105	0.230	0.183	0.082
1759	0.431	0.099	0.194	0.198	0.079
1760	0.423	0.099	0.198	0.206	0.075
1761	0.427	0.088	0.223	0.188	0.073
1762	0.433	0.086	0.239	0.175	0.067
1763	0.448	0.080	0.264	0.138	0.069
1764	0.451	0.075	0.267	0.143	0.064
1765	0.446	0.071	0.268	0.152	0.063
1766	0.448	0.071	0.257	0.160	0.063
1767	0.444	0.064	0.263	0.169	0.060
1768	0.443	0.059	0.271	0.172	0.055
1769	0.440	0.054	0.274	0.177	0.054
1770	0.434	0.054	0.276	0.183	0.054
1771	0.428	0.047	0.275	0.192	0.058
1772	0.412	0.043	0.287	0.210	0.057
1773	0.402	0.043	0.283	0.210	0.062
1774	0.403	0.040	0.275	0.220	0.062
1775	0.397	0.040	0.276	0.224	0.063
1776	0.396	0.040	0.273	0.225	0.065
1777	0.383	0.051	0.271	0.231	0.065
1778	0.361	0.056	0.288	0.229	0.066
1779	0.361	0.066	0.299	0.208	0.066
1780	0.367	0.074	0.286	0.209	0.064
1781	0.361	0.079	0.282	0.203	0.076
1782	0.387	0.067	0.258	0.199	0.089
1783	0.368	0.094	0.241	0.197	0.100
1784	0.348	0.100	0.230	0.203	0.118
1785	0.357	0.097	0.218	0.198	0.130
1786	0.360	0.096	0.215	0.190	0.139
1787	0.358	0.095	0.220	0.182	0.146
1788	0.355	0.096	0.219	0.203	0.128
1789	0.338	0.093	0.219	0.181	0.169
1790	0.334	0.083	0.220	0.180	0.183

Table 5.8   Proportional distribution of global power warships, 1714–1815

Year	Great Britain	Netherlands	France	Spain	Rusia
1791	0.331	0.080	0.216	0.192	0.182
1792	0.332	0.096	0.219	0.199	0.179
1793	0.347	0.092	0.205	0.200	0.182
1794	0.350	0.087	0.195	0.195	0.176
1795	0.349	0.067	0.219	0.192	0.173
1796	0.363	0.045	0.223	0.197	0.175
1797	0.380	0.044	0.227	0.186	0.164
1798	0.411	0.045	0.196	0.184	0.165
1799	0.399	0.047	0.192	0.186	0.175
1800	0.401	0.046	0.185	0.191	0.176
1801	0.401	0.046	0.183	0.193	0.177
1802	0.398	0.046	0.185	0.194	0.176
1803	0.389	0.046	0.201	0.191	0.173
1804	0.382	0.047	0.216	0.179	0.176
1805	0.413	0.044	0.200	0.162	0.181
1806	0.419	0.045	0.211	0.136	0.188
1807	0.442	0.042	0.218	0.125	0.173
1808	0.443	0.042	0.214	0.125	0.176
1809	0.507	0.045	0.243		0.205
1810	0.500	0.043	0.268		0.189
1811	0.505		0.311		0.184
1812	0.503		0.330		0.167
1813	0.483		0.353		0.163
1814	0.516		0.303		0.181
1815	0.523		0.309		0.168

Table 5.9   Proportional distribution of global power seapower, 1816–1945

Year	GB	FRN	RUS	USA	GER	JAP
1816	0.660	0.175	0.130	0.031		
1817	0.609	0.189	0.165	0.038		
1818	0.615	0.183	0.166	0.036		
1819	0.589	0.198	0.166	0.050		
1820	0.588	0.201	0.156	0.056		
1821	0.586	0.211	0.159	0.045		
1822	0.567	0.238	0.162	0.034		
1823	0.558	0.245	0.162	0.036		
1824	0.573	0.231	0.154	0.042		
1825	0.554	0.231	0.167	0.048		
1826	0.582	0.214	0.148	0.057		

Table 5.9 Proportional distribution of global power seapower, 1816–1945

Year	GB	FRN	RUS	USA	GER	JAP
1827	0.574	0.222	0.148	0.058		
1828	0.540	0.251	0.154	0.056		
1829	0.552	0.232	0.161	0.057		
1830	0.524	0.259	0.166	0.052		
1831	0.538	0.236	0.170	0.058		
1832	0.518	0.231	0.179	0.074		
1833	0.513	0.236	0.184	0.069		
1834	0.503	0.231	0.190	0.077		
1835	0.495	0.220	0.217	0.068		
1836	0.482	0.214	0.221	0.083		
1837	0.499	0.198	0.222	0.081		
1838	0.486	0.207	0.224	0.084		
1839	0.476	0.200	0.216	0.074		
1840	0.482	0.224	0.214	0.082		
1841	0.481	0.234	0.211	0.076		
1842	0.472	0.227	0.207	0.095		
1843	0.503	0.235	0.205	0.058		
1844	0.465	0.245	0.206	0.084		
1845	0.473	0.232	0.223	0.074		
1846	0.493	0.233	0.203	0.072		
1847	0.480	0.241	0.203	0.077		
1848	0.475	0.247	0.195	0.085		
1849	0.462	0.232	0.216	0.092		
1850	0.476	0.230	0.211	0.084		
1851	0.462	0.227	0.220	0.093		
1852	0.472	0.216	0.228	0.084		
1853	0.474	0.209	0.232	0.086		
1854	0.513	0.236	0.187	0.064		
1855	0.551	0.239	0.148	0.063		
1856	0.505	0.269	0.148	0.080		
1857	0.504	0.246	0.168	0.083		
1858	0.489	0.266	0.146	0.099		
1859	0.467	0.341	0.116	0.077		
1860	0.493	0.323	0.117	0.068		
1861	0.574	0.304	0.063	0.060		
1862	0.401	0.398	0.047	0.150		
1863	0.449	0.315	0.051	0.187		
1864	0.490	0.269	0.077	0.165		
1865	0.401	0.273	0.118	0.209		
1866	0.475	0.278	0.139	0.109		
1867	0.493	0.299	0.116	0.092		
1868	0.514	0.276	0.132	0.079		
1869	0.503	0.287	0.144	0.068		
1870	0.477	0.292	0.153	0.075		
1871	0.467	0.247	0.151	0.073	0.062	

123

Table 5.9 Proportional distribution of global power seapower, 1816–1945

Year	GB	FRN	RUS	USA	GER	JAP
1872	0.465	0.223	0.164	0.082	0.061	
1873	0.477	0.221	0.158	0.088	0.057	
1874	0.456	0.207	0.156	0.104	0.066	
1875	0.443	0.208	0.155	0.074	0.097	0.024
1876	0.434	0.222	0.157	0.069	0.094	0.025
1877	0.432	0.225	0.157	0.053	0.112	0.023
1878	0.431	0.229	0.138	0.064	0.104	0.036
1879	0.429	0.240	0.141	0.062	0.094	0.037
1880	0.522	0.274	0.102	0.052	0.041	0.010
1881	0.508	0.297	0.094	0.056	0.038	0.008
1882	0.498	0.311	0.094	0.051	0.038	0.009
1883	0.489	0.324	0.082	0.049	0.038	0.019
1884	0.481	0.335	0.075	0.051	0.040	0.019
1885	0.477	0.348	0.076	0.047	0.040	0.014
1886	0.479	0.302	0.115	0.041	0.039	0.025
1887	0.483	0.282	0.116	0.044	0.029	0.028
1888	0.499	0.263	0.112	0.054	0.043	0.030
1889	0.533	0.238	0.107	0.064	0.037	0.023
1890	0.521	0.244	0.105	0.064	0.046	0.021
1891	0.481	0.239	0.105	0.069	0.088	0.020
1892	0.476	0.238	0.093	0.076	0.101	0.017
1893	0.454	0.227	0.102	0.110	0.092	0.016
1894	0.436	0.239	0.105	0.113	0.091	0.017
1895	0.458	0.222	0.107	0.101	0.094	0.019
1896	0.467	0.218	0.100	0.094	0.089	0.034
1897	0.428	0.219	0.099	0.098	0.087	0.070
1898	0.425	0.203	0.090	0.131	0.079	0.073
1899	0.393	0.181	0.094	0.141	0.108	0.084
1900	0.392	0.178	0.104	0.152	0.096	0.080
1901	0.392	0.166	0.100	0.153	0.118	0.073
1902	0.405	0.146	0.103	0.149	0.131	0.069
1903	0.405	0.136	0.108	0.155	0.137	0.060
1904	0.419	0.124	0.108	0.168	0.137	0.045
1905	0.411	0.124	0.098	0.187	0.147	0.034
1906	0.392	0.119	0.080	0.196	0.132	0.083
1907	0.363	0.114	0.103	0.188	0.152	0.080
1908	0.368	0.108	0.058	0.212	0.167	0.088
1909	0.373	0.108	0.054	0.199	0.187	0.081
1910	0.442	0.052	0.040	0.206	0.223	0.039
1911	0.404	0.077	0.043	0.199	0.239	0.040
1912	0.389	0.068	0.063	0.185	0.229	0.067
1913	0.391	0.087	0.079	0.156	0.221	0.066
1914	0.436	0.051	0.051	0.128	0.282	0.051
1915	0.422	0.067	0.067	0.111	0.256	0.078

124 *Global Overview*

Table 5.9 Proportional distribution of global power seapower, 1816–1945

Year	GB	FRN	RUS	USA	GER	JAP
1916	0.424	0.071	0.051	0.141	0.242	0.071
1917	0.415	0.066	0.057	0.142	0.236	0.085
1918	0.411	0.065	0.047	0.159	0.234	0.084
1919	0.374	0.071	0.061	0.448	0.000	0.078
1920	0.371	0.074	0.051	0.399	0.000	0.131
1921	0.356	0.081	0.051	0.402	0.000	0.136
1922	0.320	0.102	0.048	0.404	0.000	0.150
1923	0.346	0.097	0.047	0.389	0.000	0.146
1924	0.335	0.106	0.052	0.375	0.016	0.143
1925	0.350	0.094	0.052	0.369	0.024	0.138
1926	0.336	0.095	0.055	0.360	0.033	0.151
1927	0.336	0.113	0.053	0.343	0.031	0.152
1928	0.334	0.116	0.053	0.337	0.028	0.150
1929	0.324	0.132	0.054	0.328	0.025	0.139
1930	0.322	0.127	0.054	0.334	0.025	0.140
1931	0.292	0.134	0.061	0.351	0.024	0.149
1932	0.292	0.136	0.064	0.371	0.026	0.167
1933	0.286	0.123	0.063	0.342	0.050	0.170
1934	0.288	0.126	0.061	0.294	0.081	0.183
1935	0.279	0.118	0.061	0.312	0.089	0.173
1936	0.273	0.111	0.060	0.309	0.122	0.156
1937	0.278	0.104	0.060	0.299	0.140	0.150
1938	0.285	0.119	0.057	0.288	0.146	0.135
1939	0.259	0.130	0.056	0.278	0.093	0.167
1940	0.273	0.127	0.055	0.273	0.091	0.182
1941	0.283	0.000	0.043	0.326	0.109	0.239
1942	0.300	0.000	0.040	0.380	0.080	0.200
1943	0.294	0.000	0.039	0.412	0.078	0.176
1944	0.286	0.000	0.061	0.510	0.041	0.102
1945	0.350	0.050	0.075	0.500	0.000	0.025

figure in the 5.4–5.8 set displays a pattern of choppy descent at best, with numerous short-term reversals in the direction of movement. Moreover, the degree of decay prior to the onset of another global transitional struggle tends to vary. In the decade prior to 1580, the Portuguese relative position declined dramatically to 20 per cent. The most rapid period of Dutch decay occurred in the middle of its leadership cycle – taking place in conjunction with the end of the Thirty Years War and the rise of the English naval challenge – rather than toward the end of the cycle. By 1688, the Dutch share had fluctuated between 22 and 26 per cent for over a decade.

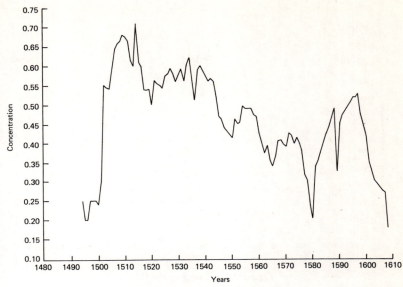

Figure 5.4   Long cycle I

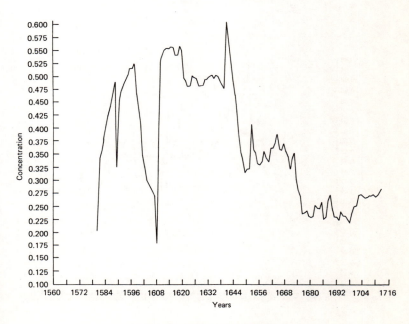

Figure 5.5   Long cycle II

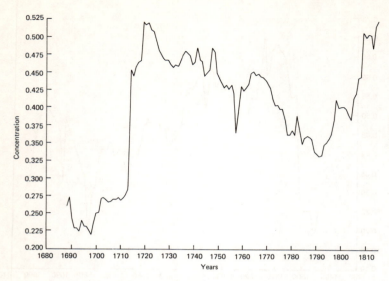

Figure 5.6 Long cycle III

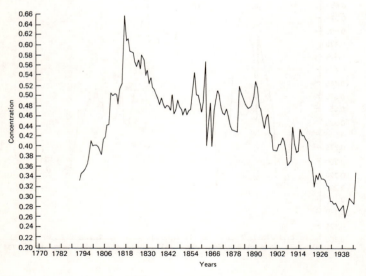

Figure 5.7 Long cycle IV

The Long Cycle of World Leadership 127

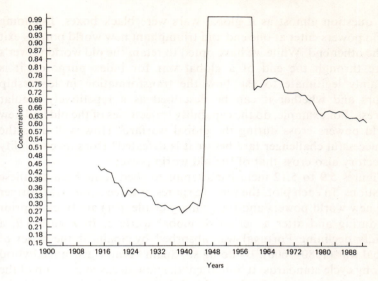

Figure 5.8 Long cycle V

The British position immediately prior to 1792, however, was more similar to their pre-1914 position than to the pre-war positions of their Portuguese and Dutch predecessors. While the Portuguese and Dutch decay patterns resemble downward staircases, with successive step-like decrements, the eighteenth-century British erosion was more prolonged. With the exception of a brief and temporary plunge during the Seven Years War, the rate of relative decay only began to accelerate a few years after the conclusion of that mid-cycle war. But even so, the British continued to maintain a respectable 33 per cent share by 1792. Similarly, the British were able to take advantage of innovations in naval technology to retard or 'stretch out' their positional decay throughout most of the nineteenth century. Only in the 1890s and the beginning of significant German and American naval building programmes is there a rapid downturn resulting in a share loss of about 17 points in about as many years. Despite this decline, however, the introduction of the Dreadnought enabled the British to enter the First World War with an even stronger position than they had had in 1792.

Most of our attention in this section has been focused on the periods between global wars. What happens during global wars? The approach we have taken to constructing the long cycle series treats this question almost as if global wars were black boxes. Declining world powers enter at one end and triumphant new world powers exit at the other end. While we have opted to retain the old world power's share through the end of a global war for index purposes, it is certainly legitimate to ask how the transformation in leadership occurs and whether it can be described as a repetitively regular process. For example, do the capability trajectories of the old and new world powers cross during the global warfare? How well does the unsuccessful challenger fare before it is defeated? Does its capability trajectory also cross that of the old world power?

Figures 5.9 to 5.12 inclusive attempt to shed some light on these questions. In each plot, the relative shares of three actors (the former and new world powers and the primary challenger) are tracked prior to, during and after a period of global warfare. In Figure 5.9, a rapidly declining Portugal was absorbed by Spain at the onset of global war (1580–1608). By doing so, Spain became a strange hybrid by long cycle standards. It 'inherited' the now-decayed position of the old world power (and its warships) but it still had to build the

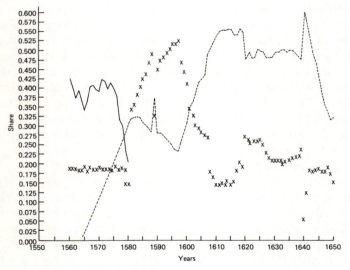

Note: Portuguese share (solid line)
Spanish share (XXXX)
Netherlands share (broken line)

Figure 5.9 Capability trajectories in global war (1560–1650)

The Long Cycle of World Leadership

requisite naval foundation before it could fully claim the role of systemic leader. Consequently, its global war role was part former leader and part challenger. To be successful, moreover, Spain had to defeat England (not plotted in Figure 5.9) and the newly emerging United Provinces of the Netherlands. At the onset of warfare, Spain rapidly developed a formidable capability that was only temporarily set back by the outcome of the first attempt to invade England (1588). It was only toward the end of the transitional struggle that the ascending Dutch position surpassed that of the weakening Spanish.

The global war of 1688–1713 was a bit more complex. The first challenge to the Dutch came from Cromwellian England in the mid-seventeenth century. Despite three Anglo-Dutch wars, the systemic outcome was rather inconclusive. This is well illustrated in Figure 5.10. The English relative share surpassed the Dutch position between 1649 and 1666 but the English failed to maintain their naval momentum. The French challenge in the late 1660s began about the same time that the English were faltering. The French building programme managed to place them in the position of leading naval power at least

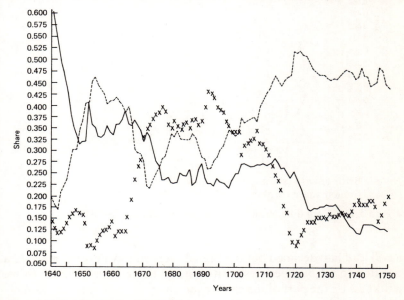

Note: Netherlands share (solid line)
English share (broken line)
French share (XXXX)

Figure 5.10 Capability trajectories in global war (1640–1750)

in terms of ship numbers from 1671 to 1700 only to be forced to give way to the re-ascendant English. In this case then, the naval capabilities of both primary challenger and the new world power passed those of the declining world power well in advance of the global war. Yet, somewhat as in the previous global war, the new world power had to be concerned primarily with defeating the challenger rather than in competing with the declining world power.

The naval competition situation in the next global war phase (1792–1815) was much less ambiguous (see Figure 5.11) than the situation characterising the second half of the seventeenth century. The British

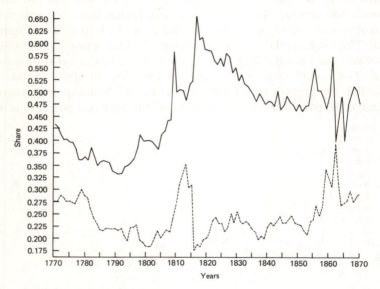

Note: British share (solid line)
French share (broken line)

Figure 5.11 Capability trajectories in global war (1770–1870)

naval lead had declined but the French were simply never in much of a position to seriously contest British naval power. A similar maritime weakness on the part of the challenger was exhibited again in the most recent global war phase (1914–45), as depicted in Figure 5.12. In this case, however, the structural ambiguity was most prominent in the years between the First and Second World Wars. At the end of the First World War, the United States was in a position to outbuild the

The Long Cycle of World Leadership

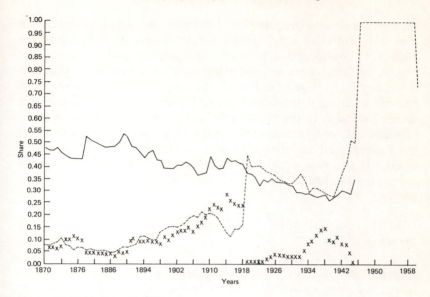

Note: British share (solid line)
United States share (broken line)
German share (XXXX)

Figure 5.12 Capability trajectories in global war (1870–1958)

British navy. Although Figure 5.12 shows the United States passing the British position in 1919, the circumstances were not quite so clear-cut. In 1919, the United States navy was out-spending the British navy but the British retained the lead in the number of battleships. If the United States had carried out its planned fleet expansion, it is highly questionable whether the British would have been in a financial position to participate in a naval arms race. But, instead, the two states compromised at rough parity and froze the size of their fleets from the 1920s into the early 1930s. It was only during the Second World War that the United States position *vis-à-vis* the British was clarified radically.

The outstanding regularity of the global war phase is the emergence of the new world power as the predominant naval power. The time that this becomes apparent within the global war phase has varied but, with the exception of the Napoleonic Wars, it is usually more toward the end, rather than at the beginning, of the global war phase. Precisely who the new world power must best in terms of naval

132 *Global Overview*

capabilities is more irregular. In 1580–1608, the Dutch needed to win over a hybrid challenger/'former' world power. By the time of the 1688–1713 confrontation between the challenger and the new world power, the Dutch were no longer in contention for the leadership role. A century later, it was the French challenger that never managed to become a serious contender, at least at sea. The new world power succeeded itself. In the twentieth century, the Anglo-German naval race certainly contributed to the outbreak of global war in 1914. Yet the fundamental naval competition turned out to be between the allied, old and new world powers. As in the 1688–1713 struggle, the old power had little choice but to concede the succession of the new power.

SUMMARY

Engaged in by a relatively small number of global powers as participants, the long cycle of world leadership is a cyclical process of seapower concentration and deconcentration that is bracketed by periodic global wars. Beginning in 1494, four cycles, averaging 107 years in length, have been completed. The fifth is still underway. The general pattern can be characterised as a period of intensive struggle over systemic leadership (global war) followed by the emergence of a single state with a preponderance in seapower (the world power). The world power's global-reach capability advantage provides an essential part of the foundation for world leadership. But this foundation is subject to erosion. The post-global war era of high concentration gives way to deconcentration and successively lower levels of seapower concentration. As the deconcentration process proceeds, the structural incentives and opportunities for challenging the world power improve until the onset of a new phase of global war ushers in another leadership transitional struggle and another opportunity to transform the system's power structure. The cycle is completed when a new world power emerges from the period of global war.

6 The Future of Seapower

In this chapter we shall briefly recapitulate and highlight the evidence that has been put together in this survey, and end with a discussion of the likely role of seapower in global politics in the decades ahead. Granted that seapower has had a great past; but what about its future?

THE EVIDENCE SO FAR

We will start with the two questions we advanced in the form of propositions in the first chapter.

To begin with, does the evidence show that all the world powers, in the modern world system, have also been sea (or ocean) powers exercising command of the sea?

Our evidence shows that over the past 500 years, four states, over a sequence of five instances, have, in orderly succession, possessed a monopoly of seapower and have therefore also exercised command of the sea over substantial periods: not just Britain in her famed nineteenth-century *Pax Britannica*, but also the United States after 1945, Britain in the eighteenth century, the Netherlands in the seventeenth, and Portugal in the sixteenth. Table 5.3 summarises this basic finding and shows that states earlier described as world powers and filling other important roles in world affairs, have also maintained naval concentration values in excess of 0.500, most notably in the decades following the close of a global war.

This finding documents, for the first time, that the influence and impact of seapower is coextensive with the entire modern system. The Mahanian thesis that is quite well understood in relation to Britain and the United States may now be seen to extend back to the Netherlands, and to Portugal, and to provide a firm basis for assessing the entire modern experience.

Our second question concerned the permanence of the position thus attained. Was monopoly of seapower a lasting condition or was it subject to shifts, associated with changes in the occupancy of the role of world leadership?

This second question, too, is illuminated by our evidence. Table 5.3 implies, and Table 5.4 documents the finding that the condition of monopoly of seapower (that is seapower concentration of 0.500 and above) so obviously and prominently in evidence at the close of one global war has never remained at that high level for the entire period but tended to decline, reflecting also associated changes in political conditions. The period of monopoly was invariably of limited duration and was regularly transformed into one of more even competition.

A most important implication of this finding is the cyclicality of the global political process. We document the fact that periods of high concentration have regularly been followed by others of lower concentration. This periodic fluctuation in naval power concentration is one basic manifestation of the long cycle in global politics and may be visually inspected in Figure 5.3.

Taken together, these two principal findings allow us to demonstrate a significant pattern in the evolution of seapower over a period of 500 years, and they also offer firm support for the theory of long cycles.

CIRCULATION OF GLOBAL POWERS

Our research highlights not only the fluctuating role of world powers. It also produces clear criteria by which to assess the contribution of other major actors to the management of politics at the global level.

There is hardly a term more frequently used in the literature of International Relations than that of 'powers' – major powers, superpowers, great powers. But there is also surprisingly little attempt to lend precision to these expressions and to analyse the criteria by which assignments to, and deletions from, such a category might be made. The roster of 'great powers' is most often compiled from what are understood to be the opinions, undoubtedly expert but not clearly demarcated, of historians. Such lists as those of Levy (1983, p. 47) are based essentially on judgemental criteria.[1]

Our own research is based on the concept of global power. Central to it are two notions – first, that it is based on objective capabilities and resources, as embodied in fleets in being (not potential that might be mobilisable but navies actually in existence in a particular year); and second, that, in the world picture, we need to distinguish between regional powers, that are significant chiefly in terms of one particular 'narrow sea' such as Sweden in the Baltic, or Venice in the Mediterranean, and others that use their resources for world-wide operations

The Future of Seapower

upon the ocean and for world-significant puposes. That is also why, in our title, we employ the expression 'global' politics.

In practice, these two criteria combined mean that the global powers are those that contend for world leadership and in a serious way. Global power status, then, has been, and remains, the capability to compete for the world leadership stakes, and to participate in global systemic decisions; it includes the world powers, both current, and maybe also past and future ones, and the most serious challengers to that role, in past and future global wars in particular. It includes both the conventionally well-known 'seapowers' and also all the major 'continental' or 'land' powers.

Our list of global powers is therefore a firmly operationalised and carefully measured list of contenders for global status. Viewed over time, as in Table 6.1, it offers a picture of the circulation of these élite members of modern international society in its entire experience.

Several interesting points emerge in relation to Table 6.1. The number of powers with capabilities significant enough to serve as sources of the 'supply of order' at the global level has consistently

Table 6.1   Circulation of powers in the global political system (1494–1993)

Global powers on the eve of global war		Subtractions (−) and additions (+) in subsequent cycle
	(England, France, Portugal, Spain)	
1494	4	− 1 (Portugal) + 1 (Netherlands)
1580	4	0
1688	4	+ 1 (Russia)
1792	5	− 2 (Netherlands, Spain)
		+ 3 (United States, Germany, Japan)
1914	6	− 4 (Britain, France, Germany, Japan)
(1993)	2	

been a small one. The total, for half a millenium, is only nine. At any given point in time, the number was obviously even smaller. In the first two cycles this nucleus of the global political system, was made up of just four powers, and it is these four that have also formed the nucleus of the modern system of nation-states. The number rose to five in the next cycle and, as though in an orderly progression, and despite considerable coming and going, reached six in the period up to

136   *Global Overview*

1945. It is only the end of the Second World War that marked a drastic change in the number of globally-capable powers, the exit of four of them and the reduction in the overall number to two, at this time of writing and foreseeably until 1993.

It would seem then that the nuclear global political system slowly and gradually expanded in respect of number of participants, from four to six by 1914. But the change in the scale of global politics between 1850 and 1950 raised the size of the stakes in this contest and brought the number of serious participants in it down to two.

All the global powers have been nation-states. This suggests that the course of the long cycle has been linked to that other important dynamic process of world politics, the rise of the nation-state system. Two states that are absent from our list but often figure in the historians' lists of European great powers, the Ottoman Empire, and the House of Austria (or the Austro-Hungarian Empire after 1867) were not nation-states but multi-ethnic empires of the pre-modern kind, mostly engaged in fighting each other on land; neither ever deployed a strong naval force capable of braving the oceans. Their traditional-type organisation visibly handicapped their global orientation, even though their regional significance in the Mediterranean was undoubted. Also significant in the same area and in the sixteenth century, was Venice, a prosperous city-state on the eve of the modern era but unable or unwilling to make or to lead (as France and Spain were then doing in their areas) transition to an Italian nation-state. The Italy that did emerge in the second half of the nineteenth century, a successor to the maritime glories of Venice, and of Genoa, was late in the stakes for nation-state status, and too late, ill-equipped and ill-located for a global role in the twentieth century. Yet another traditional organisation was the Chinese Empire. In its Confucian framework it had trouble adjusting to the emerging framework of nation-states and a global role in spite of significant potential for maritime enterprise shown especially between the years 1000 and 1500.

The data show that a rise to global status is negatively related to pre-modern political organisation and positively correlated with nation-statehood. The first four global powers – in particular, England, France, Portugal and Spain – with oceanic resources second to none in their time, all reached nation-state status at about the time they could be regarded as global powers, and as a group they became the nucleus of, at first, the European, and then the contemporary world system of nation-states.

The Future of Seapower 137

The small number of global powers since 1945 is a notable departure from the pattern of the previous four to five centuries of global politics. It is worthwhile to ask: is this a pattern that is going to last through this entire cycle and possibly the next, or will there be, once again, new entrants into the ranks of global powers (on terms as defined in this analysis, requiring a substantial stake in the instruments of global reach, in particular a minimum of 10 per cent of major warships)?

PROSPECTS FOR NEW GLOBAL POWERS

We have now had some four decades of systemic experience with just two global powers (or, as they are often called, the two superpowers). What does the experience of the past 500 years tell us about the chances for new powers joining their ranks at this point in the cycle, and over the next three or four decades?

The experience of the modern system suggests that entry to global power status via a strong naval commitment can occur at any point in 'system-time'. For example, in the case of the Netherlands, or Russia, the process coincided with their involvement in global wars. In the case of Germany and Japan, it occurred roughly at mid-point between two global wars. For the United States it was a case of early entry and late commitment. In other words the fact that we have so far had only two global powers in the current cycle does not mean that we cannot have additions to these ranks over the next half-century or so (that is in the next two phases of system-time).

What might a list of possible candidates look like? Or, in other words, which countries might in the foreseeable future embark on a substantial drive toward global (sea) power? At this time, such a list should include Western Europe (the European Community); Japan, China, and India. The evaluation of this list should show both inherent national capabilities for global reach, and the ability to mobilise them for global purposes. For purposes of casting the question in more concrete terms we shall also ask of each candidate if they might be able to field what appears to be the present minimum stake of global status: a fleet of some ten to twenty nuclear ballistic submarines, together with the necessary complement of attack submarines and the nucleus of a space (surveillance) system. We notice immediately that the question of naval power cannot be discussed in

138   *Global Overview*

isolation from the question of the distribution of nuclear weapons, and ultimately also from the arrangements for space.

Western Europe, in the political shape of the European Community, is an obvious and important candidate. It is obvious because within its confines may be found a number of states that for most of the modern period and until quite recently were global powers. We might single out Britain and France, which even after 1945 retained a unique role of distinction in international politics, acquired legitimate status as nuclear-weapon states and, in the mid-1980s, were in possession of a sizeable fleet of nuclear-missile boats (Britain, four; France, six) which, when refitted with new multiple warheads, would constitute a notable deterrent force. Our position (see Chapter 10) is that by themselves, neither the British, nor the French, forces satisfy the criteria of forces of global reach in the era since the Second World War. Nor do we anticipate Britain or France independently regaining global power status. But what if they both merged into a unified European Community political and command structure?

Today's European Community brings together, not just Britain and France, but also the Netherlands, the German Federal Republic, Portugal and Spain, each with its own distinct memories of global prominence. Technically, and resource-wise, they would make a formidable combination, especially on the sea. But whether they do so in the next three to four decades will depend very much on political factors – as it must, this being a move of prime political significance.

Merger as a mode of constructing new global powers has not been altogether unusual in the modern experience. Spain rose to a global role through the union of Castile and Aragon; the Netherland provinces came together at Utrecht in resistance to Philip II; Britain entered upon the Union with Scotland in her first cycle; and Germany built a federal union not long before mounting a challenge for world status, and proceeded to build a federal navy as a principal common organisation of the empire. Indeed, it can be argued that the preferred political organisation for contemporary global status is federal and multiplex, as evidenced by the constitutional structures of the United States and the Soviet Union, and as might be expected in a large system whose management is beyond the capacity of any simple nation-state.

What might be the political conditions in which state members of the European Community would decide upon a merger which would create a force meeting the criteria of global status? The principal ones would have to do with (i) the weakening of NATO, concurrent with a

The Future of Seapower

decline of American leadership; and (ii) the withering of the Soviet threat, concurrent with a weakening of the Soviet Union, for reasons of economic difficulty or internal instability; both conditions coinciding with demands and opportunities for an assertion of a distinct European identity under European leadership.

A unification of Western Europe on the Prussian model (that is unity centred on one state) is probably unlikely but the evolution of unity on the American model (unity based on a collaborative axis of two or three key states and the acquiescence of others) is entirely conceivable. A joint deterrent force of some ten to twenty ballistic submarines, regularly modernised, and combined with the necessary defensive systems could easily serve as an obvious focus of political unification. Such a force would obviously be expensive both in terms of political commitment and in terms of economic and budgetary resources (a fleet of twenty Trident boats costs as much as $85 billion). The rudiments of a European space organisation are already in place.

Overall, however, while not describing such a course as probable (in particular, as of 1993 – a 500-year benchmark), we must include it in the calculus of possibilities for the longer haul. It would appear more likely if the world were heading toward another global war; it might be less of a possibility if alternatives to the next global war were being constructed in a deliberate manner.

Somewhat similar considerations apply to Japan. That prosperous, well organised and now highly-developed society has the capacity to mount a force of global reach within the space of maybe two decades from the time such a decision is taken. That is, of course, a long lead-time but late starters usually enjoy advantages too, such as avoiding false starts and other mistakes of the pioneers.

As in the case of Europe the basic considerations will be political; they will be both internal, having to do with the country's own conception of its role in the world, and with the prohibitions and inhibitions surrounding the development of military forces and the use of nuclear weapons; and also external, the decisive relationships being those with the United States, China, and the Soviet Union. If American leadership should falter, or the Soviet Union lose stability, conditions of change might be at hand. A European move toward autonomy could also serve as an example and a precedent.

In respect to both India and China, on the other hand, the proximate limitations have to do with resources rather than with the basic thrust toward an autonomous position. As the second most

140 *Global Overview*

populous country in the world, India is an important and complex, if somewhat fragile, political system. While a minimal capacity might already be in place, India's status as a nuclear-weapon state remains uncertain. Her naval capacity is limited and her military deployments basically are regional in character, sufficient to confront Pakistan, and possibly even China, but are not likely to have global significance in the coming decades.

As the world's most populous country China is in a similar if somewhat stronger situation. She is a nuclear-weapon state, with more than a minimal capacity for strategic missile deployment. China currently has two nuclear-missile submarines and maybe four more under construction and development. She also has the rudiments of a space launching organisation. As we have seen, she has a not insignificant maritime tradition.

Among China's liabilities, on the other hand, is the persisting security problem on her northern borders; throughout her history that problem has impeded her constructive participation in global matters. As in the case of India, but in contrast with Europe and Japan, there is also a basic scarcity of resources, but lesser degree of involvement in the existing framework of global political relationships, hence ultimately greater incentive for asserting global autonomy. Even if global standing may not be attained in the relative near-term of two or three decades, it is sure to be pursued in the more long-range future.

It is the conclusion of this brief survey that over the next three to four decades some small addition – of one or two – to the current number of two global powers would not be altogether surprising. This survey excludes from consideration the regional powers, nuclear and otherwise, that have risen or might arise in some parts of the world, for instance in South America, Africa, or the Near East. These would be unlikely, though, to have a serious naval component and alter the basic outlines of the global political structure.

DOES SEAPOWER HAVE A FUTURE?

As long as a large portion of the earth's surface is covered with water, navies will be needed to guard the seas and to help to maintain order among those using that resource and employing it as a medium of communication. But the crucial question is: for how long will navies of global reach remain a strategic indicator of global-power status?

The Future of Seapower   141

Will they continue telling us the striking and unambiguous story they have done for the past half-millenium?

Navies have been useful as indicators of global status because in global wars, those great tests of strength that selected world leadership and ratified major policies, they fought the decisive battle (such as Trafalgar) that effected a systemic decision at the global level. Moreover, because the decisive battles were encounters between the principal warships of the two sides, a ratio of the warships of the major powers was a good predictor of the outcome of such a battle, and of the global war as a whole. While the decisive battle as a rule conferred the command of the sea and – what followed from it – control over the global layer of communications, it did not produce instantaneous success: great land campaigns also had to be fought, invariably with the help of coalition partners supplying a large portion of the non-naval forces (as demonstrated in the Russian campaign, or at Leipzig and Waterloo). Hence the viability of the naval-strength indicator ultimately rests upon the maritime character of the decisive battles in past global wars.

The question for the future then becomes: what will be the character of the systemic decision in the coming cycle? Will it take the form, in the first place, of a global war, and if so, what is the probable character of the decisive battle of the next world war? In the second place, we must examine the possibility that the systemic decision in the next cycle will assume a form other than that of a global war. In such a contingency, what would remain of the significance of seapower? In this last section we enter the realm of technological and political innovation in the next cycle, that is, ground which almost by definition is uncharted.

Let us review three types of decisive global battle that might conceivably be fought in the next global war and by reference to which the forces that will determine the outcome of such a battle may be determined. We might distinguish among the following:

(1) a surface battle fought by carriers;
(2) a battle involving under-sea forces, that is submarines;
(3) a battle in space.

A CARRIER BATTLE

The major surface combatants at the close of the Second World War were the aircraft-carriers: in a most effective way, they fused traditio-

142 *Global Overview*

nal considerations of seapower with the latest developments in air power. Since 1945, United States superiority in carriers has been unsurpassed; the deployment of these powerful ships in such sensitive areas of the globe as the Mediterranean or the Indian Ocean has provided some of the most visible and spectacular symbols of American involvement in world politics. At the time of writing (1985) the US Navy has thirteen of these huge, nuclear-armed vessels (four of them nuclear-powered) available for deployment and by the year 2000, presumably, will still have about that same number.

The Soviet interest in aircraft-carriers dates back to before the Second World War, and in the 1970s assumed the form of a class of smaller, helicopter-carrier types of about 40 000 tons. But it is only recently that the Soviet Union has apparently decided to enter the competition in heavy carriers. Mentioned by Admiral Gorshkov as early as 1979, one such ship (*circa* 75 000 tons) has been under construction since 1983; but its full commissioning, after launching, and full sea trials, is not expected to take place until the early 1990s. This makes it clear that the Soviets' current position of inferiority in this category is unlikely to be changed over the next decade or two; it does show, though, that they have not altogether given up on carriers and are still prepared to invest more in this expensive weapon system.

But is a battle between carrier fleets, such as were fought in the Pacific in the Second World War, a likely scenario of the future world war? Probably not, because of the increasing vulnerability of these fleets to tracking and sensing devices, and the development of inexpensive weapons for destroying them. Similar considerations apply to strikes executed by carrier forces against a major power. This is not to say that carriers will not have their uses but only that their significance as the principal battleships of the navy, and the fighters of the decisive battle, hence also the foundation of global status, is likely to diminish gradually in the future. Impressive symbols of global reach though they are, they will unavoidably become ever more vulnerable and expensive.

UNDER-SEA POWER

Ever since Hiroshima, it has been possible to envisage the shape of the next decisive battle as a massive nuclear exchange. That nuclear duel is often visualised as an affair of quite short duration – a matter of a few hours or few days of sustained bombardment. But that would

The Future of Seapower

hardly be the end of it all: as likely as not and if life itself survived the initial shock of the nuclear holocaust, hostilities would continue for a prolonged period, probably taking the form of 'broken-back' warfare. Like earlier global wars, the next one too would consist of two major elements: the decisive global battle (the nuclear exchange), and a prolonged period of land warfare of the coalition type ('broken-back').

In general imagination, the nuclear duel is often thought of chiefly as a matter of massive salvoes fired by land-based intercontinental ballistic missiles (ICBMs). Since the rise to prominence of the great rockets in the 1950s, nuclear warfare has tended to be simplified into a form of artillery barrage. Defence strategies in this field, such as current Strategic Defence Initiative (SDI) plans, are aimed at defeating the threat of ICBMs.

Yet students of nuclear-weapon systems have long been aware that a substantial proportion of nuclear capacity of both superpowers is now deployed at sea. Table 4.5 has shown that between 1971 and 1980 between 33 and 43 per cent of deliverable warheads of *both sides* taken together were already found in submarines; for the United States alone that proportion already exceeded 50 per cent in 1976. If to that is added the nuclear-weapon inventory of the large carriers on sea station, it becomes clear that the most recent trend has been gradually to diminish the role of ICBMs in the nuclear-deterrence picture, even though the Soviet Union remains more heavily committed to land-based missiles than is the United States.

Other trends stemming principally from the effects of the computer revolution on weapons systems have accentuated this tendency. The principal motor of change may well be increasing accuracy, both of land- and of sea-based missiles. The high precision of current ground-to-ground missiles makes them vulnerable to surprise attack because no amount of silo hardening is likely to be adequate protection for a near-direct hit. Thus fear of a first strike in a crisis becomes a form of instability.

Until recently, land-based missiles could be expected to achieve higher accuracy than sea-based missiles but accuracy approaching that of land missiles is now claimed for Trident II, a weapon that entered production in 1984 and that will become operational in 1989. This means that in the next decade the chief threat of a surprise attack might well come from submarines, a trend that could lead to a further erosion of the value of static ICBMs (unless mobile forms of deployment will become prevalent). In such conditions, the decisive weapon

144 *Global Overview*

of the next few decades would become submarines, and the decisive nuclear battle, one fought by submarines launching their nuclear missiles while being pursued by hunter–killer boats of the other side. Only countries with an adequate arsenal of ballistic and attack submarines could be considered to wield adequate nuclear deterrence.

If increasing accuracy of sea-based missiles is the dominant trend in nuclear innovation, then submarine forces are likely to be the principal element entering into global power calculations of the next few decades. The chief qualifying assumption is the persistent and continuing difficulty in locating submerged submarines. Much technical ingenuity is currently being expended on devising technologies to overcome this problem. One such device, a mechanical suckerfish would attach itself to the hull of a submarine and, equipped with the newest in electronics, signal its location over long distances (Dyson, 1984). This would, of course, greatly increase the vulnerability of submarine forces. Should such a breakthrough occur, and should it become possible to locate submarines at all times, the value of undersea forces would obviously decline. So far, however, the opaqueness of the sea serves as the guarantor of nuclear stability.

SPACE SYSTEMS

President François Mitterrand was quoted by W. R. Hearst Jr (26 April 1985) as having said in a recent interview that 'whoever controls the sky will rule the world'. Francis Bacon, and Sir Walter Raleigh, whom we quoted in Chapter 1 on the rule of the sea, would both have applauded such a statement.

In a work such as this, the temptation is great to extend the Mahanian terminology we have been using so far: seapower, decisive battle, command of the sea, to the analysis of the military issues of space. For space power is a good candidate for being named a yet higher-order power-medium, in the same sense in which in Chapter 1 we referred to seapower, but now superior to it.

Is not space likely to be the high ground of future conflict? Does it not confer greater mobility, require higher technology, carry greater symbolic content and truly global significance? Is it not arguable, moreover, as Freeman Dyson puts it (in *Weapons and Hope*, 1984) that the 'perennial squabbles of mankind' might be made less dangerous 'by a move of the arena of military activity from the earth into space?' Could not warfare in space become, as oceanic warfare has

The Future of Seapower

been for the past half-millenium, a comparatively decent and humane method of conducting global warfare in a yet higher-order power-medium?

There is no need to exaggerate the decency and the humaneness of warfare conducted by higher-order power instruments. Oceanic warfare of the past 500 years, often of a high degree of intensity, has also gone step-in-step with steadily more costly and damaging campaigns on land. Space warfare, even if defence-oriented, would not be likely to be separable from heavy fighting on earth.

While thinking about space let us distinguish, too, between contemporary space capabilities, which mostly concern forms of information-gathering and processing (through reconnaissance, early warning, guidance, communications, etc.), and future capabilities, which might become available several decades from now, and which might include navigable space craft, not excluding space battleships.

Present-day, and over-the-horizon, space systems are substantially earth-bound: the observation satellites, the space shuttle, or the space station all operate in fixed orbits around the earth and cannot leave their orbits except in pre-planned trajectories. In other words, they are not truly navigable. Nor are the operational characteristics of space to be thought of as directly analogous to those of the sea: space is transparent and it is difficult to hide in; nor is space at present a means of reaching some desirable destination at the other end of the journey; inter-planetary trade is not in the cards as yet and control over it could not be an incentive comparable with those motivating, for example, the exploratory and later naval activities of the Portuguese.

In this vein, Dyson ridicules the attempt to apply Mahanian concepts to space and sees the military future of space in a 'defence-dominated' context. In his view, space deployments should take the form of an inconspicuous and invulnerable force of a multitude of small vehicles designed to monitor activities on earth. Such space forces might allow a disarmed world to settle down more comfortably by providing protection against the risks of surprise attack. Dyson does not explain the political basis or the command structure of such a force.

Space systems might also be seen as the eyes and ears of today's global forces. An attack on them would be likely to be the opening shot of the decisive battle of the next global war. It might thus also be the event that could trigger such a global war.

In the more distant future though, if and when navigable spacecraft

146 *Global Overview*

are built, notions of the command of space might begin to make better sense. Innovation along such lines is likely to proceed but is unlikely to be significant within the next two or three decades.

Space could ultimately become the high ground of world politics but we need not run too far ahead of ourselves. It is also possible that some other form of innovation might take mankind in a direction altogether unforeseeable, and in a manner drastically altering the character of the decisive battle, and the forces required for fighting it. It is the nature of innovations that they can never be properly anticipated.

POLITICAL INNOVATION

This exploration of the future has ranged widely but over a terrain that is in the main technical. Innovation has concerned weapons and other instruments for winning battles and fighting the next global war. But arguably the most important innovation that needs to be considered might come from an altogether different direction for it could assume the shape of an invention or design to substitute for global war as a systemic process of decision-making.

We must bear in mind the possibility that the world will not experience another global war. Indeed, given the likely cost of such a catastrophic event, and the distinct possibility that it might end life on this earth, we ought to take such a possibility with the uttermost seriousness. It is the inertia of the past that prevents us from giving our inventiveness a free rein and getting a good hold on this important question.

A global war might be avoided in the next 50–100 years in two sets of circumstances:

(1) if nuclear deterrence holds;
(2) or if a substitute is found/developed for the functions global war performed in the past half millenium.

If nuclear deterrence holds over such a long period, and the security of critical regions and essential weapon systems remains unimpaired, then seapower in the form of under-sea forces will be likely to be a part of that process, and will remain a prominent component of the status of global power. The validity of such forces rests, of course, upon the small but finite possibility that they might be used in battle. It must be qualified by the probability of technical breakthroughs that

The Future of Seapower 147

would render the forces, especially the submarines, vulnerable to a surprise attack.

In such conditions the threat value (and danger) of strategic weapons would remain even while the fundamental function of forces of global reach – that of winning a global war and thereby rendering a macro-decision on global leadership and policies – will not be performed. One might anticipate difficulties in global policy-making because of the absence of such decision-making, and because the ordinary working of the global system would tend to throw up ever new problems for decision. This might create a situation that is observed in super-stable regimes, those that persist, apparently without change, such as would be caused by elections, or coup or civil war, until the time when they explode in great outbursts of revolutionary tumult. We would expect such a super-stable, non-decision, system gradually to evolve a substitute form of decision-making or else to break up into disorder.

If a substitute is indeed found or invented, what might the effect be on seapower, both in its own right and as an index of global status? In the short run, probably small. In the long run, the validity of this predictor to success in global decision-making would tend to fade into oblivion, possibly also via transfer into space. For if its use cannot ever be even contemplated then its continued and expensive maintenance will become self-evidently superfluous.

*   *   *

In response to our question: does seapower have a future? it is our tentative prognosis that seapower does have a future in the current cycle. That future is based, in our judgement, principally on fleets of nuclear submarines of the ballistic and attack varieties. Beyond the next few decades the outlook is more clouded; space begins to enter into serious consideration and political innovation might dominate the entire field.

CONCLUDING COMMENTS

We have, in Part I of this book, dissected and discussed one basic dimension of global politics: that of polarity or power concentration. It tells us something about the military resources of global reach, their distribution, and the likelihood of future changes.

148 *Global Overview*

Polarity is quite basic to political analysis because the ups and downs of power concentration tell us a good part of the story of long cycles. But the power base is not everything that needs to be covered in this multiplex tale of world politics. Other basic dimensions are system time, the conflicts engendered in the give-and-take of the decision process and the strength of forces for systemic innovation (the coalition dimension). We now know a good deal about system time because that is the stuff of long cycles but much more work needs to be accomplished, and other books must be written, before we have an equally firm grip on 'conflicts' and 'coalitions'.

Part II
Country Data

The second part of this study presents the data on national naval capabilities on the basis of which the global picture of Part I was constructed.

Two distinctions are basic to this more particularised presentation, that between global and regional powers, and that between world powers and the other global powers.

Global powers are distinguished from regional powers, as explained at some length in Chapter 2, principally by the size of their battle fleets (number of capital warships as compared with that of the global powers) and by the scope of their operational range, which must be oceanic in order to qualify as global. Our primary focus in Chapters 7 to 9 therefore is on the oceanic powers. By contrast, Chapter 10 presents the evidence justifying the exclusion of a number of navies from the 'global' category on the grounds that they did not meet the size criterion (10 per cent) and that their operations were primarily regional in scope. The non-global powers of that last chapter are in fact all regional powers and, as such, fall into a distinct and important political category but one that is necessarily confined in spatial range and impact.

Within the category of global powers we distinguish between the four world powers (in Chapters 7 and 8), and the five other global powers (in Chapter 9), most of whom have in fact, at one time or another, been major challengers (France, Spain, Germany, Japan), fighting on the losing side of one or the other of the five global wars that are of principal interest to students of long cycles. The one exception is Russia/USSR that was on the winning side of the last three such wars but has moved into a challenger's position in the current cycle.

Each country section presents the year-by-year quantitative series with an indication of the relevant sources, and a descriptive–narrative account designed to add a minimum of background to the bare bones of the statistical materials, with emphasis on conditions favouring or hindering the development of seapower, organisational, locational and logistic problems, and the major strategic dilemmas and opportunities.

7 The World Powers: Was Portugal the First World Power?

Just as the last two chapters have painted the big picture of long cycles in their unfolding over the centuries, the present chapter singles out for special and detailed attention one single world power, namely Portugal, whose standing appears to be the least secure and the most questionable. To that end it asks the important question: which was the power that was prominent in the management of the global system at the very onset of that system? Was it Portugal as predicted by long cycle theory (Modelski, 1978)?

To answer the question it is necessary to look at two sets of data relevant to measuring seapower: the evidence for (i) ocean-going activities (as distinct from coastal and regional maritime activities) and (ii) the distribution of ocean-going warships (because a world power is one whose share of such warships equals or exceeds one half of the global powers' total of such capacity). The task is therefore not merely to count the number of Portuguese warships and compare that figure to that for other global powers, but (ignoring for the moment the fact that accurate figures on these matters are not readily available) also to clarify what role was played by Portugal in the global system and what an oceanic warship was in that period, bearing in mind that that role was only just then being invented and was still in the process of crystallisation toward the classical form it assumed in the later Dutch and British systems. Finally, it must also be kept in mind that the role of Portugal in world affairs is probably the most controversial among the world powers.

GLOBAL OPERATIONS AND GLOBAL ASPIRATIONS

Which were the powers whose plans and whose operations might qualify them for global rather than for regional status in the fifteenth and sixteenth centuries? For anyone acquainted with the main thrust of world history in that age there seems little possibility to doubt that the strategies of the King of Portugal were the first to assume concrete

152   *Country Data*

shape and were the grandest both in design and in execution. They were first set in motion in 1415 with an impressive amphibious expedition to Ceuta, a Moroccan trading city on the Mediterranean side of the Straits of Gibraltar (see also Table 10.10). They were continued in the following two decades by the occupation and settlement of the Atlantic islands of Azores and Madeira. In the 1480s, after building a trading network along the coasts of West Africa and capturing the gold trade of Guinea the King's men and his ships reached the southern tip of Africa. The plans and strategies were also the boldest because from an early stage onward they appeared to aim at supplanting the central artery of the economy of the old world – the China–India–Egypt–Europe route – and at creating an alternative to it around Africa.

To carry out that design, from 1500 onward, fleets were dispatched to the Indian Ocean, serious naval engagements were fought and the first oceanic trade routes, together with a new organisation of intercontinental relations, were put in place. Nothing of comparable boldness and single-mindedness in world politics as well as world economics was planned and carried out until the English and the Dutch decided to mount an attack on that same system late in the sixteenth century.

As distinct from the single-mindedness of Portuguese strategies, the policies of the Spanish monarchy, while drawing on the greater wealth and power of the new union between Castile and Aragon, were dispersed among a number of objectives. Until 1492, these objectives were primarily local and included the re-establishment of domestic political stability, the building of a nation-state, and the conquest of Granada, although they did also include an interest in the Canaries, maintained against the Portuguese in the Treaty of Alcacovas (1479). After 1492, first priority was given to regional Mediterranean and European policies such as the containment of France, then control of Italy, resistance to the Ottoman Empire, and generally the pursuit of Hapsburg dynastic aspirations. Such global exploration as was undertaken by Columbus, spectacular though it was in its ultimate results, was based on Portuguese experience and was in the first place aimed at the same goals as those the King of Portugal had set for himself – the opening of a new route to Asia. And as such it did not prove successful. Hence, for some two to three decades, the American project remained marginal to Spain's policy, even though a pattern of territorial settlement was developed in Cuba and Haiti, and the maritime effort was not inconsiderable (a total of sixty-two ships and

The World Powers: Was Portugal the First? 153

a number of caravels, lightly armed, sailed in six expeditions between 1492 and 1502).

Aspirations to global reach similar to the Portuguese were still in evidence in 1519–22 when a Spanish fleet of five small ships led by Magellan, a Portuguese captain, succeeded in circumnavigating the world. Although it was a historical landmark, the expedition was far from being an unqualified success. Magellan himself lost his life on a Philippine island and only one of his ships returned safely home. Two other expeditions ran into similar trouble and brought only conflict with Portugal, already strongly entrenched in the Moluccas (the source of many of the spices). In view of these difficulties, negotiations were once more entered with Portugal (Treaty of Zaragoza, 1529) wherein, against a handsome indemnity, Spain agreed to halt her operations 17 degrees east of the Moluccas, and thus to abandon global aspirations. Only in the following generation did Spain return to the Philippines, with the establishment of a first settlement on Cebu in 1564–5, and the founding of Manila in 1570. The annual Manila galleon from Mexico then came to link Acapulco with China.

In the meantime the conquests of Cortes in Mexico (1521) and Pizarro in Peru (1531) produced results that were at first imperial and territorial but that, in the event, created a new major intercontinental trade route between Seville and the New World. That route began to flourish after 1535 when shipments of gold and silver to Spain reached the annual rate of 1 million ducats. By 1555 when that rate had doubled, the route assumed European significance; it became a legend at the end of the century when the rate peaked at 8 million ducats annually in 1591–5 (Elliott, 1963, p. 184). Long before that time, serious security problems had arisen, and naval precautions had to be taken to protect the route. Spain's oceanic navy was born of these problems, and a trans-Atlantic convoy system came to be gradually established. Thus Spain's record is one of considerable success in the imperial mode in the Americas, but with inattention to problems of global organisation until quite late in the period. As Mattingly (1963, p. 24) summarises the issue: 'in spite of her vast transatlantic empire Spain never had to be an Atlantic sea power. The only regular fighting force in Atlantic waters had been her "galleons of the India guard".'

Early in the sixteenth century, England did not undertake any global operations. Henry VII turned down Columbus' demand for his support (Parry, 1963, p. 170), but a few years later, he lent some backing to John Cabot's efforts to explore the northern coasts of North America. These efforts did not bear much fruit. Attempts to

Country Data

find a north-west passage (Frobisher, 1583) or the route to Muscovy (1554, 1586) were none too successful either. The first real break-through came when John Hawkins sailed in three small ships in 1562, on the first of his slaving ventures to Hispaniola (via Sierra Leone). While that particular project ended in disaster in 1566 (high-level Spanish policy insisting on maintaining the monopoly of access to colonies), from 1571 onward the Caribbean became the scene of intermittent privateering in which Francis Drake (Hawkins' cousin) was the central figure. But not until Drake carried out his own circumnavigation in 1577–80, were global aspirations clearly asserted, and in 1585 Drake returned to the Spanish Indies with a fleet of twenty sail. Thus, the English record is one of expressions of interest but no exercise of naval power until 1585.

To start with, the Netherlanders were closely associated with the global operations both of the Portuguese, and of the Spaniards by about 1500. Antwerp became the northern distribution-point for Portuguese spices and the purchasing-point for supplies needed to equip the fleets of the Indies. Charles, a Netherlander by birth, became King of Spain and Holy Roman Emperor. But the Low Countries did not really participate actively and directly in those matters, and by the middle of the century became absorbed in their own internal and revolutionary troubles. Their attention did not turn to global problems until about 1590 when it became obvious that the Iberian world system was coming under attack from several quarters. The first Dutch circumnavigation of the globe was then effected by Oliver van Noord in 1598 (Hall, 1955, p. 231). The Dutch Navy that took shape in the naval battles of 1573–4, which gave it control of the waters around Holland and Zealand, played a part in the Battle of the Armada (1588) by helping to prevent the junction of the Spanish fleet with the Spanish Army in Flanders, but it did not become a global force until the last decade of the century.

England, and the Netherlands, did not challenge the Portuguese world order until quite late in the first cycle, but when they did, they did so with great intensity and ultimately, with complete success. France was the first to issue a major challenge, earlier in the cycle, but with less of a single-minded dedication and mostly in the context of her European struggle with the Hapsburgs. Privateers from Dieppe, for instance, were pursuing Spanish shipping in the 1520s (they seized three ships taking Aztec treasures to Charles V in 1523). In 1530 Portuguese shipping was subjected to raids and even Lisbon was blockaded from a distance. Francis I publicly denied the legitimacy of

The World Powers: Was Portugal the First? 155

the Iberian world partition: '*Le soleil luit pour moi comme pour les autres; et je voudrais bien voir l'article du Testament d'Adam qui m'exclut du partage*' (quoted in Tramond, 1947, p. 81).

And he too sent out expeditions in search of 'gold, spices and a passage to Asia'. Jacques Cartier sailed three times up the Gulf of St Lawrence, between 1534 and 1541, but he failed. A French navy briefly surged in the 1540s and 1550s but the expansion was based chiefly on the Mediterranean model of the galley fleet and had little impact on oceanic relations. Attempts at settlements were made at Rio in Brazil (1555–8) and in Florida (1562–5) but they failed in part because they were Calvinist and could not attract sufficient home backing. Until 1559, French privateers constituted 'the principal danger' to Spanish shipping (Parry, 1963, p. 197). But when the time came to make a settlement with Charles V and his successor, France abandoned her claims to oceanic freedom and conceded maritime dominion in exchange for territorial gains in Europe. As wars of religion began to divide France from 1560 onward, the anti-Spanish party in France, based on the Huguenots, came to merge their efforts with the Netherlanders and the English. Filippo Strozzi equipped for the King a war-fleet of carracks (more than eighty vessels in all) at Bordeaux in 1572, for the initial purpose of blockading La Rochelle (Braudel, 1976, pp. 1107–9). In 1581–3, after the Spanish conquest of Portugal, Strozzi led the French expedition to the Azores, possibly with designs upon Brazil, but was defeated by a Spanish force in two sea battles near Terceira. No new French effort on a global scale appeared until the next century.

The French challenge was basically an Atlantic problem; in the Indian Ocean matters were different but not entirely unrelated. Just prior to the modern era, the most spectacular event in the maritime region had been the seven great expeditions mounted by China and led by Chung Ho between 1405 and 1435. Six of these occurred in the reign of just one emperor, Yung Lo, the third of the Ming dynasty who, following the consolidation of Ming rule, thought it desirable also to project his power outside China. In the words of the official historian, he sent out great fleets in order to 'spread out the knowledge of [his] majesty and virtue'; 'every country became obedient to the imperial commands' and in return sent envoys to offer tribute (Needham, 1971, pp. 488 ff). These 'treasure' fleets called on Java, Sumatra, Malacca, Ceylon, Siam, Cochin, Calicut, Ormuz and even reached the coast of Africa.

What is so impressive about these fleets is their size and range. The

156   *Country Data*

first fleet consisted of sixty-two 'treasure' ships (of up to nine masts) and was manned by 27 800 officers and men. The ships were ocean-going junks especially built for this purpose in government shipyards, well equipped and armed with bombards. The fleet apparently never fought a naval action but they did carry out some military operations in Ceylon; 'those who refused to submit were subdued by military force' (Pelliot, 1931, p. 273). In size they were superior to the fleets that Portugal dispatched to that same region a few decades later. The symmetry of these two movements, as though 'provoked by the rhythms of history', has been noticed by scholars since the nineteenth century.

The expeditions stopped as suddenly as they began. China turned inward and her navy 'simply fell to pieces' (Needham *et al.*, 1971, p. 526). Maritime activities and trade were discouraged and the Portuguese stepped into the void created by the Chinese withdrawal. By mid-sixteenth century they even acquired a foothold in China, at Macao, from which they organised trade missions to Japan, Goa, and soon Manila.

Apart from China, in the first decade of the sixteenth century the major opposition to Portuguese operations came from the Mameluk rulers of Egypt, who in turn had the backing of Venice. Responding to the pleas of their trade partners who included the Hindu ruler of Calicut, the Sultan of Gujerat, and the Yemenis, the Mameluks equipped a substantial fleet at Suez and proceeded to fight the Portuguese in Indian waters in 1507–9 (Serjeant, 1963, pp. 14–18) but they were defeated decisively at Diu in 1509. The next serious problem arose only when the Ottoman Turks, after capturing Syria and Egypt (1517) and Iraq (1534–5) and in the context of their wars against Spain and Persia, also set up a challenge in the Indian Ocean. But for the Ottomans the Indian Ocean never became a principal theatre of operations.

The Ottoman Empire was, of course, at that time, a major Mediterranean naval power. After the battle of Preveza (1538) and until the battle of Lepanto (1571) it had 'supremacy over almost the entire Mediterranean' (Braudel, 1976, p. 905). It was, moreover, fighting primarily Spain (and even Portugal, via Algiers and Morocco), and was therefore an ally of France. Thus it is not surprising that in the Indian Ocean too it would come into conflict with the Iberian world order. In 1538, a Turkish naval expedition based on the Red Sea seized Aden, and mounted a strong attack on Portuguese-held Diu. In 1542, Portuguese-allied Ethiopia came under heavy pressure. Basra

The World Powers: Was Portugal the First? 157

was seized in 1546 and, in the course of the war against Persia (also cooperating with Portugal), naval attacks were launched in Diu, Muscat and Ormuz. In 1558 Turkish gunners assisted in a naval onslaught on Malacca from Atjeh. The result of this was the revival of the Red Sea pepper route (channelled from Atjeh to Jeddah by Gujerati ships) and a significant attenuation of the Portuguese monopoly (as documented by Braudel, 1976, pp. 545 ff). Yet the Turks never won a clear victory on the ocean. The Mediterranean galleys they employed proved no match against the great ships of Portugal.

This brief survey shows that the only power systematically engaged in global operations throughout most of the period ending in 1580 was Portugal. It was she who fought the significant naval engagements; who organised and guarded the one new major artery of world trade from Asia to Europe. The runner-up was Spain who, by 1535, had created the second major new trade route: the Atlantic route to the New World. But this route had to be protected: transatlantic convoys were launched in wartime in the 1540s, and as a more permanent institution in the 1560s (cf. Table 3.2). In turn, the Portuguese route to the East was challenged by the Ottoman-organised competition based on the Red Sea. Most of the time, though, such organised violence as was employed against these two trade arteries took the form of corsair activities and small scale operations. Oceanic enterprise had to be learnt before they could be undertaken in earnest. That stage was reached in England and the Netherlands only in the 1580s, and it is only then that general naval activity on the oceans took off. Global seapower was thus born, and could be observed, first, in the creation and consolidation of new global trade routes, and then, in the deliberate effort to disrupt them and to capture the wealth they represented, and ultimately, to replace the old system by a new one.

THE OCEANIC 'WARSHIPS' OF THE SIXTEENTH CENTURY

What ships did the sixteenth century's global powers, or the potential global powers, have to establish their will upon the ocean? What were the ships that constituted a capacity for naval operations?

The classic warship of the pre-oceanic (or pre-modern) era was the Mediterranean war galley. For some 2000 years this was the dominant

158 *Country Data*

naval weapon of the maritime powers: propelled by oars and by sail, low-lying and open to the sea, independent of the wind but bound to stay close to the shore, carrying a large crew (200 seemed standard) that doubled as attack force when the enemy was close-in and a ramming and boarding could be effected. In fifteenth-century Venice, galleys were of two types: heavy galleys (*galie grosse* or *galleasses*) for high-value cargo and also for serving in war fleets, and light galleys (*galie sotil*) which were more purely military in function.

Galleys served well in the Mediterranean, and with the spread of Italian models, in Western Europe in the fourteenth and fifteenth centuries. They were also seen operating at times on the coasts of the Atlantic. At that time, Aragon, Castile and Portugal each had a galley force. A Portuguese galley squadron, for instance, fought in the Channel on England's side in 1384–90, during the Hundred Year's war against France (which was, in turn, assisted by a Castilian force). In the modern era, galley fleets continued as local defence forces, for instance off Lisbon or Cadiz or in the Straits of Gibraltar. Four 'Galleys of Portugal' even sailed in the Great Armada of 1588. Mediterranean sea warfare continued to be conducted by galley fleets. But theirs clearly was a technology whose time had passed; it was adapted neither to the open ocean nor to sailing global distances.

When the King of Portugal first launched his expedition of discovery along the coasts of Africa, his preferred instrument of exploration was the caravel, a light vessel of maybe up to 100 tons, easy to build, manoeuvrable and excellent for navigating close to the coast. It was in fact a new type of ship innovated by the Portuguese (*circa* 1430–1440) for their special needs. It was also well armed. 'For a long time' wrote a Portuguese chronicler 'the caravels of Portugal were very much feared on the sea' (De Resende, quoted by Cipolla, 1965, p. 81).

But the caravel was unsuited for global operations, for carrying men or cargo over long distances, for fighting bigger ships, for carrying heavier armament, or for braving the heavy seas off the coast of northern Europe. For such purposes larger ships were required and the model became the northern trading ship known as the carrack. This was a fairly large ship by the standards of the time, 300–500 tons at first (but there were some very large Mediterranean round ships too), one that stood high in the water, afforded shelter to the crew and passengers, and could carry cargo and an impressive armament of guns.

Early in the sixteenth century there was a burst of rivalry in the building of large carrack-type ships by West European rulers; notable

The World Powers: Was Portugal the First? 159

examples of such ships were '*Great Michael*' of Scotland (1512, soon sold to France) or '*The Great Harry*' of England (1514, 1000 tons). It was the Portuguese who took the matter most seriously and for whom that type of ship, named by them the *nau* or 'Great Ship', first became the basic instrument of long distance operation.

This period, the decades around 1500, was also a time of certain significant naval innovations, in all of which Portuguese shipbuilders took a leading part. In addition to improvements in the navigational capacity of the carrack through a reduction of hull width in proportion to the length, the introduction of multiple masts, and multiple sails per mast, two other decisive changes were then effected: the cutting of ports into the main hull (traditionally ascribed to a Brest shipbuilder *circa* 1500, but possibly earlier (cf. Clowes, 1897–1903, I, p. 412), thus greatly increasing the possible fire-power of a ship; and the introduction of bronze guns (replacing iron guns) thus improving their reliability and safety. This last point meant that in addition to being a heavy importer of Northern artillery, Portugal also became a substantial consumer of copper; an average of 200 tons *circa* 1500, (cf. Cipolla, 1965, p. 31), although much of it was also re-exported.

It is reported of Joao (John) II of Portugal (died 1495), who is also credited with devising the technique of skimming shot over the water in anticipation of the broadside method, that 'he used to spend much money in building great vessels manned with guns' (De Resende, quoted by Cipolla, 1965, p. 80). When a Portuguese fleet arrived at Corfu in 1501 to assist in the war against the Ottomans it 'made the Venetians gape' and made their commander comment on the 'incredible quantity of artillery and the troop-carrying capacity of the Portuguese ships' (Weinstein, 1960, p. 170). Joao II was also 'obsessed' with an ambition to build a 1000-ton carrack, bigger and better than any constructed up to his time and with such heavy sides that no artillery could pierce them. Such a ship was indeed constructed during his reign, though she did not prove very manoeuvrable (Duffy, 1955, pp. 49–50). But by the turn of the century such large ships were becoming commonplace and in preparation for the assault on the route to India Portugal proceeded to design and launch an impressive fleet of Great Ships that came to form the core of her operations of discovery. The fleets that annually sailed to the East were predominantly made up of *naus*. The naval operations in the Indian Ocean, too, initially relied heavily on the Great Ships. The 1517 expedition to Aden, for instance, consisted of a fleet of thirty-nine sail, fifteen of which were *naus*. The squadron sent to Hormuz in

160 *Country Data*

1520 included eleven *naus* and two galleons out of a total of twenty-five ships (Serjeant, 1963, pp. 170–1). Without the Great Ship there would have been no global operations. This was the ship that founded the new global system, but was it a warship?

That is, indeed, a good question. The *nau* was not really a specialised warship (as at that time only the ships of Henry VII and VIII's navy were, even though they too were later lent to commercial operators). Its functions included, as occasion demanded, carrying passengers and cargo over long distances and it became the principal carrier of spices on their way to Lisbon (just the way the great war-galleys of Venice did it in the fifteenth century). On the other hand, the *nau* was, as a rule, state-owned (the direct property of the King, as in England) for Portuguese naval matters were in the great majority state-organised and owned. She was armed with guns, and served, as we have seen, as the backbone of Portuguese expeditions. It soon also became the largest ship on the oceans and gave symbolic expression to the significance of the Portuguese world project.

The Great Ship was the major ship of the first decades of the sixteenth century. But quite soon it came to be supplemented on the oceans by the galleon, a ship more nearly specialised to military functions. While there is no official definition it is widely agreed that the galleon represented the evolution of the carrack-type ship toward greater manoeuvrability and speed and heavier armament. The ship became longer and narrower, with a characteristic galleon beak-head (resembling that of a galley). All writers also stress that in practice the difference between *nau* and galleon was far from absolute, the terms often being used interchangeably; though in the later decades the *nau* became pre-eminently the cargo-carrier. But the galleon, too, was frequently pressed into commercial service, and both Portuguese and Spanish galleons were commonly used to ferry bullion from the Guinea coast or across the Atlantic.

The origin of the galleon is uncertain. Parry (1963, pp. 83–4) claims the first design for a Venetian shipbuilder between 1526 and 1530. Cipolla (1965, pp. 84–5, citing Anderson, *Sailing Ship*, p. 126) indicates a Spanish origin and notes that, in Venice, early sixteenth-century experiments with the sailing ship for naval action were discarded until the following century. Padfield (1979, p. 110) is uncertain whether the galleon was evolved in the Atlantic war against privateers or by Venetians out of the great *galleasses*. Standard reference works obscure the evolution of the galleon, play down the

The World Powers: Was Portugal the First? 161

Spanish role and totally ignore the vital Portuguese one. Mattingly (1959, p. 195) is one of the few writers who is prepared, albeit grudgingly ('perhaps') to grant priority of development to Portugal.

The evidence of the basic Portuguese ship-lists compiled by Enrique Quirino da Fonseca (1926) demonstrates beyond any doubt that the galleon was a specialised warship that the Portuguese brought into sustained use in the Indian Ocean as early as 1515 and that became widely used in their navy by 1530.

The Fonseca list is not an inventory of ships that is derived from archival documents or from official compilations. The Portuguese archives perished in the Lisbon earthquake of 1755. Fonseca's listing is an attempt to reconstruct the evidence about Portugal's pioneering ships from their first mentions in extant literary sources, chronicles, histories and other narratives of voyages and catastrophes at sea. Seldom is the date of construction, or the year of decommissioning known for these ships; for some, the size or the armament is recorded. Happily, though, the ships are listed by classes, and the *naus* and the galleons are shown separately. Table 7.1 reproduces the information on all the eighty-four galleons known to have been in service between 1515 and 1580.

Besides documenting the priority of Portuguese development and use of this first true oceanic warship, Table 7.1 shows, most importantly, that the major part of the Portuguese galleons of that period operated in the Indian Ocean. Of the eight ships for which information is available on the place of construction, seven were in fact built in India (including at least three in Cochin). In the first fifteen years after 1515 (by which time Portuguese rule had been firmly established) the great majority of galleons mentioned in the sources (seventeen out of twenty-one) were operating in the East. The first galleon on da Fonseca's list (*Piedade*) is a well-armed ship sailing in Indian waters in 1515. As early as 1518 the standard armament of a Portuguese galleon apparently consisted of thirty-five guns (Diffie and Winius, 1977, p. 280). The first reference to an operational use of galleons occurs in a report, already cited, on the composition of a fleet sailing to Hormuz in 1520. Galleons may have been particularly useful in enforcing Portugal's policies of controlling and taxing sea-borne trade in these areas. In the Spanish traffic across the Atlantic the first galleon appears only in 1524 and 1525 (two two-way crossings; could these be experimental cruises?) followed by more numerous instances after 1539 (Chaunu and Chaunu, 1955–6, II, p. 159; VI, pp. 160 ff). It

Table 7.1 Portuguese galleons, 1515–80

Year of first notice	Name	Remarks
1515	N.S. da Piedade	In India; armed with 28 pieces; 80 tons
1519	S. Antonio	Lost in Lisbon
	S. Denis (1)	Built in India; 300 tons
1520	Samorim Grande	Built in India; still in service in 1532; 150 tons
	S. Jorge (1)	Built in Cochin, armed with 28 pieces; 150 tons
1521	S. Marcos	In India
	S. Mateus	'the best in India'; armed with 22 major pieces of artillery
1522	Flor do Mar	Part of Embassy to Pope Adrian, 1522
	S. Tiago Lam.	Built in India; 150 tons
1523	S. Espirito	Sailing in India, 1523
	S. Joao (1)	Still in service, 1537
	S. Leao	In India; 160 tons
1524	S. Jorge (2)	In India, lost 1524
	S. Luis	Built in India; still there in 1538; armed with 16 major pieces
1525	N.S. da Conceicao	250 tons
	Espadarte	Sailing for India
	S. Jeronimo	250 tons; sailing for India and Malacca
	S. Miguel	In India; 300 tons
	S. Rafael	In India; 300 tons
1527	Samorim Pequeno	In India, still there in 1538
1528	Reis Magos	In India
1530	S. Vicente	Served in Brazil and Morocco
1533	S. Joao (2) Botafogo	Built in Lisbon; armed with 366 bronze pieces; in capture of Tunis 1535; still afloat, 1580
	S. Salvador	In India, 1533; on patrol off Portugal, 1537
1536	S. Jorge (3)	Armed with 30 pieces; 200 tons
1537	S. Denis (2)	Still there in 1550
1538	S. Bartolomeu	
	S. Bernardo	
	S. Boaventura	
	Bufara	
1539	S. Cruz	In India
1541	N.S. da Annunciada	Built in Cochin
	Coulao	In India
	S. Luis (2)	Built in Cochin, 1541

Table 7.1   Portuguese galleons, 1515–80

Year of first notice	Name	Remarks
1542	S. Catarina	
	Santissima Trindade	In India
	S. Tiago	Sailing 1542–59
1543	Esperanca	On patrol off Portugal
	S. Paulo	In armada of three galleons off Morocco
1547	Botica	Also described as a caravel
	N.S. da Rosario	Sailing for India
1548	S. Joao (3)	Sailing for India, 1548; lost 1552
1550	Biscainho	
	S. Juliao	In India
	S. Lourenco	In India, 1550–4
	O. Velho	
1551	S. Jeronimo (2)	Sailing for India in 1551
1552	Samorim (3)	
	Sta Cruz (2)	In India
	S. Pedro (1)	In India
	S. Tome (1)	Sailing East between 1552 and 1556
1554	S. Mateus (2)	Mentioned between 1554 and 1559
1556	S. Vicente (2)	In India, still sailing in 1567
	S. Marcos (2)	Part of Invincible Armada, 1588; 790 tons, 33 pieces of artillery
	S. Sebastiao	Went to India, 1558; lost in combat with Achin vessel, 1565
1559	S. Boaventura (2)	
	S. Francisco (1)	In India
	S. Tiago Maior	Lost, 1584
1560	S. Pedro (2)	In the Indies; 520 tons
	Drago	In India
	S. Lourenco (2)	In India, returned to Portugal, 1575
1565	S. Cruz (3)	
	Sta Maria da Esperanca	In India
	S. Pedro de Rates	Sailing for India
1566	S. Cristovao	
	S. Joao (4)	1100 tons; 50 artillery pieces; part of Invincible Armada
1567	S. Estevao (1)	In India
	S. Joao Baptista (1)	
	S. Joao Evangelista	
	Sta Maria	In India

164 *Country Data*

Table 7.1   Portuguese galleons, 1515–80

Year of first notice	Name	Remarks
	Mestre da Ferraria	
	S. Rafael (2)	Sailing for India, 1567
	Reis Magos (2)	In seafight with English ship in the Indies, 1586
1568	*S. Pedro e S. Paulo*	In India
1570	*S. Gabriel*	Sailing for India, 1570
	S. Juliao (2)	For India
	S. Leao (2)	For India
	S. Luis (3)	For India
	S. Matias	For India, 'very powerful'
	Santissima Trindade (2)	For India
1574	*Sta Catarina* (2)	
	S. Denis (3)	In India
	S. Martinho	In Moroccan expeditions, 1574, 1578; flagship of the Invincible Armada, 1588
1577	*S. Antonio* (3)	In India

Note: Tonnages presumably refer to Portuguese tons. One Portuguese ton was equal to three Venetian *botte*. If at this period one Venetian *botte* equals 0.6 metric ton deadweight (Lane, 1973, pp. 479–80), then one sixteenth-century ton equals 1.8 metric ton. Some galleon names are used more than once as is indicated by the numbers in parentheses following popular ship names.

Source: da Fonseca (1926, pp. 630–58).

would therefore be safe to conclude that Portuguese naval campaigns and operations in the Indian Ocean created the demand for a specialised warship that became the galleon.

Godinho (1982, vol. III, p. 50) reports that an inventory taken in 1537 showed, among ships either anchored, or expected, in Lisbon, in addition to sixteen *naus*, seven galleons capable of undertaking the voyage to India. When Spain finally perfected its convoy system in the 1560s, galleons of 250–500 ton became the standard escorts and they performed well in that task. In the 1570s both Spain and England brought into service a number of highly effective 600-ton galleons. Ultimately the English and the Dutch carried the design to perfection for the galleon became the predecessor of the ship-of-the-line and, ultimately, the modern battleship.

The World Powers: Was Portugal the First? 165

While the *nau* and the galleon both evolved to establish and to lend substance to one great trade artery, the galleon found its next major use in protecting the other great emerging trade route, across the Atlantic, and finally became the best instrument for attacking both routes and for creating alternatives to them. To assess naval capacity we therefore need to know, in the first place, about both *naus* and galleons (while ignoring caravels and other minor types), but as time goes on, we also see the *nau* become powerless as a source of security and instrument of naval operations and by the end of the century fall prey to English and Dutch galleons. They could not be considered as sources of seapower beyond 1580.

We may remark in passing on England's early lead in the evolution of specialised high-seas warships. Henry VII deemed it of importance to build some such vessels specially for war instead of hiring them from merchants (Clowes, 1897–1903, I, p. 404) as Spain did. Henry VIII continued that practice. English observers early became aware that the Channel was the route of Europe's then most important trade circuit, that between Flanders and Spain, including also the traffic from Genoa and Venice to Bruges and then Antwerp. 'With the sea under English dominion, Spain and Flanders flourished only by the permission of England' said the anonymous author of the 'Libel of English Policie' (written *circa* 1430; Clowes, 1897–1903, I, pp. 350–2). England herself had a strong stake in the export of wool to the Low Countries too. Hence a specialised force was needed both to keep peace in the Channel by suppressing piracy and to have the capacity to control that traffic if the need arose. Thus solutions to problems were being attempted in the late fifteenth century that prefigured solutions to global problems of the next period.

Nor was Henry VII unaware of the role of the sea for the stability of his reign. He spent sixteen years of his youth and early manhood in Britanny and returned to England by sea at the head of an invasion force to claim the throne for the House of Tudor. For at least another decade he had to fight off challenges to his rule from others who were trying a similar route with the support of France and the Netherlands. The English navy founded by the Tudors was at first only of regional significance but the principles underlying its foundation especially in its preoccupation with trade routes were very much in advance of their time.

166 *Country Data*

AN ESTIMATE OF PORTUGAL'S NAVAL STRENGTH

If in the sixteenth century the core of naval strength was constituted by the carrack-type Great Ship (the *nau*), and later by the galleon, what was Portugal's inventory of these ships each year between 1494 and 1580? No such figures are directly available and all that can be done is to attempt an estimate based upon existing evidence and some reasonable assumptions.

One overall figure of the maritime strength of Portugal is that of '300 ocean-going ships' *circa* 1536 (Boxer, 1969, p. 56, citing contemporary sources). This is not really helpful because even though 'ocean-going' does constitute a relevant category and is meant to exclude local and short-range craft, it is not a figure purporting to give an inventory of Great Ships or of galleons either. It is likely to include caravels and also *navios* of all kinds, including various trading and supply ships. But it might be usefully contrasted with the figure for English shipping in 1575: twenty-four Royal Navy ships and 135 other ships of over 100 tons in size (Clowes 1897–1903, I, p. 422).

The basic source, once again, is the Fonseca listing, both for *naus* and for galleons, for the year of their 'first mention'. To translate this list into an annual inventory, an assumption needs to be made about the average life-span of these ships.

The Useful Life of Great Ships

There is not too much information on this subject except a statement (Duffy, 1955, p. 60) suggesting that the life-span was indeed a short one: three or four round trips between Lisbon and Goa seemed to be about the limit. If two years are taken as the length of a round trip, this would give a life of only six to eight years. Boxer also thought that the average ship of the *carreira* 'seldom . . . lasted as long as a decade' (Boxer, 1969, p. 210). Another, more indirect, piece of evidence is even more sobering. The Chaunus' analysis shows that for the entire period 1504–1650 (but with information available largely after 1570) the average life of a ship engaged in Spain's Atlantic trade (for those ships for which age information is available) was only six years (Chaunu and Chaunu, 1955–6, VI, pp. 170 ff). For 1576–80 and for forty-nine ships out of 512, the average age was eight years. It is also relevant that the average age of the twenty-four major ships of the Royal Navy engaged in the Battle of the Armada was 12.6 years in

The World Powers: Was Portugal the First? 167

1588. Bear in mind also that the Portuguese data relate only to ships travelling along the long, arduous and punishing track of the *Carreira*. Not all the units of the fleets of Portugal travelled that route all the time; the galleons stayed in the Indian Ocean or around the home bases and may have had a less stressful life.

Another set of data concerns loss of ships because of shipwreck and also capture. This is quite well documented for the Indies route (Godinho, 1982, vol. III, p. 49); these were:

    1500–50:   53 or 54
    1500–1650:   154–159

In other words, this random process of losses at sea averaged out at close to one ship per year. The losses did however become particularly severe in the decade of 1551–60 when a total of sixteen to twenty such ships were apparently lost in incidents giving rise to a new literary genre that came to be known as *historia tragico-maritima*.

It is the conclusion of this analysis that the average lifespan of a *nau* may reasonably be set at eight years, and that of a galleon at ten years. *Naus* listed as lost at sea in the year of first mention shall not be counted at all.

PORTUGUESE SHIPBUILDING

All the evidence seems to suggest that most of Portugal's ships were Portuguese-built. In the sixteenth century, shipbuilding and biscuit manufacture (for ship stores) were the country's 'only important' (and royal) industries (de Oliveira Marques, 1976; I, p. 170). In the first two decades of activities in the East 'Portuguese shipwrights' built '231 ships of all classes' (Duffy, 1955, p. 50), that is 11.6 units per year. Shipyard capacity seems to have been quite substantial. For instance, for the fleet of 1503 the following ships were being constructed: in Lisbon, two *naus*: one of 700 tons and another of 500 tons; at Oporto, one of 450 tons; at Madeira, two of 350 tons, and at Setubal, one of 160–70 tons (Godinho, 1982, vol. III, p. 50). That makes six major ships under construction in just one year, equal to about the strength of the English Navy that same year. Viana, a base for fishing off the North American coast, also had its shipyards.

A total of 138 ships sailed to the Indian Ocean in the decade after 1500, and most of them were *naus*. Almost immediately, Portuguese

168 *Country Data*

shipbuilding was aided by the establishment of shipyards and gun foundries in the East. When Francisco de Almeida sailed for India in 1505, he was instructed to build galleys both at Angediva and at Cochin. The first Great Ship (800 tons) was built at Cochin in 1511–12 (Magalhaes Godinho, 1982, III, p. 50). Similar facilities were also established at Goa (by Albuquerque in 1515; Prestage, 1929, pp. 59–60); Damao and Macao. Owing to the high quality of the teak, ships built in India were in fact thought to be better and longer-lasting than those of metropolitan construction. Rio de Janeiro, using Brazilian timber, also became a centre of construction.

Some reduction in building activity apparently occurred in part as a reflection of the economic crisis setting in after 1540 but was also partly offset by the rising average tonnage of the major ships built. In the first third of the sixteenth century, the Great Ships on the Indian route averaged 400 tons; in the second third, their size ranged between 500 and 1000 tons, with a 'normal' size of about 600 tons.

Given this analysis, the King of Portugal's inventory of *naus* and galleons emerges as shown in Table 7.2 and Figure 7.1 The series shows a rapid rise to a peak of over 100 in the 1510s followed by gradual decline. The figures document substantial global strength for Portugal through most of the relevant period and the possibility for a monopoly of seapower in the regions of its major interest including the South Atlantic, the Indian Ocean, the Far East and some of the Pacific.

Yet it is also worth bearing in mind that these data are reconstructed from fragmentary data of available names. Other evidence suggests that the actual figures might have been, in some years, even higher. For instance, we know that in 1500–2, three fleets sailed from Lisbon for India with a total of 42 *naus* (Almeida, 1929, VI, p. 433); moreover, in 1501 the King also sent a fleet of some thirty ships including five major ships (apparently *naus*), with about 3000 men on board to the Eastern Mediterranean, to aid the Venetians against the Ottomans (Weinstein, 1960, pp. 70–1). Yet Table 7.2 shows only twenty-one *naus* for 1502, and twenty-four for 1503. In 1537, Lisbon alone is known to have harboured seven galleons, and there must have been several others on eastern station. Yet the 1537 number in Table 7.2 encompasses only six galleons (see also Table 7.1). The estimates presented here therefore tend to err in the conservative direction.

The World Powers: Was Portugal the First?   169

Table 7.2   Portugal's estimated annual number of *naus* and galleons
1494–1580

Year	Number of warships	Year	Number of warships	Year	Number of warships
1494	3	1521	63	1548	37
1495	3	1522	62	1549	40
1496	3	1523	60	1550	40
1497	4	1524	64	1551	50
1498	4	1525	66	1552	45
1499	4	1526	62	1553	44
1500	5	1527	54	1554	48
1501	5	1528	51	1555	52
1502	21	1529	38	1556	44
1503	24	1530	41	1557	44
1504	26	1531	39	1558	44
1505	36	1532	38	1559	36
1506	52	1533	44	1560	34
1507	61	1534	41	1561	30
1508	69	1535	38	1562	26
1509	93	1536	36	1563	28
1510	91	1537	40	1564	23
1511	93	1538	45	1565	23
1512	112	1539	41	1566	24
1513	103	1540	43	1567	32
1514	91	1541	38	1568	35
1515	89	1542	43	1569	34
1516	80	1543	42	1570	39
1517	63	1544	44	1571	39
1518	58	1545	38	1572	38
1519	62	1546	42	1573	38
1520	50	1547	38	1574	38
				1575	37
				1576	32
				1577	25
				1578	21
				1579	21
				1580	18

Source: Based on da Fonseca (1926, pp. 630 ff).

GLOBAL DISTRIBUTION

So much for the overall size of the Portuguese seapower. What, then,
might have been the deployment of these forces among the several foci

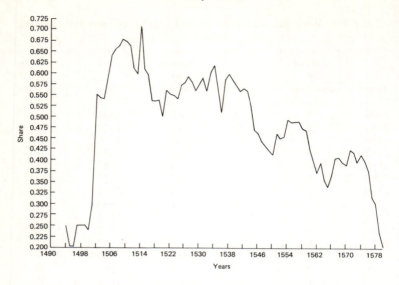

Figure 7.1   Portuguese relative capability share, 1494–1580

of maritime activity? Four such major components may be distinguished.

(1) The 'home fleet'. This included a powerful force of galleons for commerce protection, and other major ships being held in readiness, in reserve or being overhauled, or newly fitted out. Almeida (1929, VI, p. 433) reports that both King Manuel (1495–1520) and King Joao III (died 1555) each had at their disposal three squadrons: one for coastal defence, based on Lisbon; one for the coast of the Algarvae and the straits of Gibraltar, and a third one for the islands (Azores, Madeira). The coastal defence force, also referred to as the Armada da Portugal, alone carried 1300 men.

As already noted, in 1537 the following were found at Lisbon: seven galleons (from 280 to 100 tons) and sixteen *naus* ranging from 650 to 150 tons. In 1544 the Armada of Portugal was asked to protect Spanish shipping passing the Azores on their way back from the New World (a permanent force may have been established in 1552: Reynolds, 1974, p. 127). In 1567 a squadron of six galleons was cooperating with a Spanish one off Cape St Vincent (Chaunu and Chaunu, 1955–6, pp. 261, 337). In the 'Invincible' Armada of 1588 (which had no more than some two dozen first-line warships) the

The World Powers: Was Portugal the First? 171

squadron of Portugal, the lead squadron with the fleet commander on board, consisted of ten large galleons (Mattingly, 1959, 1963; Clowes, 1897–1903, I, p. 598). The Brazil and Guinea protection squadrons may have been detached from the main base at Lisbon; two galleons may have been fairly regularly engaged in carrying gold from La Mina (Guinea) to Lisbon between 1534 and 1561.

(2) The first Viceroy of India, Almeida, created a permanent Indian Ocean force *circa* 1509 (Reynolds, 1974, p. 129). This included the Armada of Malabar, patrolling the Western coast of India, and the Armada del Norte, guarding the Northern approaches. Each year, at monsoon time, these would be sent out to enforce the system of passes (*cartazas*) whereby merchants, in exchange for convoys and protection would pay customs duties in Portuguese ports. These armadas would also be the nucleus of forces that could strike at enemies or come to the rescue of beleaguered outposts. In 1531, Governor Nono da Cunha mounted a '400-ship' attack on Diu and failed; but the Portuguese soon established themselves in Diu by invitation and by 1538 repulsed a strong Ottoman force of seventy-two ships that withdrew when their Gujerati allies stopped supplying them and a relief fleet was approaching (Diffie and Winius, 1977, pp. 287 ff).

(3) Viceroy Albuquerque created another permanent force of ten ships in the Malacca Straits in 1511 (Reynolds, 1974, p. 130). Its task was to patrol the straits and collect taxes on all passing traffic; also to watch over the restive rulers of Malaya and Sumatra, to protect the Moluccas, sources of the luxury spices of cloves and nutmeg, and to guard the routes to Macao and Japan.

(4) In view of the distances separating Portugal and its eastern outposts, a substantial number of ships must also usually have been in transit; these were the ships of the *Carreira da India*, for major ships were rare on the route to Brazil. The average size of the fleet sailing from Lisbon in the 1530s was seven ships while another fleet of somewhat smaller size was advancing in the opposite direction.

Table 7.3 is a record of sailings on Portugal's *Rota do Capo* (the Cape route). It shows both the decennial rate of sailings from Lisbon, and the annual averages both for sailings from Lisbon and for the return trip from the East. The numbers are those for *navios* (ships), for not all these fleets were composed of major ships. Thus Cabral's fleet of 1500 consisted of ten *naus* and three other ships. But in later years these were predominantly the major ships. The last column shows the 'surplus' of ships (arrivals in the East minus departures

172 *Country Data*

Table 7.3   Sailings in the *Carreira da India (navios)*

	Total departing Lisbon	Annual averages		
		Arriving east	*Departing east*	*Surplus*
1500–9	138	13–14	7	6–7
1510–19	96	9	6	3
1520–29	76	6	4	2
1530–39	80	7	n.d.	n.d.
1540–49	61	5–6	5	0–1
1550–59	51	4	4–5	0–1
1560–69	49	4	4	0
1570–79	54	5	4	1

Source: Based on Godinho (1982, vol. III, p. 49).

from the East) that indicates the number of ships retained in the East. It will be seen that that surplus vanishes to zero by the 1540s. By that time we may suppose the Lisbon–Goa or Malacca–Lisbon round trip to have become fairly routinised and settled down to mainly commercial traffic. The mobility of seapower had been reduced, though not eliminated, and the needs of the eastern squadrons met mostly from local resources. Arguably, by 1540 the *carreira* had become a cargo fleet, clearly differentiated from the war fleet.

But that conclusion could be premature. All the King's ships were armed and all could be pressed back into naval operations if the need arose. Bear in mind, too, that in the Battle of the Armada only the core of the English fleet was composed of the Royal Navy (thirty-four ships); among the total number of ships engaged on the English side, which was 197, many were merchant ships, ships fitted out by the City of London, coasters and so forth. Mostly they were smaller than the Navy ships but as many as eighty-two were 100 tons or larger. Hence British seapower too found expression in battle in part through the mobilisation of ships other than pure warships.

A final estimate of Portugal's naval strength will thus depend on the importance attached in the latter part of the cycle, to the King's *naus*. It seems fairly certain that at the end of this era they were primarily commercial carriers. In the reorganisation of Portugal's India trade in 1570 and 1576 a greater role was given to private interests, hence to increased differentiation of function. The question then is at what

The World Powers: Was Portugal the First? 173

point we need to stop regarding the *naus de carga* as part of naval strength.

It seems clear that by the onset of global warfare in 1580 their military capacity had deteriorated considerably. But would it not be justified to say that this role reversal had occurred around 1540? Yet unlike the ships of the Atlantic trade they needed no convoys. Their strength and weight on distant routes meant security on the way and kept interlopers out until 1590. In Table 7.4, showing Portuguese naval dispositions, it is easy to distinguish the *naus de carga*, primarily the ships in transit, and at Lisbon, from others more clearly devoted to naval operations proper. Thus probably one-third of the major ships were engaged in high-value cargo operations under conditions of enhanced security, while two-thirds remained in primarily naval and protective roles. Right up to 1580 Portuguese *naus* supplemented the galleons in the role of providing security much in the same way in which Venetian heavy galleys (and China's 'treasure ships') combined trading and naval functions.

Table 7.4   Estimated distribution of Portugal's major ships, 1537

Dispositions	*Naus*	*Galleons*	*Total*
Home base (especially Lisbon)	16	7	23
Indian Ocean forces	6	2	8
Malacca Straits	1	2	3
In transit	5	1	6
TOTAL	28	12	40

Table 7.4 summarises an informed guess about the world-wide distribution of Portuguese seapower in 1537. It is an attempt to bring the total of major ships (forty) in line with the estimate for that year in Table 7.2. But if that figure is compared with other evidence of Portuguese naval strength in that year, including the Lisbon inventory (twenty-three major ships in that harbour alone), the knowledge about the *naus* in transit in the *Carreira* (five departed Lisbon for Goa in March 1537, and ten the following year in April), as well as the force of '400 ships' that attacked Diu only six years earlier, it becomes clear that this estimate, too, may well be on the conservative side.

174   *Country Data*

Portuguese seapower was, in its day and for its time, immensely impressive, yet much of it was veiled in secrecy by deliberate policies and also remained inaccessible to European observers because it was unfolding on distant oceans; hence it has tended to be ignored both in contemporary appraisals and by more recent scholarship.

CONCLUSION

Was Portugal then the first world power? The answer is yes, it most certainly was, and most strikingly so in the first four decades after 1500. It was the first and, until about 1540, the only powerfully active on the world ocean. It was the leader of the age of discoveries, and also the leader in the evolution of the three most important types of ship that dominated the age of discoveries: the caravel, the Great Ship, and the galleon. Moreover, until about 1540, it also had a preponderant numerical share of such major oceanic ships and deployed them in a manner calculated to maintain the command of the sea in crucial areas.

This heroic and then golden age of Portuguese seapower came to an end in mid-century because of the declining significance of the spice trade, partly because of the revival of the Red Sea route, the peak in spice deliveries in Lisbon being reached in 1547; also because of the rising costs of maintaining fleets and bases and severe losses of ships in the 1550s, leading to state bankruptcy in 1560; and also because of the onset of the international economic crisis of 1544–61 that wrought a reorientation of economic activities away from Antwerp toward Seville, and the rising intolerance and illiberality at home and in relations with the world. Nonetheless, Portugal remained the only power with a global distribution of forces until the 1560s.

The principal challenger to Portugal's world position was Spain. The treasures of the New World (and silver in particular) became more important than the spices of the East, and the value of the Atlantic trade overtook that of Portugal's with the Orient probably in the 1530s. Moreover, Spanish silver was indispensable to that Portuguese trade and made for Lisbon's dependence on Seville. Spain reappeared in the Philippines in the 1560s but otherwise the challenge was largely non-confrontational, with the attention absorbed mostly by the French encroachments in the Atlantic and by Ottoman pressures in the Indian Ocean.

The Iberian partition of the world in 1494 had nearly eliminated

The World Powers: Was Portugal the First? 175

opportunities for friction and had indeed forged a community of interests in the defence of the monopoly privileges thus created. Portuguese and Spanish fleets cooperated against French and later English and Dutch corsairs and privateers in the Atlantic and against Barbary pirates in the Mediterranean. In fact, Portuguese predominance on the ocean remained outwardly unaffected for some time longer because Spain's naval effort after 1560 was concentrated on the Mediterranean and in the Low Countries. Only when a truce was reached with the Sultan at Istanbul (*circa* 1578) were its energies freed once again for the world ocean. Spain's invasion of Portugal, that followed in 1580, was the 'turning-point of the century', opening 'the great battle for control of the Atlantic and world domination' (Braudel, 1976, p. 1176).

Table 7.5   The Great Ships of Portugal: *Naus Portuguesas*, 1494–1580

Year of first notice	Name	Remarks
1487	*Figa* (?)	Crew of fifty
1489	*S.M. da Nazare*	Launched, 1489
	Bretoa (2)	
1497	*S. Rafael*	100 tons; in da Gama's fleet, burnt off the coast of Mozambique, 1497
	S. Gabriel (1)	120 tons; in da Gama's fleet
1500	*El-Rei*	
	Anunciada (1)	
1502	*Anunciada* (2)	
	Batecabello	
	Borreco	
	Bretoa (3)	
	Vera Cruz (1)	
	Esmeralda	
	Flor de la Mar (1)	400 tons; shipwrecked off Sumatra, 1511
	S. Helena (1)	
	S. Jeronimo (1)	
	Julia (1)	
	Leitoa (1)	
	Lionarda (1)	
	S. Martinho (1)	
	S. Pantaleao (1)	
	S. Paulo (1)	
	S. Rafael (2)	

176

Table 7.5   The Great Ships of Portugal: *Naus Portuguesas*, 1494–1580

Year of first notice	Name	Remarks
1503	*N.S. da Conceicao* (1)	
	Faial	
	Rainha (2)	Disappeared off Portugal, 1503
	S. Caterina de Monte Sinai	100 tons; private owners (?); lost sailing to India, 1503
	Taforeia	Dismantled in Malacca, 1510
	S. Tiago (1)	Sank, 1505
1504	*S. Antonio* (2)	
	Rei (1)	Burnt in Cochin for nails, 1511
1505	*S. Antonio* (3)	
	S. Antonio (4)	
	S. Bartolomeo (1)	
	S. Bartolomeo (2)	
	Bela	Abandoned on voyage to India, 1505
	N.S. da Conceicao (2)	
	S. Cristovao (2)	Private owner
	S. Espirito (2)	300 tons
	Bom Jesus (1)	
	S. Jorge (1)	
	Lionarda (2)	
	Madalena (1)	Private owner?
	S. Tiago (2)	
1506	*S. Antonio* (5)	
	S.M. de Ajuda (1)	
	Aveiro	400 tons
	Botafogo (3)	
	Cirne (1)	Burnt for nails, 1512
	Condona	
	S. Espirito (3)	
	S. Gabriel (2)	
	Graca (1)	
	S. Jorge (2)	
	Judia	Privately owned
	N.S. da Luz (1)	
	N.S. da Luz (2)	Sank, 1517
	S. Maria (4)	
	S. Maria da Pena	Shipwrecked off Mozambique, 1506
	Rei (2)	
	S. Tiago (3)	
	S. Vincente (1)	Shipwrecked on way to India, 1506

177

Table 7.5 The Great Ships of Portugal: *Naus Portuguesas*, 1494–1580

Year of first notice	Name	Remarks
1507	*S. Antonio* (6)	
	Belem	
	N.S. da Conceicao (3)	
	N.S. da Conceicao (4)	
	San Cristovao (3)	
	S. Gabriel (3)	Shipwrecked at sea, 1509
	S. Joao (2)	Lost off Goa, 1510
	Leitoa (2)	
	Meri	600–800 tons?
1508	*S. Antonio* (7)	
	Bernalda	
	Botafogo (4)	
	S.M. do Campo	
	Cervalha	
	S. Cruz (1)	Shipwrecked, 1508
	Galega (1)	
	S. Joao (3)	
	S. Marta (1)	
	Ribalta	
	Rosario (1)	
1509	*Amory*	
	S. Ana (1)	
	S. Antonio (8)	
	Anunciada (3)	
	S. Boaventura (1)	
	Botafogo (5)	
	S. Clara (2)	Private owners
	N.S. da Conceicao (5)	
	S. Cristovao (4)	
	S. Cristovao (5)	
	S. Cruz (2)	
	Galega (2)	Grounded in Mozambique, 1510
	Giroa	
	Graca (2)	Private owners
	S. Juliao (4)	
	Lionarda (3)	
	Madalena (2)	
	Nazare (3)	
	S. Rafael (3)	
	Flor da Rosa (1)	
	S. Sebastiao (1)	
	S. Tiago (4)	Private owners
	Trindade (1)	
	S. Vincente (2)	

178

Table 7.5   The Great Ships of Portugal: *Naus Portuguesas*, 1494–1580

Year of first notice	*Name*	*Remarks*
1510	*S. Agostinho* (1)	Private owner
	N.S. da Ajuda (2)	
	S. Ana (2)	Crew of 70
	S. Antonio (9)	
	S. Bartolomeu (3)	
	S. Bartolomeu (4)	
	S.M. do Campo (2)	
	Julioa (2)	450 tons, private owners
	Rainha (3)	
	S. Sebastiao	Sank on the way to India, 1520
	S.M. da Vitoria (1)	
	S.M. da Ajuda (3)	
	Belem (2)	
	Bretoa (4)	Crew of 29
1511	*S. Cristovao* (6)	
	S. Cruz (3)	
	S. Eufemia (1)	Private owners
	Joia	
	S. Pedro	
	Piedade (1)	
	S. Catarina de Monte Sinai (2)	
	S. Tiago (5)	
1512	*Ajuda* (4) *Grande*	
	Ajuda (5) *Pequena*	
	Ajuda (6)	
	S. Antonio (10)	Lost, 1512
	S. Antonio (14)	
	Botafogo (6)	
	Bretam	
	Cabaia	
	Cirne (2)	
	N.S. da Conceicao (6)	
	N.S. da Conceicao (7)	
	S. Cruz (4)	
	S. Espirito (4)	Shipwrecked on way to India, 1512
	S. Eufemia (2)	
	S. Joao (4)	Built in India
	S. Juliao (1)	
	Madalena (3)	
	Piedade (2)	
	Rumesa	

179

Table 7.5   The Great Ships of Portugal: *Naus Portuguesas*, 1494–1580

Year of first notice	Name	Remarks
	S.M. da Serra (1)	
	S. Catarina de Monte Sinai (3)	700 tons; built in India; disappeared in 1530
	S. Tiago (6)	
	S. Tome (1)	150 tons; built in Cochin
	Virtudes	
1513	*S. Antonio* (11)	Lost, 1513
	Anunciada (4)	
	Botafogo (7)	
	S. Cristovao (7)	
	Piedade (3)	
1514	*S.M. da Ajuda* (7)	
	S. Juliao (2)	
	S.M. da Luz (3)	
1515	*S. Antonio* (12)	
	N.S. da Conceicao (8)	
	S. Elena (2)	Private owners
	S.M. da Serra (2)	
1516	*Nazare* (4)	
1517	*S. Agostinho* (2)	
	S. Antonio (13)	
	Nazare (5)	
	Nazare (6)	
	S. Tiago (7)	
	S. Tiago (8)	40–80 tons
1518	*S.M. da Ajuda* (8)	80–110 tons
	Annunciada (5)	
	Bretam (2)	
	Espera	80–110 tons
	Celestina	40–80 tons
	S. Jeronimo (2)	
	S. Juliao (3)	
	Reis Magos (1)	
	S. Mateus (1)	
1519	*S. Antonio* (15)	Shipwrecked off Arabia, 1520
	Belem (3)	
	N.S. da Conceicao (9)	Private owners
	S. Maria da Estrela (2)	Private owners
	Graca (3)	
	Guadelupe (1)	
	S. Jeronimo (3)	Abandoned, 1519; was it a galleon?

180

Table 7.5   The Great Ships of Portugal: *Naus Portuguesas*, 1494–1580

Year of first notice	Name	Remarks
	S. Jeronimo (4)	
	S. Rafael (4)	
	Flor da Rosa (2)	
	S. Tome (2)	Private owners
1520	*Burgalesa*	
	N.S. da Conceicao (10)	Private owners
	Espadarte (1)	
	S. Joao (5)	
	Nazare (7)	Crew of 400; disappeared, 1523
	S. Rafael (5)	
1521	*S. Antonio* (16)	
	S. Bartolomeo (3)	
	Burgalesa (2)	
	Samorim (1)	
	S. Clara (3)	
	N.S. da Conceicao (11)	250 tons
	S. Espirito (5)	
	S. Helena (3)	
	S. Joao (6)	
	S. Jorge (3)	
	Madalena (4)	
	S.M. da Serra (3)	Set afire in Diu, 1521
	S. Miguel (1)	
	S. Antonio (17)	Shipwrecked, 1527
	S. Espirito (6)	
	Loba	Private owners
	S. Miguel (2)	Shipwrecked in Mozambique, 1523
	S. Salvador (2)	
1524	*Barbosa*	Lost, 1524?
	S. Jorge (4)	Valued at 250 000 *cruzados* when lost in 1524
	N.S. da Piedade (4)	
	S. Roque (1)	350 tons
	S. Sebastiao (3)	500 tons; shipwrecked on way to India, 1527
1525	*S. Eufemia* (3)	
	Flor de la Mar (2)	
	S. Miguel (3)	Private owners; valued at 250 000 *cruzados* when disappeared on return from India in 1537

181

Table 7.5   The Great Ships of Portugal: *Naus Portuguesas*, 1494–1580

Year of first notice	Name	Remarks
	S.M. do Paraiso (1)	Lost on way back from India, 1526
	Flor da Rosa (3)	Shipwrecked on way to India, 1528
	Corpo Santo	Valued at 250 000 *cruzados*; lost, 1525
	S. Vincente (3)	Valued at 250 000 *cruzados* when lost off Lisbon, 1525
1526	*S.M. do Espinheiro*	
	Flor da Rosa (4)	
	S.M. da Rosa (1)	
	S.M. da Vitoria (2)	
1527	*N.S. da Conceicao* (12)	Shipwrecked 1527
	S. Tiago (9)	
1528	*S.M. da Ajuda* (9)	
	Samorim (2) *Pequeno*	Lost in Diu, 1528
	S.M. do Castelo (1)	
	S. Espirito (7)	
	S.M. de Monserrate (1)	
1529	*N.S. da Conceicao* (13)	
	S. Jorge (5)	
	S. Jose (1)	
	S.M. da Nazare (8)	
1530	*S.M. da Ajuda* (10)	
	S.M. Barbara (1)	
	S. Bartolomeu (4)	
	N.S. das Candeias (1)	
1531	*Vera Cruz* (2)	
	S. Cruz (5)	
	S.M. da Esperanca (1)	Lost, 1531
	Trinidade (2)	Disappeared, 1531
1532	*Cufturca?*	800 tons
	Graca (4)	Lost off Melinde, 1545
	Reis Magos (2)	
1533	*Anunciada* (6)	
	S. Bartolomeu (5)	
	Cirne (3)	
	S. Clara (4)	
	Espera (2)	Private owners

182

Table 7.5   The Great Ships of Portugal: *Naus Portuguesas*, 1494–1580

Year of first notice	Name	Remarks
	Graca (5)	
	Bom Jesus (2)	Lost in 1533 on way to India
	S. Joao (7)	
	S. Marta (2)	
	S. Sebastiao (4)	
1534	*S. Antonio* (18)	
	Graca (6)	
	Rainha (4)	
1535	*N.S. da Conceicao* (14)	
	Esperanca (2)	
	S.M. do Espinheiro (2)	
1536	*S. Andre* (1)	
	Grifo	Private owners; shipwrecked, 1543
1537	*S. Antonio* (19)	
	S. Clara (5)	
	S. Cruz (6)	
	S. Denis	
	S. Lourenco (1)	
	S. Paulo (2)	
	S. Pedro (2)	
	Siciao	
1538	*S. Antonio* (20)	
	Burgalesa (3)	
	Fieis de Deus	
	Galega (3)	
	Junco	
	S. Catarina de Monte Sinai (4)	
1539	*S. Paulo* (3)	
1540	*S. Filipe* (1)	
1541	*S. Espirito* (8)	Valued at 200 000 *cruzados* when shipwrecked off Melinde, 1542
1542	*S. Mateus* (2)	
	S. Salvador	Private owners; lost, 1549
	S. Tome	
	Nau Urca	
	Nau Zambuco	Shipwrecked on way to India 1552
1543	*S. Filipe* (2)	Private owners
	S. Tome (4)	
	S.M. da Vitoria (3)	
1544	*Espera* (3)	
	S. Espirito (9)	Private owners

183

Table 7.5   The Great Ships of Portugal: *Naus Portuguesas*, 1494–1580

Year of first notice	Name	Remarks
	Flamenga	Shipwrecked on way back from India, 1558
	S. Pedro	Private owners
1545	*S. Espirito* (10)	
	S. Tome (5)	Private owners, lost, 1547
1546	*Galega* (6)	
	Flor de la Mar (3)	Lost on way to India, 1549
1547	*S. Boaventura* (2)	Lost, 1554
	Boquiqua?	
	Burgalesa (4)	
	Burgalesa (5)	
	S. Cruz (7)	Lost on way to India, 1547
	S. Denis (2)	
	Grangeira?	
1548	*S.M. de Ajuda* (11)	
	S.M. do Rosario (2)	
	S. Sebastiao (5)	
	Trindade (3)	
1549	*S.M. da Ajuda* (12)	
	S. Bento	Lost off Natal, 1559
	S. Cruz (8)	Lost on way back from India, 1555
1550	*S. Ana* (3)	
	S. Joao (8)	
1551	*Algarvia* (1)	
	Algarvia (2)	Privately owned; lost, 1551
	Barrileira	Privately owned; disappeared, 1554
	S. Bento (1)	Sank *en route* to Flanders, 1551
	Espadarte (2)	
	Ginha?	
	Bom Jesus (3)	Privately owned
	Misericordia (1)	
	Retenta?	Privately owned
	S. Salvador (5)	Privately owned
	S. Salvador (6)	Privately owned
	Serveira?	
1552	*S. Jeronimo* (5)	Lost, 1552
	S. Tiago (10)	Lost, 1553
1553	*S. Antonio* (21)	Lost, 1553
	N.S. da Barca	Crew of 200; lost, 1559
	Burgalesa? (6)	Lost, 1553
	S.M. do Loreto (1)	Privately owned
	S. Salvador (3)	

184

Table 7.5   The Great Ships of Portugal: *Naus Portuguesas*, 1494–1580

Year of first notice	Name	Remarks
1554	*Conceicao* (15)	
	S. Francisco (1)	
	S. Paulo (4)	Privately owned; built in India; lost off Sumatra, 1560
	N.S. das Reliquias	Lost, 1558
	S.M. da Vitoria (4)	Lost, 1556
1555	*S. Marta* (3)	
1556	*Graca* (7)	1,000 tons; lost, 1559
	S. Juliao (5)	
	Flor de la Mar (4)	Lost off Mozambique, 1564
	S. Vincente (4)	
1557	*Aguia* (1)	Carried 1,137 persons when lost, 1560
	S.M. dos Anjos	
	S. Antonio (22)	
	Assuncao (2)	Private owners
1558	*Castelo* (2)	
	Rainha (5)	
	Tigre	Lost, 1566
1559	*Algarvia* (3)	
1560	*Cedro*	Privately owned
	Drago	Was it a galleon?
1561	*S. Tiago* (11)	
1562	*Chagas* (1)	Built in Goa
	S.M. da Esperanca (3)	
	S. Martinho (2)	Built in India; lost, 1563
1563	*Algarvia* (4)	Privately owned; lost, 1565
	S. Filipe (3)	Privately owned; lost, 1563
1564	*S. Barbara* (2)	
1565	*S. Rafael* (6)	
1966	*S. Clara* (6)	250 tons
	S. Francisco (2)	Lost, 1573
	Reis Magos (3)	
	N.S. dos Remedios (1)	
1567	*Anunciada* (7)	
	S.M. de Belem (4)	
	Reis Magos (4)	Lost, 1573
1568	*S. Catarina* (1)	
	S. Clara (7)	Lost off Brazil, 1573
	Fe	
	S. Maria (5)	
1569	*Assuncao*	250 tons
	S. Clara (8)	
	S. Espirito (11)	

185

Table 7.5 The Great Ships of Portugal: *Naus Portuguesas*, 1494–1580

Year of first notice	Name	Remarks
1570	*N.S. do Castelo* (3)	
	S. Gabriel (4)	
	S. Leao	
	S. Luis (1)	Lost, 1582
	S. Tiago (12)	300 tons; taken by French corsairs, 1570
1573	*S. Gregorio*	
1574	*S. Barbara* (3)	
	Bom Jesus (4)	
	S. Lourenco (2)	
1575	*S. Cruz* (9)	
	S. Joao (9)	Lost, 1577
	S. Pedro (4)	Lost, 1578
	S. Sebastia (6)	
1576	*S. Jorge* (6)	Lost off Mozambique, 1576
1577	*S. Antonio* (23)	
	Boa Viagem (1)	
1578	*S. Rafael* (7)	
1579	*Trindade* (4)	
1580	*S. Francisco* (3)	
	S. Joao (10)	
	S. Salvador (7)	

Note: Some ship names are used more than once as is indicated by the numbers in parentheses following popular names.

Source: da Fonseca (1926, pp. 696–707, 724–7).

8 The World Powers: The Netherlands, Great Britain, and the United States

Of the four world powers since 1494, Portugal, admittedly, is the most controversial case. The preceding chapter, as a consequence, devoted considerable space to its case for oceanic leadership in the sixteenth-century global political system. Great Britain, the United States and the United Provinces of the Netherlands, are much less controversial. Therefore it is not surprising that each of these three states has had a great deal written about the ebb and flow of its political fortunes and naval successes. Accordingly in this chapter we shall review all three cases with a selective focus on their strategic contexts and choices, the development of their naval organisations, and some of the factors involved in their global asendancy and decline as leading naval powers.

While the political history of each world power possesses unique facets, there are also a number of commonalities. For instance, the rise to world power and lead navy status has been neither 'natural' nor inevitable but depended instead on policy decisions made during wartime, and particularly during global wars. Indeed all three states required global wars to achieve their lead positions. Later wars – and here again global wars have particular significance – also contributed to the Dutch and British failure to retain global leadership. Moreover, it is well worth noting that each world power played a major formative role in the development of its successor – as a source of threat, a model, and as an alliance partner. In this respect, each successive world power has stood on the shoulders of its immediate predecessor while, at the same time, contributing to the task of global management successively more extensive resources. In the process, the world power role has evolved and so too has the potential for global leadership and political management.

THE UNITED PROVINCES OF THE NETHERLANDS

Viewed within the context of an evolving global system, Portugal's prototypical leadership was partially achieved by default in the sense that Portuguese oceanic capabilities were developed well in advance of its subsequent competitors. Portugal's successor as the global system's world power – the United Provinces of the Netherlands – can also claim an early start on its competition. But it can be argued that many of the attributes – including the early lead – that facilitated the rise of the Dutch ultimately contributed to their decline as well.

The coastal cities and provinces of the northern Netherlands and Flanders developed early specialisations in fishing and maritime trade – occupations that historically have had important and obvious implications for the development of naval resources. During the fifteenth century, both activities had been advanced, respectively, by innovations in preserving herring and by the forceful acquisition of commercial supremacy in the Baltic region. This latter position, in turn, was aided by advancements in Dutch shipbuilding. Needing to adjust to the relative shallowness of the northern Netherlands harbours, Dutch ships tended to be round, wide, and relatively flat-bottomed. Such characteristics gave these ships comparative advantages in terms of carrying capacity, manoeuvrability, crew size, and transportation costs. While offering definitive benefits for the eventual establishment of a global reach capability, the intensive fishing-trade specialisation and even the ways in which Dutch ships were built proved later to be liabilities for maintaining a position of predominance in the seventeenth-century global system.

The strong commercial orientation of the Dutch cities was directly responsible for the unusually loose structure of the Dutch Republic. The Union of Utrecht (1579) brought together seven provinces and eight times as many towns in a heterogeneous coalition in revolt against Spain. Institutions with centralising potential evolved – the legislative States-General and the *Stadtholderate*. But the States-General was restricted by provincial particularism, a need for unanimity on important questions, the inability to tax, and by extreme limitations on the actual decision-making powers of the delegates. In contrast, the position of the *Stadtholder* tended to be occupied by successive Princes of Orange who usually favoured some form of greater political integration, especially in wartime. Yet more decision-making power for the *Stadtholder* meant less autonomy for the

188   *Country Data*

provinces, whose resistance was often led by the richest province of the seven, Holland. In 1622, Hugo Grotius described the outcome:

> Unity is, according to the pact of union, restricted to foreign affairs, but as regards administration, the Republic is an agglomeration of independent republics, and each province contains an individual nation and forms a complete state (quoted in Barker, 1906, p. 160).

As a consequence, the United Provinces of the Netherlands, at least for most of their history, were unable to achieve much in the way of institutionalised leadership or well-coordinated state administration – two important factors in the establishment and maintenance of a state navy.

The initial naval forces of the Dutch provinces were privateers (the Sea Beggars) whose activities had preceded the formalisation of the revolt against Spain. Not always discriminating in the selection of their targets, the Sea Beggars had experienced some difficulty in establishing a secure base of operations in the early 1570s. The capture of Brill in 1572 resolved this problem and gave the incipient revolt a much-needed boost in momentum and morale. By 1573, local command at sea was acquired.

Until 1589, however, naval activities against Spain remained largely uncoordinated and were dependent, for the most part, on the initiatives of various individuals and towns. A central admiralty board was created in 1589 to coordinate the five traditional provincial admiralties (Amsterdam, Rotterdam, North Holland, Zeeland, and Friesland). Each provincial admiralty separately was expected to equip and service its own ships with revenues collected by taxing shipping and occasional subsidies. A nominal command structure was established by naming the *Stadtholder* to head the central admiralty board but with only limited powers over policy and strategy. Thus, Dutch naval efforts in the late sixteenth and early seventeenth centuries tended to depend on the specific policies of the five admiralties. And since three of the admiralties were located within one province, naval leadership and the majority of the ships were often supplied by Holland.

This highly decentralised approach created an assortment of problems that were never fully resolved. Teitler (1977, p. 98) mentions several command structure problems, at least one of which may have been unique to the Netherlands in comparison with the other global powers. The problem concerned the authority of each admiralty to name its own slate of admirals thereby creating situations in which combined fleets would either possess too many flag officers or too many independent squadrons. The solution, which created its own set of problems, was to name somebody, often with little naval experience (in one case a cavalry officer and, at other times, leading politicians) to act as the primary fleet commander. Thus the most qualified naval officers could only aspire to vice-admiral positions. The vice-admiral nevertheless was the best-paid public servant of the Republic, according to Sir William Temple (1972, p. 133), with an early 1670s income two and a half times as high as the salary for the pensioner of Holland.

Problems of command notwithstanding, the principal functions of the late sixteenth-century Dutch navy or navies consisted of fighting on inland waterways, providing protection for fishing fleets and escorts for convoys, as well as blockading the ports of the southern Netherlands, an effort which contributed to the defeat of the Great Armada of 1588. Only occasionally (e.g. 1599, 1606, 1607) were relatively large fleets assembled for more offensive attacks on Spanish shipping in the Atlantic.

Although the ships were much smaller than those of their Spanish opponents, the United Provinces at least had access to a large number of them. Boxer (1965, p. 69) claims that as many as 2000 merchantmen were available for transformation into war-capable ships in 1588. But even this apparent advantage concealed several liabilities. When ships were needed, the admiralties tended to draft ships, crews, and officers as opposed to maintaining regular squadrons. This practice seriously retarded the development of specialised naval vessels for combat purposes and since officers alternated between military and commercial pursuits, naval tactics and fleet discipline suffered as well. For this reason, the Dutch navy retained a strong appreciation for the old-fashioned, individualistic, ship-to-ship, boarding/mêlée type of combat. The dependence on merchantmen also meant the Dutch warships would tend to carry fewer guns than were increasingly needed, especially in the second half of the seventeenth century.

Another related and persistent feature of decentralised Dutch naval practices was the tendency to respond to military emergencies after they began by building up their fleets and to reduce their naval costs drastically as soon as they were at peace again. Although or because the truce with Spain after 1609 was restricted primarily to European waters, the size of the Netherlands navy was cut back in 1609, expanded in the early 1620s, and then reduced severely in 1648. In

190 *Country Data*

1652, when the first war with the English began, it was discovered that only thirty-eight ships were ready for conversion to naval duty. Yet by the end of the same year, at least seventy-eight warships were at sea (Rowen, 1978, pp. 67, 72). It was only after the first Anglo-Dutch war that some consideration was given by the Amsterdam admiralty to creating a permanent battle fleet, nearly thirty years after a small but permanent cadre of officers had been established (1626) by the same provincial admiralty.

The resumption of hostilities with Spain in 1621 ushered in a new era of naval combat on a much grander scale than had been experienced in the late sixteenth century. The blockade of the southern Netherlands ports was resumed as one of the principal naval functions preoccupying as much as half of the Dutch fleet. Another principal task consisted of protecting – primarily from Flemish privateer attacks from Dunkirk – what had become the world's largest merchant and fishing fleets. The extent of this threat, which bears a close resemblance to the later French *guerre de course* and German U-boat campaigns, is demonstrated by the very large number of ship losses sustained in the North Sea and Atlantic and credited by Israel (1982) to the Flemish privateers and Spain's *armada de Flandes*:

Ships captured or sunk

1627–30	886 (includes English ships)
1631–2	488
1633–7	about half the number lost in 1628–32
1642–46	525

In addition to the blockade which the above figures indicate was less than completely successful, large convoys of at least forty ships, accompanied by armed escorts, were organised for the southern (France and the Mediterranean) and northern (Baltic and Russia) destinations. Some resources were also finally allocated to the development of *schepen van force* – larger warships with greater fire-power intended for these blockade/convoy duties (Israel, 1981, p. 110). At the same time, nonetheless, Dutch naval combat continued against the Chinese around Macao, the Portuguese throughout the Asian theatre and around Brazil, and the Spanish in the Caribbean and Pacific.

Despite these far-flung responsibilities, the Dutch were ultimately able to break the back of Spanish seapower at the Battle of the Downs

The Netherlands, Great Britain and the USA

(1639). In several respects the circumstances of this action reveal the strengths and weaknesses of the Dutch naval effort. A small Dutch squadron with approximately a dozen or so warships intercepted a large Spanish fleet carrying troops to the southern Netherlands. Over a period of several weeks, the size of the Dutch fleet was reinforced to nearly 100 ships. While the Dutch managed to sink, capture, or run aground roughly two-thirds of their opponent's fleet, the Spanish troops still managed to reach their objective. Moreover, the effort proved to be so expensive for the provincial admiralties that no blockade could be mounted in the following year, and this led to a resurgence in the privateering activities based in Dunkirk (see above for the 1642–6 losses).

Generally, the financial and administrative position of the Dutch navy is thought to have been substantially reformed in the 1650s and 1660s thanks to the intensive demands associated primarily with the first and second Anglo-Dutch wars. In the third Anglo-Dutch war, however, the United Provinces were faced with simultaneous threats at sea and from the land. Artillery and powder shortages on land in 1672 forced a reduction in the number of ships that could be armed. Army priorities increasingly began to prevail over those of the navy, a factor accelerated institutionally by the wider powers granted to the *Stadtholder* in this period.

By the last third of the seventeenth century, the Dutch were barely able to hold off the English challenge of the 1650s and 1660s and were confronted by the emergence of a second maritime challenger in France. In fact, in the thirty-one years following the end of the Thirty Years War in 1648, the Dutch were at war with England, France, Sweden, or some combination of the three for eighteen years. Despite the escalation in the number and size of ships required, the United Provinces managed to remain in the game but could no longer aspire to anything resembling naval leadership. Franks (1942, pp. 108–9) argues that this development was an inevitable function of geography:

Holland was put out of the competition by reason of its shallow harbours. While France and England, with their wide and deep harbours, could construct three and four deckers of 110 or 120 guns and displacing 2500 tons, Holland could never go very much beyond a mere 700-tonner without being compelled to keep the vessel perpetually upon the high seas . . . The final defeat of Holland was a mere matter of time and mathematics.

192 *Country Data*

The decline of the United Provinces is of course much more complicated and certainly encompasses non-naval factors as well. Indeed, if one wished to stress 'geographical' factors, a stronger case could be made for the fact that the Dutch were confronted with two adjacent, rising seapowers that could and did attack the Netherlands from multiple fronts. In any event, the Dutch clearly had problems remaining militarily competitive at sea. In the global war period, 1688–1700, Symcox's data suggests that the Dutch constructed as many warships as either the French or English (Symcox, 1974, pp. 235–7). But at the same time, the United Provinces were required to assume greater military responsibilities on land in the Wars of the League of Augsburg and Spanish Succession than had been customary. At sea, their alliance with the English tended to relegate them to a junior partnership.

According to Boxer (1965, pp. 105–6), participation in these global wars increased the size of the national debt by a factor of about 4.5 and placed a particularly heavy debt burden on the three maritime provinces due to the extreme reluctance of the four land provinces to contribute to wartime naval expenditures. After 1713, then, unusually strong incentives for economising prevailed. The serial consequences for the navy are well illustrated by Bruijn's detailed counts of Dutch ships-of-the-line armed with 50 or more guns: 1714–77; 1724–42; 1733–45; 1742–35; 1751–32 (Bruijn, 1970, p. 7). The reduction in strength was also most heavily felt in the first- and second-class warship categories.

As the navy declined in size during an era of relatively low demand for warships, its ships became increasingly obsolete (partly because of conservative shipbuilding practices), corruption became more common, and naval service became less attractive (Teitler, 1977, pp. 158–161). Interestingly, Teitler also notes that eighteenth-century naval-strengthening plans were interpreted as anti-British in nature and therefore unattractive to those Dutch politicians who favoured stronger ties with Britain. In any event, the long eighteenth-century decay of the Dutch navy was arrested, briefly, by the fourth Anglo-Dutch war in the early 1780s. Again the fleet was refurbished but by this time it had seen little combat for several generations and was unable to contribute much to the French–Spanish–Dutch coalition. A decade later (1794) French cavalry were able to capture the ice-locked Dutch fleet at Texel. After this embarrassment, the navy of the Batavian Republic was gradually whittled down in a number of unsuccessful efforts to break the British blockade. The ships that

The Netherlands, Great Britain and the USA

survived were eventually absorbed into the French fleet. A list of sources for statistics on Dutch warships is given in Table 8.1, and the relative capability share of the Netherlands is shown in Figure 8.1. Table 8.2 gives the estimated annual number of Dutch warships from 1579 to 1810.

Table 8.1   Sources on Dutch warships, 1572–1815

Blok (1975)	Mahan (1892)
Boxer (1965)	Masson and Muracciole (1968)
Brenton (1823–5)	Memain (1936)
Bruijn (1970)	Nicolas (1949, 1958)
Callender (1924)	Owen (1938)
Chalmers (1794)	Pemsel (1977)
Charnock (1800–3)	de Peyster (1905)
Clark (1970b)	Pontalis (1885)
Clowes (1897–1903)	Renaut (1932)
Coombs (1958)	Reynolds (1974)
Cooper (1970)	Richmond (1946, 1953)
Cowburn (1965)	Robison and Robison (1942)
Dickson and Sperling (1970)	Rose (1921a)
Dirks (1890)	Rowen (1978)
Dupuy and Dupuy (1977)	Silburn (1912)
Edler (1911)	Southworth (1968)
Ehrman (1953)	Temple (1972)
Franks (1942)	Ten Raa and De Bas (1911)
Fuller (1955)	Tramond (1947)
Graham (1972)	Vecchj (1895)
Hanotaux (1932)	Vreugdenhil (1938)
James (1886)	Wilcox (1966)
de Jonge (1869)	Wilson (1904)
Lloyd (1965a)	Wilson (1957)

ENGLAND/GREAT BRITAIN

According to our data, in the number of capital ships, the British (English before 1707) navy led the other global powers for some 261 of the 500 years (or about 52 per cent) that are being examined in this study. It is hardly surprising then that so many historians and/or former naval personnel have chosen to write on its evolution and activities. Fortunately, it is not our purpose to compete with this extensive literature. We only need to extract some of the more salient features that serve our own organisational and strategic emphases.

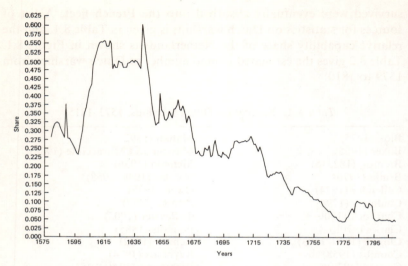

Figure 8.1 Netherlands relative capability share, 1579–1810

Table 8.2 The United Provinces of Netherlands: estimated annual number of warships, 1567–1859

Year	Number of warships	Sources on numbers of warships
1567	–	18 (Reynolds, 1974)
1572	–	24 (Southworth, 1968)
–	–	
1579	25	
1580	27	
1581	29	
1582	32	
1583	34	
1584	36	
1585	37	
1586	39	
1587	40	80 w/guns (de Jonge, 1869; Dirks, 1890)
1588	40	
1589	40	
1590	39	
1591	39	
1592	39	

195

Table 8.2 The United Provinces of Netherlands: estimated annual number of warships, 1567–1859

Year	Number of warships	Sources on numbers of warships
1593	38	
1594	38	
1595	38	
1596	37	
1597	37	
1598	37	73 (Southworth, 1968)
1599	37	70 (Graham, 1972); 73 (Robison and Robison, 1942; Dirks, 1890)
1600	38	
1601	40	
1602	41	
1603	43	
1604	44	
1605	45	
1606	46	
1607	48	
1608	49	
1609	51	
1610	53	
1611	54	
1612	56	
1613	57	
1614	59	
1615	60	60 w/guns (de Jonge, 1869; Dirks, 1890)
1616	60	60 w/guns (de Jonge, 1869; Dirks, 1890)
1617	66	
1618	72	
1619	78	
1620	84	
1621	90	
1622	96	
1623	102	
1624	108	
1625	114	
1626	120	
1627	127	
1628	133	133 w/guns (de Jonge, 1869; Dirks, 1890)
1629	134	
1630	135	
1631	135	
1632	136	
1633	137	

196

Table 8.2 The United Provinces of Netherlands: estimated annual number of warships, 1567–1859

Year	Number of warships	Sources on numbers of warships
1634	137	
1635	138	
1636	139	
1637	139	
1638	104	
1639	141	105 w/guns (Reynolds, 1974); 70 (Hanotaux, 1932); 18 (Charnock, 1800–3)
1640	141	
1641	142	
1642	143	143 w/guns (de Jonge, 1869; Dirks, 1890)
1643	130	
1644	118	
1645	104	
1646	92	
1647	81	
1648	70	'70' w/guns (Vreugdenhil, 1938)
1649	66	'66' w/guns (Vreugdenhil, 1938)
1650	70	'70' w/guns (Vreugdenhil, 1938); 160 w/30+ (Nicolas, 1958); 150 w/20+ (Charnock, 1800–3); '125' (Pontalis, 1885); 120 w/guns (Charnock, 1800–3)
1651	72	'72' w/guns (Vreugdenhil, 1938); 150 (Charnock, 1800–3)
1652	124	'124' w/guns (Vreugdenhil, 1938); 149 w/guns/[50] (Pontalis, 1885); 112 (Wilson, 1957); 102 (Rose, 1921a); 100 (Blok, 1975; Callender, 1924); 38–78 (Rowen, 1978); 66 (Memain, 1936); 60 w/40+ (Pemsel, 1977); [76] (Cooper, 1970)
1653	106	'106' w/guns (Vreugdenhil, 1938); 154 w/guns (de Jonge, 1869); 125 (Rowen, 1978); 102 (Charnock, 1800–03)
1654	106	'106' w/guns (Vreugdenhil, 1938); 125 (Southworth, 1968), 121 w/20+ (Clowes, 1897–1903); 101 w/guns (de Jonge, 1869); [86] (Rowen, 1978)
1655	81	'81' w/30+ (Vreugdenhil, 1938)
1656	78	'78' w/30+ (Vreugdenhil, 1938)
1657	78	'78' w/30+ (Vreugdenhil, 1938)
1658	84	'84' w/30+ (Vreugdenhil, 1938)
1659	79	'79' w/30+ (Vreugdenhil, 1938); [48 w/40+] (Ten Raa and De Bas, 1911)
1660	78	'78' w/30+ (Vreugdenhil, 1938)
1661	82	'82' w/30+ (Vreugdenhil, 1938)

197

Table 8.2   The United Provinces of Netherlands: estimated annual number of warships, 1567–1859

Year	Number of warships	Sources on numbers of warships
1662	83	'83' w/30+ (Vreugdenhil, 1938)
1663	87	'87' w/30+ (Vreugdenhil, 1938)
1664	95	'95' w/30+ (Vreugdenhil, 1938); 120 w/38+ (Charnock, 1800–03)
1665	93	'93' w/30+ (Vreugdenhil, 1938); 133 w/guns/ 97 w/30+ (de Jonge, 1869); 130–40 (Wilson, 1957); 115 (Pontalis, 1885); 100–20 (Charnock, 1800–3); 103 (Clowes, 1897–1903; Memain, 1936; Tramond, 1947; Wilcox, 1966; Nicolas, 1958; Silburn, 1912); 72 w/40+ (Ten Raa and De Bas, 1911)
1666	96	'96' w/30+ (Vreugdenhil, 1938); 104 w/guns/84 w/30+ (de Jonge, 1869); 103 (Nicolas, 1958); 96 (Silburn, 1912); 93 (Pontalis, 1885); 85 (Robison and Robison, 1942); [84 w/30+] (Clowes, 1897–1903); 84 (Richmond, 1953); [100+] (Temple, 1972)
1667	95	'95' w/30+ (Vreugdenhil, 1938); 86 w/guns/64 w/30+ (de Jonge, 1869); [72 w/40+] (Ten Raa and De Bas, 1911); [48 w/30+] (Rowen, 1978)
1668	94	'94' w/30+ (Vreugdenhil, 1938)
1669	94	'94' w/30+ (Vreugdenhil, 1938)
1670	96	'96' w/30+ (Vreugdenhil, 1938); 30–40 (Temple, 1972)
1671	80	'80' w/40+ (Vreugdenhil, 1938); [72 w/40+] (Ten Raa and De Bas, 1911); [56] (Rowen, 1978); 48 (Pontalis, 1885)
1672	77	'77' w/40+ (Vreugdenhil, 1938); 91 (Silburn, 1912; Southworth, 1968); 90 (Charnock, 1800–3); 75 (Pontalis, 1885; Reynolds, 1974); 72 w/40+ (Rowen, 1978); 72 w/40+ (Ten Raa and De Bas, 1911)
1673	70	'70' w/40+ (Vreugdenhil, 1938); 70 (Charnock, 1800–3); 60–4 (Southworth, 1968); 48 (Pontalis, 1885)
1674	63	'63' w/40+ (Vreugdenhil, 1938); 74 in European waters (Nicolas, 1949); 152 w/guns/49 w/40+ (de Jonge, 1869)
1675	63	'63' w/40+ (Vreugdenhil, 1938); 136 w/guns (Franks, 1942)
1676	51	'51' w/40+ (Vreugdenhil, 1938); [18] (Southworth, 1968)

198

Table 8.2   The United Provinces of Netherlands: estimated annual number
of warships, 1567–1859

Year	Number of warships	Sources on numbers of warships
1677	51	'51' w/40+ (Vreugdenhil, 1938)
1678	53	'53' w/40+ (Vreugdenhil, 1938)
1679	54	'54' w/40+ (Vreugdenhil, 1938)
1680	54	'54' w/40+ (Vreugdenhil, 1938)
1681	54	'54' w/40+ (Vreugdenhil, 1938)
1682	61	'61' w/40+ (Vreugdenhil, 1938)
1683	61	'61' w/40+ (Vreugdenhil, 1938)
1684	61	'61' w/40+ (Vreugdenhil, 1938)
1685	65	'65' w/40+ (Vreugdenhil, 1938); 82 w/guns/ 50 w/50+ (de Jonge, 1869)
1686	53	'53' w/40+ (Vreugdenhil, 1938)
1687	55	'55' w/40+ (Vreugdenhil, 1938)
1688	66	'66' w/40+ (Vreugdenhil, 1938); 90–100 (Richmond, 1953); 70 (Reynolds, 1974); 69 (Ehrman, 1953); 66 (Bromley and Ryan, 1971); 53 (Ehrman, 1953); 50 (Vecchj, 1895)
1689	71	'71' w/40+ (Vreugdenhil, 1938); 69 (Cowburn, 1965); 50 (Pemsel, 1971); [c. 100] (Boxer, 1965)
1690	61	'61' w/40+ (Vreugdenhil, 1938); 63 [1–4] (Ehrman, 1953); [c. 200] (Boxer, 1965)
1691	60	'60' w/50+ (Vreugdenhil, 1938); 44 w/50+ (de Jonge, 1869); [35] (Nicolas, 1958); [c. 100] (Boxer, 1965)
1692	61	'61' w/50+ (Vreugdenhil, 1938); 36 (Charnock, 1800–3; Reynolds, 1974; Silburn, 1912); [c. 100] (Boxer, 1965)
1693	65	'65' w/50+ (Vreugdenhil, 1938); 46 w/50+ (de Jonge, 1869); 41 (Charnock, 1800–3); [c. 100] (Boxer, 1965)
1694	73	'73' w/50+ (Vreugdenhil, 1938); 49 w/50+ (de Jonge, 1868); [c. 100] (Boxer, 1965)
1695	74	'74' w/50+ (Vreugdenhil, 1938); 43 w/50+ (de Jonge, 1869); [c. 100] (Boxer, 1965)
1696	73	'73' w/50+ (Vreugdenhil, 1938); [c. 100] (Boxer, 1965)
1697	73	'73' w/50+ (Vreugdenhil, 1938); [c. 100] (Boxer, 1965)
1698	72	'72' w/50+ (Vreugdenhil, 1938)
1699	81	'81' w/50+ (Vreugdenhil, 1938)
1700	86	'86' w/50+ (Vreugdenhil, 1938); 84 (Charnock, 1800–3)

199

Table 8.2   The United Provinces of Netherlands: estimated annual number of warships, 1567–1859

Year	Number of warships	Sources on numbers of warships
1701	86	'86' w/50+ (Vreugdenhil, 1938); 30 (Dickson and Sperling, 1970); [50] (Clark, 1970b)
1702	89	'89' w/50+ (Vreugdenhil, 1938); 53 (Richmond, 1946); 50 (Pemsel, 1977); 35 w/50+ (de Jonge, 1869); [35] (Owen, 1938)
1703	88	34 w/50+ (de Jonge, 1869); [42] (Coombs, 1958); [22 in European waters] Owen, 1938)
1704	87	35 w/50+ (de Jonge, 1869); [20 in European waters] Owen, (1938)
1705	86	35 w/50+ (de Jonge, 1869); [31 in European waters] (Owen, 1938)
1706	85	30 w/50+ (de Jonge, 1869); [25 in European waters] (Owen, 1938)
1707	84	32 w/50+ (de Jonge, 1869); [26 in European waters] (Owen, 1938)
1708	83	31 w/50+ (de Jonge, 1869); [25 in European waters] (Owen, 1938)
1709	82	30 w/50+ (de Jonge, 1869); [23 in European waters] (Owen, 1938)
1710	81	[14 in European waters] (Owen, 1938)
1711	80	50 (Charnock, 1800–3); 40 (Richmond, 1946)
1712	79	
1713	78	
1714	77	77 w/50+ (Bruijn, 1970)
1715	73	
1716	70	
1717	66	
1718	63	
1719	59	
1720	56	
1721	53	
1722	49	
1723	45	
1724	42	
1725	42	
1726	43	
1727	43	
1728	43	
1729	43	
1730	44	
1731	44	
1732	44	

200

Table 8.2 The United Provinces of Netherlands: estimated annual number of warships, 1567–1859

Year	Number of warships	Sources on numbers of warships
1733	45	45 w/50 + (Bruijn, 1970)
1734	43	
1735	40	
1736	39	
1737	37	
1738	35	
1739	33	
1740	30	
1741	29	29 w/50 + (de Jonge, 1869)
1742	35	35 w/50 + (Bruijn, 1970)
1743	35	
1744	34	
1745	34	
1746	33	23 (Dirks, 1890)
1747	33	
1748	33	
1749	33	
1750	33	
1751	33	33 w/50 + (Bruijn, 1970)
1752	32	
1753	31	
1754	29	
1755	29	
1756	29	
1757	27	
1758	27	
1759	25	
1760	25	
1761	23	
1762	23	
1763	21	
1764	20	
1765	19	
1766	19	
1767	17	
1768	16	
1769	15	
1770	15	
1771	13	
1772	12	26 w/50 + /12 w/60 + (de Jonge, 1869)
1773	12	
1774	11	

201

Table 8.2 The United Provinces of Netherlands: estimated annual number of warships, 1567–1859

Year	Number of warships	Sources on numbers of warships
1775	11	
1776	11	11 w/60+ (Edler, 1911)
1777	14	
1778	16	
1779	19	
1780	22	44 w/50+ /22 w/60+ (Charnock, 1800–3); '34'/[29] (Renaut, 1932); 25 (de Peyster, 1905); 22 (Richmond, 1946); [26] (Edler, 1911)
1781	25	'25'/[12] (Brenton, 1823–5); 17 (Boxer, 1965)
1782	22	46 w/50+ (Dirks, 1890); 40 w/50+ /27 w/60+ (de Jonge, 1869)
1783	32	46 (Boxer, 1965); 46 w/50+ /32 w/60+ (de Jonge, 1869); '33' (Chalmers, 1894)
1784	33	
1785	33	
1786	34	40 w/50+ (de Peyster, 1905)
1787	35	
1788	36	
1789	37	46 w/50+ /37 w/60+ (de Jonge, 1869); 44 w/52–74 (Vecchj, 1895)
1790	34	2 w/60+ (de Jonge, 1869)
1791	32	2 w/60+ (de Jonge, 1869)
1792	38	'49' (James, 1886; Lloyd, 1965a; Dupuy and Dupuy, 1977); 2 w/60+ (de Jonge, 1869)
1793	35	50 (Pemsel, 1977); 49 (Mahan, 1892; Wilson, 1904); [46] (Richmond, 1946); 2 w/60+ (de Jonge, 1869)
1794	33	2 w/60+ (de Jonge, 1869)
1795	25	2 w/60+ (de Jonge, 1869)
1796	16	22 w/50+ /16 w/60+ (de Jonge, 1869)
1797	16	
1798	16	12–16/2 w/60+ /9 captured by British (Robison and Robison, 1942)
1799	16	
1800	15	
1801	15	15 w/60+ (de Jonge, 1869); 7 (Masson and Muracciole, 1968)
1802	15	
1803	15	'16' (Richmond, 1946); '15'/[5] (Fuller, 1955); [20] (Pemsel, 1977)
1804	15	[6] (Robison and Robison, 1942)
1805	14	

202   *Country Data*

Table 8.2   The United Provinces of Netherlands: estimated annual number
of warships, 1567–1859

Year	Number of warships	Sources on numbers of warships
1806	14	14 w/60+ (de Jonge, 1869)
1807	14	
1808	14	
1809	13	17 (Richmond, 1946)
1810	13	13 w/60+ (de Jonge, 1869); 10 (Brenton, 1823–5)
–	–	
1859		5 (Pemsel, 1977)

Note: In this table and the others that follow of a similar nature, a set of
symbols is used to qualify the numerical information presented:
quotation marks denote the total number of ships regardless of their
sea-going condition; brackets [] indicate the number of ships believed
to be actually capable of going to sea. The absence of either quotation
marks or brackets signifies that no qualifications were provided by the
source(s). Slashes and the abbreviation for 'with' (w/) are used when
several types of numbers are supplied by a source and/or when
information on the number of guns carried is provided.

Despite its later predominance, England, in a somewhat contradictory fashion, was one of the first states to develop a relatively
permanent naval force and yet its navy was also one of the slowest to
develop as a competitive entity. An explanation for this early but slow
development is not particularly difficult to generate. England's early
start can be attributed in part to the necessities and opportunities of
geography and geopolitical history. Its slowness to develop was also
partially due to geography but, more fundamentally, to a shortage of
financial resources. While the geography, if not its interpretation,
remained constant, English/British decision-makers eventually were
able to overcome the financial limitations for several hundred years
before the costs of naval warfare once again became too expensive.

It is possible to go back to the Roman invasion of Britain,
adventuring Irish monks, King Alfred's ninth-century naval victories
over Danish raiders, William's eleventh-century Norman Conquest of
the Saxons, which a defending Saxon fleet failed to prevent, English
participation in the Mediterranean Crusades via the sea, and several
centuries of intermittent, medieval warfare between the English and

The Netherlands, Great Britain and the USA

the French, which called for ferrying English troops to the continent as at Agincourt (1415), or grappling with French fleets at sea (as at the Battle of Sluys, 1340). Nevertheless, the point of this historical digression is to suggest that England's insular geography historically has not meant political and military insularity. The interest in north-west Europe, parts of which were English-controlled at times, has been long-standing if for no other reason than its convenience as a launching-point for invasions of the British Isles. As a consequence, one of the strongest threads of continuity in the annals of English/British naval history is the strategic imperative of preventing maritime invasions from first the Danes, and later the French, the Spanish, and the Germans.

As we know, the repeated attempts at invasion have proved unsuccessful since 1066 (with the possible exception of 1688). Both in part because of, and despite, this clear strategic imperative (albeit of intermittent intensity) the state's organisation of a naval defence was developed early but in only a limited way. English Kings had long maintained small collections of ships for various purposes but they very quickly developed a reliance on mobilising privately-owned vessels in crisis periods. An exchange relationship between the Crown and towns on the English Channel coast (the Cinque Ports) had been established even prior to the Norman Conquest. In return for some amount of autonomy and trading privileges, the towns were expected to supply fifty-seven ships with crews for fifteen days per year. If they were needed for a longer period of time, the ships and crews were available for hire. The Cinque Ports gradually became less important as their harbours filled with silt, but it is only after the advent of the Tudors in the late fifteenth century that a beginning was made in breaking away from the dependence on rented fleets.

Henry VII (1485–1509) initiated the practice of subsidising the construction of vessels larger than needed for commercial purposes in the late 1480s, perhaps in imitation of Spanish practices (Oppenheim, 1961, p. 37). He also had the first dry dock built at Portsmouth in 1495–7. But the first genuine expansion of the royal fleet was instituted under Henry VIII (1509–47) who, confronted with increased French and Scottish naval activity, tripled the number of ships inherited from Henry VII. Additional dockyards were built at Deptford and Woolwich. The Navy Board – a committee to oversee naval administration – was created in 1532 under the leadership of the Lord High Admiral (a post first established in 1391). Perhaps most importantly, Henry VIII is also credited with introducing heavy guns

204   *Country Data*

aboard ships – a development which became crucial to subsequent English naval strategy.

Henry VIII enjoyed the advantage of confiscated monastery property to help to pay for his naval expansion – an advantage not available to his immediate successors although Edward VI (1547–53) did build a fourth dockyard at Chatham in 1550. Elizabeth I (1558–1603) was also in no financial position to expand the English fleet. During her reign, however, emphasis was placed, under the supervision of Hawkins, on rebuilding the royal fleet with new 'race-built' galleons.

The Elizabethan era is frequently associated with substantial English maritime expansion. Yet the expansion that occurred took place primarily in the private sector. In the last third of the sixteenth century, France's European position had disintegrated into internal warfare. Spain then replaced France as England's principal source of external warfare. It was no coincidence that Spain also appeared to have developed a monopoly relationship with the most lucrative portions of the New World. While the flow of transatlantic wealth enhanced Spain's European capabilities, the lightly-defended treasure fleets had proved to be tempting targets since the 1520s. Moreover, Spanish attempts to suppress the Dutch revolt contributed to the further polarisation of Western Europe into Protestant and Catholic camps just as it more specifically increased the perceived threat for the English of an expanding European power directly across the Channel.

Within this general context, English attacks on Spanish Atlantic and Caribbean shipping began to increase in the late 1560s. Representing ostensibly private and sometimes quasi-official ventures, Howarth (1974, p. 121) offers a rather romantic conceptualisation of what he calls the 'sport of baiting Spaniards'. Neither war, nor trade, nor conquest, the English attacks were partially a game with cheering sections at home, and partially an extension of Channel piracy traditions. To stay within the game rules, one had to make sufficient profit to share with the Crown without causing so much trouble that Spain declared war on England. While there is something to be said for the game analogy, Andrews (1984, p. 363) supplies a more realistic summary:

> In the maritime struggle which ensued the English with no great traffic of their own to defend and with the riches of Iberian commerce exposed to their attack, predictably adopted the usual tactics of have-nots at war with possessors and developed a persuasive campaign of plunder.

The Netherlands, Great Britain and the USA   205

In other words, the English possessed a relatively weak navy and little trade of their own to protect. Thus, they emphasised a *guerre de course* strategy before and after the war broke out in 1585. The 1588 defeat of the first Spanish Armada provides only a partial exception to this atypical emphasis on English naval weakness. The defence against the Armada capitalised on the past hundred years of Tudor naval preparations. The naval organisation and dockyard infrastructure facilitated the rapid mobilisation of a small royal fleet, greatly expanded by the incorporation of a large number of privately-owned vessels. Henry VIII's heavy guns and Hawkins' fast ships dictated the defensive strategy of avoiding close contact with the troop-laden Spanish galleons while firing their heavier cannon at long range. Aided by the vagaries of weather and Spanish tactical errors, the English were able to prevent the Spanish invasion but they lacked the financial resources and navy size to launch a concerted naval offensive against Spain. Occasional efforts to seize Iberian bases or to mount blockades proved unsuccessful; hence the reliance on the cheaper tactics of commerce raiding.

At the end of the war (1604) the English royal fleet was not much larger than it had been at the end of Henry VIII's reign. But the prizes of more than 100 Spanish and Portuguese vessels (Andrews, 1984, p. 248) taken by the English did little to encourage the continued growth of Spanish shipbuilding while it did facilitate the near-doubling of the English merchant marine. Despite the commercial expansion, the next forty years are usually characterised as a period of royal naval decline. The Thirty Years War diverted any potential European threat. Piracy increased but the navy's few ships were too heavy and slow to catch them. Naval administration languished as corruption and court favouritism increased under the Stuarts. Charles I (1625–49) demonstrated more interest in naval affairs than had his father, James I (1603–25), but Charles' attempts to obtain fleet-financing ('Ship Money' taxes) only aggravated further his constitutional disputes with Parliament which led to the outbreak of civil war in the 1640s.

The English civil wars laid the foundation for the first real expansion of the state's fleet. Most of the navy sided with Parliament and contributed to that side's victory by limiting the effectiveness of the royalist fleet and by preventing any European assistance coming to the aid of the royalists. The English navy emerged from the civil wars with more ships, improved financing (this time resulting from confiscated royalist property) and more talented operational leadership. The 'Generals-at-Sea' appointed by Cromwell are particularly no-

206 *Country Data*

table for their introduction of a greater sense of military discipline ('Fighting Instructions') into English fleet operations, from which emerged the formalisation of the line-ahead tactical formation and, later, the standardisation of ships-of-the-line. The 1651 Navigation Act further enhanced the need for a strong naval capability to enforce its protectionist provisions, as did the related outbreak of the first of a series of Anglo-Dutch wars.

General-at-Sea Monck pithily summarised the motivations behind the war of 1652–4 (and the next two as well: 'The Dutch have too much trade, and the English are resolved to take it from them' (quoted in Kennedy, 1976, p. 48). What is particularly interesting to note is that the war began with a commerce-raiding strategy:

The aim was to cut Dutch sea-borne trade and fishing – with the acquisition of ships and cargoes as an important bonus – hence ruin Dutch commerce and threaten the very existence of the Dutch state ... time enough to tackle the Dutch fleet when it came to the defence of its merchantmen. It was only later, when merchant shipping was as important to England as it was to the Dutch in mid-century, that the enemy battle fleet became the prime target (Padfield, 1979, p. 191).

With each successive Anglo-Dutch war (the second in 1665–7 and the third in 1672–4) the strategic emphasis shifted from simple commerce raiding toward battle-fleet clashes over the control of the English Channel, blockades of the Dutch ports, and even combined land and sea operations with the unsuccessful attempt to invade the Netherlands from the sea in 1672. We need not go as far as Lewis (1948, p. 30), who contends that 'there was no true permanent national maritime fighting force before Cromwell', to recognise the period between the end of the 1640s and the beginning of the 1670s as a watershed for the development of the English navy. Prior to this time, it had been useful for coastal defence and commerce raiding. During the Anglo-Dutch wars, as well as an Anglo-Spanish one (1656–60), however, the navy began to be transformed into the type of long-range, offensive weapon needed for global competition – as was demonstrated by naval actions in the Atlantic, Caribbean, Mediterranean, and Baltic theatres in these years.

The Restoration did little to detract from the advances made in naval development. On the contrary, Samuel Pepys' managerial skills vastly improved the navy's administrative and support infrastructure

The Netherlands, Great Britain and the USA 207

in the 1660s and 1670s. For instance, senior naval officers finally began to receive a partial salary in non-war years – a practice which amounted to a significant step toward a permanent officer corps. Promotion procedures were improved. Some progress was also made in standardising ship-of-the-line ratings.

French naval reforms under Colbert in the same era, nonetheless, gave France an offensive edge when global war broke out in 1688. A French fleet was able to land troops in Ireland and the 1690 battle at Beachy Head over control of the English Channel was a defeat for the Anglo-Dutch fleet. Yet the French chose not to take advantage of this victory and, instead, reverted to a commerce raiding strategy. Two years later, the question of control of the Channel was decided at La Hogue when a French invasion fleet was defeated decisively. After 1692, the basic pattern of Anglo-French warfare for the next 123 years was established. With some exceptions, France concentrated on its land campaigns within Europe and commerce raiding at sea. England or Great Britain concentrated on mounting blockades, protecting commercial convoys, engaging in naval skirmishes in more distant waters (Caribbean, Mediterranean, and Indian Ocean) with only occasional fleet encounters (usually in the early phases of war as at Quiberon Bay in 1759), and supplementing its ground efforts with subsidised allies.

French commerce raiding certainly had some impact. Kennedy (1976, pp. 72, 79, 85, 93, 131), for example, offers the following civilian ship-loss figures: 1693–7, 4000; 1701–3, 3250; 1739–48, 3238; 1793–1815, 11 000. But these losses must be interpreted within the context of a rapidly-expanding British commercial fleet. Whether or not France or Spain lost more, or as many, ships in specific eighteenth-century wars, the proportional damage was always more severely felt on the side opposing Britain and this was often an important factor in the financial problems of Britain's opponents. Great Britain may have suffered setbacks from time to time in European land warfare, but it usually experienced far fewer problems in oceanic warfare. Control of the sea therefore was translated into global leadership. While Britain remained vulnerable in European land-fighting, it still managed to contain much of the fighting to the European continent.

The one major exception was the internationalised phase of the American War of Independence when the strategic circumstances of Anglo-French rivalry were reversed. Several generations after its first rise to world power status, Britain, with widespread commitments

208   *Country Data*

and without allies, was involved in North American land-warfare while its French, Spanish, and Dutch opponents were able to concentrate on maritime operations. Even so, the British were able to cut their losses and gave up no more than the thirteen rebellious colonies. Naval leadership was regained decisively in the global conflict of the Napoleonic Wars, and particularly at Trafalgar (1805).

These successes were not achieved without experiencing a variety of problems. The financial problems of the navy were ameliorated substantially by fiscal/debt innovations for raising governmental revenue introduced during the 1688–1713 global warfare (Rasler and Thompson, 1983). The tendency to allow the fleet to decay in times of peace was at least weakened by trade and colonial expansion, scientific explorations, and, for a while, in the post-1714 era, the possibility of an attempt to restore Stuart rule. Personnel problems were persistent. Crews were always difficult to obtain for reasons that may best be summarised by an observer in 1759:

> No man will be a sailor who has contrivance enough to get himself into a jail; for being in a ship is being in jail with the chance of being drowned . . . a man in jail has more room, better food and commonly better company (attributed to Dr Samuel Johnson and quoted in Tute, 1983, p. 72).

As it worked out, going to jail and joining the navy were not mutually-exclusive activities in eighteenth-century Britain. Impressment of civilians was another favoured recruitment technique.

There were also structural problems. As early as the mid-sixteenth century, an organisational split in terms of functions had developed between the Navy Board and its former head, the Lord High Admiral. The Navy Board specialised in questions concerning material and funding while the Admiralty (which evolved from the Admiral's office) concentrated on operational policies. Whether, and how well, the system worked tended to depend on the variable abilities of the individuals involved to work together. Eventually, the Admiralty, under the leadership of a First Sea Lord, absorbed the Navy Board and its functions, but not until 1832.

Nonetheless, the British navy emerged from the Napoleonic War with little in the way of genuine competition at sea. Throughout much of the global war of 1792–1815 Great Britain actually possessed many more ships-of-the-line than it could either need or could afford to keep afloat (217 in 1815, according to Walker, 1860). But then many

The Netherlands, Great Britain and the USA

of these surplus vessels were captured prizes, much in need of repair, and frequently used as prison-ships or storage depots – and therefore should not be counted (and are not in our calculations) as even potential components of the battle fleet. For example, in enumerating 192 ships-of-the-line possessed in 1799, von Pivka (1980, p. 171) includes thirty-five ships used for guard, hospital and prison functions, nine receiving ships, twenty-two 'in ordinary', and twenty-four still being built. At the end of the war, the ships in poor shape were sold or scrapped and a substantial proportion of the active fleet was put 'in ordinary' – the older form of mothballing. As the theoretical size of the fleet was reduced to a number which was still much larger than the combined fleets of other states, the absence of any overt naval threat and the nature of the navy's nineteenth-century functions meant that as few as nine to twenty-seven ships-of-the-line, in conjunction with a variety of smaller ships, were actually needed at sea in any given year (see Bartlett, 1963, p. 342).

The nineteenth-century functions of the British navy included the 'collective good' duties of suppressing piracy and the slave trade in the Atlantic and Indian Oceans and the Mediterranean and China Seas, as well as extensive charting and exploration assignments. Interventions in civil wars, participation in British colonial warfare where feasible, and showing the flag and keeping the peace via gunboat diplomacy throughout the world were also characteristic of the *Pax Britannica* era, in which the British were formally involved in only one war (the mid-century Crimean) against another European power.

To carry out these functions, an extensive network of bases and dockyard facilities was established incrementally. Nineteenth-century additions to such earlier bases as Port Royal (Jamaica), Gibraltar, Halifax, and Port Mahon (Minorca) included Malta, Trincomalee, Falkland Islands, Aden, Hong Kong, Bermuda, Singapore, Lagos, Cyprus, Alexandria, Mombasu, Zanzibar, and Wei-hai-wei. In conjunction with this global-base network, naval forces were clustered at thirteen points (or fewer) around the world. At mid-century, a naval station was designed for each of the following sectors: North America, West Indies, West Africa, the Cape of Good Hope, the southeastern coast of South America, the Pacific, East Indies, China, and the Mediterranean, as well as the Home fleet. An Irish station was sometimes kept and, at later points, Australian and English Channel squadrons were also maintained.

Industrialisation came late and reluctantly to the British navy and was usually forced on the Royal Navy by French innovations

210   *Country Data*

intended to achieve naval parity through technological breakthroughs. From the perspective of the world's strongest wooden sailing-navy, the incentives to convert to steam and ironclads at the possible risk of a loss of leadership were less than compelling. Yet the conversions were made eventually and, in the process, Britain's technological lead enabled it to maintain its naval lead.

However, the technological lead, which, in any event, began to erode in the last quarter of the nineteenth century, could not suppress the re-emergence of naval competition – first from traditional sources such as the French and the Russians, and then from relatively new challengers, Germany, Japan, and the United States. As the size of ships and their armaments increased, and as the number of competitive fleets rose, naval expenditures climbed dramatically (see Table 4.4). Now that the British had real competition, the strategic choice was to try to maintain the world-wide scale of operations carried out in an earlier era without much competition or reduce its commitments and reconcentrate British naval forces. The level of expenditures associated with attempting to maintain the *status quo* and the sheer number and distribution of potential naval opposition – in particular, the German naval expansion close to home – persuaded British decision-makers to pursue the con-solidation approach in the first few years of the twentieth century. In brief, the steps taken involved withdrawing all but two battleships (in the Mediterranean) to home waters, merging or abandoning all the foreign stations, making arrangements for Japanese and French naval support in Asia and the Mediterranean respectively, building new naval bases at home on the North Sea, while at the same time participating in an Anglo-German naval race which included the introduction of the Dreadnought-class battleship in 1906.

When the First World War began, most of the British fleet was stationed in the North Sea and English Channel to inhibit any attempt on the part of the weaker German fleet to emerge from its own bases. With a few deviations, such as the Battle of Jutland in 1916, this surface fleet stand-off situation prevailed throughout the war. Once again, the emphasis was placed on commerce protection against the *guerre de course*. German surface raiders were eliminated fairly early in the war but the escalating U-boat attacks proved more difficult to control. Pemsel's data on Allied shipping losses (in thousands of tons) attri-buted to submarine attacks illustrates the quantitative nature of the problem: 1914, 3; 1915, 1193; 1916, 2209; 1917, 6236; 1918, 2814 (Pemsel, 1971, pp. 161–2). Precisely the same problem emerged in the

Second World War although the surface context had been altered significantly by the opposing combination of the German, Italian, and Japanese naval efforts, the early loss of the French fleet, and Britain's own weaker naval status. Allied shipping losses to submarine attacks climbed more quickly this time: 1939, 509; 1940, 2477; 1941, 2329; 1942, 6546; 1943, 2735; 1944, 776; 1945, 246 (Pemsel, 1977, p. 136; shown in thousand tons). In both world wars the severely threatened British were aided by the reluctance of Germany to exploit its U-boat weapon fully and also by the intervention of the United States. Convoy tactics (not adopted until 1917 in the First World War), new ship construction to replace the losses, broken codes, and the development of new detection technology in the Second World War all played roles in eventually curbing the submarine threat.

Yet it is clear that Britain's strategic position had changed from its earlier ability to absorb the damages sustained in commerce raiding. As Kennedy points out:

> The greatest flaw in the British over-estimation of the effects of their sea power lay in the associated calculation that, whilst the blockade was steadily sapping the enemy's strength, the superior economic resources of the Empire would be assembled to provide the eventual retribution; that, just as Britain's combined maritime and financial pressure had caused the collapse of the Dutch and French challenges in the seventeenth and eighteenth centuries, so too it would undermine the German threat in the twentieth. Yet this assumption ... was based upon the fallacy that Britain's productive strength, her control of raw materials and especially her financial resources, were as well equipped to withstand war now as they had been in the era of her rise to economic supremacy in the western world – which clearly was no longer the case (Kennedy, 1976, p. 312).

In sum, Britain emerged from the First World War no longer the world power and too poor to maintain its long-standing naval leadership. Consequently, naval parity with the United States was accepted in 1922 to avoid another naval race it could not win. By the end of the Second World War, it became obvious that in the future it would no longer be able to afford to maintain a globally competitive navy.[1] Sources of statistics relating to British warships are listed in Table 8.3, whilst Table 8.4 shows an estimate of England/Great Britain's annual number of warships from 1494–1860, and Table 8.5

212   *Country Data*

lists actual numbers of British battleships for each year from 1861 to
1945. Figure 8.2 shows England/Britain's relative capability share
from 1494 to 1945.

Table 8.3   Sources for English/British warships, 1494–1860

Albion (1926)	James (1886)
Almanach de Gotha	Jenkins (1973)
Anderson (1935)	de Jonge (1869)
Anderson (1961, 1972)	Lacour-Gayet (1902, 1905)
Archibald (1968)	Lloyd (1961, 1965a, 1965b)
Barfleur (1907)	Loir (1893)
Bartlett (1963)	Mahan (1890, 1892)
Baugh (1965, 1977)	Marcus (1961)
Benians (1940)	Mattingly (1959)
Bourne (1939)	Memain (1936)
Brenton (1823–5)	Merriman (1961)
Bromley and Ryan (1971)	Moreau de Jonnes (1835)
Bruun (1963)	Nicolas (1958, 1973)
Busk (1859)	Oppenheim (1961)
Chalmers (1794)	Owen (1938)
Charnock (1800–3)	Parker (1979)
Clark (1970a)	Parry (1971)
Clowes (1897–1903)	Pemsel (1977)
Cobden (1862)	Penn (1913)
Colledge (1969)	de Peyster (1905)
Cooper (1970)	Pontalis (1885)
Corbett (1900)	Powell (1962)
Cowburn (1965)	Reynolds (1974)
Derrick (1806)	Richmond (1946, 1953)
Dorn (1963)	Robison and Robison (1942)
Dupuy and Dupuy (1977)	Rose (1921a, 1921b, 1940a, 1940b)
Edler (1911)	Rowen (1978)
Ehrman (1953)	Silburn (1912)
Fernandez Duro (1972–3)	Stevens and Westcott (1943)
Franks (1942)	Thomazi (1950)
Frere-Cook and Macksey (1975)	Tramond (1947)
Fuller (1955)	Vecchj (1895)
Graham (1965)	Vovard (1948)
de la Gravière (1879)	Walker (1860)
Hampson (1959)	Wilcox (1966)
Hannay (1909)	Wilson (1904)
Headlam (1921)	Wilson (1957)

Table 8.4 England/Great Britain's estimated annual number of warships, 1494–1860

Year	Number of warships	Sources on numbers of warships
1494	6	'6' (Colledge, 1969)
1495	6	'6' (Colledge, 1969)
1496	6	'6' (Colledge, 1969)
1497	6	'6' (Colledge, 1969)
1498	5	'6' (Colledge, 1969)
1499	6	'6' (Colledge, 1969)
1500	6	'6' (Colledge, 1969)
1501	6	'6' (Colledge, 1969)
1502	6	'6' (Colledge, 1969)
1503	6	'6' (Colledge, 1969)
1504	6	'6' (Colledge, 1969)
1505	6	'6' (Colledge, 1969)
1506	6	'6' (Colledge, 1969)
1507	6	'6' (Colledge, 1969)
1508	6	'6' (Colledge, 1969)
1509	6	'6' (Colledge, 1969)
1510	7	'7' (Colledge, 1969)
1511	9	'9' (Colledge, 1969)
1512	19	'19' (Colledge, 1969); 45 (Derrick, 1806)
1513	19	'19' (Colledge, 1969); 1 (Parker, 1979)
1514	17	'17' (Colledge, 1969)
1515	17	'17' (Colledge, 1969)
1516	17	'17' (Colledge, 1969)
1517	18	'18' (Colledge, 1969); 14 (Derrick, 1806); 12 (Archibald, 1968)
1518	18	'18' (Colledge, 1969)
1519	19	'19' (Colledge, 1969)
1520	19	'19' (Colledge, 1969)
1521	16	'16' (Colledge, 1969); 13 (Derrick, 1806, Archibald, 1968)
1522	15	'15' (Colledge, 1969)
1523	17	'17' (Colledge, 1969)
1524	18	'18' (Colledge, 1969)
1525	14	'14' (Colledge, 1969)
1526	12	'12' (Colledge, 1969)
1527	10	'10' (Colledge, 1969)
1528	10	'10' (Colledge, 1969)
1529	9	'9' (Colledge, 1969)
1530	9	'9' (Colledge, 1969)
1531	8	'8' (Colledge, 1969)
1532	8	'8' (Colledge, 1969)
1533	8	'8' (Colledge, 1969)

214

Table 8.4   England/Great Britain's estimated annual number of warships, 1494–1860

Year	Number of warships	Sources on numbers of warships
1534	7	'7' (Colledge, 1969)
1535	9	'9' (Colledge, 1969)
1536	9	'9' (Colledge, 1969)
1537	9	'9' (Colledge, 1969)
1538	9	'9' (Colledge, 1969)
1539	10	'10' (Colledge, 1969)
1540	11	'11' (Colledge, 1969)
1541	11	'11' (Colledge, 1969)
1542	12	'12' (Colledge, 1969)
1543	12	'12' (Colledge, 1969)
1544	18	'18' (Colledge, 1969)
1545	22	'22' (Colledge, 1969); 16 (Stevens and Westcott, 1943)
1546	24	'24' (Colledge, 1969); 20 (Archibald, 1968)
1547	24	'24' (Colledge, 1969); 30 (Charnock, 1800–3)
1548	24	'24' (Colledge, 1969); 32 (Oppenheim, 1961); 14 (Archibald, 1968); 13 (Derrick, 1806)
1549	25	'25' (Colledge, 1969); 35/[29] (Oppenheim, 1961); 20 (Derrick, 1806); 10 (Archibald, 1968)
1550	25	'25' (Colledge, 1969)
1551	26	'26' (Colledge, 1969); 29/[12] (Oppenheim, 1961)
1552	25	'25' (Colledge, 1969); 29/[8] (Oppenheim, 1961); 10 (Archibald, 1968)
1553	24	'24' (Colledge, 1969)
1554	21	'21' (Colledge, 1969); 29 (Oppenheim, 1961)
1555	17	'17' (Colledge, 1969)
1556	19	'19' (Colledge, 1969)
1557	19	'19' (Colledge, 1969); 24 (Oppenheim, 1961); 21 (Derrick, 1806; Archibald, 1968)
1558	19	'19' (Colledge, 1969); 23/[22] (Charnock, 1800–3, Richmond, 1946; Cowburn, 1965); 21 (Derrick, 1806; Stevens and Westcott, 1943; Archibald, 1968)
1559	18	'18' (Colledge, 1969); 25/[6] (Oppenheim, 1961)
1560	21	'21' (Colledge, 1969); [0] (Oppenheim, 1961)
1561	22	'22' (Colledge, 1969)
1562	24	'24' (Colledge, 1969)
1563	23	'23' (Colledge, 1969)
1564	23	'23' (Colledge, 1969)
1565	23	'23' (Colledge, 1969); 24 (Derrick, 1806; Archibald, 1968)

Table 8.4 England/Great Britain's estimated annual number of warships, 1494–1860

Year	Number of warships	Sources on numbers of warships
1566	22	'22' (Colledge, 1969)
1567	24	'24' (Colledge, 1969)
1568	25	'25' (Colledge, 1969)
1569	25	'25' (Colledge, 1969)
1570	25	'25' (Colledge, 1969)
1571	25	'25' (Colledge, 1969)
1572	25	'25' (Colledge, 1969)
1573	28	'28' (Colledge, 1969)
1574	28	'28' (Colledge, 1969)
1575	28	'28' (Colledge, 1969)
1576	28	'28' (Colledge, 1969)
1577	30	'30' (Colledge, 1969)
1578	28	'28' (Colledge, 1969); 24 (Derrick, 1806; Busk, 1859; Archibald, 1968)
1579	28	'28' (Colledge, 1969)
1580	29	'29' (Colledge, 1969); 25 (Rose, 1921a)
1581	29	'29' (Colledge, 1969)
1582	29	'29' (Colledge, 1969)
1583	29	'29' (Colledge, 1969)
1584	29	'29' (Colledge, 1969)
1585	30	'30' (Colledge, 1969)
1586	32	'32' (Colledge, 1969)
1587	33	'33' (Colledge, 1969)
1588	33	'33' (Colledge, 1969); 34 (Derrick, 1806; Archibald, 1968); 25 (Stevens and Westcott, 1943), 25 w/100 tons+ (Mattingly, 1959); 17 (Charnock, 1800–3)
1589	33	'33' (Colledge, 1969)
1590	35	'35' (Colledge, 1969)
1591	35	'35' (Colledge, 1969)
1592	35	'35' (Colledge, 1969)
1593	35	'35' (Colledge, 1969)
1594	36	'36' (Colledge, 1969)
1595	36	'36' (Colledge, 1969)
1596	39	'39' (Colledge, 1969)
1597	39	'39' (Colledge, 1969); 44 (Corbett, 1900)
1598	39	'39' (Colledge, 1969)
1599	36	'36' (Colledge, 1969); 42 (Derrick, 1806; Archibald, 1968)
1600	35	'35' (Colledge, 1969)
1601	35	'35' (Colledge, 1969)
1602	35	'35' (Colledge, 1969); 32 (Charnock, 1800–3)

216

Table 8.4 England/Great Britain's estimated annual number of warships, 1494–1860

Year	Number of warships	Sources on numbers of warships
1603	34	'34' (Colledge, 1969); 42 (Busk, 1859); 40 (Derrick, 1806; Archibald, 1968); 39 (Penn, 1913); 31 (Richmond, 1953); 29 (Richmond, 1946); [29] (Cowburn, 1965)
1604	31	'31' (Colledge, 1969); 37 (Penn, 1913); 32 (Derrick, 1806; Archibald, 1968); 31 [1–4] (Corbett, 1900)
1605	31	'31' (Colledge, 1969)
1606	31	'31' (Colledge, 1969)
1607	31	'31' (Colledge, 1969); '37'/[3] (Rose, 1921a), 37 (Marcus, 1961; Cowburn, 1965); 32 (Archibald, 1968)
1608	30	'30' (Colledge, 1969)
1609	30	'30' (Colledge, 1969)
1610	31	'31' (Colledge, 1969); 40 (Silburn, 1912)
1611	30	'30' (Colledge, 1969)
1612	30	'30' (Colledge, 1969)
1613	31	'31' (Colledge, 1969)
1614	31	'31' (Colledge, 1969)
1615	32	'32' (Colledge, 1969)
1616	34	'34' (Colledge, 1969)
1617	34	'34' (Colledge, 1969)
1618	31	'31' (Colledge, 1969); '43'/[27] (Richmond, 1946); '41'/[8] (Penn, 1913); 27 (Marcus,1861); 26 Archibald, 1968); 15 (Corbett, 1900)
1619	33	'33' (Colledge, 1969); '43'/[23] (Penn, 1913)
1620	34	'34' (Colledge, 1969)
1621	36	'36' (Colledge, 1969)
1622	37	'37' (Colledge, 1969)
1623	39	'39' (Colledge, 1969)
1624	36	'36' (Colledge, 1969); 31 [1–4] (Clowes, 1897–1903; Cowburn, 1965); 28 w/20+ (Clowes, 1897–1903); 27 w/20+ (Archibald, 1968)
1625	40	'40' (Colledge, 1969)
1626	46	'46' (Colledge, 1969)
1627	53	'53' (Colledge, 1969)
1628	50	'50' (Colledge, 1969)
1629	47	'47' (Colledge, 1969)
1630	44	'44' (Colledge, 1969)
1631	44	'44' (Colledge, 1969); 40 (Penn, 1913)
1632	43	'43' (Colledge, 1969)
1633	44	'44' (Colledge, 1969); 50/17 w/40+ (Derrick, 1806); 32 w/20+ (Archibald, 1968)

217

Table 8.4 England/Great Britain's estimated annual number of warships, 1494–1860

Year	Number of warships	Sources on numbers of warships
1634	46	'46' (Colledge, 1969)
1635	43	'43' (Colledge, 1969); 19 (Clowes, 1897–1903)
1636	44	'44' (Colledge, 1969); 45 (Cowburn, 1965); 27 (Clowes, 1897–1903)
1637	46	'46' (Colledge, 1969); 55 (Cowburn, 1965)
1638	46	'46' (Colledge, 1969)
1639	46	'46' (Colledge, 1969)
1640	46	'46' (Colledge, 1969); 40 (Cooper, 1970; Parker, 1979)
1641	45	'45' (Colledge, 1969); 42 (Busk, 1859); 42 [1–6]/31 [1–4] (Archibald, 1968)
1642	46	'46' (Colledge, 1969); '41' [1–6]/35 (Powell, 1962); 19 (Oppenheim, 1961)
1643	55	'55' (Colledge, 1969); 36 (Oppenheim, 1961; Clowes, 1897–1903); 30 [1–6]/80 [1–6] + armed merchantmen (Powell, 1962); 18 (Richmond, 1953)
1644	56	'56' (Colledge, 1969); 36 (Oppenheim, 1961; Richmond, 1953); 30 [1–6]/52 [1–6] + armed merchantmen (Powell, 1962)
1645	57	'57' (Colledge, 1969); 34 (Oppenheim, 1961); 29 [1–6]/55 [1–6] + armed merchantmen (Powell, 1962)
1646	66	'66' (Colledge, 1969); 45 (Oppenheim, 1961); 42 [1–6]/63 [1–6] + armed merchantmen (Powell, 1962)
1647	69	'69' (Colledge, 1969); 45 [1–6]/64 [1–6] + armed merchantmen (Powell, 1962); 43 (Oppenheim, 1961)
1648	63	'63' (Colledge, 1969); 39 [1–6] (Powell, 1962); 14 (Charnock, 1800–3)
1649	73	'73' (Colledge, 1969); '68' w/guns (Anderson, 1935)
1650	80	'80' (Colledge, 1969); '76' w/guns (Anderson, 1935)
1651	91	'91' (Colledge, 1969); '86' w/guns (Anderson, 1935); c. 95 (Cooper, 1970); 41 (Charnock, 1800–3)
1652	124	'124' (Colledge, 1969); '117' w/guns (Anderson, 1935); 97 [1–6] (Archibald, 1968); 85 Wilson, 1957; Parker, 1970); 20 [1–3] (Clowes, 1897–1903); [106] (Pontalis, 1885)
1653	134	'134' (Colledge, 1969); '132' w/guns (Anderson, 1935); 154 (Nicolas, 1958); 117 w/20+ (de Jonge, 1869), 99 [1–6]/88 [1–4] (Charnock, 1800–3)

218

Table 8.4 England/Great Britain's estimated annual number of warships, 1494–1860

Year	Number of warships	Sources on numbers of warships
1654	140	'140' (Colledge, 1969); '144' w/guns (Anderson, 1935); 131 w/guns (de Jonge, 1869; Pontalis, 1885); [60] (Rowen, 1978)
1655	109	'109' (Colledge, 1969); '89' [1–4] (Anderson, 1935)
1656	103	'103' (Colledge, 1969); '82' [1–4] (Anderson, 1935)
1657	99	'99' (Colledge, 1969); '79' [1–4] (Anderson, 1935)
1658	95	'95' (Colledge, 1969); '78' [1–4] (Anderson, 1935); '145' [1–6]/'73' [1–4] (Derrick, 1806; Archibald, 1968)
1659	95	'95' (Colledge, 1969); '80' [1–4] (Anderson, 1934)
1660	96	'96' (Colledge, 1969); '79' [1–4] (Anderson, 1935); c. 160 (Cooper, 1970); '154' [1–6]/'76' [1–4] (Derrick, 1806; Archibald, 1968)
1661	95	'95' (Colledge, 1969); '79' [1–4] (Anderson, 1935)
1662	94	'94' (Colledge, 1969); '77' [1–4] (Anderson, 1935)
1663	94	'94' (Colledge, 1969); '77' [1–4] (Anderson, 1935)
1664	94	'94' (Colledge, 1969); '75' [1–4] (Anderson, 1935)
1665	103	'103' (Colledge, 1969); '91' [1–4] (Anderson, 1935); 160 (Wilson, 1957; Parker, 1970); 109 (Memain, 1936; Tramond, 1947; Nicolas, 1958; Wilcox, 1966; Pontalis, 1885; Silburn, 1912); 114 (Charnock, 1800–3); 109/35 [1–3]/35 [4–6]/21 armed merchantmen, Pemsel, 1977)
1666	99	'99' (Colledge, 1969); '85' [1–4] (Anderson, 1935); 109/80 w/30 + /72 w/40 + /50 w/50 + (Clowes, 1897–1903); 89 (Charnock, 1800–3); 88 (Silburn, 1912); [80] (Robison and Robison, 1942); [76] (Richmond, 1953)
1667	78	'78' (Colledge, 1969); '65' [1–4] (Anderson, 1935)
1668	78	'78' (Colledge, 1969); '64' [1–4] (Anderson, 1935)
1669	80	'80' (Colledge, 1969); '66' [1–4] (Anderson, 1935)
1670	83	'83' (Colledge, 1969); '68' [1–4] (Anderson, 1935)
1671	52	'52' (Colledge, 1969); '63' [1–4] (Anderson, 1935); 132 [1–6] (Lacour-Gayet, 1902); 132 (de la Gravière, 1879)
1672	50	'50' (Colledge, 1969); '64' [1–4] (Anderson, 1935); 65 (Clowes, 1897–1903; Silburn, 1912; Pontalis, 1885)
1673	54	'54' (Colledge, 1969); '67' [1–4] (Anderson, 1935); c. 60 (Charnock, 1800–3)
1674	56	'56' (Colledge, 1969); '69' [1–4] (Anderson, 1935); 92 (Richmond, 1953)
1675	60	'100' [1–6]/'76' [1–4] (Derrick, 1806; Archibald, 1968); 92 w/guns (Franks, 1942)

219

Table 8.4   England/Great Britain's estimated annual number of warships, 1494–1860

Year	Number of warships	Sources on numbers of warships
1676	61	'61'[1–6]/'77' [1–4] (Derrick, 1806; Archibald, 1968)
1677	62	'62' (Busk, 1859); '75'/[23] (Albion, 1926); 55 w/40 + (James, 1886)
1678	69	'69' (Colledge, 1969); '83' [1–4] (Anderson, 1935); '77' [1–6]/'58' [1–4] (Archibald, 1968)
1679	80	'80' (Colledge, 1969); '96' [1–4] (Anderson, 1935); [76] [1–6] (Charnock, 1800–3)
1680	79	'79' (Colledge, 1969); '96' [1–4] (Anderson, 1935)
1681	81	'81' (Colledge, 1969); '98' [1–4] (Anderson, 1935)
1682	79	'79' (Colledge, 1969); '97' [1–4] (Anderson, 1935)
1683	81	'81' (Colledge, 1969); '98' [1–4] (Anderson, 1935)
1684	81	'81' (Colledge, 1969); '98' [1–4] (Anderson, 1935); 104 [1–4] (Charnock, 1800–3)
1685	82	'127' [1–6]/'108' [1–4] (Derrick, 1806; Archibald, 1968)
1686	80	'80' (Colledge, 1969); '97' [1–4] (Anderson, 1935)
1687	79	'79' (Colledge, 1969); '101' [1–4] (Anderson, 1935); 37 (Clark, 1970a)
1688	78	'78' (Colledge, 1969); '97' [1–4] (Anderson, 1935); '108' [1–6]/'100' [1–4] (Richmond, 1953; Archibald, 1968; Silburn, 1912); '100' [1–4] (Ehrman, 1953; Vecchj, 1895; 99 [1–4] (Clowes, 1897–1903; 95/[40] (Charnock, 1800–3)
1689	74	'74' (Colledge, 1969); '91' [1–4] (Anderson, 1935); '127' [1–6]/'107' [1–4] (Archibald, 1968); 100 (Bromley and Ryan, 1971; Cowburn, 1965; Pemsel, 1977)
1690	71	'71' (Colledge, 1969); '90' [1–4] (Anderson, 1935)
1691	68	'68' (Colledge, 1969); '67' [1–4] (Anderson, 1935); 91/57 w/50 + (Nicolas, 1958)
1692	70	'70' (Colledge, 1969); ; '70' [1–4] (Anderson, 1935); 63 (Charnock, 1800–3; Silburn, 1912; Reynolds, 1974)
1693	81	'81' (Colledge, 1969); '83' [1–4] (Anderson, 1935); 68 w/50 + /99 w/40 + (Chalmers, 1794)
1694	87	'87' (Colledge, 1969); '90' [1–4] (Anderson, 1935)
1695	97	'97' (Colledge, 1969); '105' [1–4] (Anderson, 1935)
1696	99	'99' (Colledge, 1969); '107' [1–4] (Anderson, 1935)
1697	107	'107' (Colledge, 1969); '114' [1–4] (Anderson, 1935); '192' [1–6]/'119' [1–4] (Archibald, 1968)
1698	115	'115' (Colledge, 1969); '126' [1–4] (Anderson, 1935); '181' [1–6]/'129' [1–4] (Archibald, 1968); 128 (Silburn, 1912)

220

Table 8.4 England/Great Britain's estimated annual number of warships, 1494–1860

Year	Number of warships	Sources on numbers of warships
1699	117	'117' (Colledge, 1969); '128' [1–4] (Anderson, 1935)
1700	115	'115' (Colledge, 1969); '127' [1–4] (Anderson, 1935); '136'/[66] (Richmond, 1953)
1701	117	'117' (Colledge, 1969); '131' [1–4] (Anderson, 1935); '130' (Merriman, 1961); 129 [1–4] (Vecchj, 1895)
1702	124	'124' (Colledge, 1969); '125' [1–4] (Anderson, 1935); '130' [1–4] (Charnock, 1800–3; Richmond, 1953); 128 (Silburn, 1912); 117 [1–4] (Bourne, 1939); [115] [1–4] (Baugh, 1977); [111] (Owen, 1938); [110] [1–4] (Merriman, 1961; Pemsel, 1977); [102] (Chalmers, 1794); 100 (Bromley and Ryan, 1971); [90] [1–4] (Charnock, 1800–3); [74] (Chalmers, 1794
1703	117	'117' (Colledge, 1969); '121' [1–4] (Archibald, 1968); [127] [1–4] (Baugh, 1977); [79] Chalmers, 1794)
1704	119	'119' (Colledge, 1969); [121] [1–4] (Baugh, 1977); [96] (Owen, 1938); [95] [1–4] (Merriman, 1961); [74] (Chalmers, 1794)
1705	121	'121' (Colledge, 1969); [115] [1–4] (Baugh, 1977); 79 (Chalmers, 1794)
1706	120	'120' (Colledge, 1969); '129' [1–4] (Archibald, 1968); [115] [1–4] (Baugh, 1977); [106] [1–4] (Merriman, 1961); [78] (Chalmers, 1794)
1707	114	'114' (Colledge, 1969); [112] [1–4] (Baugh, 1977); [100] (Owen, 1938); [72] (Chalmers, 1794)
1708	123	'123' (Colledge, 1969); '135' [1–4] (Archibald, 1968); [112] [1–4] (Baugh, 1977); [103] [1–4] (Merriman, 1961); [98] (Owen, 1938); [69] (Chalmers, 1794)
1709	124	'124' (Colledge, 1969); [114] [1–4] (Baugh, 1977); 100 (Bromley and Ryan, 1971); [67] (Chalmers, 1794)
1710	129	'129' (Colledge, 1969); [109] [1–4] (Baugh, 1977); [95] [1–4] (Merriman, 1961); [62] (Chalmers, 1794)
1711	129	'129' (Colledge, 1969); '135' [1–4] (Archibald, 1968); [112] [1–4] (Baugh, 1977); [59] (Chalmers, 1794)
1712	130	'130' (Colledge, 1969); [88] [1–4] (Baugh, 1977); [53] [1–4] (Merriman, 1961)
1713	128	'128' (Colledge, 1969); '133' [1–4] (Derrick, 1806; Archibald, 1968)
1714	127	'127' (Colledge, 1969); '131' [1–4] (Merriman, 1961; Archibald, 1968); 131 [1–4] (Clowes, 1897–1903); [45] (Merriman, 1961)

Table 8.4 England/Great Britain's estimated annual number of warships, 1494–1860

Year	Number of warships	Sources on numbers of warships
1715	124	'124' (Colledge, 1969); '131' [1–4] (Baugh, 1977)
1716	122	'122' (Colledge, 1969)
1717	122	'122' (Colledge, 1969)
1718	122	'122' (Colledge, 1969)
1719	121	'121' (Colledge, 1969)
1720	120	'120' (Colledge, 1969)
1721	122	'122' (Colledge, 1969); '124' [1–4] (Derrick, 1806; Archibald, 1968); 124 (Anderson, 1961)
1722	119	'119' [1–4] (Colledge, 1969)
1723	121	'121' [1–4] (Colledge, 1969)
1724	121	'121' [1–4] (Colledge, 1969)
1725	120	'120' [1–4] (Colledge, 1969)
1726	117	'117' [1–4] (Colledge, 1969)
1727	116	'116' [1–4] (Colledge, 1969); '124' [1–4] (Archibald, 1968; Baugh, 1977); 124 (Mahan, 1890; Clowes, 1897–1903) 123 [1–4] (Silburn, 1912); [38] (Charnock, 1800–3)
1728	113	'113' [1–4] (Colledge, 1969)
1729	113	'113' [1–4] (Colledge, 1969)
1730	111	'111' [1–4] (Colledge, 1969); '124' [1–4] (Archibald, 1968); 119 [1–4] (Charnock, 1800–3)
1731	112	'112' [1–4] (Colledge, 1969)
1732	113	'113' [1–4] (Colledge, 1969)
1733	113	'113' [1–4] (Colledge, 1969)
1734	115	'115' [1–4] (Colledge, 1969)
1735	117	'117' [1–4] (Colledge, 1969)
1736	121	'121' [1–4] (Colledge, 1969)
1737	123	'123' [1–4] (Colledge, 1969)
1738	123	'123' [1–4] (Colledge, 1969)
1739	118	'118' [1–4] (Colledge, 1969); '124' [1–4] (Richmond, 1946; Archibald, 1968); '121' [1–4] (Baugh, 1965); 116 (Fernandez Duro, 1972–3); [83] (Richmond, 1946); [81] (Charnock, 1800–3); [68] [1–4] (Baugh, 1977); [35] (Anderson, 1961)
1740	116	'116' [1–4] (Colledge, 1969); 120 (Wilson, 1957; Lacour-Gayet, 1902); [80] [1–4] (Baugh, 1977)
1741	119	'119' [1–4] (Colledge, 1969); [87] [1–4] (Baugh, 1977)
1742	117	'117' [1–4] (Colledge, 1969); '125' [1–4] (Archibald, 1968; Baugh, 1965); 124 (Nicholas, 1973); [86] [1–4] (Baugh, 1977)
1743	116	'116' [1–4] (Colledge, 1969); [88] [1–4] (Baugh, 1977)

222

Table 8.4   England/Great Britain's estimated annual number of warships, 1494–1860

Year	Number of warships	Sources on numbers of warships
1744	107	'107' [1–4] (Colledge, 1969); '128' [1–4] (Archibald, 1968); 120 (Dorn, 1963); 90 (Mahan, 1890); [88] [1–4] (Baugh, 1977)
1745	110	'110' [1–4] (Colledge, 1969); '125'/[101] (Baugh, 1965); [92] [1–4] (Baugh, 1977); [78] (Richmond, 1946)
1746	112	'112' [1–4] (Colledge, 1969)
1747	122	'122' [1–4] (Colledge, 1969); 126 (Mahan, 1890)
1748	123	'123' [1–4] (Colledge, 1969); '138' [1–4] (Derrick, 1806; Archibald, 1968); '131' [1–4] (Charnock, 1800–3); 124 (Nicolas, 1958); [89] (Chalmers, 1894)
1749	114	'114' [1–4] (Colledge, 1969); '126' [1–4] (Baugh, 1977)
1750	116	'116' [1–4] (Colledge, 1969); '126' [1–4] (Derrick, 1806; Archibald, 1968)
1751	116	'116' [1–4] (Colledge, 1969); '131'/[116] (Baugh, 1965); 116 (Lacour-Gayet, 1902)
1752	115	'115' [1–4] (Colledge, 1969); 132 [1–4] (Clowes, 1897–1903)
1753	117	'117' [1–4] (Colledge, 1969); '132' (Derrick, 1806; Archibald, 1968)
1754	118	'118' [1–4] (Colledge, 1969); 142 (Vovard, 1948)
1755	119	'119' [1–4] (Colledge, 1969); '134' [1–4] (Archibald, 1968); 108 [1–4] (Charnock, 1800–3); [c. 100] (Jenkins, 1973); 98 (Richmond, 1946); [89] (Vecchj, 1895); 75–80 (Parry, 1971)
1756	117	'117' [1–4] (Colledge, 1969); '142' [1–4] (Archibald, 1968); 142 (Rose, 1921b); 131 [1–4] (Charnock, 1800–3); 130 (Mahan, 1890; Dupuy and Dupuy, 1977); 120 (Pemsel, 1977); 89 (Loir, 1893)
1757	95	'95' w/60+ (Colledge, 1969)
1758	103	'103' w/60+ (Colledge, 1969)
1759	109	'109' w/60+ (Colledge, 1969); 113 (Parry, 1979)
1760	107	'107' w/60+ (Colledge, 1969); '155' [1–4]/'127' w-60+ (Archibald, 1968); '155' [1–4] (Clowes, 1897–1903); 127 (Silburn, 1912); 120 (Mahan, 1890)
1761	111	'111' w/60+ (Colledge, 1969); 120 (Mahan, 1890)
1762	116	'i16' w/60+ (Colledge, 1969); '163' [1–4]/'139' w/60+ (Archibald, 1968); 141 [1–4] (Clowes, 1897–1903; Anderson, 1961)

223

Table 8.4 England/Great Britain's estimated annual number of warships, 1494–1860

Year	Number of warships	Sources on numbers of warships
1763	117	'117' w/60+ (Colledge, 1969); '133' [1–4] (Walker, 1860); '118' (Barfleur, 1907)
1764	120	'120' w/60+ (Colledge, 1969); '158' [1–4]/'136' w/60+ (Derrick, 1806; Archibald, 1968); '135' [1–4] (Walker, 1860)
1765	120	'120' w/60+ (Colledge, 1969); '136' [1–4] (Walker, 1860); 109 (Wilcox, 1966)
1766	120	'120' w/60+ (Colledge, 1969); '136' [1–4] (Walker, 1860); 62 (Headlam, 1921); 56 (Lloyd, 1965a)
1767	118	'118' w/60+ (Colledge, 1969); '152' [1–4]/'133' w/60+ (Derrick, 1806; Archibald, 1968); '133' [1–4] (Walker, 1860)
1768	121	'121' w/60+ (Colledge, 1969); '132' [1–4] (Walker, 1860)
1769	122	'122' w/60+ (Colledge, 1969); '139' [1–4] (Walker, 1860)
1770	121	'121' w/60+ (Colledge, 1969); '141' [1–4] (Walker, 1860); 40 (Richmond, 1946)
1771	118	'118' w/60+ (Colledge, 1969); '154' [1–4]/'144' w/60+ (Derrick, 1806; Archibald, 1968); '135' [1–4] (Walker, 1860)
1772	115	'115' w/60+ (Colledge, 1969); '137' [1–4] (Walker, 1860)
1773	111	'111' w/60+ (Colledge, 1969); '133' [1–4] (Walker, 1860)
1774	110	'110' w/60+ (Colledge, 1969); '133' [1–4] (Walker, 1860)
1775	108	'108' w/60+ (Colledge, 1969); '143' [1–4]/'131' w/60+ (Archibald, 1968); 131 (Clowes, 1897–1903), '131' [1–4] (Walker, 1860); (Lloyd, 1961)
1776	109	'109' w/60+ (Colledge, 1969); '126' [1–4] (Walker, 1860); 122 w/60+ (Edler, 1911)
1777	106	'106' w/60+ (Colledge, 1969); '142' [1–4]/'125' w/60+ (Derrick, 1806; Archibald, 1968); '126' [1–4] (Walker, 1860)
1778	104	'104' w/60+ (Colledge, 1969); '152' [1–4]/'131' w/60+ (Archibald, 1968); 150 (Stevens and Westcott, 1943); 137/122 w/60+ (de Jonge, 1869); 131 (Silburn, 1912); '126' [1–4] (Walker, 1860); 126 (Busk, 1859); 72 (Lacour-Gayet, 1905)
1779	104	'104' w/60+ (Colledge, 1969); c. 150 (Mahan, 1890); '133' [1–4] (Walker, 1860)

224

Table 8.4 England/Great Britain's estimated annual number of warships, 1494–1860

Year	Number of warships	Sources on numbers of warships
1780	109	'109' w/60+ (Colledge, 1969); '164' [1–43]/'144' w/60+ (Derrick, 1806; Archibald, 1968); '143' [1–4] (Walker, 1860); 130 (Pemsel, 1977); 122 (de Peyster, 1905)
1781	114	'114' w/58+ (Colledge, 1969); '153' [1–4] (Walker, 1860)
1782	126	'126' w/60+ (Colledge, 1969); '184' [1–4]/'161' w/60+ (Derrick, 1806; Archibald, 1968); '156' [1–4] (Walker, 1860)
1783	125	'125' w/60+ (Colledge, 1969); '197' [1–4]/'174' w/60+ (Archibald, 1968); 174 (Clowes, 1897–1903; Silburn, 1912; Anderson, 1961); '173' [1–4] (Walker, 1860); '145'/[117]/[109] (Chalmers, 1794); [100] (Brenton, 1823–5); 68 (Lloyd, 1965a)
1784	115	'115' w/60+ (Colledge, 1969); '168' [1–4] (Walker, 1860)
1785	121	'121' w/60+ (Colledge, 1969); '151' [1–4] (Walker, 1860)
1786	127	'127' w/60+ (Colledge, 1969); '166' [1–4]/'149' w/60+ (Derríck, 1806; Archibald, 1968); '149' [1–4] (Walker, 1860)
1787	132	'132' w/60+ (Colledge, 1969); '139' [1–4] (Walker, 1860); [40] (Richmond, 1946)
1788	133	'133' w/60+ (Colledge, 1969); '146' [1–4] (Walker, 1860)
1789	134	'134' w/60+ (Colledge, 1969); '165' [1–4]/'148' w/60+ (Archibald, 1968); '147' [1–4] (Walker, 1860); '141'/[115] (Bruun, 1963); 118 w/60+ (Vecchj, 1895); 101 (Lloyd, 1965a)
1790	137	'137' w/60+ (Colledge, 1969); '144' [1–4] (Walker, 1860); '126'/97 [1–4]/'110'/[90] w/60+ (Archibald, 1968); 146 (Silburn, 1912); [93] (Richmond, 1946; Benians, 1940)
1791	133	'133' w/60+ (Colledge, 1969); '144' [1–4] (Walker, 1860); 115 (Loir, 1893)
1792	132	'132' w/60+ (Colledge, 1969); '163'/[86] [1–4]/'146'/[79] w/60+ (Archibald, 1968); '141' [1–4] (Walker, 1860); '141' (Wilson, 1904); '140' (Chalmers, 1794); '129'/[82] (Clowes, 1897–1903); 115 (Lloyd, 1965a; Dupuy and Dupuy, 1977); '87'/[60] (James, 1886)
1793	132	'132' w/60+ (Colledge, 1969); '161' [1–4]/'141'

225

Table 8.4   England/Great Britain's estimated annual number of warships, 1494–1860

Year	Number of warships	Sources on numbers of warships
		w/60+/'140' [1–3] (Archibald, 1968); 157 (Charnock, 1800–3); '141' [1–4] (Walker, 1860); '115' (Stevens and Westcott, 1943; Richmond, 1946; Lloyd, 1965b); 115 (James, 1886; Mahan, 1892; Wilson, 1904; Pemsel, 1977); 113/[75] [1–3] (Clowes, 1897–1903); 113 (Vecchj, 1895); '113'/[93] (Rose, 1940a); 93 (Parry, 1971); [26] (Hannay, 1909)
1794	133	'133' w/60+ (Colledge, 1969); 145 (Busk, 1859); '140' [1–4] (Walker, 1860); '117' (Hampson, 1959); 117 [1–3] (Clowes, 1897–1903); 117 (Vecchj, 1895)
1795	131	'131' w/60+ (Colledge, 1969); '163' [1–4]/'145' w/60+/'144' [1–3] (Archibald, 1968); '145' [1–4] '144' [1–3] (Walker, 1860); 114 [1–3] (Clowes, 1897–1903); 114 (Vecchj, 1895); '113'/[26] (James, 1886); '110'/[89–91] (Hampson, 1959)
1796	129	'129' w/60+ (Colledge, 1969); '160' [1–4]/'159' [1–3] (Walker, 1860); '160' (Wilson, 1904); '116'/[105] w/60+ (James, 1886); '116' [1–3] (Clowes, 1897–1903); 116 (Vecchj, 1895)
1797	139	'139' w/60+ (Colledge, 1969); '184' [1–4]/'161' w/60+/'160' [1–3] (Archibald, 1968); '160' [1–3] (Walker, 1860); 124 (Brenton, 1823–5); 116 [1–3] (Clowes, 1897–1903)
1798	147	'147' w/60+ (Colledge, 1969); '172' [1–3] (Walker, 1860); 135 (Mahan, 1892); 120 [1–3] (Clowes, 1897–1903)
1799	135	'135' w/60+ (Colledge, 1969); '197' [1–4]/'176' w/60+/'173' [1–3] (Archibald, 1968); '177' [1–3] (Walker, 1860); 125 [1–3] (Clowes, 1897–1903)
1800	132	'132' w/60+ (Colledge, 1969); 197 (Charnock, 1800–3); '179' [1–3] (Walker, 1860); 123 [1–3] (Clowes, 1897–1903)
1801	131	'131' w/60+ (Colledge, 1969); '202' (Mahan, 1892); '200' [1–4]/'180' w/60+/'179' [1–3] (Archibald, 1968); '177' [1–3] (Walker, 1860); [144] (Silburn, 1912); '127'/[100] (James, 1886); 127 [1–3] (Clowes, 1897–1903)
1802	129	'129' w/60+ (Colledge, 1969); 189 (Stevens and Westcott, 1943); '180' [1–3] (Walker, 1860); '126'/[104] (James, 1886); 126 [1–3] (Clowes, 1897–1903); [104] (Rose, 1940b)

226

Table 8.4   England/Great Britain's estimated annual number of warships, 1494–1860

Year	Number of warships	Sources on numbers of warships
1803	128	'128' w/60+ (Colledge, 1969); '197' [1–4]/'177' w/60+ /'176' [1–3] (Archibald, 1968); '177' [1–3] (Walker, 1860); 126 (Fernandez Duro, 1972–3); 120 (Thomazi, 1950); [120] (Pemsel, 1977); 115 (Richmond, 1946); '111' (Fuller, 1955); '111'/[32] (James, 1886); 111 [1–3] (Clowes, 1897–1903); [23] (Rose, 1940b)
1804	122	'122' w/60+ (Colledge, 1969); '190' [1–3] (Walker, 1860); 175 (Busk, 1859); '115'/[75] (James, 1886); 115 [1–3] (Clowes, 1897–1903); [105] (Robison and Robison, 1942); [81] (Rose, 1940b)
1805	130	'130' w/60+ (Colledge, 1969); '199' [1–4]/'175' w/60+ /'174' [1–3] (Archibald, 1968); '176' [1–3] (Walker, 1860); '116'/[83] (James, 1886); 116 [1–3] (Clowes, 1897–1903)
1806	129	'129' w/60+ (Colledge, 1969); '189' [1–3] (Walker, 1860); '120'/[104] (James, 1886); 120 [1–3] (Clowes, 1897–1903); [104] (Rose, 1940b)
1807	148	'148' w/60+ (Colledge, 1969); '212' [1–3] (Walker, 1860); '123'/[103] (James, 1886); 123 [1–3] (Clowes, 1897–1903)
1808	149	'149' w/60+ (Colledge, 1969); '228' [1–3] (Walker, 1860); '126'/[113] (James, 1886); 126 [1–3] (Clowes, 1897–1903)
1809	148	'148' w/60+ (Colledge, 1969); '247' [1–3] (Walker, 1860); '127'/[113] (James, 1886); 127 [1–3] (Clowes, 1897–1903; Richmond, 1946)
1810	151	'151' w/60+ (Colledge, 1969); '248' [1–3] (Walker, 1860); '124'/[108] (James, 1886); 124 [1–3] (Clowes, 1897–1903)
1811	148	'148' w/60+ (Colledge, 1969); '246' [1–3] (Walker, 1860); '124'/[107] (James, 1886); 124 [1–3] (Clowes, 1897–1903)
1812	154	'154' w/60+ (Colledge, 1969); 245 (Busk, 1859); '242' [1–3] (Walker, 1860); 191 (Frere-Cook and Macksey, 1975); '120'/[102] (James, 1886); 120 [1–3] (Clowes, 1897–1903); 108 (Richmond, 1946)
1813	145	'145' w/60+ (Colledge, 1969); '248' [1–3] (Walker, 1860); '124'/[102] (James, 1886); 124 [1–3] (Clowes, 1897–1903)
1814	131	'131' w/60+ (Colledge, 1969); '240' [1–3] (Walker, 1860); 240 (Fuller, 1955); 130 including frigates/

227

Table 8.4 England/Great Britain's estimated annual number of warships, 1494–1860

Year	Number of warships	Sources on numbers of warships
		[99] (Graham, 1965); '118'/[99] [1–3] (Archibald, 1968); '118'/[99] (James, 1886); 118 [1–3] (Clowes, 1897–1903)
1815	134	'134' w/60+ (Colledge, 1969); 240 (Lloyd, 1965b); 218 (Busk, 1859); '217' [1–3] (Walker, 1860); '214' (Anderson, 1972); '214'/[72–80] (Bartlett, 1963); '109'/[47] (James, 1886); 109 [1–3] (Clowes, 1897–1903)
1816	130	'130' w/60+ (Colledge, 1969); '192' [1–3] (Walker, 1860); '100'/[30] (James, 1886)
1817	124	'124' w/60+ (Colledge, 1969); '145' [1–4]/'137' [1–3] (Walker, 1860); '109'/[79] (Bartlett, 1963); '98'/[14] (James, 1886)
1818	127	'127' w/60+ (Colledge, 1969); '144' [1–4]/'135' [1–3] (Walker, 1860); '109'/[78] (Bartlett, 1963); '100'/[13] (James, 1886)
1819	118	'118' w/60+ (Colledge, 1969); '142' [1–4]/'132' [1–3] (Walker, 1860); '103'/[13] (James, 1886)
1820	118	'118' w/60+ (Colledge, 1969); 146 (Busk, 1859); '145' [1–4]/'135' [1–3] (Walker, 1860); '114'/[17] [1–4]/'105'/[14] [1–3] (Archibald, 1968); '105'/[14] [1–3] (Archibald, 1968); '105'/[14] (James, 1886); [49] (Graham, 1965)
1821	114	'114' w/60+ (Colledge, 1969); '143' [1–4]/'133' [1–3] (Walker, 1860)
1822	110	'110' w/60+ (Colledge, 1969); [146] (Padfield, 1972); '136' [1–4]/'126' [1–3] (Walker, 1860); [68] (Bartlett, 1963; Anderson, 1972)
1823	109	'109' w/60+ (Colledge, 1969); '132' [1–4]/'122' [1–3] (Walker, 1860)
1824	107	'107' w/60+ (Colledge, 1969); '103' [1–4]/'102' [1–3] (Walker, 1860)
1825	100	'100' w/60+ (Colledge, 1969); 120 (Busk, 1859); '118' [1–3] (Walker, 1860)
1826	96	'96' w/60+ (Colledge, 1969); '119' [1–3] (Walker, 1860); '96'/[74] (Bartlett, 1963)
1827	92	'92' w/60+ (Colledge, 1969); '114' [1–3] (Walker, 1860)
1828	91	'91' w/60+ (Colledge, 1969); 138 (Moreau de Jonnes, 1835); '111' [1–3] (Walker, 1860); '92'/[16] [1–3] (Bartlett, 1963)
1829	91	'91' w/60+ (Colledge, 1969); '110' [1–3] (Walker, 1860); '94'/[14] [1–3] (Bartlett, 1963)

228

Table 8.4   England/Great Britain's estimated annual number of warships, 1494–1860

Year	Number of warships	Sources on numbers of warships
1830	86	'86' w/60+ (Colledge, 1969); 131 (*Almanach de Gotha*); '108' [1–3] (Walker, 1860); '92'/[17] [1–3] (Bartlett, 1963); 106 (Busk, 1859; Cobden, 1862)
1831	85	'85' w/60+ (Colledge, 1969); '106' [1–3] (Walker, 1860); '90'/[14] [1–3] (Bartlett, 1963)
1832	82	'82' w/60+ (Colledge, 1969); '102' [1–3] (Walker, 1860); '88'/[15] [1–3] (Bartlett, 1963); [14] (Graham, 1965)
1833	84	'84' w/60+ (Colledge, 1969); '97' [1–3] (Walker, 1860); '83'/[14] [1–3] (Bartlett, 1963)
1834	82	'82' w/60+ (Colledge, 1969); '104' [1–3] (Walker, 1860); '88'/[16] [1–3] (Bartlett, 1963)
1835	81	'81' w/60+ (Colledge, 1969); '103' [1–3] (Walker, 1860); '87'/[13] [1–3] (Bartlett, 1963); 58 (Anderson, 1972)
1836	79	'79' w/60+ (Colledge, 1969); '97' [1–3] (Walker, 1860)
1837	77	'77' w/60+ (Colledge, 1969); '93' [1–3] (Walker, 1860); '79'/[21] [1–3] (Bartlett, 1963)
1838	76	'76' w/60+ (Colledge, 1969); '92' [1–3] (Walker, 1860); '78'/[18]/[20] [1–3] (Bartlett, 1963)
1839	77	'77' w/60+ (Colledge, 1969); '91' [1–3] (Walker, 1860); '78'/[21] [1–3] (Bartlett, 1963); [c. 30] (Graham, 1965)
1840	78	'78' w/60+ (Colledge, 1969); '95' [1–3] (Walker, 1860); '77'/[23] [1–3] (Bartlett, 1963); 89 (Busk, 1859; Cobden, 1862)
1841	77	'77' w/60+ (Colledge, 1969); '99' [1–3] (Walker, 1860); '78'/[27] [1–3] (Bartlett, 1963); '73' (Bartlett, 1963)
1842	76	'76' w/60+ (Colledge, 1969); '93' [1–3] (Walker, 1860); '75'/[24] [1–3] (Bartlett, 1963)
1843	76	'76' w/60+ (Colledge, 1969); '96' [1–3] (Walker, 1860); '78'/[18] [1–3] (Bartlett 1963)
1844	75	'75' w/60+ (Colledge, 1969); '97' [1–3] (Walker, 1860); '78'/[11] [1–3] (Bartlett, 1963)
1845	73	'73' w/60+ (Colledge, 1969); '106'/[23] [1–4]/'87'/[16] [1–3] (Archibald, 1968); '100' [1–3] (Walker, 1860); 88 (Busk, 1859); '77'/[9] [1–3] (Bartlett, 1963)
1846	73	'73' w/60+ (Colledge, 1969); '94' [1–3] (Walker, 1860); '71'/[12] [1–3] (Bartlett, 1963)
1847	73	'73' w/60+ (Colledge, 1969); '95' [1–3] (Walker, 1860); '72'/[13] [1–3] (Bartlett, 1963)

229

Table 8.4   England/Great Britain's estimated annual number of warships, 1494–1860

Year	Number of warships	Sources on numbers of warships
1848	73	'73' w/60+ (Colledge, 1969); 121 (*Almanach de Gotha*); '95' [1–3] (Walker, 1860); '71'/[17] [1–3] (Bartlett, 1963)
1849	70	'70' w/60+ (Colledge, 1969); '96' [1–3] Walker, (1860); '76'/[21] [1–3] (Bartlett, 1963)
1850	70	'70' w/60+ (Colledge, 1969); 95 (*Almanach de Gotha*); '93' [1–3] (Walker, 1860); 86 (Busk, 1859; Cobden, 1862); '71'/[13] (Bartlett, 1963)
1851	71	'71' w/60+ (Colledge, 1969); '94' [1–3] (Walker, 1860)
1852	73	'73' w/60+ (Colledge, 1969); '95' [1–3] (Walker, 1860); 73 (Bartlett, 1963)
1853	76	'76' w/60+ (Colledge, 1969); '94' [1–3] (Walker, 1860); 70 (Vecchj, 1895)
1854	78	'78' w/60+ (Colledge, 1969); '91' [1–3] (Walker, 1860)
1855	80	'80' w/60+ (Colledge, 1969); '90' [1–3] (Walker, 1860)
1856	77	'77' w/60+ (Colledge, 1969); '90' [1–3] (Walker, 1860)
1857	76	'76' w/60+ (Colledge, 1969); '94' [1–3] (Walker, 1860)
1858	76	'76' w/60+ (Colledge, 1969); '94' [1–3] (Walker, 1860); 94 (Cobden, 1862)
1859	78	'78' w/60+ (Colledge, 1969); '93' [1–3] (Walker, 1860); 68/36 screw/32 sail (Pemsel, 1977)
1860	76	'76' w/60+ (Colledge, 1969)

Note: In this table and Table 9.2, a bracketed hyphenated number (e.g., 1–3 through 1–6) refers to the ship-of-the-line classes or ratings encompassed by the ship number which may also be bracketed if it refers to seaworthy ships. See also Note to Table 8.2.

230   *Country Data*

Table 8.5   British battleships, 1861–1945

Year	Number of ships	Year	Number of ships	Year	Number of ships
1861	2	1890	22	1919	44
1862	5	1891	22	1920	39
1863	7	1892	23	1921	37
1864	12	1893	24	1922	24
1865	16	1894	19	1923	24
1866	22	1895	19	1924	21
1867	25	1896	21	1925	21
1868	29	1897	24	1926	18
1869	30	1898	29	1927	20
1870	37	1899	18	1928	20
1871	38	1900	22	1929	20
1872	40	1901	24	1930	20
1873	42	1902	29	1931	15
1874	43	1903	32	1932	15
1875	40	1904	38	1933	15
1876	40	1905	43	1934	15
1877	45	1906	45	1935	15
1878	45	1907	50	1936	15
1879	44	1908	41	1937	15
1880	7	1909	43	1938	15
1881	8	1910	10	1939	14
1882	8	1911	14	1940	15
1883	10	1912	21	1941	13
1884	10	1913	27	1942	15
1885	10	1914	34	1943	15
1886	13	1915	38	1944	14
1887	16	1916	42	1945	14
1888	17	1917	44		
1889	21	1918	44		

THE UNITED STATES

One military historian summarised the early naval history of the
United States in the following way:

> British naval power had been the enemy's principal strategic asset in
> the War of the Revolution, a timely accession of Allied naval power
> produced American victory at the end, and the major strategic

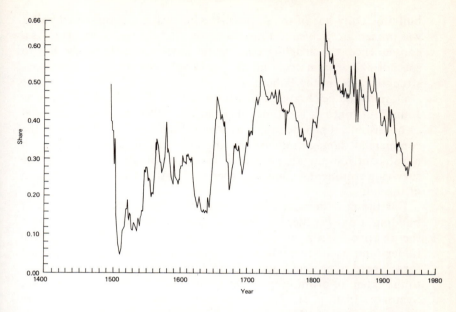

Figure 8.2   English/British relative capability share, 1494–1945

preoccupations of the new United States almost inevitably became naval (Weigley, 1973, p. 40).

Almost inevitably or not, the genesis of United States naval power was characterised by an unusually reluctant flavour and was highlighted by a series of hesitantly-taken false starts. During the revolutionary war, a variety of American navies developed under the supervision of the Continental Congress and its Marine Committee, individual army commanders, and a majority of the separate colonies. At the very beginning of the war (1775–6), the Continental Congress authorised the conversion of several merchantmen and the construction of three ships-of-the-line as well as a relatively large number of frigates – many of which were never launched because of shortages in men, supplies, and expenditures, cost overruns, or destruction while

Country Data

building. Only one of the ships-of-the-line was ever completed and it was immediately given to France shortly after the end of the war. As a consequence, the fledgling continental navy had little choice but to specialise in commerce raiding, with only one or two squadron-strength raids on the Bahamas.

Despite the celebrated successes achieved by individuals such as John Paul Jones, it is estimated (Bradford, 1984, p. 6) that unofficial or quasi-official privateering was about three times as effective as the commercial damage inflicted by the continental navy. The French naval contribution at Yorktown in 1781 notwithstanding, all the surviving continental ships had been sold within two years of the end of the war.

For the next decade, decision-makers debated the advantages of building a navy, generally splitting along party/sectional lines over the relative merits of ships-of-the-line versus smaller commerce raiders and harbour gunboats. Proponents of a strong navy argued for the need to protect trade and the desirability of naval deterrence – to the extent of promoting a 1786 version of Tirpitz's risk theory (see Symonds, 1980, p. 21). Opponents emphasised the large expenditure required and stressed the absence of any real need for a strong navy. It was argued that, rather than creating a deterrent effect, attempts to build a high-profile navy might simply invite an attack from the leading naval power, Great Britain.

A direct naval threat was finally brought about by the outbreak of war in Europe in 1792 which led, in turn, to the expansion of North African piracy and more frequent attacks on American shipping. In response, the construction of six large frigates (large enough to take care of the pirates but not so large as to offend Great Britain) was authorised in late 1794 for use against Algiers. However, a treaty was negotiated before the ships could be completed. It was then determined to build only three which were to remain unequipped until another emergency should arise. Such a contingency did arise in 1797 thanks to French privateering and British attacks. The three frigates were launched and twelve more (as well as nine galleys) were built. A Navy Department was created in 1798 and, a year later, the construction of six ships-of-the-line was approved (but not completed because of a change in administration).

The frigate force was employed in the wars with Tripoli and Morocco (1801–5) giving rise to the first US Mediterranean squadron, but no larger ships were authorised until after war with Great Britain

The Netherlands, Great Britain and the USA

was renewed in 1812. Four ships-of-the-line were approved in 1813 but none could be launched during the war. Aside from the encouraging small ship combat of the Great Lakes theatre, the strategy of commerce raiding again predominated but the British blockade did even greater damage to American shipping and governmental revenues. After the war, a brief burst of naval enthusiasm led to the construction authorisation of nine line ships (most of which were completed but not sent to sea) and twelve frigates. Governmental economy, the absence of an overt European threat in conjunction with the emerging *Pax Britannica*, the growing preoccupation with continental expansion, and the very nature of the US navy's missions (protecting trade in relatively obscure parts of the world, chasing pirates, and suppressing the slave trade) all worked against the perceived need for ships-of-the-line. Instead:

> For more than a half century afterward, American naval policy was based on a militiaman concept; a few small and relatively weak vessels patrolled far-flung stations while citizens in the homeland remained blissfully confident that, in case of an overt threat, citizen sailors would volunteer in droves to serve aboard makeshift warships or to work the coastal artillery. The more ambitious notion of influencing other parts of the world by projecting American force overseas was clearly rejected (Symonds, 1980, p. 13).

Yet the smaller ships were used and deployed on a fairly extensive scale. In addition to the Mediterranean squadron (1801–6, and resumed in 1815), other squadrons were stationed in the West Indies (1816–41), the Pacific (from 1821), the coast of Brazil (from 1826), the East Indies (from 1835), and Africa (from 1843). Only in 1841 was a Home squadron, absorbing the West Indies station, created. Moreover, naval support did prove useful in the Mexican War (1846–8) and the navy was also the vehicle for three Asian projections of force (in China, Japan, and Korea) to obtain commercial privileges between 1842 and 1871.

The American Civil War (1861–5) provided a temporary departure from the weak navy pattern. In the course of the war, the Union navy expanded from forty-two vessels to 671 ships (including seventy-one armour-clads), which, according to Buhl (1978, p. 146), rivalled the British navy in size and modernity and clearly outspent them as well (see Table 4.4). The problem was that the ships that were built in the

234 *Country Data*

early 1860s were useful for coastal blockade and river warfare duties but proved to be entirely unsuitable for oceanic cruising. In any event, this large naval force was quickly demobilised after the war (down to 238 vessels in 1867 and 147 in 1875) with a continued emphasis on using fast, wooden, sailing ships for non-coastal purposes. The foreign stations that had been abandoned during the war were resumed in 1865 and reconstituted into six squadrons: Mediterranean, North Atlantic, South Atlantic, European, Pacific, and Asiatic (Paullin, 1968, pp. 313–14).

By maintaining a low naval profile throughout the first three-quarters of the nineteenth century, the United States navy was at least able – or forced – to forgo much of the expensive European experimentation in ship design and tactical disputes over torpedoes and rams. In response to increasing domestic interest in overseas expansion and growing concern over the prospects of trade conflicts, however, the United States entered the general, late-century, naval expansion ranks in 1883 by building three steel cruisers and establishing the first Naval War College in the following year. Genuine expansion was realised in the next decade through the battleship authorisations specified in the Naval Acts of 1890 (3), 1892 (1), 1895 (2), and 1896 (3). The easy victories over the weak Spanish fleets at Manila Bay and Cuba in the 1898 Spanish–American War further advanced the cause of naval expansion. Naval bases were established in Cuba, Puerto Rico, and the Philippines. Ten more battleships were authorised in Theodore Roosevelt's administration only to be rendered obsolete by the introduction in 1906 of the Dreadnought class. The incremental response was Congressional endorsement for ten new Dreadnoughts in the next half dozen years, followed by five more in 1914–15.

In 1916, President Wilson advanced the expansion of the US navy one major step further. Responding to German and British interference with American shipping, the decision was taken to build a navy 'equal to the most powerful maintained by any nation in the world'. The first phase of this development involved the construction of sixteen more battleships and battle-cruisers and 146 smaller ships, but the ultimate goal was to have sixty capital ships by 1925 (Trask, 1984, p. 208). These plans were set aside, however, when the United States entered the First World War in 1917. Faced with a primary mission of anti-submarine warfare in the Atlantic, building priorities were shifted to more appropriate smaller vessels (e.g. destroyers). After the conclusion of the war, a British–American agreement was struck to

The Netherlands, Great Britain and the USA

exchange British support for the League of Nations for a temporary postponement of the 1916 construction plan. To avoid a naval arms race in which neither side was in a position to participate, the 1922 Washington Treaty established a ten-year moratorium on battleship building, which was later extended by a further five years in 1930. What this meant for the US navy was that only three battleships of the 1916 authorisation entered the fleet and fifteen older battleships and battle-cruisers were scrapped.

Ten years prior to the American entry into the First World War, the multiple stations of the US navy had been consolidated into the Atlantic and Pacific fleets plus a small Asiatic squadron with all battleships concentrated in the Atlantic fleet. In 1919, roughly half the battleships were sent to the Pacific in anticipation of eventual conflict with Japan. War Plan Orange was gradually refined to envisage a holding operation in the difficult-to-defend Philippines until the strenthened Pacific fleet could arrive to defeat the Japanese in a classical fleet clash. In the late 1930s, however, American planning priorities shifted back to the Atlantic and the German threat.

When the Japanese did attack in late 1941, contingency plans had to be revised drastically to play down the anticipated role of battleships in favour of task-force tactics organised around the surviving aircraft-carriers. While the Pacific theatre was initially designated a secondary priority, by 1942–3, it was receiving a share of resources and attention that was generally on a par with the European theatre. After the Battles of the Coral Sea (1942) and Midway (1943) the primarily American forces in the Pacific had forced the Japanese into a defensive war of attrition that would eventually exhaust the Japanese resource base. Beyond the increasing inability to replace warships, especially carriers, and in contrast to the Battle of the Atlantic, the Japanese merchant marine lost approximately 83 per cent of its total shipping – largely because of submarine attacks (approximately 60 per cent of the losses were accounted for by submarines, according to data found in Pemsel, 1977, p. 164, and Weigley, 1973, p. 309).

At the end of the Second World War the US navy found itself in a position of relative strength very similar to the one experienced by Britain at the end of the Napoleonic Wars. Yet the usual post-war problems with demobilisation and reduced budgets were aggravated in this case by the possibility that atomic warfare and air power had greatly reduced the need for a conventional navy and by the movement to reduce the navy's autonomy through unification of the various armed services. The latter threat receded but the threat to the navy's continued significance (and funding) could only be countered by creating a naval niche in the strategic-weapon delivery system. Carrier-based bombers initially served this function in the 1950s but gradually gave way to the development of the sea-launched ballistic missile capability in the 1960s. Concurrent with the early efforts to create a nuclear delivery role, the Korean War broke out in 1950 and resurrected the perceived need for conventional armed forces. In particular, the US navy benefited by a nearly two-thirds expansion of shipping during the war.

In the late 1960s and early 1970s, the US navy encountered two comparatively new developments. Unlike the Korean War, the war in Vietnam (1965–73), although similar in operational nature, contributed to the declining size of the navy because of postponements and cancellations in new procurement projects at a time when the Second World War generation vessels were reaching the end of their normal service lives (see Korb, 1985, pp. 337–8). Nor was the attitudinal climate in the post-Vietnam years conducive to funding extensive ship construction. Overlapping in time with the US navy's decline in size, Soviet naval activities and fleet size visibly expanded leading to the usual disputes about the naval challenger's ultimate intentions and which side had more or better ships. Within this setting, the Reagan administration initiated a movement toward US naval expansion beginning with the 1983 fiscal year budget. Plans current at the time of this writing call for a projected 1989 force encompassing fifteen carriers, 100 nuclear attack submarines, forty-three ballistic missile submarines (twelve in the most recent Ohio class), and approximately 500 other ships (Breemer, 1983, pp. 30–1). At present, four fleets operate in the Atlantic (Second), eastern Pacific (Third), Mediterranean (Sixth), and western Pacific/Indian Ocean (Seventh), serviced by a network of some forty-four overseas bases of various sizes in 1983. Figure 8.3 shows the United States' relative capability share from 1816 to 1993, while Table 8.6 shows the estimated annual number of United States warships in the years 1816–60, and Table 8.7 shows the actual number of American battleships annually for the years 1861–1945.

Tables 8.8 and 8.12 inclusive, represent the annual calculations of the United States' evolving sea-launched ballistic missile and nuclear-attack submarine capabilities. In the Soviet case (see Chapter 9), the sketchy details on missile-refitting force the analyst to match the categorical number and type of warheads with the mix of submarine missile platforms (submarine classes). The more complete informa-

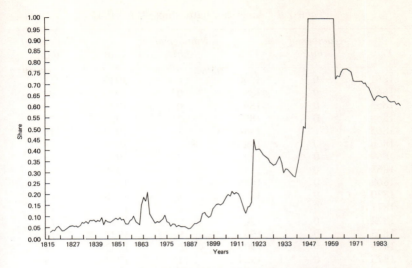

Figure 8.3   US relative capability share, 1816–1993

Table 8.6   United States' estimated annual number of warships, 1816–60

Year	Number of warships	Year	Number of warships	Year	Number of warships
1816	2	1831	5	1846	6
1817	2	1832	5	1847	6
1818	2	1833	5	1848	6
1819	3	1834	5	1849	6
1820	3	1835	5	1850	6
1821	3	1836	5	1851	6
1822	3	1837	5	1852	6
1823	3	1838	6	1853	6
1824	3	1839	6	1854	6
1825	4	1840	6	1855	6
1826	4	1841	7	1856	6
1827	4	1842	7	1857	5
1828	5	1843	6	1858	5
1829	5	1844	6	1859	5
1830	5	1845	6	1860	5

Source: US Department of the Navy (1969).

238 *Country Data*

Table 8.7   American battleships, 1861–1945

Year	Number of ships	Year	Number of ships	Year	Number of ships
1861	0	1890	0	1919	18
1862	0	1891	0	1920	20
1863	0	1892	0	1921	19
1864	0	1893	3	1922	21
1865	0	1894	3	1923	18
1866	0	1895	3	1924	18
1867	0	1896	3	1925	18
1868	0	1897	3	1926	18
1869	0	1898	3	1927	17
1870	0	1899	4	1928	17
1871	0	1900	8	1929	15
1872	0	1901	9	1930	15
1873	0	1902	9	1931	15
1874	0	1903	10	1932	15
1875	0	1904	11	1933	15
1876	0	1905	12	1934	15
1877	0	1906	15	1935	15
1878	0	1907	22	1936	15
1879	0	1908	20	1937	15
1880	0	1909	21	1938	15
1881	0	1910	4	1939	15
1882	0	1911	6	1940	15
1883	0	1912	8	1941	15
1884	0	1913	8	1942	19
1885	0	1914	10	1943	21
1886	0	1915	10	1944	25
1887	0	1916	14	1945	20
1888	0	1917	15		
1889	0	1918	17		

tion on American submarine missile conversion and MIRVing practices permits the analyst to concentrate directly on the type of missiles carried (Table 8.8). Table 8.9 then aggregates the number of warheads for each missile type. Next, each warhead type is associated with certain performance characteristics; Tables 8.10 and 8.11 aggregate equivalent megatonnage (EMT) and lethality (CMP) respectively. The following schedule was used to make the various calculations discussed in Chapter 4:

Table 8.8   United States nuclear ballistic submarines: multiple class estimates (according to the type of missiles carried) 1960–93

| | Polaris | | | | | |
Year	A-1	A-2	A-3	Poseidon	Trident*	Total
1960	3					3
1961	5	1				6
1962	5	4				9
1963	5	11				16
1964	5	13	11			29
1965	5	13	15			33
1966	2	13	25			40
1967		13	28			41
1968		13	28			41
1969		13	28			41
1970		8	29	4		41
1971		8	23	10		41
1972		8	17	16		41
1973		8	12	21		41
1974		5	13	23		41
1975		3	10	28		41
1976			13	28		41
1977			10	31		41
1978			10	31		41
1979			10	31		41
1980			5	31		36
1981			1	23	8/1	33
1982				19	12/2	33
1983				19	12/3	34
1984				19	12/4	35
1985				19	12/6	37
1986				16	12/8	36
1987				16	12/8	36
1988				13	12/8	33
1989				9	12/8/2	31
1990				5	12/8/3	28
1991				4	12/4/5	25
1992				2	12/6/7	27
1993				1	12/5/9	27

*The first number refers to submarines converted from Poseidon to Trident. The second number refers to Ohio class submarines with C-4 missiles. The third number refers to Ohio class submarines with D-5 missiles.

Table 8.9 United States nuclear ballistic submarines: warhead estimates, 1960–93

Year	Polaris			Poseidon	Trident	Total
	A-1	*A-2*	*A-3*			
1960	48					48
1961	80	16				96
1962	80	64				144
1963	80	176				256
1964	80	108	176			464
1965	80	208	240			528
1966	32	208	400			640
1967		208	448			656
1968		208	448			656
1969		208	448			656
1970		128	464	640		1232
1971		128	368	1600		2096
1972		128	272	2560		2960
1973		128	192	3360		3680
1974		80	208	3680		3968
1975		48	160	4480		4688
1976			208	4480		4688
1977			160	4960		5120
1978			160	4960		5120
1979			160	4960		5120
1980			80	4960		5040
1981			16	3680		4912
1982				3040	1920	4960
1983				3040	2112	5152
1984				3040	2304	5344
1985				3040	2688	5728
1986				2560	3072	5632
1987				2560	3072	5632
1988				2080	3072	5152
1989				1440	3456	4896
1990				800	3648	4448
1991				640	3264	3904
1992				320	4032	4352
1993				160	4224	4384

Table 8.10 United States nuclear ballistic submarines: warhead equivalent megatonnage estimates, 1960–93

| Year | Polaris | | | Poseidon | Trident | Total |
	A-1	*A-2*	*A-3*			
1960	41.4					41.4
1961	69.0	13.8				82.8
1962	69.0	55.2				124.2
1963	69.0	151.7				220.7
1964	69.0	179.3	60.2			308.5
1965	69.0	179.3	82.1			330.4
1966	27.6	179.3	136.8			343.7
1967		179.3	153.2			332.5
1968		179.3	153.2			332.5
1969		179.3	153.2			332.5
1970		110.3	158.7	74.9		343.9
1971		110.3	125.9	187.2		423.4
1972		110.3	93.0	299.5		502.8
1973		110.3	65.7	393.1		569.1
1974		69.0	71.1	430.6		510.7
1975		41.4	54.7	524.2		620.3
1976			71.1	524.2		595.3
1977			54.7	580.3		635.0
1978			54.7	580.3		635.0
1979			54.7	580.3		635.0
1980			27.4	580.3		607.7
1981			10.9	430.6	262.7	704.2
1982				355.7	414.7	770.4
1983				355.7	456.2	811.9
1984				355.7	497.7	853.4
1985				355.7	580.6	936.3
1986				299.5	663.6	963.1
1987				299.5	663.6	963.1
1988				243.4	663.6	907.0
1989				168.5	746.5	915.0
1990				93.6	788.0	881.6
1991				74.9	829.5	904.4
1992				37.4	870.9	908.3
1993				18.7	912.4	931.1

242

Table 8.11   United States nuclear ballistic submarines: warhead lethality estimates, 1960–93 (counter military potential)

| | Polaris | | | | | |
Year	A-1	A-2	A-3	Poseidon	Trident	Total
1960	165.5					165.5
1961	275.8	55.2				331.0
1962	275.8	220.7				496.5
1963	275.8	606.9				882.7
1964	275.8	717.2	240.8			1233.8
1965	275.8	717.2	328.8			1321.3
1966	110.3	717.2	547.2			1374.7
1967		717.2	612.9			1330.1
1968		717.2	612.9			1330.1
1969		717.2	612.9			1330.1
1970		441.3	634.8	1198.1		2274.2
1971		441.3	503.4	2995.2		3939.9
1972		441.3	372.1	4792.3		5605.7
1973		441.3	262.7	6289.9		6993.9
1974		275.8	284.5	6889.0		7449.3
1975		165.5	218.9	8386.6		8771.0
1976			284.7	8386.6		8671.3
1977			218.9	9285.1		9504.0
1978			218.9	9285.1		9504.0
1979			218.9	9285.1		9504.0
1980			109.4	9285.1		9394.5
1981			21.9	6889.0	4202.5	11113.4
1982				5690.9	6635.5	12326.4
1983				5690.9	7299.1	12990.0
1984				5690.9	7962.6	13653.5
1985				5690.9	9289.7	14980.6
1986				4792.3	10616.8	15409.1
1987				4792.3	10616.8	15409.1
1988				3893.8	10616.8	14510.6
1989				2695.7	14303.2	16998.9
1990				1497.6	16146.4	17644.0
1991				1198.1	19169.3	20367.4
1992				599.0	22192.1	22791.1
1993				299.5	25215.0	25514.5

Missile type	Number of warheads	Yield (megatonnage)	Accuracy (CEP)
Polaris A-1	16	0.80	0.50
Polaris A-2	16	0.80	0.50
Polaris A-3	16	0.20	0.50
Poseidon	160	0.04	0.25
Trident I (C-4)			
conversions	128	0.10	0.25
Ohio class	192	0.10	0.25
Trident II (D-5)	192	0.10	0.15

In order to project American naval capabilities to 1993, a few assumptions need to be made. Carrier and submarine construction plans require several years for completion and do not represent information that is particularly difficult to obtain. Thus, one assumption is that the publicly announced construction schedules will be maintained. Retirement schedules also tend to be known in advance although there is a tendency to stretch them out whenever feasible. To date, retired ballistic missile submarines have not been converted to attack submarine duties. We assume that this practice will continue. We also assume a 25-year life for attack submarines and 30 years for ballistic missile submarines. Somewhat conservatively perhaps, we anticipate that only one carrier (the *Coral Sea* – scheduled to become a training ship in 1991) will be removed from front-line duties prior to 1993.

Ignoring the possibility that construction plans might be either accelerated or cut back in the near future, projecting the size of the United States' submarine fleet is a fairly straightforward numerical exercise with one exception. The unratified SALT II documents impose a limitation of 1200 MIRVed missile-launchers on both sides. The deployment of new Trident submarines will require adjustments elsewhere if the United States decision-makers choose to avoid violating the launcher ceiling. This will be all the more true if the United States proceeds with the deployment of the Peace Keeper ICBM system (fifty to 100 launchers between 1987 and 1990). While American forces did exceed the launcher ceiling in November 1986, we assume that adjustments will continue to be made and that the primary point of adjustment will be the aging ballistic missile submarines of the James Madison and Los Angeles classes (armed with Poseidon missiles) which will be retired, as they eventually would be in any event, as new Tridents are commissioned. The rate of

244 *Country Data*

retirement (see Table 8.8) will be governed by the 550 to 650 MIRVed launchers (subtracting Minuteman and the anticipated Peace Keeper launchers) ostensibly available for SLBM purposes. Table 8.12 gives the numbers of US nuclear-attack submarines annually, from 1954 to 1993.

Table 8.12   United States nuclear-attack submarines, 1954–93

Year	Number	Year	Number	Year	Number
1954	1	1968	36	1982	88
1955	1	1969	43	1983	89
1956	1	1970	46	1984	86
1957	3	1971	53	1985	88
1958	5	1972	57	1986	87
1959	7	1973	59	1987	87
1960	8	1974	62	1988	89
1961	14	1975	64	1989	85
1962	17	1976	64	1990	88
1963	17	1977	67	1991	89
1964	21	1978	72	1992	90
1965	22	1979	71	1993	91
1966	25	1980	74		
1967	31	1981	83		

9 The Other Global Powers: France, Spain, Russia/the Soviet Union, Germany, and Japan

The last two chapters have described the winners in the 500-year struggle for naval predominance and political-military ascendancy in the global system. In the present chapter, the focus shifts to the 'also-ran' competitors for global power – France, Spain, Russia/the Soviet Union, Germany, and Japan – who lost or – at least in the case of the Soviet Union – who have yet to win their struggles with the world powers. We shall consider in order of 'seniority' defined as 'years in global status' between 1494 and 1983: France (451); Spain (315); Russia/the USSR (232); Germany (75); and Japan (75). As in Chapter 8, the emphasis will be placed on generating brief synopses of national naval developments as a prelude to the provision of more detailed information on each global power's annual number of capital warships

Two themes are common to the naval experiences of these states: (i) the variability of their commitment to global reach via seapower, and (ii) the notable impact each had in their own time and place. The variability is a function of fluctuations in long-range national interest in, and priorities given to, global maritime enterprise. For France it was the perennial dilemma of continental versus maritime policy. For Spain, it was the choice between a Mediterranean or an oceanic strategy; for Russia, the varying drives toward the open sea, punctuated by a string of continental invasions; for Germany and Japan, a short burst of activity between 1900 and 1945, subject in itself to the conflicting pulls of military versus naval priorities, and preceded by long periods of deliberate non-commitment and even isolation.

But even granted this variability if not volatility of interest in seapower, the impact of it all was nonetheless there, and at times quite notable. French naval architecture and quality of naval organisation, for instance, were frequently superior to that of Britain's Royal Navy. Spain's ability to maintain the sinews of empire through its far-flung system of bases and maritime convoys was strikingly effective. Ger-

246   *Country Data*

man and Japanese technical innovation in such fields as submarine warfare or aircraft-carrier operations were notable too. Even an obviously continental power such as Russia/the USSR has now succeeded in mounting a credible global challenge both on the sea and in space.

The net upshot of these two themes is a number of initial victories and tactical successes in global wars (e.g. Spain in the Azores, 1582–3; France's unexploited victory at Beachy Head, 1690; Germany's lead in submarine warfare in 1917 and 1941–2; or Japan's victories in 1941–2) or else victories against non-global powers (as in Russia's defeats of the Ottoman Empire or Sweden), but also a string of major defeats and few decisive victories. We shall follow these two themes throughout this entire chapter.

FRANCE

Prior to the advent of industrialisation in the late eighteenth/early nineteenth centuries, France's population size, national wealth, and apparent access to the Atlantic Ocean should have boded well for eventual French pre-eminence in the jockeying for world power. That global pre-eminence was never achieved can be attributed in part to the oscillations in French regional and global priorities. France may easily be the best example of a global power whose 'drives wobbled' between continental and maritime aspirations to the very clear detriment of its often interrupted development of seapower.

With Genoese help France acquired a royal fleet by the late thirteenth century, but for several centuries its resources were oriented primarily to Mediterranean galleys. In the sixteenth century (e.g., in 1545, 1557–9), relatively large ocean-going fleets were assembled periodically for action in the wars against the Habsburgs, when occasionally England was also an opponent. But they represented only temporary augmentations of a very small state fleet and were used primarily to ferry troops and supplies from one point to another and for the occasional sea battle in which the soldiers of one ship fought the soldiers of another ship. But during the civil wars after 1560, the French navy disappeared for all practical purposes. French maritime exploits of this period, as a consequence, were organised along private or quasi-private lines. French harassment of Spain's treasure fleets in the Caribbean and Atlantic since the 1520s by privateers, based in Dieppe among other places is one early example.

France, Spain, Russia, Germany, Japan

After 1568, and based in French sea ports, the Huguenots – one of whose leaders was Gaspar de Coligny, the Admiral of France – gave valuable help to the Sea Beggars, the original nucleus of the Dutch navy. Filippo Strozzi's attempt to intervene with a fairly large fleet in the revolt of the Azores against Spain, and his defeat in the battle of Tercerra (1582–3), is another example.

A sea-going royal fleet did not re-emerge until the 1620s with the ascension to power of Cardinal Richelieu. Richelieu, who served as first minister from 1624 to 1642, was an advocate of seapower for global purposes but he was also faced with more local problems – North African piracy and a Huguenot revolt centred at La Rochelle (a principal sea port situated on the Atlantic coast) – which required maritime solutions as well. Confronted with an absence of ships, little in the way of naval organisational infrastructure, and difficulties in even obtaining access to the Atlantic, Richelieu was forced to create a French navy from scratch. The first six ships, purchased abroad in 1624, were captured by Huguenot rebels a year later and prompted the French to seek naval assistance from the Netherlands and England. The coastal access problem, a legacy of feudalism, was resolved by Richelieu's purchase of the traditional Admiralty offices of Brittany, Guyenne, Provence, and France. Prior to this time, the incumbents had been more preoccupied with the commercial aspects of their inherited positions (e.g. customs collections) than contributing to the maritime capabilities of the French state. In addition, naval bases were established at Brest, Brouage, Le Havre (the principal shipbuilding yard), and Toulon under the centralised authority of the *Surintendant de la Marine* – an office initially occupied by Richelieu himself. More ships were also acquired from Dutch shipyards.

Ironically and with the benefit of considerable hindsight, starting with very little gave Richelieu and his naval-reform successors at least one advantage. Essentially, the absence of a merchant marine, a pool of experienced manpower, and an entrenched naval tradition were 'traded' for the freedom to take the lead in warship design:

> In general it can be observed that Richelieu experienced less difficulties in building up the material side of the navy – than in developing crews which were suited to modern ships and naval battles. This phenomenon was to determine the destiny of the French navy from the time of Richelieu to the fall of the *Ancien Régime*. The material side of the navy was usually excellently tended and in this respect the French fairly quickly established a definite lead on their direct rivals

248 *Country Data*

... This lead even went so far that these rivals began to imitate the French ships and had to admit their superior sailing qualities. On a material level one can thus speak of 'the benefit of lag'. Richelieu had to build up the French navy from scratch and in this was not hampered – as far as the ships were concerned – by all sorts of considerations as to sea trade and available merchant ships. The ships of the French [navy] could thus immediately be designed and built purely as warships (Teitler, 1977, p. 106).

Nevertheless, the impressive foundation created by Richelieu was permitted to decay for the next thirty-five years. The royal fleet did not disappear this time but Richelieu's successors were reluctant to provide adequate financial support, particularly in an era of political confusion and a lack of centralised state leadership. The fortunes of the French navy were revived only after Louis XIV came to power and in 1663, appointed Colbert to administer marine policy, in addition to policies concerning commerce, finance, and colonies. Colbert's mercantilistic programmes clearly required a strong navy and the changes introduced by Colbert brought about what may have been France's best chance to win the leadership of the global system. Non-French shipbuilders were imported and the size of the fleet was expanded at a rapid pace. The ports established by Richelieu were rebuilt and improved. Brouage was replaced by Rochefort, and Dunkirk was added to the network of home bases. A system to draft seamen, the supply of whom was and continued to be an important problem, was established in the late 1660s. Other hallmarks of organisational specialisation (an artillery corps, marines, naval medicine) were also introduced in the 1670s.

The pattern of isolated surges of interest in maritime matters was continued by Colbert's successors. Despite some early successes, the naval dimension of the wars of Louis XIV was resolved by the French defeat at La Hogue in 1692 at the hands of an English–Dutch fleet. After this failure, the French fleet was essentially restricted to its own ports in order that scarce resources could be concentrated on the army's continental campaigns. Fleet actions were replaced by the strategy of commercial raiding (*guerre de course*) to be carried out predominantly by privateers. In the second phase of the global war of 1688–1713, the French navy was again sent to sea briefly and inconclusively (1704), only to be subordinated once again to the less-expensive commerce-raiding activities.

The inability to finance the French state adequately, which became

France, Spain, Russia, Germany, Japan 249

so obvious in wartime, continued to characterise French naval policies after 1714, with predictable consequences for building, commissioning, and arming ships-of-the-line. Compounding the scarcity of financial resources were the burdens imposed by rivalries between noble and non-noble officers, the schisms between land-based naval administrators and sea-going line officers, and the tradition of incompetent and uninspired leadership. As a consequence, the French navy's greatest eighteenth-century handicap, aside from acute material shortages and the usual problems with priorities, may well have been a shortage of experience and talent. For much of the first two-thirds of the century, the navy could neither afford to practice fleet manoeuvres during peace-time nor was it permitted the opportunity to gain much experience during wartime. Financial problems and strategic priorities repeatedly intervened to emphasise the perceived luxury of maintaining a competitive naval force at sea.

The next surge in naval reform, led by Choiseul and others, took place between the Seven Years War and the War of American Independence – which may help to explain why the French navy was more successful in the latter war than in most of its other encounters with Great Britain. Older ports were rebuilt. Cherbourg had become a base in the late 1750s; Lorient was added in 1770. The rivalries between naval bureaucrats and line officers were ameliorated by cutting back the power of the naval bureaucracy and later by abolishing them altogether as a separate entity. Particularly important was the renewed availability of money for shipbuilding.

This forward momentum in organisational rebuilding was cut short by the French Revolution. Discipline eroded, sailors mutinied, noble officers were executed or encouraged to leave the service and the country. Inconsistent administrative leadership was supplied by a series of under-financed Revolutionary governments with fairly predictable results. Naval reform was again attempted when Napoleon came to power but, unlike earlier efforts, it was being tried during (as opposed to before or after) global warfare. After the Trafalgar defeat (1805), fleet encounters with the enemy were again avoided, despite continued shipbuilding, in favour of the customary fall-back position of commerce raiding.

The peace terms of 1814 insisted upon a sizeable reduction in the number of ships-of-the-line maintained by the French but this setback proved to be less than disastrous, given the small squadrons actually needed for the type of maritime fighting typical of the period prior to the Crimean War. Although less than half the fleet may have been

250 *Country Data*

capable of going to sea in any given year, the French navy still managed to see action in and around southern Europe, Madagascar, North Africa, and Central/South America. Most of the Crimean fighting was concentrated in the Black Sea area but some clashes also took place in the Baltic and Pacific. Even so, troop movements and naval bombardments of land fortifications as opposed to fleet encounters characterised much of this combat. In any event, the use of exploding shells in the Crimean War ended the military utility of wooden-hulled sailing ships.

In the evolution toward the battleship, France actually scored a short-lived lead in naval technology by launching the armoured and steam-powered *La Gloire* (1859). This explicit attempt to gain a naval edge on the traditional rival, Great Britain, seriously underestimated British industrial capabilities and France's own fluctuating interest in maritime developments. After 1871, that interest again faded for a variety of reasons including the low profile of the navy in the Franco-Prussian War.

Continental interests and priorities predominated in much of the period leading up to the First World War. But despite governmental instability, restraints on naval expenditures, and a strategic quarrel within naval circles over whether to invest in battleships or smaller ships to be used for commerce raiding, a few organisational advances were realised. The naval-base network was expanded by developing port facilities of various magnitude in Bizerta, Ajaccio, Algiers, Oran, and Saigon. The *Ecole Supérieure de Marine* was founded in 1896. France also developed an early lead in submarine forces. Nevertheless, the First World War began before the French had been able to respond significantly to the British introduction of the Dreadnought (1906) and, partially as a consequence, the French navy was relegated to an auxiliary role, primarily in the Mediterranean theatre.

Naval needs in the period immediately after the First World War continued to receive little attention. However, a naval staff was finally brought into being. More bases (Casablanca, Dakar, Diego Suarez, Port Lyautey) were established or developed. But France's naval status in the 1920s was frozen by the naval disarmament conferences, at a level well behind Great Britain, the United States, and Japan. While resented, it was not a wholly inaccurate assessment of the French naval position or even its probable potential for expansion. Naval rearmament did receive some attention in the 1930s enabling France to enter the Second World War in a better position than it had possessed immediately prior to the First World War. However, in

Table 9.1　Sources for French warships, 1494–1860

Almanach de Gotha	Lamontagne (1966)
Anderson (1961)	LAF-L'Ancienne France (1888)
Barfleur (1907)	Lavisse (1911)
Bartlett (1963)	Le Conte (1932, 1935)
Block (1875)	Lloyd (1965a, 1965b)
Bouchard (1971)	Loir (1893)
Bouret de Cresse (1824)	Lublinskaya (1968)
Brenton (1823–5)	Mahan (1890, 1892)
Bromley and Ryan (1971)	Margry (1879a, 1879b)
Bruun (1963)	Mariejol (1911)
Busk (1859)	Masson and Muracciole (1968)
Carré (1911)	Memain (1936)
Chalmers (1794)	Ministère de la Marine (1838)
Charnock (1800–3)	Moreau de Jonnes (1835)
Chasseriau (1845)	Neuville (1977)
Clark (1970a, 1970b)	Nicolas (1949, 1958, 1973)
Clowes (1897–1903)	Oppenheim (1961)
Cobden (1862)	Owen (1938)
Cole (1964)	Parry (1971)
Cooper (1970)	Pemsel (1977)
Cowburn (1965)	Penn (1913)
DeNervo (1865)	Perkins (1971)
Dorn (1963)	Pontalis (1885)
Dupuy and Dupuy (1977)	Reussner and Nicolas (1963)
Dutot (1739)	Reynolds (1974)
Edler (1911)	Richmond (1946, 1953)
Ehrman (1953)	Roncière, de la (1909–32)
Fuller (1955)	Rose (1921a, 1921b)
Gaxotte (1970)	Silburn (1912)
Grant (1908)	Southworth (1968)
Gravière (1879)	Stevens and Westcott (1943)
Hampson (1959)	Sue (1835)
Hanotaux (1932)	Symcox (1974)
Headlam (1921)	Tapie (1975)
Innes (1931)	Thomazi (1950)
James (1886)	Tracy (1975)
Jenkins (1973)	Treasure (1966)
Jonge, de (1869)	Vecchj (1895)
Jouan (1950)	Vovard (1948)
Lacour-Gayet (1902, 1905, 1911)	Wilson (1904, 1936)

252

Table 9.2   France's estimated annual number of warships, 1494–1860

Year	Number of warships	Sources on numbers of warships
1494	1	'0' (Le Conte, 1932)
1495	3	'2' (Le Conte, 1932)
1496	3	'2' (Le Conte, 1932)
1497	3	'2' (Le Conte, 1932)
1498	3	'2' (Le Conte, 1932)
1499	3	'2' (Le Conte, 1932)
1500	6	'4' (Le Conte, 1932)
1501	3	'3' (Le Conte, 1932)
1502	5	'2' (Le Conte, 1932)
1503	6	'3' (Le Conte, 1932)
1504	7	'3' (Le Conte, 1932)
1505	8	'3' (Le Conte, 1932)
1506	8	'2' (Le Conte, 1932)
1507	9	'2' (Le Conte, 1932)
1508	10	'2' (Le Conte, 1932)
1509	12	'2' (Le Conte, 1932)
1510	12	'2' (Le Conte, 1932)
1511	12	'2' (Le Conte, 1932)
1512	18	'4' (Le Conte, 1932)
1513	18	'5' (Le Conte, 1932)
1514	14	'3' (Le Conte, 1932)
1515	13	'2' (Le Conte, 1932)
1516	12	'2' (Le Conte, 1932)
1517	14	'5' (Le Conte, 1932)
1518	12	'4' (Le Conte, 1932)
1519	13	'4' (Le Conte, 1932)
1520	12	'5' (Le Conte, 1932)
1521	12	'4' (Le Conte, 1932)
1522	14	'6' (Le Conte, 1932)
1523	12	'4' (Le Conte, 1932)
1524	14	'5' (Le Conte, 1932)
1525	14	'5' (Le Conte, 1932)
1526	13	'5' (Le Conte, 1932)
1527	10	'3' (Le Conte, 1932)
1528	11	'4' (Le Conte, 1932)
1529	8	'3' (Le Conte, 1932)
1530	8	'3' (Le Conte, 1932)
1531	7	'2' (Le Conte, 1932)
1532	9	'4' (Le Conte, 1932)
1533	7	'2' (Le Conte, 1932)
1534	6	'1' (Le Conte, 1932)
1535	8	'3' (Le Conte, 1932)
1536	6	'1' (Le Conte, 1932)

Table 9.2   France's estimated annual number of warships, 1494–1860

Year	Number of warships	Sources on numbers of warships
1537	6	'1' (Le Conte, 1932)
1538	7	'1' (Le Conte, 1932)
1539	6	'1' (Le Conte, 1932)
1540	7	'1' (Le Conte, 1932)
1541	6	'1' (Le Conte, 1932)
1542	7	'1' (Le Conte, 1932)
1543	7	'1' (Le Conte, 1932)
1544	6	'0' (Le Conte, 1932)
1545	6	'0' (Le Conte, 1932)
1546	8	'1' (Le Conte, 1932)
1547	8	'2' (Le Conte, 1932)
1548	9	'3' (Le Conte, 1932)
1549	12	'5' (Le Conte, 1932)
1550	14	'7' (Le Conte, 1932)
1551	12	'4' (Le Conte, 1932)
1552	11	'4' (Le Conte, 1932)
1553	11	'4' (Le Conte, 1932)
1554	10	'3' (Le Conte, 1932)
1555	11	'5' (Le Conte, 1932)
1556	10	'3' (Le Conte, 1932)
1557	10	'3' (Le Conte, 1932)
1558	13	'6' (Le Conte, 1932)
1559	9	'3' (Le Conte, 1932)
1560	10	'4' (Le Conte, 1932)
1561	9	'3' (Le Conte, 1932)
1562	7	'2' (Le Conte, 1932)
1563	7	'2' (Le Conte, 1932)
1564	7	'2' (Le Conte, 1932)
1565	9	'4' (Le Conte, 1932)
1566	8	'3' (Le Conte, 1932)
1567	8	'2' (Le Conte, 1932)
1568	10	'4' (Le Conte, 1932)
1569	11	'5' (Le Conte, 1932)
1570	13	'6' (Le Conte, 1932)
1571	11	'4' (Le Conte, 1932)
1572	11	'4' (Le Conte, 1932)
1573	12	'5' (Le Conte, 1932)
1574	9	'2' (Le Conte, 1932)
1575	10	'3' (Le Conte, 1932)
1576	10	'3' (Le Conte, 1932)
1577	9	'3' (Le Conte, 1932)
1578	8	'3' (Le Conte, 1932)
1579	2	'2' (Le Conte, 1932)

254

Table 9.2 France's estimated annual number of warships, 1494–1860

Year	Number of warships	Sources on numbers of warships
1580	2	'2' (Le Conte, 1932)
1581	2	'2' (Le Conte, 1932)
1582	2	'2' (Le Conte, 1932)
1583	2	'2' (Le Conte, 1932)
1584	2	'2' (Le Conte, 1932)
1585	2	'2' (Le Conte, 1932)
1586	2	'2' (Le Conte, 1932)
1587	0	'0' (Le Conte, 1932)
1588	0	'0' (Le Conte, 1932)
1589	0	'0' (Le Conte, 1932)
1590	0	'0' (Le Conte, 1932)
1591	0	'0' (Le Conte, 1932)
1592	0	'0' (Le Conte, 1932)
1593	0	'0' (Le Conte, 1932)
1594	0	'0' (Le Conte, 1932)
1595	0	'0' (Le Conte, 1932)
1596	0	'0' (Le Conte, 1932)
1597	0	'0' (Le Conte, 1932)
1598	0	'0' (Le Conte, 1932)
1599	0	'0' (Le Conte, 1932)
1600	0	'0' (Le Conte, 1932)
1601	0	'0' (Le Conte, 1932)
1602	0	'0' (Le Conte, 1932)
1603	0	'0' (Le Conte, 1932); 0 armed (LAF, 1888)
1604	0	'0' (Le Conte, 1932); 0 armed (LAF, 1888)
1605	0	'0' (Le Conte, 1932); 0 armed (LAF, 1888)
1606	0	'0' (Le Conte, 1932); 0 armed (LAF, 1888)
1607	0	'0' (Le Conte, 1932); 0 armed (LAF, 1888)
1608	0	'0' (Le Conte, 1932); 0 armed (LAF, 1888)
1609	0	'0' (Le Conte, 1932); 0 armed (LAF, 1888)
1610	0	'0' (Le Conte, 1932); Tapie, 1975); 0 armed (LAF, 1888)
1611	0	'0' (Le Conte, 1932); 0 armed (LAF, 1888)
1612	0	'0' (Le Conte, 1932); 0 armed (LAF, 1888)
1613	0	'0' (Le Conte, 1932); 0 armed (LAF, 1888)
1614	0	'0' (Le Conte, 1932); 0 armed (LAF, 1888)
1615	0	'0' (Le Conte, 1932; Penn, 1913); 0 armed (LAF, 1888)
1616	0	'0' (Le Conte, 1932); 0 armed (LAF, 1888)
1617	0	'0' (Le Conte, 1932); 0 armed (LAF, 1888)
1618	0	'0' (Le Conte, 1932); 0 armed (LAF, 1888)
1619	4	'4' (Le Conte, 1932); 0 armed (LAF, 1888)
1620	5	'5' (Le Conte, 1932); 0 armed (LAF, 1888)

255

Table 9.2 France's estimated annual number of warships, 1494–1860

Year	Number of warships	Sources on numbers of warships
1621	9	'9' (Le Conte, 1932); 0 armed (LAF, 1888)
1622	16	'16' (Le Conte, 1932); 0 armed (LAF, 1888)
1623	16	'16' (Le Conte, 1932); 0 armed (LAF, 1888)
1624	16	'16' (Le Conte, 1932); 0 armed (LAF, 1888; Tapie, 1975)
1625	15	'15' (Le Conte, 1932); 0 (Lublinskaya, 1968)
1626	16	'16' (Le Conte, 1932); 5 (Cowburn, 1965); 4 (Oppenheim, 1961); 0 (de la Gravière, 1879)
1627	24	'24' (Le Conte, 1932)
1628	34	'34' (Le Conte, 1932); 30 (Nicolas, 1958); 25 (Perkins, 1971)
1629	39	'39' (Le Conte, 1932); 0 (Treasure, 1966)
1630	37	'37' (Le Conte, 1932); 40 (Oppenheim, 1961)
1631	37	'37' (Le Conte, 1932); 43 (Penn, 1913); 39 (Oppenheim, 1961; Richmond, 1946)
1632	37	'37' (Le Conte, 1932)
1633	37	'37' (Le Conte, 1932)
1634	37	'37' (Le Conte, 1932)
1635	36	'36' (Le Conte, 1932); 51 (Vovard, 1948); 46 (Nicolas, 1958); 35 (Lublinskaya, 1968; Cooper, 1970; Cole, 1964)
1636	35	'35' (Le Conte, 1932); 51 (Jenkins, 1973; Lacour-Gayet, 1911); 39 (Mariejol, 1911); 35 (Cole, 1964)
1637	39	'39' (Le Conte, 1932); 41 (Loir, 1893); 38 (Cowburn, 1965)
1638	39	'39' (Le Conte, 1932); 41 (Lacour-Gayet, 1911; Tapie, 1975)
1639	39	'39' (Le Conte, 1932; Lacour-Gayet, 1911)
1640	34	'34' (Le Conte, 1932); 76 (Perkins, 1971)
1641	32	'32' (Le Conte, 1932)
1642	32	'32' (Le Conte, 1932); 85 (Perkins, 1971); 65 (Treasure, 1966; Mariejol, 1911; Nicolas, 1973); 63 (Lacour-Gayet, 1911; Memain, 1936; Nicolas, 1958; Jenkins, 1973; Hanotaux, 1932; Perkins, 1971)
1643	32	'32' (Le Conte, 1932); 24 (Rose, 1921a)
1644	32	'32' (Le Conte, 1932); 22 (de la Roncière, 1909–32)
1645	34	'34' (Le Conte, 1932)
1646	37	'37' (Le Conte, 1932)
1647	37	'37' (Le Conte, 1932); 22 (Mahan, 1890)
1648	35	'35' (Le Conte, 1932); '42' w/guns/'22' [1–5] (Le Conte, 1935); 40–2 (de la Roncière, 1909–32)

256

Table 9.2 France's estimated annual number of warships, 1494–1860

Year	Number of warships	Sources on numbers of warships
1649	35	'35' (Le Conte, 1932); '39' w/guns/'20' [1–5] (Le Conte, 1935); 30 (LAF, 1888)
1650	35	'35' (Le Conte, 1932); '31' w/guns/'16' [1–5] (Le Conte, 1935)
1651	31	'31' (Le Conte, 1932); '30' w/guns/'18' [1–5] (Le Conte, 1935); 25 (Ehrman, 1953); 20 (Bromley and Ryan, 1971); [2–3] (de la Roncière, 1909–32)
1652	27	'27' (Le Conte, 1932); '30' w/guns/'18' [1–5] (Le Conte, 1935); 30 (Charnock, 1800–3; Jenkins, 1973); [2–3] (de la Roncière, 1909–32)
1653	27	'27' (Le Conte, 1932); '29' w/guns/'18' [1–5] (Le Conte, 1935); [2–3] (Lavisse, 1911; de la Roncière, 1909–32)
1654	26	'26' (Le Conte, 1932); '29' w/guns/'18' [1–5] (Le Conte, 1935); [2–3] (Lavisse, 1911; de la Roncière, 1909–32)
1655	25	'25' (Le Conte, 1932); '18' [1–5] (Le Conte, 1935); [2–3] (Lavisse, 1911; de la Roncière, 1909–32)
1656	28	'28' (Le Conte, 1932); '19' [1–5] (Le Conte, 1935); [2–3] (Lavisse, 1911; de la Roncière, 1909–32)
1657	29	'29' (Le Conte, 1932); '20' [1–5] (Le Conte, 1935); [2–3] (Lavisse, 1911; de la Roncière, 1909–32)
1658	30	'30' (Le Conte, 1932); '20' [1–5] (Le Conte, 1935); [2–3] (Lavisse, 1911; de la Roncière, 1909–32)
1659	30	'30' (Le Conte, 1932); '21' [1–5] (Le Conte, 1935); 18 (Loir, 1893); [2–3] (Lavisse, 1911; de la Roncière, 1909–32)
1660	33	'33' (Le Conte, 1932); '21' [1–5] (Le Conte, 1935); 30 (Innes, 1931); [2–3] (Lavisse, 1911; de la Roncière, 1909–32)
1661	25	'25' (Le Conte, 1932); '25' [1–5] (Le Conte, 1935); 30 (Mahan, 1890); 22 (Perkins, 1971); 20 (Vovard, 1948; Reynolds, 1974; Oppenheim, 1961); 20/[2–3]/18 w/30+ (Nicolas, 1958); 18 (de la Roncière, 1909–32; Cole, 1964); 16 w/30+ (Memain, 1936); [8] (LAF, 1888); [2–3] (Lavisse, 1911; de la Roncière, 1909–32)
1662	28	'28' (Le Conte, 1932); '26' [1–5] (Le Conte, 1935); 17 (Memain, 1936)
1663	29	'29' (Le Conte, 1932); '28' [1–5] (Le Conte, 1935); '20–22'/[2–3] (Lavisse, 1911); 20 (Memain, 1936)
1664	30	'30' (Le Conte, 1932); '34' [1–5] (Le Conte, 1935); 25 (Memain, 1936); [0] (Charnock, 1800–3)

257

Table 9.2   France's estimated annual number of warships, 1494–1860

Year	Number of warships	Sources on numbers of warships
1665	39	'39' (Le Conte, 1932); '43' [1–5] (Le Conte, 1935); 32 (Memain, 1936)
1666	51	'51' (Le Conte, 1932); '43' [1–5] (Le Conte, 1935); '130' (Richmond, 1953); 70 (Loir, 1893); 55 (Memain, 1936); 50 (Mahan, 1890); 40 (Bouchard, 1971); 34 (Nicolas, 1958)
1667	61	'61' (Le Conte, 1932); '64' [1–5] (Le Conte, 1935); 110 (Pontalis, 1885); 93 (Cowburn, 1965); 64 (Memain, 1936)
1668	70	'70' (Le Conte, 1932); '72' [1–5] (Le Conte, 1935); 78 (Memain, 1936)
1669	76	'76' (Le Conte, 1932); '81' [1–5] (Le Conte, 1935); 158 [1–5] (Ehrman, 1953); 119 (LAF, 1888); '20'/[2–3] (Grant, 1908); 20 (Treasure, 1966); 8 (Gaxotte, 1970)
1670	99	'99' (Le Conte, 1932); '99' [1–5] (Le Conte, 1935); 121 [1–5] (Vecchj, 1895); 120 [1–5] (Nicolas, 1949); 116 [1–5]/Bouchard, 1971); 12 (Gaxotte, 1970)
1671	81	'81' (Le Conte, 1932); '108' [1–5]/'82' [1–4] (Le Conte, 1935); 196 (Mahan, 1890); 119 (Chasseriau, 1845)
1672	83	'83' (Le Conte, 1932); '113' [1–5]/'85' [1–4] (Le Conte, 1935); 120 (Pontalis, 1885); 50 (Charnock, 1800–3); 36 (Silburn, 1912)
1673	86	'86' (Le Conte, 1932); '112' [1–5]/'86' [1–4] (Le Conte, 1935); 196 (Mahan, 1890)
1674	87	'87' (Le Conte, 1932); '112' [1–5]/'88' [1–4] (Le Conte, 1935)
1675	90	'90' (Le Conte, 1932); '116' [1–5]/'91' [1–4] (Le Conte, 1935)
1676	86	'86' (Le Conte, 1932); '110' [1–5]/'89' [1–4] (Le Conte, 1935)
1677	84	'84' (Le Conte, 1932); '105' [1–5]/'85' [1–4] (Le Conte, 1935); 270 (Reynolds, 1974); 116 [1–5]/90 [1–4] (de la Roncière, 1909–32; Lavisse, 1911; Cole, 1964)
1678	79	'79' (Le Conte, 1932); '102' [1–5]/'83' [1–4] (Le Conte, 1935); 128 [1–4] (Ehrman, 1953); 113 (Chasseriau, 1845); 104 (Sue, 1835)
1679	83	'83' (Le Conte, 1932); '110' [1–5]/'87' [1–4] (Le Conte, 1935)
1680	86	'86' (Le Conte, 1932); '109' [1–5]/'88' [1–4] (Le Conte, 1935); 100 + (Bouret de Cresse, 1824)

258

Table 9.2 France's estimated annual number of warships, 1494–1860

Year	Number of warships	Sources on numbers of warships
1681	84	'84' (Le Conte, 1932); '109' [1–5]/'87' [1–4] (Le Conte, 1935); [115] [1–5]/95 [1–4] (Dutot, 1739; Charnock, 1800–3; Vecchj, 1895); 100+ (Bouret de Cresse, 1824)
1682	85	'85' (Le Conte, 1932); '112' [1–5]/'91' [1–4] (Le Conte, 1935); 120 (Margry, 1879a); 100+ (Bouret de Cresse, 1824)
1683	90	'90' (Le Conte, 1932); '116' [1–5]/'95' [1–4] (Le Conte, 1935); 117 [1–5]/86 [1–4] (de la Roncière, 1909–32); 117 [1–5] (Symcox, 1974); 107 w/24+ (Mahan, 1890)
1684	91	'91' (Le Conte, 1932); '117' [1–5]/'96' [1–4] (Le Conte, 1935)
1685	89	'89' (Le Conte, 1932); '117' [1–5]/'96' [1–4] (Le Conte, 1935); 120 w/50+ (Nicolas, 1949, 1958); 121 (Chasseriau, 1845); 96 (1–4) (Memain, 1936)
1686	88	'88' (Le Conte, 1932); '112' [1–5]/'91' [1–4] (Le Conte, 1935); [.705] (Symcox, 1974)
1687	89	'89' (Le Conte, 1932); '113' [1–5]/'91' [1–4] (Le Conte, 1935); 120 (Mahan, 1890)
1688	92	'92' (Le Conte, 1932); '113' [1–5]/'92' (Le Conte, 1935); '130'/[118] [1–5] (Symcox, 1974); 118 (Vovard, 1948); 99 [1–4] (Memain, 1936); 93 [1–4] (Ehrman, 1953); 80 (Richmond, 1953)
1689	96	'96' (Le Conte, 1932); '108' [1–5]/'86' [1–4] (Le Conte, 1935); 200 (Reynolds, 1974); 113 [1–4] (Bromley and Ryan, 1971); [96] (Charnock, 1800–3); 80 (Clark, 1970a, Pemsel, 1977)
1690	100	'100' (Le Conte, 1932); '106' [1–5]/'88' [1–4] (Le Conte, 1935); 120 (Chasseriau, 1845); 105 (Ehrman, 1953); 96 (Charnock, 1800–3); 105 [1–4]/129 [1–5] (Neuville, 1977); 105 [1–4] (Lacour-Gayet, 1902)
1691	114	'114' (Le Conte, 1932); '121' [1–5]/'105' [1–4]/'87' [1–3] (Le Conte, 1935); 96 (Charnock, 1800–3)
1692	115	'115' (Le Conte, 1932); '117' [1–5]/'100' [1–4]/'81' [1–3] (Le Conte, 1935); 131 (Chasseriau, 1845); 101 (Charnock, 1800–3); 96 (Charnock, 1800–3); 95 (Lacour-Gayet, 1905); [90] (Nicolas, 1958); 88 (Nicolas, 1973); 63 (Charnock, 1800–3); 44 (Reynolds, 1974)
1693	122	'122' (Le Conte, 1932); '130' [1–5]/'112' [1–4]/'96' [1–3] (Le Conte, 1935); 95 w/40+/87 w/50+ (Chalmers, 1794); 70 (Clark, 1970a)

259

Table 9.2   France's estimated annual number of warships, 1494–1860

Year	Number of warships	Sources on numbers of warships
1694	120	'120' (Le Conte, 1932); '132' [1–5]/'144' [1–4]/'99' [1–3] (Le Conte, 1935); 55 (Nicolas, 1958)
1695	125	'125' (Le Conte, 1932); '139' [1–5]/'120' [1–4]/'1–4' [1–3] (Le Conte, 1935); 137 [1–5] (Symcox, 1974)
1696	122	'122' (Le Conte, 1932); '139' [1–5]/'112' [1–4]/'98' [1–3] (Le Conte, 1935); 135 (Chasseriau, 1845; Nicolas, 1958); 135 w/40+ (Vovard, 1948)
1697	119	'119' (Le Conte, 1932); '127' [1–5]/'110' [1–4]/'96' [1–3] (Le Conte, 1935); c. 70 (Charnock, 1800–3)
1698	118	'118' (Le Conte, 1932); '122' [1–5]/'106' [1–4]/'93' [1–3] (Le Conte, 1935)
1699	118	'118' (Le Conte, 1932); '121' [1–5]/'104' [1–4]/'91' [1–3] (Le Conte, 1935)
1700	118	'118' (Le Conte, 1932); '121' [1–5]/'104' [1–4]/'91' [1–3] (Le Conte, 1935); '107' (Clark, 1970b; Owen, 1938); [50] (Richmond, 1953)
1701	118	'118' (Le Conte, 1932); 90+ (Jenkins, 1973); 50 w/o ammunition (de la Roncière, 1909–32)
1702	96	'96' (Le Conte, 1932); '135'/[84] (Bromley and Ryan, 1971); 100 (Nicolas, 1949; Pemsel, 1977); 90 w/50+ (Charnock, 1800–3)
1703	101	'101' (Le Conte, 1932); '114' (Owen, 1938)
1704	104	'104' (Le Conte, 1932)
1705	106	'106' (Le Conte, 1932)
1706	105	'105' (Le Conte, 1932); 120 (Chasseriau, 1845)
1707	108	'108' (Le Conte, 1932)
1708	99	'99' (Le Conte, 1932); 78 (Charnock, 1800–3); 70 (Charnock, 1800–3)
1709	96	'96' (Le Conte, 1932)
1710	92	'92' (Le Conte, 1932)
1711	86	'86' (Le Conte, 1932)
1712	77	'77' (Le Conte, 1932); 96 (Chasseriau, 1845); 87 w/44+ (Lacour-Gayet, 1902); 85 (Vovard, 1948)
1713	68	'68' (Le Conte, 1932)
1714	66	'66' (Le Conte, 1932); [66] (Nicolas, 1949); 55 [1–5]/ 45 [1–4] (Lamontagne, 1966)
1715	60	'60' (Le Conte, 1932); 66 (Vovard, 1948; Nicolas, 1958); 40 (Lacour-Gayet, 1902); 30 at Toulon (Carré, 1911)
1716	48	'48' (Le Conte, 1932); 69 [1–5] (Bromley and Ryan, 1971)
1717	43	'43' (Le Conte, 1932)
1718	32	'32' (Le Conte, 1932)

260

Table 9.2   France's estimated annual number of warships, 1494–1860

Year	Number of warships	Sources on numbers of warships
1719	23	'23' (Le Conte, 1932); '49' (Wilson, 1936); 49 (Margry, 1879a); 49 [1–5] (Anderson, 1961)
1720	22	'22' (Le Conte, 1932)
1721	23	'23' (Le Conte, 1932)
1722	27	'27' (Le Conte, 1932)
1723	30	'30' (Le Conte, 1932)
1724	35	'35' (Le Conte, 1932)
1725	36	'36' (Le Conte, 1932); 51 (Neuville, 1977); 30 (Wilson, 1936)
1726	36	'36' (Le Conte, 1932)
1727	38	'38' (Le Conte, 1932); 56 (Lamontagne, 1966)
1728	37	'37' (Le Conte, 1932); 51 [1–6] (Lacour-Gayet, 1902)
1729	37	'37' (Le Conte, 1932); 54 [1–6] (Lacour–Gayet, 1902); 45 (Jouan, 1950; Vovard, 1948)
1730	37	'37' (Le Conte, 1932); 51 [1–5] (Wilson, 1936); 51 (Loir, 1893; Carré, 1911); [45] (Nicolas, 1949)
1731	40	'40' (Le Conte, 1932); 54 (Carré, 1911)
1732	39	'39' (Le Conte, 1932); 66 (Lamontagne, 1966); 45 armed (Margry, 1879a)
1733	39	'39' (Le Conte, 1932); 30 (Margry, 1879b)
1734	40	'40' (Le Conte, 1932); 45 (Lacour-Gayet, 1902)
1735	41	'41' (Le Conte, 1932); [15] (Wilson, 1936)
1736	41	'41' (Le Conte, 1932)
1737	41	'41' (Le Conte, 1932)
1738	44	'44' (Le Conte, 1932)
1739	47	'47' (Le Conte, 1932); 60 + (Carré, 1911); '50' (Richmond, 1946; Anderson, 1961); 49 [1–4] (Wilson, 1961); 48 (Charnock, 1800–3)
1740	47	'47' (Le Conte, 1932); '41'/[28–25] (Wilson, 1936); 41 (Lacour-Gayet, 1902)
1741	45	'45' (Le Conte, 1932); 51 (Chasseriau, 1845)
1742	46	'46' (Le Conte, 1932); '48'/[25] (Nicolas, 1949; Vovard, 1948)
1743	46	'46' (Le Conte, 1932); 40–45 (Wilson, 1936); 35 (LAF, 1888)
1744	46	'46' (Le Conte, 1932); 50 (Jouan, 1950); 45 (Mahan, 1890)
1745	47	'47' (Le Conte, 1932); [45] (Dorn, 1963)
1746	44	'44' (Le Conte, 1932)
1747	37	'37' (Le Conte, 1932); 31 (Mahan, 1890)
1748	41	'41' (Le Conte, 1932); [45–50] (Carré, 1911); 31 (Charnock, 1800–3); '30'/[9] (Jenkins, 1973; Lacour-Gayet, 1902); 30 (Margry, 1879b; Nicolas, 1958); [30] (Vovard, 1948); 1 (Chasseriau, 1845)

Table 9.2   France's estimated annual number of warships, 1494–1860

Year	Number of warships	Sources on numbers of warships
1749	47	'47' (Le Conte, 1932)
1750	53	'53' (Le Conte, 1932); 38 (Nicolas, 1958)
1751	55	'55' (Le Conte, 1932); 57 (Nicolas, 1958); 38 (Lacour-Gayet, 1902)
1752	58	'58' (Le Conte, 1932)
1753	59	'59' (Le Conte, 1932)
1754	62	'62' (Le Conte, 1932); 63 (Nicolas, 1958); 57 [1–4]/50 [1–3] (Margry, 1879b; Lacour-Gayet, 1902); 57 (Vovard, 1948; Anderson, 1961)
1755	63	'63' (Le Conte, 1932); '63'/[45] (Richmond, 1946); c. 60 (Parry, 1971); 58 (Carré, 1911); 45 (Jenkins, 1973); [45] (Nicolas, 1958); 60/[45] (Vecchj, 1895)
1756	67	'67' (Le Conte, 1932); 82 (Rose, 1921b); 72 (Charnock, 1800–3); 70 (Pemsel, 1977); 63–72 (Dorn, 1963); '63'/[45] (Mahan, 1890); 63 (LAF, 1888; Chasseriau, 1845; Dupuy and Dupuy, 1977); '60'/ [45] (Barfleur, 1907); 60 (Loir, 1893)
1757	71	'71' (Le Conte, 1932)
1758	59	'59' (Le Conte, 1932); 77 (Mahan, 1890)
1759	49	'49' (Le Conte, 1932); c. 56 (Parry, 1971); 42 (Mahan, 1890)
1760	50	'50' (Le Conte, 1932)
1761	58	'58' (Le Conte, 1932); 44 (Rose, 1921b); [0] (Mahan, 1890)
1762	64	'64' (Le Conte, 1932); c. 40 (Jenkins, 1973); [40] (Mahan, 1890)
1763	69	'69' (Le Conte, 1932); 44 (Tracy, 1975); 40 (Mahan, 1890; Lacour-Gayet, 1902); [40] (Nicolas, 1958)
1764	71	'71' (Le Conte, 1932)
1765	72	'72' (Le Conte, 1932); '63'/[36] (Tracy, 1975); 62 (Chasseriau, 1845); 44 (Carré, 1911)
1766	69	'69' (Le Conte, 1932); 64 (Rose, 1921b); 40 (Lloyd, 1965a); [39–42] (Tracy, 1975); 36 (Jouan, 1950)
1767	70	'70' (Le Conte, 1932)
1768	74	'74' (Le Conte, 1932); '59'/[41] (Tracy, 1975)
1769	76	'76' (Le Conte, 1932); 63 (Tracy, 1975)
1770	77	'77' (Le Conte, 1932); 64 (Mahan, 1890; Chasseriau, 1845; Carré, 1911; Lloyd, 1965a; Jenkins, 1973); [64] (Nicolas, 1958); 58 (Tracy, 1975)
1771	76	'76' (Le Conte, 1932); [64] (Vovard, 1948; Lacour-Gayet, 1902)
1772	80	'80' (Le Conte, 1932); 66 (Chasseriau, 1845); 61/[47] (Tracy, 1975)

262

Table 9.2   France's estimated annual number of warships, 1494–1860

Year	Number of warships	Sources on numbers of warships
1773	78	'78' (Le Conte, 1932); 66 (Chasseriau, 1845; Anderson, 1961); 62 w/50+ (Lacour-Gayet, 1902)
1774	75	'75' (Le Conte, 1932); 79 (Vovard, 1948); 66 (Jenkins, 1973)
1775	75	'75' (Le Conte, 1932); 79 (Vovard, 1948); 54 (Tracy, 1975)
1776	75	'75' (Le Conte, 1932); 79 (Vovard, 1948); 63 w/60+ (Edler, 1911); [40] (Lacour-Gayet, 1905)
1777	75	'75' (Le Conte, 1932); 79 (Vovard, 1948); [50] (Tracy, 1975); [42] (Lacour-Gayet, 1905)
1778	83	'83' (Le Conte, 1932); 94 [1–3] (Charnock, 1800–3); 84 (Loir, 1893); 80 (Southworth, 1968; Stevens and Westcott, 1943); [80] (Mahan, 1890); 79 (Vovard, 1948); 73 (Chasseriau, 1845); 68 (Busk, 1859; Cobden, 1862); 65 w/50+ (Richmond, 1946); 63 w/64+ (de Jonge, 1869); [47] (Tracy, 1975)
1779	86	'86' (Le Conte, 1932); 94 [1–3] (Charnock, 1800–3); 79 (Vovard, 1948); 78 (Headlam, 1921; Chasseriau, 1845)
1780	85	'85' (Le Conte, 1932); 94 [1–3] (Charnock, 1800–3); 81 (Anderson, 1961); 80 (Pemsel, 1977); 79 (Nicolas, 1949; Vovard, 1948); [79] (Nicolas, 1949; Vovard, 1948); [79] (Nicolas, 1958); 78 (Lacour-Gayet, 1905; Jenkins, 1973)
1781	89	'89' (Le Conte, 1932); 94 [1–3] (Charnock, 1800–3)
1782	84	'84' (Le Conte, 1932); 94 [1–3] (Charnock, 1800–3); [60] (Nicolas, 1958)
1783	82	'82' (Le Conte, 1932); '82' (Chalmers, 1794)
1784	76	'76' (Le Conte, 1932)
1785	74	'74' (Le Conte, 1932)
1786	76	'76' (Le Conte, 1932); 63 (Hampson, 1959)
1787	81	'81' (Le Conte, 1932)
1788	82	'82' (Le Conte, 1932)
1789	87	'87' (Le Conte, 1932); '86'/[28] (Dorn, 1963; Bruun, 1963); 72 (LAF, 1888); 71 (Lacour-Gayet, 1905; Jenkins, 1973; Nicolas, 1958); [71] (Vovard, 1948); 64 w/60+ (Vecchj, 1895); [63] (Lacour-Gayet, 1905)
1790	90	'90' (Le Conte, 1932)
1791	87	'87' (Le Conte, 1932); 86 (Mahan, 1890; Loir, 1893; Vovard, 1948); 82 (Chasseriau, 1845)

263

Table 9.2   France's estimated annual number of warships, 1494–1860

Year	Number of warships	Sources on numbers of warships
1792	87	'87' (Le Conte, 1932); 88 (Nicolas, 1958); 86/[27] (James, 1886); 83 (Chasseriau, 1845); [83] (Thomazi, 1950); 76 (Lloyd, 1965a); '76'/[38] (Dupuy and Dupuy, 1977); '73'/[27] (Wilson, 1904)
1793	78	'78' (Le Conte, 1932); '82' (James, 1886); 80 (Pemsel, 1977); 77 (Chasseriau, 1845); '76'/[27] (Lloyd, 1965b); '76'/[65] (Masson and Muracciole, 1968); 76 (Stevens and Westcott, 1943; Wilson, 1904; Parry, 1971; Mahan, 1892; Rose, 1940b); [76] (Clowes, 1897–1903; Richmond, 1946); [74] (Vovard, 1948); [67] (Lloyd, 1965a); 63 (Hampson, 1959)
1794	84	'84' (Le Conte, 1932); 77 (Busk, 1859); '56'/[47] (Hampson, 1959)
1795	82	'82' (Le Conte, 1932); 78 (Chasseriau, 1845); 32 (Brenton, 1823–5)
1796	79	'79' (Le Conte, 1932)
1797	83	'83' (Le Conte, 1932)
1798	70	'70' (Le Conte, 1932); 80 (Mahan, 1892)
1799	65	'65' (Le Conte, 1932); 54 (Charnock, 1800–3)
1800	61	'61' (Le Conte, 1932); 46 (Chasseriau, 1845); '40' (Masson and Muracciole, 1968)
1801	60	'60' (Le Conte, 1932); 83 (Nicolas, 1973); 52 (Chasseriau, 1845); 51 (Loir, 1893; Vovard, 1948); 39 (Mahan, 1892); [13] (Masson and Muracciole, 1968)
1802	60	'60' (Le Conte, 1932); 46 (Chasseriau, 1845; Thomazi, 1950); 45 (Stevens and Westcott, 1943)
1803	66	'66' (Le Conte, 1932); 60 (Thomazi, 1950); [40] (Pemsel, 1977); 33 (Richmond, 1946); [23] (Fuller, 1955)
1804	69	'69' (Le Conte, 1932); 51 (Chasseriau, 1845); 50 (Busk, 1859)
1805	63	'63' (Le Conte, 1932); 49 (Chasseriau, 1845)
1806	65	'65' (Le Conte, 1932); 39 (Chasseriau, 1845); 32 (James, 1886)
1807	73	'73' (Le Conte, 1932); 37 (Thomazi, 1950); 35 (Chasseriau, 1845)
1808	72	'72' (Le Conte, 1932); 80 (James, 1886); 43 (Chasseriau, 1845)
1809	71	'71' (Le Conte, 1932); 60 (Richmond, 1946); 45 (Chasseriau, 1845); ave. 60 (Thomazi, 1950); 42/[27] (Vecchj, 1895)

264

Table 9.2   France's estimated annual number of warships, 1494–1860

Year	Number of warships	Sources on numbers of warships
1810	81	'81' (Le Conte, 1932); 58 (Brenton, 1823–5); 56 (Chasseriau, 1845); 27 (Brenton, 1823–5); ave. 60 (Thomazi, 1950)
1811	91	'91' (Le Conte, 1932); 58 (Brenton, 1823–5); 57 (Chasseriau, 1845); ave. 60 (Thomazi, 1950)
1812	101	'101' (Le Conte, 1932); 113 (Busk, 1859); 60–70 (Richmond, 1946) 64 (Chasseriau, 1845); 59 (Brenton, 1823–25); 58 (Brenton, 1823–5); ave. 60 (Thomazi, 1950); [56] (Jenkins, 1973)
1813	106	'106' (Le Conte, 1932); 71 (Chasseriau, 1845); 71 armed (Thomazi, 1950); [71] (Nicolas, 1958); ave. 60 (Thomazi, 1950)
1814	77	'77' (Le Conte, 1932); 103 (Lloyd, 1965b; Loir, 1893; Vovard, 1948; Mahan, 1890); 69 (Chasseriau, 1845; Block, 1875); ave. 60 (Thomazi, 1950)
1815	79	'79' (Le Conte, 1932); 103 (Lloyd, 1965b, Fuller, 1955; Nicolas, 1973); 83 (Vecchj, 1895); 71 (Reussner and Nicolas, 1963); 69; (Busk, 1859); 55 (Chasseriau, 1845); 53 (Vovard, 1948); 50 (Jenkins, 1973)
1816	77	'77' (Le Conte, 1932); 70 afloat or in construction (Vovard, 1948); c. 50 (Bartlett, 1963)
1817	72	'72' (Le Conte, 1932); 68 (DeNervo, 1865); 31 (Loir, 1893)
1818	72	'72' (Le Conte, 1932); 45 (DeNervo, 1865)
1819	69	'69' (Le Conte, 1932); 31 (Vovard, 1948)
1820	69	'69' (Le Conte, 1932); 58 (Busk, 1859); 48 (DeNervo, 1865; Block, 1875)
1821	65	'65' (Le Conte, 1932); 48 (Chasseriau, 1845)
1822	64	'64' (Le Conte, 1932); 58 (Padfield, 1972); 46 (Jenkins, 1973); [8] (Vovard, 1948)
1823	67	'67' (Le Conte, 1932); [8] (Vovard, 1948)
1824	67	'67' (Le Conte, 1932); 59 (Moreau de Jonnes, 1835); [8] (Vovard, 1948)
1825	62	'62' (Le Conte, 1932); 58 (Busk, 1859); [8] (Vovard, 1948)
1826	62	'62' (Le Conte, 1932); [8] (Vovard, 1948)
1827	65	'65' (Le Conte, 1932); [8] (Vovard, 1948)
1828	64	'64' (Le Conte, 1932); [8] (Vovard, 1948)
1829	65	'65' (Le Conte, 1932); [8] (Vovard, 1948)
1830	63	'63' (Le Conte, 1932); 53 (Busk, 1895); 36 *Almanach de Gotha*); 33 (Chasseriau, 1845; Thomazi, 1950); [8] (Vovard, 1948)

Table 9.2   France's estimated annual number of warships, 1494–1860

Year	Number of warships	Sources on numbers of warships
1831	62	'62' (Le Conte, 1932); [8] (Vovard, 1948)
1832	61	'61' (Le Conte, 1932); [8] (Vovard, 1948)
1833	59	'59' (Le Conte, 1932); 33 (Block, 1875); [8] (Vovard, 1948)
1834	58	'58' (Le Conte, 1932); 33 *Almanach de Gotha*), [8] (Vovard, 1948)
1835	60	'60' (Le Conte, 1932); [8] (Chasseriau, 1845; Vovard, 1948)
1836	56	'56' (Le Conte, 1932); [11] (Chasseriau, 1845); [8] (Vovard, 1948)
1837	54	'54' (Le Conte, 1932); '40'/[20] (M. Marine, 1838); 40 (Jenkins, 1973); 20 (Block, 1875); [10] (Chasseriau, 1845); [8] (Vovard, 1948)
1838	55	'55' (Le Conte, 1932); '49'/[10] (Bartlett, 1963); 11 (Chasseriau, 1845); [8] (Vovard, 1948)
1839	51	'51' (Le Conte, 1932); 15 (Chasseriau, 1845); [8] (Vovard, 1948)
1840	53	'53' (Le Conte, 1932); 44 (Busk, 1859); '20'/[17[(Chasseriau, 1845); [8] (Vovard, 1948)
1841	53	'53' (Le Conte, 1932); [20] (Chasseriau, 1845)
1842	52	'52' (Le Conte, 1932); [20] (Chasseriau, 1845)
1843	52	'52' (Le Conte, 1932); [20] (Chasseriau, 1845)
1844	52	'52' (Le Conte, 1932); [20] (Chasseriau, 1845)
1845	52	'52' (Le Conte, 1932); 46 (Busk, 1859); '23'/[12] (Chasseriau, 1845)
1846	52	'52' (Le Conte, 1932)
1847	51	'51' (Le Conte, 1932)
1848	52	'52' (Le Conte, 1932); '40'/[10] (*Almanach de Gotha*)
1849	52	'52' (Le Conte, 1932)
1850	47	'47' (Le Conte, 1932); 45 (Busk, 1859)
1851	48	'48' (Le Conte, 1932)
1852	48	'48' (Le Conte, 1932); 27 (Bartlett, 1963)
1853	54	'54' (Le Conte, 1932); 40 (Vecchj, 1895)
1854	57	'57' (Le Conte, 1932)
1855	54	'54' (Le Conte, 1932)
1856	55	'55' (Le Conte, 1932)
1857	56	'56' (Le Conte, 1932); 45 (Block, 1875)
1858	54	'54' (Le Conte, 1932); 50 (Busk, 1859)
1859	53	'53' (Le Conte, 1932); 47 (Pemsel, 1977)
1860	52	'52' (Le Conte, 1932)

Note: See Notes to Tables 8.2 and 8.4. LAF refers to L'Ancienne France.

266 *Country Data*

Table 9.3   French battleships, 1861–1945

Year	Number of ships	Year	Number of ships	Year	Number of ships
1861	1	1890	10	1919	7
1862	6	1891	10	1920	7
1863	6	1892	10	1921	7
1864	6	1893	10	1922	6
1865	11	1894	10	1923	6
1866	12	1895	9	1924	6
1867	16	1896	10	1925	6
1868	16	1897	13	1926	6
1869	16	1898	14	1927	6
1870	18	1899	8	1928	6
1871	17	1900	9	1929	6
1872	16	1901	10	1930	6
1873	16	1902	10	1931	5
1874	16	1903	11	1932	5
1875	16	1904	11	1933	5
1876	18	1905	11	1934	5
1877	19	1906	11	1935	5
1878	21	1907	13	1936	5
1879	20	1908	9	1937	5
1880	3	1909	9	1938	7
1881	4	1910	0	1939	7
1882	4	1911	0	1940	7
1883	5	1912	0	1941	–
1884	5	1913	2	1942	–
1885	6	1914	4	1943	–
1886	7	1915	6	1944	–
1887	9	1916	7	1945	2
1888	9	1917	7		
1889	9	1918	7		

1940 the French fleet at Oran was destroyed by the British; another part of the navy was scuttled at Toulon in 1942. Several years of fighting both sides (i.e. the Vichy resistance to US and British attacks in West and North Africa) took its toll of personnel and equipment. The French emerged from the Second World War on the winning side but with an extremely marginal naval position greatly dependent on ships borrowed from or given to them by their allies.[1] Table 9.1 lists the sources of information on French warships; Figure 9.1 reveals France's relative capability share; Table 9.2 shows the estimated number of French warships each year from 1494 to 1860 and Table 9.3 enumerates the French battleships annually from 1861 to 1945.

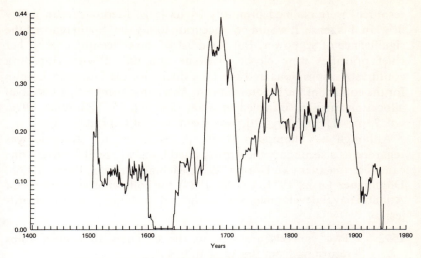

Figure 9.1   French relative capability share, 1494–1945

SPAIN

We need not underestimate the strength of Spain's naval tradition. Both Castile and Aragon, the two kingdoms from which Spain began to be constructed after 1469, had significant maritime interests and involvements. Aragon's were those of Mediterranean expansion, giving it responsibilities in the Balearic Islands, in Sardinia, and Sicily and Naples. The conquest of Granada (1492), helped by a naval effort, increased Castile's commitment to a Mediterranean strategy too and helped to set it on a course of confrontation with the Ottomans in North Africa. On the ocean, on the other hand, Spain by the Treaty of Tordesillas (1494) in effect conceded the first place to Portugal, thereby confirming the superiority which the Portuguese had attained in the naval war with Spain in the Gulf of Guinea in 1475–9.

In our context, therefore, and for most of the sixteenth century, Spain was something of a major exception, in respect of organisation because while obviously a major actor, she did not have a permanent oceanic sailing navy. Well into the 1570s, Spain's official naval

268 *Country Data*

resources were claimed primarily by its large Mediterranean galley fleet. In this sense, it would be inaccurate to say that Spain ignored the significance of seapower. But for most of the sixteenth century, her chief priorities were closer to home and linked with Hapsburg continental aspirations and the long duel with the Ottoman Empire for the control of the Mediterranean. As a consequence, Spain's naval allocations may have tripled between 1534 and 1573 (Braudel, 1976, vol. 2, p. 841), but very little was spent west of Gibraltar.

Although as Thompson (1976, p. 15) notes, the Atlantic was regarded as a secondary theatre expected largely to fend for itself, one can piece together (see Haring, 1918; Richmond, 1953; Parry, 1966b; Dominguez Ortiz, 1971; Lynch, 1984) the following chronology of Atlantic naval developments which helped to change Spanish priorities:

1512	Two caravels are sent to the Canaries to protect ships returning from the West Indies
1513	Two caravels are sent to patrol Cuban coasts
1518	The *averia*, a shipping tax for naval defence is first instituted
1520s	The first tentative attempts to enforce convoys are begun
1521–23	The level of Spanish shipping to the West Indies is reduced to its 1513–15 level by French privateers
1527–28	The level of Spanish shipping to the West Indies is reduced again by the addition of English privateers
1528	An *armada para la guardia de costa y navios de Indies* is established with an unknown station
1542	Convoys are reintroduced when war with France breaks out
1559–64	Almost all shipping to the West Indies is organised in armed convoys. The first escort consists of one 36-gun galleon. The number of escorts gradually escalates to eight and later to eighteen
1570	The *armada del mar oceano* is established as the first permanent royal fleet (eight ships) to protect the eastern end of the transatlantic routes
1574	Galleys are sent to the Indies for coastal patrol purposes
1582	The first permanent squadron in the Caribbean is established. However, it consists of two galleys, one of which is wrecked shortly after arrival and the crew of the other vessel soon mutinies. The difficulty of obtaining rowers renders the squadron's existence intermittent at best
1588	A severe shortage of convoy escorts leads to the develop-

France, Spain, Russia, Germany, Japan 269

ment of the *zabra* as a light treasure carrier with sufficient speed to outrun privateers

1590   The *armada del mar oceano* becomes a regular budget item

1598   The *armada de las islas de barlovento*, the Caribbean defence squadron is re-established with six frigates but is soon diverted to convoy duty and after 1606 is assigned to Spanish waters until 1640

Spanish transatlantic shipping and the rich treasure fleets quickly became tempting targets for north-west European attackers. Yet their early attacks were not regarded as so threatening as to require the development of full-scale naval protection. Instead, convoy procedures were developed with armed escorts contracted either by merchants themselves or the Spanish government. Throughout much of this period, Spanish kings evaded the need for a permanent navy either by seizing foreign vessels when needed in emergencies or by hiring merchant ships. The building of ships larger than was necessary for commercial purposes was also encouraged by royal subsidies. Given the frequent need for emergency acquisitions, the damages sustained, and the slow rate of reimbursement, it is unlikely that any of these practices, which continued well into the seventeenth century, benefited the long-term development of Spanish shipbuilding and commercial fleets.

Official Spanish resources and attention began shifting away from the Mediterranean and toward the Atlantic in the 1570s. A small nucleus for an Atlantic fleet was created by the establishment in 1570 of the *armada del mar oceano* and augmented by the availability of ten to twelve royal Portuguese galleons after 1580. The strategic need for a permanent fleet was facilitated moreover by French operations in the Azores (1582–3), the Dutch rebellion, and semi-official and official English attacks in the Caribbean. But the most important impetus for creating a royal navy was the decision to make an attempt to solve many of Spain's strategic problems by invading England. To accomplish this imposing task, all Spain's potential naval resources would have to be mobilised. The 1588 Armada which brought together as many as 130 vessels, of which a little more than half were considered capable of fighting other warships, relied heavily on improvised merchant ships in addition to some twenty-four royal warships (ten Portuguese galleons, ten *armada del mar oceano* galleons, and four New Spain *flota* great ships). The failure of the first armada attempt was followed by several more equally unsuccessful

270   Country Data

efforts in the next decade. But in the process of attempting to invade England (or Ireland), Spain was finally forced to build a permanent navy.

As a naval power, late sixteenth/early seventeenth century Spain was characterised by a number of liabilities – many of which persisted into the early nineteenth century. Tactically, Spain attempted to rely on Mediterranean tactics of ramming and boarding and fighting what were essentially land battles at sea. A Spanish officer in the 1588 Armada summarised this problem quite accurately when asked whether Spain could defeat England in the coming sea battle:

> Of course we shall win. It is very simple. It is well known that we fight in God's cause. So, when we meet the English, God will surely arrange matters so that we can grapple and board them, either by sending some strange freak of weather or, more likely, just by depriving the English of their wits. If we can come to close quarters, Spanish valour and Spanish steel (and the great masses of soldiers we shall have on board) will make our victory certain. But unless God helps us by a miracle the English, who have faster and handier ships than ours, and many more long-range guns and who know their advantage just as we do will never close with us at all, but stand aloof and knock us to pieces with their culverins without our being able to do them serious hurt. So we are sailing against England in the confident expectation of a miracle (quoted in Frere-Cook and Macksey, 1975, pp. 31–2).

As suggested above and closely related to their tactical doctrine, Spanish ships tended to be under-gunned or out-ranged by the cannon of their opponents. War with the Dutch and English also restricted the supply of materials (copper, tar, timber, sail cloth, hemp) needed to build guns and ships and to keep them afloat. Parry (1966b, p. 158) notes that as a consequence between 1590 and 1610 Spanish ships aged quickly and were increasingly prone to wrecking. Naval manpower was also, seemingly always, in short supply and what men were available preferred the higher wages associated with civilian shipping.

A weak and weakening economy, provincial separatist tendencies, and governmental finances dependent on the regularity of the treasure fleets and often over-committed to the past and future demands of land warfare, of course, were less than supportive of the type of sustained capital investment necessary to build and maintain a state

France, Spain, Russia, Germany, Japan 271

fleet. This problem was further aggravated by a proclivity for stripping the transatlantic and Caribbean protection forces and diverting them to European combat. Trying to coordinate all these problems was a succession of absolutist regimes that were fairly typical of their era – under-institutionalised, not too blessed with talented monarchs, and subject to the rise and fall of the occasional strong minister.

Despite all these various liabilities, Spain was able to field a competitive, albeit rarely successful, navy for intermittent periods of time. The late 1580s and the 1590s constituted one such period. A naval secretariat had been created in 1586. A royal dockyard was built around 1607. Nevertheless, the first decade and half of the 1600s was a period of fiscal stringency and corresponding naval decay. For a few years, naval resource priorities even reverted to the Mediterranean galley fleet.

North African corsair activity is credited with stimulating an overhaul of the navy between 1617 and 1623, including the construction of some seventy new ships. In 1621, the *armada del mar oceano* was expanded and its budget doubled (Elliott, 1963, p. 322). New bases were established such as the frigate squadron stationed at Ostend and Dunkirk (*armada de Flandes*) in 1626 – to engage in extensive, and successful, cruiser warfare against Dutch shipping – and the *armada de la mar del sur* created to protect the Callao (Peru) to the Panama Isthmus route in the Pacific. The creation of a Baltic naval base in northern Germany was even considered briefly.

This spurt of reform, in conjunction with continental setbacks, was cut short by three successive shocks. In 1628, the Dutch finally managed to intercept and capture the entire New Spain *flota*, the annual convoy of treasure to Spain. In 1639, a large fleet transporting troops to Flanders was intercepted and soundly defeated again by the Dutch (Battle of the Downs) with a loss of approximately 67 per cent of the fleet. A year later even further losses were experienced by a fleet sent to Brazil in 1638 to retake Pernambuco from the Dutch. Very few ships were left to respond to the Portuguese revolt in 1640 and financial difficulties this time barred a rebuilding of the Spanish fleet.

One indicator of the severity of the situation was the need to depend on the English navy for Atlantic troop transport escorts in 1640 (Powell, 1962, p. 5). The Spanish navy did not disappear in 1639–40 but it was forced to function on a much smaller scale after this point throughout the largely land-oriented warfare of the rest of the seventeenth century. By the 1690s, the *armada del mar oceano* had been reduced to about 40 per cent of its 1621 size. A decade later,

272   *Country Data*

Coxe (1815, vol. 1, p. 120) asserts that the navy had diminished to a small collection of armed trading vessels and a few galleons. Kamen (1969, p. 59) disagrees somewhat and finds twenty warships of unspecified type operating in the Atlantic and Caribbean in 1701. Yet he also points out that no *Tierra Firme* fleet (Spain to Panama) sailed between 1697 and 1705 and that the French navy was primarily responsible for protecting the returning silver fleets in 1708, 1709 and 1712.

After the conclusion of the War of the Spanish Succession, the navy was revived through the purchase in 1717 of twenty warships constructed in France. The collective longevity of these new acquisitions was not great. Sent to Sicily in 1718 as part of an attempt to recover some of Spain's former Italian territory, the new fleet was thoroughly mauled by the British at the Battle of Cape Passaro. However, between 1727–36 and 1741–54, a succession of influential ministers (Patino, Campillo, and Ensenada), with backgrounds in the naval ministry (created in 1714), predominated in the Spanish government and sequentially, were able to rebuild the navy into a force of respectable strength, at least in terms of ship-of-the-line numbers if not effectiveness.

Between the War of Jenkin's Ear (which began in 1739) and Spanish participation in the internationalised War of American Independence (1779–83), the navy was employed intermittently at sea, usually in opposition to the British and frequently as an adjunct of the French navy. If no spectacular successes were achieved at least there were no devastating defeats. Yet by the end of the eighteenth century, the Spanish navy had once more slid into decay. Von Pivka provides the following status report for 1792:

If the condition of the French navy was poor, that of the Spanish navy was verging on the terrible. Still an active colonial power, corruption in the upper echelons of Spanish society and government had reduced her armed forces to the status of paper tigers. Dockyards were derelict, ships neglected, crew morale low due to the injustice of a promotion system where money completely outweighed seniority or merit. The government was too torpid to use their fleet properly and after Trafalgar they had little to fight with (von Pivka, 1980, p. 31).

France, Spain, Russia, Germany, Japan 273

After 1804, the Spanish navy was again operating in conjunction with the French navy against the British. The inequality of the Franco-Spanish naval partnership is perhaps best summarised by Napoleon's alleged 1805 order to one of his admirals to count two Spanish ships equal to one French ship (Mahan, 1892, vol. 1, p. 78). At Trafalgar in the same year, two-thirds of the Spanish fleet contingent were sunk, captured, or badly damaged. Table 9.4 lists the sources of information on Spanish warships; Figure 9.2 illustrates Spain's relative capability share, and Table 9.5 gives the estimated annual number of Spanish warships from 1494 to 1836.

Table 9.4   Sources on Spanish warships, 1494–1836

Almanach de Gotha	Lloyd (1965a)
Anderson (1961)	Lynch (1969)
Ballesteros y Beretta (1932)	Mahan (1890, 1892)
Bourne (1939)	March y Labores (1854)
Brenton (1823–5)	Mattingly (1959)
Callender (1924)	McKee (1963)
Canaga Arguelles (1826)	Merriman ((1934)
Chalmers (1794)	Moreau de Jonnes (1835)
Charnock (1800–3)	Muhmann (1975)
Cooper (1970)	Nicolas (1958)
Corbett (1898)	Olague (1950–1)
Coxe (1815)	Olesa Munido (1968)
Desdevises Du Dezert (1899)	Oppenheim (1961)
Dupuy and Dupuy (1977)	Pemsel (1977)
Elliott (1963)	Perkins (1971)
Fernandez Duro (1972–3)	de Peyster (1905)
Graham (1972)	Reynolds (1974)
Haring (1918)	Richmond (1946, 1953)
Headlam (1921)	de la Roncière (1909–32)
Hume (1927)	Silburn (1912)
Ibanez de Ibero (1943)	Southworth (1968)
James (1886)	Thompson (1976)
Kamen (1969)	Tracy (1975)
Lacour-Gayet (1902)	Vecchj (1895)
Laughton (1892)	Wilson (1904)

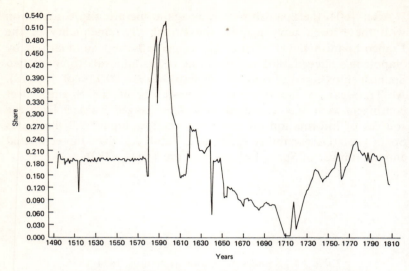

Figure 9.2 Spanish relative capability share, 1494–1808

Table 9.5 Spain's estimated annual number of warships, 1494–1836

Year	Number of warships	Sources of numbers of warships
1494	2	
1495	3	
1496	3	
1497	3	
1498	3	
1499	3	
1500	4	
1501	3	
1502	7	
1503	8	
1504	9	
1505	11	
1506	15	
1507	17	
1508	19	
1509	26	
1510	25	

275

Table 9.5   Spain's estimated annual number of warships, 1494–1836

Year	Number of warships	Sources on numbers of warships
1511	26	
1512	34	
1513	32	
1514	28	
1515	27	
1516	25	
1517	22	
1518	20	
1519	21	
1520	19	
1521	21	
1522	21	
1523	20	
1524	22	
1525	21	
1526	20	
1527	17	
1528	16	
1529	13	
1530	13	
1531	12	
1532	13	
1533	14	
1434	12	
1535	13	
1536	12	
1537	13	
1538	14	
1539	13	
1540	14	
1541	13	
1542	14	
1543	14	
1544	16	
1545	15	
1546	17	
1547	16	
1548	16	
1549	18	
1550	18	
1551	20	
1552	19	
1553	18	

276

Table 9.5   Spain's estimated annual number of warships, 1494–1836

Year	Number of warships	Sources on numbers of warships
1554	18	c. 100 substantial vessels (Graham, 1972)
1555	16	
1556	17	
1557	17	
1558	17	
1559	14	
1560	15	
1561	14	
1562	13	
1563	13	
1564	12	
1565	13	
1566	12	
1567	15	
1568	16	
1569	16	
1570	18	
1571	17	
1572	17	
1573	18	105 (Southworth, 1968)
1574	17	
1575	18	
1576	16	
1577	15	
1578	13	
1579	13	
1580	13	400 Portuguese vessels pre-empted for war purposes (Silburn, 1912)
1581	31	
1582	40	2 galleons/16 smaller ships in Azores fleet (Merriman, 1934)
1583	40	
1584	45	
1585	51	23 + 10 pinnaces + 22 armed merchantmen (Corbett, 1898)
1586	57	104 Spanish + 92 Portuguese of 100 tons + (Richmond, 1953); 12 Portuguese galleons in European waters (Mattingly, 1959)
1587	64	106 (Thompson, 1976); c. 10 men-of-war (McKee, 1963)
1588	70	131 (Thompson, 1976); 109 combat vessels (Graham, 1972); 85–95/21 galleons (Mattingly, 1959); 73 in battle line (Merriman, 1934); 60–70 men-of-war of 300 + tons (Southworth, 1968)

277

Table 9.5   Spain's estimated annual number of warships, 1494–1836

Year	Number of warships	Sources on numbers of warships
1589	35	c. 71 (Graham, 1972); 33 galleons (Richmond, 1953)
1590	60	100 (Thompson, 1976); 60 ocean-going men-of-war (Richmond, 1953); [50 with 30 galleons] (Graham, 1972)
1591	66	55/36 galleons (Thompson, 1976); 20 galleons (Reynolds, 1974)
1592	69	
1593	71	
1594	75	37/25 galleons (Thompson, 1976)
1595	79	
1596	81	100/30 galleons (Graham, 1972)
1597	84	136/60 galleons (Graham, 1972); 130/60 men-of-war (Richmond, 1953); 84 armed (Haring, 1919); 84 (Thompson, 1976)
1598	67	67 (Thompson, 1976); 24 galleons (Merriman, 1934)
1599	58	38 galleons and great ships (Graham, 1972)
1600	51	
1601	40	78 (Richmond, 1953); 40/20 galleons (Graham, 1972); 33/32 galleons (Thompson, 1976)
1602	37	
1603	33	
1604	31	21 galleons (Thompson, 1976)
1605	30	
1606	29	19 galleons (Thompson, 1976)
1607	29	
1608	17	17–20 galleons (Thompson, 1976)
1609	16	
1610	14	14–18 galleons (Thompson, 1976)
1611	14	
1612	15	
1613	15	
1614	16	28/24 galleons (Thompson, 1976)
1615	16	[4 galleons] (Thompson, 1976)
1616	17	17/13–15 galleons/[4 galleons] (Thompson, 1976)
1617	22	4–13 (Thompson, 1976)
1618	26	26/22 galleons (Thompson, 1976)
1619	27	26/27 (Thompson, 1976)
1620	46	46 in the 1620s (Lynch, 1969); 36/30 galleons (Thompson, 1976)
1621	48	78 (Olesa Munido, 1968); 76 (Fernandez Duro, 1972–3); 60 (Ibanez de Ibero, 1943); 46 (Elliott, 1963); 27–31/21–5 galleons (Thompson, 1976)
1622	51	38–51/30 galleons (Thompson, 1976)

278

Table 9.5 Spain's estimated annual number of warships, 1494–1836

Year	Number of warships	Sources on numbers of warships
1623	55	38–40 (Thompson, 1976)
1624	55	38–40 (Thompson, 1976)
1625	60	[108] (Hume, 1927); 60–70 (Richmond, 1953)
1626	60	49/46 galleons (Thompson, 1976)
1627	60	36 (Oppenheim, 1961)
1628	59	
1629	58	
1630	57	
1631	57	
1632	56	
1633	55	55 (Fernandez Duro, 1972–3)
1634	57	
1635	58	
1636	60	
1637	62	
1638	64	87 (Cooper, 1970)
1639	70	89 (Charnock, 1800–3); 77 (Reynolds, 1974); 70 (Hume, 1927; Callender, 1924; Richmond, 1953); 67 (Southworth, 1968); 70/50 warships (Cooper, 1970); 70 with 58 lost at Downs (Pemsel, 1977)
1640	12	
1641	30	
1642	50	50 (Perkins, 1971)
1643	48	
1644	46	
1645	45	
1646	43	
1647	41	
1648	40	40 (de la Roncière, 1909–32)
1649	37	
1650	33	
1651	30	30 (Charnock, 1800–3)
1652	29	
1653	29	
1654	29	
1655	30	
1656	28	
1657	27	
1658	27	
1659	27	
1660	26	
1661	25	
1662	25	

279

Table 9.5   Spain's estimated annual number of warships, 1494–1836

Year	Number of warships	Sources on numbers of warships
1663	25	
1664	25	
1665	24	
1666	24	
1667	23	
1668	23	
1669	23	
1670	22	
1671	21	
1672	21	
1673	21	
1674	21	
1675	20	
1676	19	
1677	19	
1678	19	
1679	19	
1680	18	
1681	17	
1682	17	
1683	17	
1684	17	
1685	16	
1686	16	17 (Fernandez Duro, 1972–3)
1687	17	
1688	18	
1689	19	
1690	20	20 in the Atlantic in the 1690s (Lynch, 1969)
1691	21	
1692	22	
1693	23	3 in the Pacific (Lynch, 1969)
1694	24	
1695	24	
1696	24	
1697	25	
1698	25	
1699	26	
1700	26	26 (Olesa Munido, 1968); [7] (Richmond, 1953); several galleons (Desdevises Du Dezert, 1899)
1701	23	13 (de la Roncière, 1909–32); [8] (Nicolas, 1958)
1702	20	20 (Kamen, 1969)
1703	17	
1704	14	

280

Table 9.5   Spain's estimated annual number of warships, 1494–1836

Year	Number of warships	Sources on numbers of warships
1705	11	
1706	9	
1707	6	
1708	3	
1709	0	0 (Bourne, 1939)
1710	0	
1711	0	
1712	0	
1713	0	
1714	0	
1715	6	
1716	11	
1717	17	
1718	22	c. 22 (Mahan, 1890); 22 (Olague, 1950–51); 22/18 lost (Desdevises Du Dezert, 1899)
1719	3	c. 2–3 (Mahan, 1890)
1720	5	
1721	7	
1722	9	
1723	12	
1724	14	
1725	17	
1726	19	
1727	22	c. 30 (Charnock, 1800–3)
1728	24	24 (Desdevises Du Dezert, 1899); Olague, 1950–1); 18 (Ibanez de Ibero, 1943)
1729	25	
1730	27	
1731	28	
1732	30	
1733	31	
1734	33	45 (Lacour-Gayet, 1902)
1735	34	34 w/60 + (Olague, 1950–1; Desdevises Du Dezert, 1899)
1736	36	36 (Muhmann, 1975)
1737	41	41 (Fernandez Duro, 1972–3); 33 (Anderson, 1961)
1738	42	42 (Muhmann, 1975)
1739	41	'41' (Richmond, 1946); 41 (Muhmann, 1975); 33 (Fernandez Duro, 1972–3)
1740	40	
1741	38	
1742	37	
1743	35	

281

Table 9.5 Spain's estimated annual number of warships, 1494–1836

Year	Number of warships	Sources on numbers of warships
1744	34	12 w/50+ (Laughton, 1892)
1745	32	[c. 32] (Richmond, 1946)
1746	34	34 (Fernandez Duro, 1972–3)
1747	35	22 (Mahan, 1890)
1748	36	
1749	37	
1750	38	
1751	40	
1752	42	
1753	43	
1754	45	49 (Ballesteros y Beretta, 1932); 45 (Muhmann, 1975)
1755	45	'40' (Richmond, 1946)
1756	46	46 (Mahan, 1890; Dupuy and Dupuy, 1977)
1757	46	
1758	47	47 (Muhmann, 1975); 44 (Olague, 1950–1; Desdevises Du Dezert, 1899; Canaga Arguelles, 1826; Ballesteros y Beretta, 1932; Moreau de Jonnes, 1835)
1759	50	51 (Charnock, 1800–3); c. 50 (Mahan, 1890)
1760	52	52 (Muhmann, 1975); [47] (Fernandez Duro, 1972–3)
1761	49	56 (Southworth, 1968); c. 50 (Mahan, 1890); 49 (Olague, 1950–1; Desdevises Du Dezert, 1899; Ballesteros y Beretta, 1932)
1762	47	c. 60 (Mahan, 1890); 47 (Coxe, 1815)
1763	36	37 (Desdevises Du Dezert, 1899); 36 (Ballesteros y Beretta, 1832)
1764	38	36 (Tracy, 1975)
1765	41	39 (Tracy, 1975)
1766	43	64–83 (Headlam, 1921); 39 (Tracy, 1975)
1767	45	38 (Tracy, 1975)
1768	47	42 (Tracy, 1975)
1769	49	49–52 (Tracy, 1975)
1770	51	51 (Olague, 1950–1; Desdevises Du Dezert, 1899; Ballesteros y Beretta, 1932)
1771	53	[44] (Tracy, 1975)
1772	56	63 (Tracy, 1975)
1773	58	
1774	60	64 (Olague, 1950–1; Desdevises Du Dezert, 1899; Ballesteros y Beretta, 1932); 60 (Muhmann, 1975); 58 (Fernandez Duro, 1972–3; Anderson, 1961); 53 (Tracy, 1975)

282

Table 9.5   Spain's estimated annual number of warships, 1494–1836

Year	Number of warships	Sources on numbers of warships
1775	61	61 (Muhmann, 1975); 60 (Richmond, 1946)
1776	62	62 (Edler, 1911)
1777	64	63/[38] (Tracy, 1975)
1778	66	67 (Olague, 1950–1; Desdevises Du Dezert, 1899); 66 (Ballesteros y Beretta, 1932); 62 (de Jonge, 1869); 60 (Mahan, 1890; Southworth, 1968); [50] (Tracy, 1975)
1779	60	60 (Headlam, 1921; Mahan, 1890); [60] (Olague, 1950–1); 40 (Coxe, 1815); [32] (Desdevises Du Dezert, 1899)
1780	62	77 (Charnock, 1800–3); (de Peyster, 1905)
1781	64	
1782	65	
1783	67	'67' (Chalmers, 1794)
1784	67	
1785	67	
1786	67	
1787	67	67 (Ibanez de Ibero, 1943; 50 armed (Desdevises Du Dezert, 1899)
1788	76	76 (Muhmann, 1975); 66 (Coxe, 1815); 64 (Moreau de Jonnes, 1835)
1789	72	72 (Anderson, 1961); 72 w/58+ (Vecchj, 1895)
1790	74	
1791	77	
1792	79	79 (Muhmann, 1975); '76'/[56] (James, 1886); '76' (Lloyd, 1965a); 56 (Dupuy and Dupuy, 1977)
1793	76	'76'/[60] (Richmond, 1946); '76'/[56] (Mahan, 1892; Wilson, 1904); 60 (Pemsel, 1977)
1794	74	
1795	72	[46] (Fernandez Duro, 1972–3)
1796	70	
1797	68	
1798	66	76 (Ibanez de Ibero, 1943; March y Labores, 1854; Olague, 1950–1; Desdevises Du Dezert, 1899); 66 (Ballesteros y Beretta, 1932)
1799	63	76 (Desdevises Du Dezert, 1899); 63 (Ballesteros y Beretta, 1932)
1800	63	
1801	63	
1802	63	
1803	63	63 (Richmond, 1946); [30] (Pemsel, 1977)
1804	57	
1805	51	51 mobilised (Desdevises Du Dezert, 1899)

France, Spain, Russia, Germany, Japan 283

Table 9.5   Spain's estimated annual number of warships, 1494–1836

Year	Number of warships	Sources on numbers of warships
1806	42	42 (Ballesteros y Beretta, 1932); '42'/12 armed [12] (Ballesteros y Beretta, 1932)
1807	42	[12] (Ballesteros y Beretta, 1932)
1808	42	42 (Moreau de Jonnes, 1835; Fernandez Duro, 1972–3); [12] (Ballesteros y Beretta, 1932)
1809		[12] (Ballesteros y Beretta, 1932)
1810		25 (Brenton, 1923–5); [12] (Ballesteros y Beretta, 1932)
1811		[12] (Ballesteros y Beretta, 1932)
1812		11 (Brenton, 1823–5); [12] (Ballesteros y Beretta, 1932)
1813		[12] (Ballesteros y Beretta, 1932)
1814		'21' (Fernando Duro, 1972–3); [12] (Ballesteros y Beretta, 1932)
1815		[12] (Ballesteros y Beretta, 1932)
1817		42/16 armed (Moreau de Jonnes, 1835)
1830		6 (Moreau de Jonnes, 1835)
1834		3 (Fernandez Duro, 1972–3)
1835		3 (Moreau de Jonnes, 1835)
1836		3 (*Almanach de Gotha*)

Note: See Notes to Table 8.2.

RUSSIA/THE SOVIET UNION

Of the five global powers under review in this chapter, it is probably fair to say that the development of Russian naval power took place in spite of some of the most formidable obstacles faced by any members of the five-state group to the development of a maritime orientation. A major advantage, on the other hand, has been the alignment of Russia on the side of the oceanic coalitions in three global wars – beginning with Peter the Great's leaning toward Britain and the Netherlands after 1700, through Russia's participation in most of the coalitions against Napoleon, and to the role played in the twentieth century's two world wars. Nevertheless, many of the obstacles have persisted well into the twentieth century.

In the first place, the development of an ocean-going navy presumes

284 *Country Data*

some degree of access to an ocean. In spite of gradual expansion, the central Muscovy state remained virtually landlocked – although Arkhangelsk, created as a fortified monastery in 1584, was the principal port of Russia until the creation of St Petersburg in 1703. Nor was it possible to achieve and hold onto the maritime access that was eventually acquired without struggle. Strong regional powers – the Ottomans in the south-east and Sweden in the north-east – initially blocked the way. But even when their opposition was overcome by force, the geopolitical circumstances of the Black and Baltic Seas rendered further access beyond these local, regional waters less than guaranteed. Yet, the fact that the Russian navy did eventually acquire multiple approaches to the sea in the north (White Sea), the north-east (Baltic Sea), the south-east (Black Sea), and the west (Pacific) – all fairly distant from one another – made it increasingly difficult to defend these maritime venues simultaneously and concentrate naval strength when necessary. Seasonal bad weather and ice in three of the four outlets only complicated matters further.

Russia was slow – probably the slowest of the European powers – to create an industrial infrastructure that would facilitate economic growth and/or support the creation and maintenance of a competitive navy. In the absence of a native infrastructure, the development of a Russian navy was highly dependent on foreign technology. Ivan the Terrible began the process of bringing in Western European instructors, designers, and skilled workers in the mid-to-late sixteenth century but it was Peter the Great (ruling from 1682 to 1725) who was most responsible for creating a foundation for constructing fleets on the basis of Dutch and English experience. After the successful seizure of Azov (1696) due in part to the efforts of a newly-built galley fleet, a large shipbuilding programme was announced and more than fifty Russians were sent for training in Venice, England, and Holland. Small ship squadrons were established at Taganrog (Black Sea) and Arkhangelsk (White Sea). Within the next decade, a naval academy (Moscow), a principal dockyard (St Petersburg), and a Baltic naval base (Kronstadt) had been created. By 1725, several additional shipbuilding facilities had been built, an Admiralty administrative structure was erected, and a second Baltic naval base (Revel-Tallin) was founded. In the course of these activities and in the context of the Northern Wars, Russia acquired, with British help, through purchase abroad and construction at home, the core of a ship-of-the-line fleet which enabled it to seize regional naval primacy in the Baltic in fairly short order.

France, Spain, Russia, Germany, Japan 285

However, still another handicap in the development of a Russian navy has been the familiar cycle of interest and disinterest in maritime expansion that seems to be characteristic of other states surveyed in this chapter with strong interests in, or incentives for, continental/ territorial expansion. This cycle is accentuated all the more by governmental policies that are especially sensitive to the personalities and orientations of individual rulers. As an example, Peter the Great's death in 1725 ended the first spurt of naval expansion. Governmental disinterest was particularly critical in the Russian case because of the tendency to use fir in building wooden sailing ships. The quick-rotting tendency of fir is illustrated by Woodward (1965, p. 39) who notes that as many as twenty-one ships-of-the-line had to be condemned for wood rot between 1750 and 1756. A second phase of interest in naval expansion came only in the 1770s during the reign of Catherine II. One of the more noteworthy developments of this period was the creation of a Russian Mediterranean squadron to be used in an attack on the Ottoman Empire (Battle of Chesme, 1770). The Black Sea fleet experienced expansion in this phase as well and a small Caspian fleet was also created.

The Russian navy was active during the French Revolutionary and Napoleonic Wars. It conducted joint operations with the British navy in the North Sea and Mediterranean in the late 1790s and early 1800s against the French, Dutch, and Ottoman navies. Between 1808 and 1809, coalitional shifts arrayed Britain and Sweden against Russia in the Baltic while, in the Mediterranean, the British interned the Russian squadron to ensure that it could not be used by the French. In any event, the intensive land combat in the Third Coalition phase reduced the significance of the Russian navy and, in many respects, this decline in its military priority appears to have been little altered until several years after the Crimean War.

Mitchell (1974, p. 158) accurately describes the Russian defeat of the Turkish navy at Sinope (1853) as the last Russian fleet victory. Sinope also is noted for its demonstration of the effectiveness of explosive shells and its implications for dooming the wooden ship-of-the-line. But the intervention of Britain and France restricted the wartime role of the Russian navy primarily to the 1855 scuttling of the Black Sea fleet to prevent its capture.

Russia joined the popular experimentation with ironclads in the early 1860s and even contributed a uniquely circular warship which, unfortunately, did not turn out to be a successful innovation. Yet overall fleet expansion was only moderate in this early battleship era,

286   *Country Data*

reflecting in part the adoption of a coastal defence orientation. Some attention was given to rebuilding the Black Sea fleet in the 1880s and expanding the Pacific fleet in the 1890s. But the Russo-Japanese War of 1904–5 proved to be a major setback. First, the Pacific fleet was virtually destroyed by Japanese attacks and then a substantial proportion of the Baltic fleet, forced to steam dramatically, albeit slowly, from northern Europe around Africa and south-east Asia to east Asia, was also devastated at Tsushima.

By the onset of the First World War, few steps had been taken to repair the devastating damage suffered in 1904–5. As a consequence, the Russian navy played only a very limited role in the 1914–17 conflict and emerged at the end of the war in even poorer material shape then it had begun – a state of affairs hardly helped by the additional damage sustained in the ensuing Allied intervention and the Russian civil war. One of the last acts of the civil war was the bloody suppression of a sailor's revolt at Kronstadt (March, 1921).

Prior to the rise of Joseph Stalin, the Soviet navy received little attention beyond some much-needed repairs to existing ships. Serious fleet expansion at the destroyer level was only begun in the five-year plan for 1933–7. New shipyards (Gorkiy, Molotovsk-later Severodvinsk, and Komsomolsk) were established at this time as well. Battleships and aircraft-carriers were to receive emphasis in the plan for 1937–42 but the Second World War broke out before much could be accomplished in reconfiguring the composition of the surface fleet.

Despite the existence of a rather large submarine capability, the Soviet navy played much the same minor role in the Second World War that had been performed by the Russian navy in the First World War. At the end of the war, few major surface vessels were again operational and even fewer resources were immediately available to improve the extremely weak status of the Soviet fleet. However, the Soviet Union did retain Lend–Lease vessels of various size through the late 1940s (major vessels) and mid-1950s (smaller craft). In addition, a large number of ships, encompassing almost every class in operation at the time, were acquired as prizes of war or reparations from the fleets of Germany, Italy, Japan, Finland and Rumania.

The early post-war rebuilding efforts focused on developing submarine capabilities and capitalised on captured German technology. Yet as early as 1950, a ten-year plan to expand the surface fleet that included several carriers was adopted only to be substantially modified after the death of Stalin in 1953. In the mid-to-late 1950s and into the early 1960s, the need for large surface warships was played down in favour of an emphasis on developing smaller surface ships and submarines as missile platforms to counter carrier attacks and for nuclear deterrence purposes. During this phase, operational activities tended to be restricted mainly to the coastal waters protected by the four main fleets (Baltic, Black Sea, Pacific, and Northern).

After several Middle Eastern crises, the 1962 Cuban missile crisis, and the fall of Nikita Khruschev, an increased emphasis on the production of larger surface ships became apparent to facilitate traditional force projection activities, but not at the expense of the continued stress on nuclear submarines and sea-launched ballistic missile capabilities. The return to more balanced fleet principles and considerable fleet expansion has been accompanied by an increased naval presence in the Mediterranean, the Atlantic, the Caribbean, the Indian Ocean, and the Pacific (see Weinland, 1973, 1975; Dismukes and McConnell, 1979; Watson, 1982). Through 1986, however, the Soviet navy has yet to develop an operational attack aircraft-carrier capability beyond the construction of several of the lighter carriers of the Moskva (1967–8) and Kiev (post-1976) classes which carry helicopter and VSTOL aircraft. A large deck carrier nonetheless is currently (1985) rumoured to be under construction. Table 9.6 lists the sources of information about Russian warships; Figure 9.3 illustrates the Russian/Soviet Union relative capability share and Table 9.7 gives the estimated annual number of Russian warships from 1700 to 1860, while Table 9.8 continues this information – for battleships – from 1861 to 1945.

Tables 9.9 to 9.13 inclusive represent the annual calculations of the

Table 9.6   Sources on Russian warships, 1700–1860

Almanach de Gotha	Mitchell (1949)
Anderson (1969)	Mitchell (1974)
Bain (1968)	Moreau de Jonnes (1835)
Bartlett (1963)	Morris (1977)
Brenton (1823–5)	Pensel (1977)
Bridge (1899)	Reynolds (1974)
Busk (1859)	Richmond (1946)
Charnock (1800–3)	Slany (1958)
Dmytryshyn (1977)	Schnitzler (1829)
James (1886)	Southworth (1968)
Jones (1981)	Vecchj (1895)
Kluchevsky (1960)	Woodward (1965)
Lloyd (1965a, 1965b)	

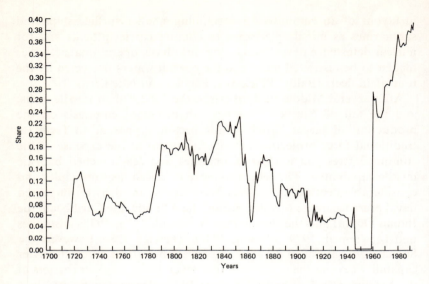

Figure 9.3   Russian/Soviet relative capability share 1714–1993

Table 9.7   Russia's estimated annual number of warships, 1700–1860

Year	Number of warships	Sources on numbers of warships
1700		0 (Anderson, 1969)
1701		0 (Anderson, 1969)
1702		0 (Anderson, 1969)
1703		0 (Anderson, 1969)
1704		0 (Anderson, 1969)
1705		0 (Anderson, 1969); 9 (Mitchell, 1974)
1706		0 (Anderson, 1969)
1707		0 (Anderson, 1969)
1708		0 (Anderson, 1969); 2 (Bridge, 1899)
1709		0 (Anderson, 1969)
1710		0 (Anderson, 1969; Mitchell, 1974)
1711		[2 in Baltic] (Anderson, 1969)
1712		3 (Bridge, 1899)
1713		5 (Bridge, 1899); 13 (Southworth, 1968); 4 (Mitchell, 1949)
1714	10	9 (Bridge, 1899); 10 (Mitchell, 1974); 40 (Charnock, 1800–3); 26 w/42–74 (Jones, 1981)

Table 9.7   Russia's estimated annual number of warships, 1700–1860

Year	Number of warships	Sources on numbers of warships
1715	17	17 (Bridge, 1899)
1716	16	16 (Bridge, 1899)
1717	15	15 (Bridge, 1899)
1718	23	20 (Bridge, 1899); [23 in Baltic] (Schnitzler, 1829)
1719	26	20 (Bridge, 1899); 28 (Jones, 1981)
1720	29	29 (Mitchell, 1974)
1721	29	[29 in Baltic] (Anderson, 1969); 22 (Bridge, 1899)
1722	29	[29 in Baltic] (Anderson, 1969); 27 (Bridge, 1899)
1723	30	[30 in Baltic] (Schnitzler, 1829)
1724	32	28 (Bridge, 1899)
1725	34	58 (Reynolds, 1974); 50 (Morris, 1977); 48 (Bain, 1968; Kluchevsky, 1960); [34 in Baltic] (Mitchell, 1974); [32 in Baltic] (Dmytryshyn, 1977)
1726	31	[12] (Slany, 1958)
1727	28	[12] (Slany, 1958)
1728	25	[25 in Baltic] (Anderson, 1969); [5–6] (Mitchell, 1974); [1–2] (Slany, 1958)
1729	24	[1–2] (Slany, 1958)
1730	22	
1731	21	
1732	19	
1733	18	
1734	17	
1735	15	15 (Slany, 1958)
1736	15	[3–5] (Slany, 1958); [20 in Baltic] (Jones, 1981)
1737	16	[3–5] (Slany, 1958)
1738	16	[3–5] (Slany, 1958)
1739	17	[3–5] (Slany, 1958)
1740	17	[17 in Baltic] (Anderson, 1969); [3–5] (Slany, 1958)
1741	14	14 (Mitchell, 1974); [13] (Woodward, 1965); [3–5] (Slany, 1958)
1742	15	
1743	17	17 (Mitchell, 1974; Woodward, 1965)
1744	20	
1745	11	
1746	24	[24 in Baltic] (Anderson, 1969; Schnitzler, 1829); '23' in Baltic (Jones, 1981)
1747	24	
1748	23	
1749	23	
1750	23	
1751	22	
1752	22	
1753	21	

290

Table 9.7   Russia's estimated annual number of warships, 1700–1860

Year	Number of warships	Sources on numbers of warships
1754	21	
1755	21	
1756	20	[20 in Baltic] (Anderson, 1969; Mitchell, 1974; Woodward, 1965)
1757	22	22 (Mitchell, 1974); '27' [21] (Jones, 1981)
1758	21	
1759	20	
1760	19	18–20 (Charnock, 1800–3)
1761	19	
1762	18	
1763	18	24 (Jones, 1981)
1764	17	
1765	17	
1766	17	
1767	16	
1768	15	'20' (Jones, 1981)
1769	15	15 (Woodward, 1965)
1770	15	13 (Woodward, 1965)
1771	16	
1772	16	
1773	17	
1774	17	
1775	17	[15 in Baltic] (Anderson, 1969)
1776	18	
1777	18	
1778	19	
1779	19	
1780	19	[15 in Baltic] (Anderson, 1969); 22 (Lloyd, 1965a); 22 w/50+ /19 w/60+ (Charnock, 1800–3)
1781	24	[17 in Baltic] (Anderson, 1969)
1782	29	[17 in Baltic] (Anderson, 1969)
1783	34	[15] (Richmond, 1946)
1784	39	
1785	44	[15 in Baltic] (Anderson, 1969)
1786	49	
1787	54	'54' (Anderson, 1969); 7 in Black Sea (Lloyd, 1965a); 5 in Black Sea (Pemsel, 1977); 17 in Baltic (Woodward, 1965)
1788	48	'48' [31]/37 in Baltic (Anderson, 1969); '54'/[30] (Mitchell, 1974); 4 in Black Sea (Woodward, 1965); 17 in Baltic (Pemsel, 1977)
1789	67	67 w/66–100 (Vecchj, 1895); '41'/[35] (Anderson, 1969); 35 in Baltic (Woodward, 1965); [21 in Baltic] (Pemsel, 1977)

291

Table 9.7   Russia's estimated annual number of warships, 1700–1860

Year	Number of warships	Sources on numbers of warships
1790	75	[29] (Anderson, 1969; Mitchell, 1974); '75' in Baltic and Black Sea (Lloyd, 1965b); 50+ (Lloyd, 1965a); 30 in Baltic (Woodward, 1965; Southworth, 1968); [16 in Black Sea] (Pemsel, 1977)
1791	73	[46 in Baltic] (Anderson, 1969); [32] (Mitchell, 1974); 31 in Baltic (Pemsel, 1977); 6 in Black Sea (Woodward, 1965); 22 in Black Sea (Anderson, 1961)
1792	71	40 (James, 1886)
1793	69	[26] (Mitchell, 1974)
1794	67	
1795	65	[21] (Mitchell, 1974)
1796	62	[40] (Mitchell, 1974); 40 (Jones, 1981)
1797	60	60/45 in Baltic/15 in Black Sea (Mitchell, 1974)
1798	59	6 in Black Sea (Woodward, 1965)
1799	59	70 (Charnock, 1800–3)
1800	58	82 (Vecchj, 1895)
1801	58	[61]/31 in Baltic (James, 1886)
1802	57	
1803	57	
1804	56	'27' in Baltic/'29' in Black Sea (Schnitzler, 1829)
1805	57	
1806	58	
1807	58	7 in Mediterranean (Pemsel, 1977)
1808	59	
1809	60	60 (Richmond, 1946)
1810	57	18 (Brenton, 1823–5)
1811	54	
1812	51	19 (Brenton, 1823–5); 30 in Baltic (Jones, 1981)
1813	49	
1814	46	
1815	43	26 (Mitchell, 1974)
1816	40	c. 40 (Bartlett, 1963)
1817	40	
1818	40	
1819	39	
1820	39	
1821	39	
1822	39	
1823	39	
1824	39	
1825	39	39/28 in Baltic/11 in Black Sea (Mitchell, 1974); '15'/[5] in Baltic (Jones, 1981)
1826	35	

292

Table 9.7   Russia's estimated annual number of warships, 1700–1860

Year	Number of warships	Sources on numbers of warships
1827	32	[8 in Baltic] (Bartlett, 1963); 32/8–9 in Baltic/8 in Mediterranean/16 in Black Sea (Schnitzler, 1829)
1828	32	32 (Moreau de Jonnes, 1835)
1829	32	
1830	32	32 (*Almanach de Gotha*)
1831	33	
1832	34	
1833	35	
1834	37	
1835	38	'12'/[8 in Black Sea] (Bartlett, 1963)
1836	39	
1837	40	
1838	41	41/[39 in Baltic and Black Sea] (Bartlett, 1963); 27 in Baltic (Anderson, 1969)
1839	41	
1840	41	66/35 in Black Sea/31 in Baltic (*Almanach de Gotha*)
1841	41	
1842	41	
1843	41	
1844	42	
1845	42	
1846	43	
1847	43	
1848	43	
1849	43	
1850	43	50 (Busk, 1859)
1851	43	
1852	43	
1853	43	60 (Vecchj, 1895); 16 in Black Sea (Pemsel, 1977)
1854	44	30 in Baltic (Anderson, 1969)
1855	30	14 scuttled in Black Sea (Pemsel, 1977)
1856	27	
1857	25	
1858	22	
1859	19	19 (Busk, 1859; Pemsel, 1977)
1860	16	

Notes: See Notes to Table 8.2

Table 9.8   Russian/Soviet battleships, 1861–1945

Year	Number of ships	Year	Number of ships	Year	Number of ships
1861	0	1890	4	1918	5
1862	0	1891	4	1919	5
1863	0	1892	4	1920	4
1864	1	1893	5	1921	4
1865	5	1894	5	1922	3
1866	6	1895	5	1923	3
1867	6	1896	5	1924	3
1868	8	1897	6	1925	3
1869	9	1898	6	1926	3
1870	13	1899	4	1927	3
1871	13			1928	3
1872	13	1900	6	1929	3
1873	13	1901	6	1930	3
1874	14	1902	7	1931	3
1875	14	1903	8	1932	3
1876	15	1904	10	1933	3
1877	16	1905	8	1934	3
1878	17	1906	4	1935	3
1879	17	1907	4	1936	3
1880	1	1908	3	1937	3
1881	1	1909	3	1938	3
1882	1	1910	0	1939	3
1883	1	1911	0	1940	3
1884	1	1912	0	1941	2
1885	1	1913	0	1942	2
1886	3	1914	4	1943	2
1887	4	1915	6	1944	3
1888	4	1916	5	1945	3
1889	4	1917	6		

Soviet Union's evolving sea-launched ballistic missile and nuclear-attack submarine capabilities. The first step in estimating the naval ballistic-missile capabilities involved determining the mix of submarine missile-platforms in commission each year (Table 9.9). The number of submarine classes is then matched with the number of warheads of a designated type carried by each submarine. Table 9.10 thus aggregates the total number of warheads theoretically at sea in each year. Next, each warhead type is believed to be associated with certain performance characteristics: Tables 9.11 and 9.12 aggregate equivalent megatonnage (EMT) and lethality (CMP) respectively.

Table 9.9   Soviet nuclear ballistic submarines: multiple class estimates, 1960–93

Year	Z-V	Golf				Hotel			Yankee		Delta				Typhoon	Total
		I	*II*	*III*	*IV*	*I*	*II*	*III*	*I*	*II*	*I*	*II*	*III*	*IV*		
1960	4	5				1										10
1961	6	12				3										19
1962	7	22				8										37
1963	7	22				9										38
1964	10	30				10										50
1965	10	30				13										53
1966	10	30				13										53
1967	10	15	10			13			1							49
1968	10	15	10			15			2							52
1969	6	15	10			10	5		8							54
1970	5	15	10				9		12							51
1971	4	12	10				8		20							54
1972	3	12	10				9		27							61
1973	2	12	10				9		32		2					67

Year	C1	C2	C3	C4	C5	C6	C7	C8	C9	C10	C11	C12	C13	C14	Total
1974	1	9	11			8		33		7						69
1975	1	9	11			8		34		11						74
1976	1	9	11			8		34		13	4					80
1977	1	9	12			8		34		14	7	1				86
1978		7	12			7	1	33	1	15	8	4				88
1979		5	13			7	1	32	1	16	6	8				89
1980		2	12	1	1	7	1	30	1	16	6	10				88
1981			10	1	1	6	1	28	1	18	4	11				81
1982			10	1		6	1	25	1	18	4	13				79
1983			10	1		5	1	24	1	18	4	14			1	79
1984			10	1		1	1	23	1	18	4	14			2	75
1985			10	1		1	1	22	1	18	4	14			3	75
1986			10	1		1	1	21	1	18	4	15			3	75
1987			19	1		1	1	17	1	18	4	15		3	4	75
1988			19	1		1	1	16	1	18	4	16		3	4	75
1989			10	1		1	1	14	1	18	4	16		4	5	75
1990						1	1	13	1	18	4	17		4	5	64
1991						1	1	11	1	18	4	17		5	6	64
1992						1	1	10	1	18	4	18		5	6	64
1993						1	1	8	1	18	4	18		6	7	64

Table 9.10   Soviet nuclear ballistic submarines: warhead estimates, 1960–93

Year	SSN4	SSN5	SSN6	SSN8	SSN17	SSN18	SSN20	SSN23	Total
1960	26								26
1961	57								57
1962	104								104
1963	107								107
1964	140								140
1965	149								149
1966	149								149
1967	104	30	16						150
1968	110	30	32						172
1969	87	45	128						260
1970	55	57	192						304
1971	44	54	320						418
1972	42	57	432						531
1973	40	57	512	24					633
1974	29	57	528	94					698
1975	29	57	544	132					762

Year									Total
1976	29	57	544	220		80			786
1977	29	60	544	280		80			993
1978	21	57	528	314	12	320			1252
1979	15	60	512	294	12	640			1533
1980	6	57	484	300	12	800			1659
1981		48	452	292	12	880			1684
1982		48	400	292	12	1040			1792
1983		45	384	292	12	1120	160		2013
1984		33	368	292	12	1120	320		2145
1985		33	352	292	12	1120	480		2289
1986		33	336	292	12	1200	480		2353
1987		33	272	292	12	1200	640	480	2929
1988		33	256	292	12	1280	640	480	2993
1989		33	256	292	12	1280	800	640	3313
1990		3	208	292	12	1360	800	640	3315
1991		3	176	286	12	1360	960	800	3597
1992		3	160	286	12	1440	960	800	3661
1993		3	128	286	12	1440	1120	960	3949

Table 9.11   Soviet nuclear ballistic submarines: warhead equivalent megatonnage estimates, 1960–93

Year	SSN4	SSN5	SSN6	SSN8	SSN17	SSN18	SSN20	SSN23	Total
1960	26								26.0
1961	57								57.0
1962	104								104.0
1963	197								107.0
1964	140								140.0
1965	149								149.0
1966	149								149.0
1967	104	39.3	13.2						156.5
1968	110	39.3	26.4						175.7
1969	87	59.0	105.6						251.6
1970	55	74.7	158.4						288.1
1971	44	70.1	264.0						378.7
1972	42	74.7	356.4						473.1
1973	40	74.7	422.4	19.8					537.1
1974	29	74.7	435.6	69.3					608.6
1975	29	74.7	448.8	108.9					661.4

1976	29	74.7	448.8	181.5					734.0
1977	29	78.6	448.8	231.0		50.4			837.8
1978	21	74.7	435.6	259.1	7.6	201.6			999.6
1979	15	78.6	422.4	242.6	7.6	403.2			1169.4
1980	6	74.7	399.3	247.5	7.6	504.0			1239.1
1981		62.9	372.9	240.9	7.6	554.4			1238.7
1982		62.9	330.0	240.9	7.6	655.2			1296.6
1983		59.0	316.8	240.9	7.6	705.6	35.2		1365.1
1984		43.2	303.6	240.9	7.6	705.6	70.4		1371.3
1985		43.2	290.4	240.9	7.6	705.6	105.6		1395.3
1986		43.2	277.2	240.9	7.6	756.0	105.6		1430.5
1987		43.2	224.4	240.9	7.6	756.0	140.8	105.6	1518.5
1988		43.2	211.2	240.9	7.6	806.4	140.8	105.6	1555.7
1989		43.2	184.8	240.9	7.6	806.4	176.0	140.8	1599.7
1990		3.9	171.6	236.0	7.6	856.8	176.0	140.8	1592.7
1991		3.9	145.2	236.0	7.6	856.8	211.2	176.0	1636.7
1992		3.9	132.0	236.0	7.6	907.2	211.2	176.0	1673.9
1993		3.9	105.6	236.0	7.6	907.2	246.4	211.2	1717.9

Table 9.12 Soviet nuclear ballistic submarines: warhead lethality estimates, 1960–93
(Counter Military Potential)

Year	SSN4	SSN5	SSN6	SSN8	SSN17	SSN18	SSN20	SSN23	Total
1960	11.5								11.5
1961	25.3								25.3
1962	46.2								46.2
1963	47.5								47.5
1964	62.2								62.2
1965	66.2								66.2
1966	66.2								66.2
1967	46.2	17.5	26.9						90.6
1968	48.8	17.5	53.9						120.2
1969	38.6	26.2	215.6						280.4
1970	24.4	33.2	323.3						380.9
1971	19.5	31.4	538.9						589.8
1972	18.7	33.2	727.5						779.4
1973	17.8	33.2	862.2	30.9					944.1
1974	12.9	33.2	889.2	108.3					1043.6

301

Year									
1975	12.9	34.9	916.1	170.1					1132.3
1976	12.9	33.2	916.1	283.6					1245.8
1977	12.9	34.9	916.1	361.0		201.6			1526.5
1978	9.3	33.2	889.2	404.7	13.4	806.4			2156.2
1979	6.7	34.9	862.2	379.0	13.4	1612.8			2909.0
1980	2.7	33.2	815.1	386.7	13.4	2016.0			3267.1
1981		28.0	761.1	376.3	13.4	2217.6			3396.4
1982		28.0	673.6	376.3	13.4	2620.8			3712.1
1983		26.2	646.7	376.3	13.4	2822.4	390.4		4275.4
1984		19.2	619.7	376.3	13.4	2822.4	780.8		4631.8
1985		19.2	592.8	376.3	13.4	2822.4	1171.2		4995.3
1986		19.2	565.8	376.3	13.4	3024.0	1171.3		5169.9
1987		19.2	458.0	376.3	13.4	3024.0	1561.6	1689.6	7142.1
1988		19.2	431.1	376.3	13.4	3225.6	1561.6	1689.6	7316.8
1989		19.2	377.2	376.3	13.4	3225.6	1952.0	2252.8	8216.5
1990		1.7	350.3	368.6	13.4	3427.2	1952.0	2252.8	8366.0
1991		1.7	296.4	368.6	13.4	3427.2	2342.4	2816.0	9265.7
1992		1.7	269.4	368.6	13.4	3628.8	2342.4	2816.0	9440.3
1993		1.7	215.6	368.6	13.4	3628.8	2732.8	3379.2	10340.1

302 *Country Data*

Table 9.13 Soviet nuclear attack and cruise-missile submarines, 1958–93

Year	Number	Year	Number	Year	Number
1958	4	1970	55	1982	108
1959	10	1971	63	1983	111
1960	15	1972	67	1984	114
1961	18	1973	68	1985	117
1962	18	1974	73	1986	119
1963	23	1975	76	1987	114
1964	27	1876	81	1988	109
1965	28	1977	83	1989	106
1966	33	1978	89	1990	105
1967	39	1979	91	1991	104
1968	42	1980	96	1992	103
1969	48	1981	101	1993	97

Although submarines are subject to refitting of newer missiles from time to time – a factor which we have tried to take into consideration whenever such information is available – the following schedule was used to make the various calculations discussed in Chapter 4:

Submarine class	Missile type	Number of warheads	Yield (megatonnage)	Accuracy (CEP)
Z-V	SSN4	2	1.00	1.50
Golf	SSN4	3	1.00	1.50
Golf II	SSN5	3	1.50	1.50
Golf III	SSN8	4	0.75	0.80
Golf IV	SSN6	4	0.75	0.70
Hotel I	SSN4	3	1.00	1.50
Hotel II	SSN5	3	1.50	1.50
Hotel III	SSN8	3	0.75	0.80
Yankee I	SSN6	16	0.75	0.70
Yankee II	SSN17	12	0.50	0.75
Delta I	SSN8	12	0.75	0.80
Delta II	SSN8	16	0.75	0.80
Delta III	SSN18	80	0.50	0.50
Delta IV	SSN23	160	0.10	0.25
Typhoon	SSN20	160	0.10	0.30

Several caveats, however, are immediately in order. The missile attribute information, as one might imagine, is somewhat speculative.

Nor is it subject to any great level of consensus. Moreover, the relevant literature also suggests that some of the missiles have been MIRVed. Various sources have indicated that the SSN6s, SSN8s, and the SSN18s are believed to have been modified in various ways but we have access to extremely little information on anything resembling the actual number of submarines carrying missiles with these multiple warheads which, by and large, would be associated with different yield and accuracy attributes than those listed above. Finally, very little information is available in open sources on the characteristics of the SSN23 and what is available tends to be contradictory. Accordingly, the SSN23 characteristics listed above should be regarded as even more speculative than the other listed attributes.

Projecting Soviet capabilities to 1993 is a different proposition from forecasting United States fleet developments (Chapter 8). In the United States, past and future construction plans are public information. Much less information is available for the Soviets. But this does not mean that we are totally in the dark. The rate of expansion during the early 1980s provides one parameter even though we should not assume that Soviet naval growth rates can simply be extended into the future. Another piece of information is supplied by the SALT I limitation of sixty-two ballistic-missile submarine hulls (excluding the Golf and Hotel classes). There are also reasons to believe that construction is more likely in some classes than in others. For example, ballistic-missile-submarine construction in the immediate future is likely to be concentrated in the Delta III/IV and Typhoon series. Finally, we also have some access to informed speculation about the future size of the Soviet Navy. MccGwire (1980, pp. 8–9) whose Soviet ship estimates have proved quite helpful in dealing with earlier decades, predicts the following array for the period 1992–5: one or two new-type large carriers, sixty to seventy-five nuclear-ballistic-missile submarines, and about 100 nuclear-powered attack submarines (after rising to a peak of 135 in 1987–8).

Combining these various ingredients, we have adopted several working assumptions in generating the Soviet data through 1993. It seems unlikely that any large carriers will be ready for sea-duty prior to about 1992. Yet there seems no reason to expect production to stop at one. Consequently, a second carrier has been forecast for 1993. Less liberally, ballistic-missile-submarine production seems to have slowed in the early 1980s. New SSBN construction averaged close to six boats per year in the period 1970–9. The average was down to about two boats per year in the half-decade 1980–84. We are

304   *Country Data*

assuming that this slow and slowing expansion will continue as more Typhoons are built and with the introduction of the new SSN23 missile planned for 1987. Yankee I class submarines will continue to be withdrawn (possibly for conversion to attack-submarines) in order to maintain the 62 hull SALT I maximum.

For attack-submarines, we simply assume the construction of five new submarines per year (based on estimates from several sources of seven new nuclear submarines of all types per year), ignore the possibility of Yankee conversions, and estimate attack-submarines retirements based on a 25-year cycle. Following these procedures, net growth remains positive up to 1986 with a peak of 119 submarines. The difference between our figures and MccGwire's prediction can presumably be traced to our different treatment of the incentives for Yankee conversions. On the other hand, our figures are eventually quite similar in the early 1990s.

GERMANY

It is customary to begin a discussion of the German navy's history at some point around the middle of the nineteenth century. Hurd and Castle (1971, pp. 55–70), however, make an interesting case for the late seventeenth century. In 1675, Brandenburg (known as Prussia after 1701), in alliance with Denmark and the Netherlands, rented a small group of armed ships from a Dutch merchant and contributed this group to the war with Sweden (allied with France). After the war, the rental arrangement was continued and expanded despite the state's minimal coastline and lack of major ports. Two West African colonies were subsequently established and serviced by the fledgling fleet. The Brandenburg navy was also used in the Atlantic and West Indies for attempts to intercept the Spanish silver fleet. In the warfare of the 1690s, in alliance with England and the Netherlands, Brandenburg ships of war were also sent to raid French commerce. Even so, it would be extremely difficult to make a direct linkage between this first naval effort, presumably too limited to meet our ship-counting conventions, and nineteenth/twentieth century developments. Official indifference is credited with the early demise of both the colonies and the fleet by 1717.

Frederick the Great (1740–86) decided not to embark on the development of a navy for fear that it might detract from the importance of his army. Continued alliance with Britain also obviated

France, Spain, Russia, Germany, Japan 305

the necessity for a navy. Prussia encouraged privateering in the Seven Years War of the mid-eighteenth century but no Prussian navy operated in the Napoleonic Wars. Some consideration was evidently given to building a navy in 1815, 1825, and again in 1832 but each time the project was abandoned as too expensive. In 1848, a Danish blockade of the Prussian coast in the First Schleswig-Holstein War did prompt the arming of several merchant vessels, which, however, saw very little combat. The situation was fairly similar during the Second Schleswig-Holstein War (1864) but by this time Wilhemshaven and Kiel had been acquired in order to develop them as naval bases and dockyards, in conjunction with a third yard in Danzig, and to improve the Prussian access to the Baltic and North Seas.

In the late 1860s, a ten-year building programme was authorised by the North German Confederation but little more than coastal defence and showing the flag was envisioned. Apart from a clash between small boats near Cuba, the Franco-Prussian War (1870–1) was also restricted to land combat. Orders were even issued prohibiting German attacks on French commerce so as to discourage French naval retaliation. Germany also declined the opportunity to acquire French warships as part of the war settlement because of the scarcity of German sailors.

In addition to the virtual absence of a naval tradition, the related lack of a naval manpower pool, and a shallow and recently-acquired coastline, the German navy of the 1870s and 1880s found itself handicapped further by service rivalries, financial restraints, geography, and doctrinal vacillation. An Imperial Admiralty was created in 1871. But until 1888, the Admiralty was headed by an army officer and the navy was clearly subordinated as a junior service to the army and its missions. Long-term building plans were subject to annual legislative review, cut-backs, and social conflicts within the domestic political system. Geographically, the Baltic and North Sea main bases were separated by Denmark and the Danish straits which increased the difficulty of planning or achieving unified fleet operations. This obstacle prevailed until the completion of the Kaiser Wilhelm Canal in 1895. Strategically, the orientation of this period involved attacking Russia while defending the coast against a French attack. Yet the German navy was probably too small and too weak to perform either task.

The accession of Wilhelm II in 1888 brought both positive and negative benefits for the navy. Technically an admiral in the British navy by courtesy of Queen Victoria, Wilhelm was definitely a naval

306   *Country Data*

enthusiast who appreciated the need for a larger navy as an important instrument in pursuing *Weltpolitik* goals. Some autonomy from the army was bestowed on the navy by a reorganisation of the naval command structure but it also gave the inconsistent emperor greater personal control over naval operations. As a consequence, no general staff organisation comparable to that of the army was developed. Strategic doctrine and ship construction preferences also continued to waver until von Tirpitz was appointed Secretary of State for the Navy in 1897.

The German navy had established stations in East Asia and the West Indies as early as 1873. In the mid-1880s, newly acquired colonies in Africa and the South Pacific justified two more naval stations (East Africa and near Australia). In the 1890s, new disputes and frictions with Great Britain, Japan (after the seizure of Tsingtao), and the United States (dating from the 1870s and Samoa) expanded the sources of potential threats and opportunities. These *Weltpolitik*-related shifts in the nature and scope of German strategic problems, even though the Russian–French problem certainly persisted, increased the need for a competitive navy, which, in turn, increased the perceived need for battleships. The essence of the German naval problem in the late 1890s, however, was how best (and at what pace) to transform a still coastal-defence-oriented force with only a very small number of battleships into a truly competitive one without precipitating a pre-emptive strike by the vastly superior British navy. A related feature of this problem was precisely how competitive the German navy needed to be.

Von Tirpitz, a firm believer in seapower supplied the following answer:

Germany must have a battle fleet so strong that, even for the adversary with the greatest sea-power, a war against it would involve such dangers as to imperil his position in the world.

For this purpose it is not absolutely necessary that the German battle fleet should be as that of the greatest naval Power, because a great naval Power will not, as a rule, be in a position to concentrate all its striking forces against us. But even if it should succeed in meeting us with considerable superiority of strength, the defeat of a strong German fleet would so substantially weaken the enemy that, in spite of a victory he might have obtained, his own position in the world would no longer be secured by an adequate fleet (quoted in Hurd and Castle, 1971, p. 121).

Von Tirpitz's 'risk theory' assumed that the world-wide commitments of Great Britain, regarded as the primary naval threat after 1896, would prevent it from concentrating its full strength in an attack on Germany. Consequently, the German navy did not require full equality with Britain's large navy. Yet as the size of Germany's fleet expanded, Britain's incentive to attack should also decline correspondingly. Accordingly, the Navy Bill of 1898 called for a six-year plan to create nineteen battleships and a number of cruisers. However, the 1900 Navy Bill, capitalising on the popular hostility to Britain's Boer War, drastically revised the 1898 plan by proposing thirty-two battleships and forty-five cruisers.

The ensuing Anglo-German naval arms race might conceivably have led to a rethinking of the assumptions underlying the risk theory. Instead, it was argued by various German decision-makers that the British could not maintain their lead forever because of their widespread imperial responsibilities and, more curiously, perceived limitations on the ability to obtain naval personnel and financing. When the British navy introduced the Dreadnought battleship and the submarine, the German navy responded with their own Dreadnoughts (after 1907) and submarine fleet (after 1906). The rate of shipbuilding was further accelerated between 1908 and 1911 but after 1911 a variety of internal and external circumstances forced a reduction in the laying-down of new ships (from four to two per year). Nevertheless, the building-rate reduction did not alter the projected or planned size of the fleet (nearly sixty pre- and post-Dreadnought battleships). The risk theory notwithstanding, a quite plausible case, in fact, can be made that von Tirpitz's ultimate goal was parity with the British and not merely deterrence at the margin (see Kennedy, 1983, pp. 129–60). Yet as noted by Lambi (1984, p. 427), the effort 'failed to provide Germany with the opportunity of becoming a major world power and . . . substantially contributed to her so-called "encirclement"'.

At the outbreak of war, almost all the German navy remained in German ports with the British fleet blocking the possibilities for putting to sea easily. A few cruisers on foreign stations, especially those of the East Asian squadron, were active initially in commerce warfare, but their threat was largely neutralised by the end of 1914 (Battle of the Falkland Islands). Few submarines were available nor was their importance fully appreciated at the beginning of the war. However, apart from occasional bombardment raids on the English coasts and the 1916 fleet clash (Battle of Jutland), which neither side

308 *Country Data*

fully exploited, the German surface fleet played a primarily passive role throughout the war. A *guerre de course* strategy using submarines against British commerce was instead adopted in 1916 and particularly emphasised in 1917. Yet, rather than forcing Britain to leave the war, the unrestricted intermittent submarine attacks ultimately facilitated the adhesion of the United States to the anti-German coalition. The last two roles played by the German navy in the First World War involved a mutiny in October 1918 when the fleet was ordered to make one last effort to break the British blockade (the order was cancelled) and the June 1919 scuttling of the interned fleet at Scapa Flow in protest over the terms of the Versailles Treaty.

The Versailles Treaty limited Germany to a half-dozen pre-Dreadnought battleships and a few light cruisers. Moreover, the construction of any submarines or airplanes was prohibited. Thus the German navy entered the inter-war era with few ships of any value, a less-than-glorious war record, severe problems in controlling the political activities of its personnel (see Bird, 1977) and domestic as well as external hostility to its continued existence. Despite the economic and political instability of post-war Germany, or perhaps because of it, the navy managed to survive more or less intact without becoming subordinated to the army and with its pre-1914 goals of fleet expansion virtually undiminished. The first 'pocket' battleship joined the fleet in 1930 but real expansion came only after Hitler's rise to power. The 1935 Anglo-German naval treaty restricting the German navy to approximately one-third the size of Britain's navy represented a potential setback but the 1938 Z-plan projected a greatly expanded 1947 fleet that would contain thirteen battleships, four aircraft-carriers, over 100 cruisers and destroyers, and nearly 250 submarines (Bekker, 1974).

The Second World War began long before the Z-plan's goals could be realised. In 1939, the German navy had only five battleships of various sizes and less than sixty U-boats which, in any event, were once again assigned a low priority in the overall war effort. Unlike 1914, however, a good proportion of the small force was at sea when the war began but its numerical weakness offered the surface fleet little choice but to avoid combat and revert to commerce raiding. Gaining access to the Norwegian and French Atlantic bases should have improved the ability to carry out this task but, ironically, it only exposed the fleet to intensive aerial bombing. In early 1942, the Atlantic bases were abandoned by heavier ships. By early 1943, Hitler had concluded that the surface navy constituted a drain on the war effort and ordered the scrapping of the capital ships with their guns to be used on land for coastal defence. The order was only partially executed.

Despite the resource competition with the needs of the surface fleet, Operation Sea Lion, and the Russian and North African fronts, the submarine capability began to improve in early 1942. Yet the increased threat posed by U-boat attacks was paralleled by the development of more effective convoy procedures and new locational technology. Most observers view the Germans as having lost the intensive struggle over the control of the Atlantic sea lanes by 1943.

Table 9.14   German battleships, 1861–1945

Year	Number of ships	Year	Number of ships	Year	Number of ships
1861	0	1890	3	1919	0
1862	0	1891	4	1920	0
1863	0	1892	4	1921	0
1864	0	1893	4	1922	0
1865	2	1894	4	1923	0
1866	2	1895	4	1924	0
1867	4	1896	4	1925	0
1868	4	1897	4	1926	0
1869	5	1898	4	1927	0
1870	5	1899	5	1928	0
1871	5	1900	5	1929	0
1872	5	1901	7	1930	0
1873	5	1902	9	1931	0
1874	5	1903	12	1932	0
1875	8	1904	14	1933	1
1876	9	1905	16	1934	2
1877	10	1906	18	1935	2
1878	9	1907	20	1936	3
1879	9	1908	18	1937	3
1880	0	1909	20	1938	4
1881	0	1910	5	1939	5
1882	0	1911	9	1940	5
1883	0	1912	14	1941	5
1884	0	1913	17	1942	4
1885	0	1914	22	1943	4
1886	0	1915	23	1944	2
1887	0	1916	24	1945	0
1888	0	1917	25		
1889	0	1918	25		

Even earlier, little capability to interrupt the 1942 Allied landings in North Africa had been demonstrated. Subsequent amphibious invasions in Italy and France also met little resistance at sea. By late 1944, the sinking of the *Scharnhorst* in the North Sea and the bombing of the *Tirpitz* in Norway had reduced the remnants of the German surface fleet to a few cruisers and destroyers stationed in the Baltic.

Table 9.14 shows the annual numbers of German battleships from 1861 to 1945, and Figure 9.4 plots the German relative capability share from 1871 to 1945.

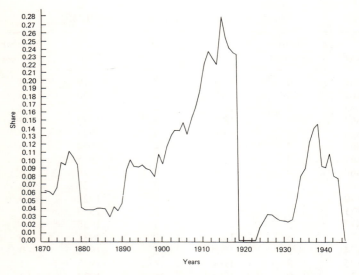

Figure 9.4   German relative capability share, 1871–1945

JAPAN

Perhaps one of the least useful generalisations to have emerged from the geopolitics literature is the notion that island nations are somehow more likely to develop seapower than nations not completely surrounded by water. Prior to the late nineteenth century, Japan definitely represented one of the many exceptions to this dubious rule. The surrounding waters did contribute to Japan's security for a long time, with help from storms as evidenced in the thirteenth-century

France, Spain, Russia, Germany, Japan 311

Mongol attempts, and certainly contributed to the retardation of the eventual incorporation of Japan into the European-centred world system. The same water barrier also acted to discourage Japanese expansion into East Asia, particularly after the Korean victory at sea in 1592 and Japan's self-imposed turn toward isolation in the seventeenth century, which included a ban on the construction of ships exceeding 50 tons as well as severe restrictions on external transactions.

Nevertheless, it was the seapower of other states – the United States' Perry mission in 1853–4 followed by Russian and British naval pressure – that was responsible for breaking down Japan's unusual success at keeping the outside world at bay for several hundred years. When the Western maritime powers developed needs for coaling stations in the eastern Pacific, in conjunction with older interests in better treatment for shipwrecked sailors and the perennial desire for new markets, the Japanese were in little position to resist the persuasiveness and technological superiority of western naval artillery.

If external seapower was ultimately responsible for the opening of Japan, it could have been argued (and was) that the only real defence required the development of a competitive Japanese naval capability. However logical or appealing such a programme might have been, it could not be achieved rapidly given the escalating technological requirements of competitive naval construction in the latter half of the nineteenth century. Japan not only lacked the industrial infrastructure, the end of isolation also undermined the Shogunate political system leading to an intermittent round of internal warfare and incipient centralisation efforts. The Shogunate navy had been initiated with the Dutch gift of a paddle-wheel steamer in 1855. But the Imperial navy was established only in 1868 and consisted of a small assortment of vessels captured in the civil-war combat with the clans. Ironically, the new navy's most powerful ship was an ironclad armoured ram which had been originally designed for the American Confederate State's navy, intercepted by the Federal navy, sold to the Shogunate navy, only to be seized finally by Imperial forces.

The Japanese navy was removed from army control and granted organisational autonomy in 1872. The Yokusaka Dockyard (Yokohama) was completed a year later with subsequent shipyards built at Kawasaki, Kure, Kobe, and Nagasaki. However, the first armoured ship to be built in Japan was not launched before 1891. In these formative years, the Japanese were heavily dependent on the Dutch in

312   *Country Data*

the 1850s but later on the British for ship construction and officer training (Etajima Naval Academy was founded in 1888) and, to a lesser extent, on the French for various forms of technical and tactical assistance. The first major expansion of the fleet consisted of three armoured ships ordered to be built in Great Britain in 1875 but genuine expansion really began in 1882 with an eight-year plan to acquire some forty-six ships of various types (thirty-two to be built abroad) with an emphasis on cruisers, torpedo boats, and gunboats. A battleship authorisation was not forthcoming until 1893.

Apart from expeditions to Formosa (1874) and Korea (1876), the Japanese navy's first combat experience took place in the Sino-Japanese War (1894–95). Although the Chinese navy was theoretically stronger at the outset, the Japanese navy experienced few problems in defeating their lesser skilled adversary in one major and several minor encounters. The Japanese army had equal success on land but after the war had ended, a Russian–German–French coalition intervened to deny Japanese control of the Liaotung Peninsula. As a consequence, the Japanese navy lost two potential bases in China (including Port Arthur). Instead, Russian, German, French, and British naval bases were soon created in the same vicinity.

One of the responses to this threatening development was a second naval expansion plan (1896) involving the construction and purchase of four battleships and a number of smaller craft. In 1903, three more battleships were ordered. But a second war, this time with Russia, broke out before the latest orders were available. In the Russo-Japanese War, two Russian fleets – the second one sent from the Baltic to replace the incapacitation of the first – were destroyed. The spectacular success at Tsushima was followed by further fleet-expansion plans in 1907 and 1910. After 1913, Japanese capital ships were built exclusively in domestic dockyards.

Japanese participation in the First World War was restricted primarily to operations against the Germans in the China Sea, the South Pacific, and the Indian Ocean. Allied requests to send naval contingents to the Mediterranean, Atlantic, and Baltic theatres were declined until 1917 when a small cruiser/destroyer squadron was finally dispatched to the Mediterranean. With the conclusion of the war and the Siberian Intervention, Japanese fleet-expansion plans held out the possibility of parity with the United States and Great Britain. However, these plans were basically shelved by the outcome of the Washington Disarmament Conferences of 1921–2. In the ensuing negotiations, Japan lost the possibility of renewing its earlier

France, Spain, Russia, Germany, Japan

alliance with Britain because of the opposition of the United States and was required to accept a third-place 5:5:3 naval ratio. The Japanese leadership's reasoning at the time was that it felt that it could not afford an arms race with the two naval leaders. Yet by accepting the limitations, it was argued, caps would be placed on the ultimate size of the British and American fleets, both of which were thought to be unlikely to expand their fleets to the maximum. More importantly, both the British and the American navies were also unlikely to be in a position to concentrate their naval strengths in the Pacific. In return, Japan received guarantees that no British naval bases would be built north of Singapore; nor would any American bases be established west of Hawaii. Consequently, Japan was granted a virtual navy monopoly in the western Pacific.

The Japanese position at subsequent conferences in 1927, 1930, and 1934–5 was complicated by domestic political turmoil which overlapped with inter-service rivalries between the army and navy, and factional disputes within the navy over preferences in strategy and foreign policy (see Sadao, 1973; Wilmott, 1982; Howarth, 1983). In 1934, the Japanese insisted unsuccessfully upon naval tonnage parity and, in 1935, formally denounced the Washington treaty limitations. During this same period, the navy began to move away from its earlier reluctance to develop air and submarine capabilities.

Within the context of the army's expanding commitments in China and rising US–Japanese tension, the navy formulated a war strategy that was predicated on the rapid establishment of a perimeter extending from Burma through the Philippines and north to the Kamchatka Peninsula. The primary naval threat would come from the US Pacific fleet which was expected to be met and defeated in the Philippines Sea area. If the perimeter could be established quickly and defended effectively, the British and the United States would be forced to accept the new reality and, presumably, negotiate some form of compromise. In 1941, the basic strategy was amended to provide for a surprise attack on Pearl Harbor to increase the time available for creating the perimeter.

The Japanese attack in late 1941 met so little resistance that steps were hastily taken to expand the perimeter in most of the possible directions. Yet the failure to destroy Pearl Harbor's dockyard and fuel facilities as well as the Pacific fleet's aircraft-carriers meant that the early decisive victory over the United States had not been fully realised. By mid-1942 (Battles of the Coral Sea and Midway) the Japanese offensive had been checked, enabling the United States to

314   *Country Data*

Table 9.15   Japanese battleships, 1861–1945

Year	Number of ships	Year	Number of ships	Year	Number of ships
1861	0	1890	0	1920	10
1862	0	1891	0	1921	10
1863	0	1892	0	1922	10
1864	1	1893	0	1923	10
1865	1	1894	0	1924	10
1866	1	1895	1	1925	10
1867	1	1896	2	1926	10
1868	1	1897	3	1927	10
1869	2	1898	3	1928	10
1870	2	1899	4	1929	9
1871	2	1900	5	1930	9
1872	2	1901	6	1931	9
1873	2	1902	6	1932	9
1874	2	1903	6	1933	9
1875	2	1904	6	1934	9
1876	2	1905	4	1935	9
1877	2	1906	10	1936	9
1878	5	1907	11	1937	9
1879	5	1908	11	1938	9
1880	0	1909	10	1939	9
1881	0	1910	0	1940	10
1882	0	1911	0	1941	11
1883	0	1912	3	1942	10
1884	0	1913	4	1943	9
1885	0	1814	4	1944	5
1886	0	1915	7	1945	1
1887	0	1916	7		
1888	0	1917	9		
1889	0	1918	9		

exploit its greater industrial-technological potential. Essentially, the United States was able to replace its losses while the Japanese, who had begun the war with fuel and ammunition shortages, found it increasingly difficult to do so. Between June 1942 and October 1944 (Battle of Leyte Gulf) the Japanese navy gradually lost most of its carrier- and sea-based air capability and, thus, was forced to concede US naval superiority. Similarly, the Japanese navy also failed to develop effective counter-measures against American submarine attacks on its shipping. A few months after the post-Hiroshima/

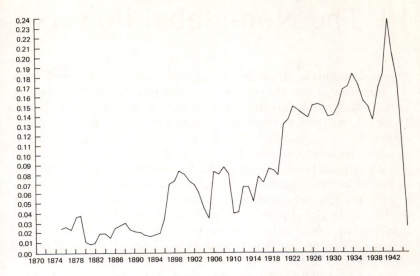

Figure 9.5 Japanese relative capability share, 1875–1945

Nagasaki surrender, the Naval ministry was abolished thereby ending the existence of the Imperial navy.[2]

Table 9.15 gives annual numbers of Japanese battleships from 1861 to 1945, and Figure 9.5 charts the Japanese relative capability share from 1875 to 1945.

10 The Non-global Powers

At various points in earlier chapters, it may have seemed as if we knew the identities of the global powers throughout the half millenium, 1494–1993, even before the data collection process was initiated. There is some truth to this impression but not as much as one might expect. Not surprisingly, we did have definite expectations about which states would be most likely to qualify and which ones would not. Long cycle theory, for example, has been fairly explicit from the outset as to the identities of the successive world powers and challengers. On this basis, and in conjunction with some familiarity with the history of global politics, it would seem reasonable to anticipate that the data would point to Great Britain as the naval leader of the nineteenth century or that United States leadership would prevail after 1945.

Indeed, if the data had contradicted safe expectations such as these, it would have been only natural at first to suspect the validity of the indicators. Still, it is one thing to possess some general sense of who the winners and losers have been and quite another to be able to specify, with the aid of empirical evidence, to what extent states led or followed or never even qualified to play in the global league. That is of course one of the principal reasons why this analysis of the distribution of seapower capabilities was initiated in the first place. Surely, it was by no means a certainty that any one state would control as much as 50 per cent or more of the available naval power capabilities at various points in time. And while it may have been reasonable to entertain some initial preconceptions about the membership parameters of the global power subsystem, there were states with debatable claims to membership – either in terms of specific cycles or at any point in time. For the marginal cases, at the very least, empirical evidence harnessed to an explicit schedule of rules, as outlined in Chapters 2, 3, and 4, is essential.

Although the data which have been presented and analysed in earlier chapters support the asserted identification of the members of the global power subset, the same data say little about the states that have been excluded from the global élite. Of course, the implication, entirely intended, is that the non-discussed states simply failed to qualify. But there is no reason to expect readers merely to take the word of the authors on this issue.

Non-global Powers

This obligation is all the more necessary given the prevailing differences of opinion over which states should be regarded as members of the élite subset of world politics. Table 10.1 selectively highlights some of these differences by contrasting Levy's (1983) and Singer's and Small's (1972) listing of great/major powers with the 1494–1993 membership listing that has emerged in this study. Assuredly, some of the disputes are readily explicable in terms of differences in procedures adopted and goals pursued. For instance, the Singer and Small Correlates of War Project takes 1816 as its beginning point. Naturally, states that rose and fell from prominence before 1816 are thereby excluded. Alternatively, both the Singer–Small and Levy undertakings attempt to introduce states in the year in which observers credit the respective states with first attaining élite status. The long cycle rules instead introduce a new global power as early as possible or feasible after the preceding global war. The United States, for example, is regarded as a global power from the first year of the fourth cycle (1816) while both Singer–Small and Levy wait until 1898

Table 10.1 Three identifications of the most significant actors in world politics

	Long cycle global powers	Levy great powers	Singer and Small major powers
Portugal	1494–1580	–	–
Spain	1494–1808	1495–1808*	–
England/ Great Britain	1494–1945	1495–1975	1816–
France	1494–1945	1495–1975	1816–1940, 1945–
Austria/ Austria-Hungary		1495–1918*	1816–1918
Ottoman Empire	–	1495–1699	–
Netherlands	1579–1810	1609–1713	–
Sweden	–	1617–1721	–
Russia/ Soviet Union	1714–	1721–1975	1816–1917, 1922–
Prussia/Germany	1870–1945	1740–1975	1816–1917, 1925-
United States	1816–	1898–1975	1898–
Italy	–	1861–1943	1860–1943
Japan	1875–1945	1905–1945	1895–1945
China	–	1949–1975	1949–

*Levy treats Austria and Spain as one United Hapsburgs actor for the 1519–1556 period.

Source: Levy (1983, p. 48) and Singer and Small (1972, p. 23).

318   *Country Data*

and the Spanish-American War to introduce the United States into their own élite circles.

There is only one state (Portugal) that appears on the long cycle list that is completely absent from the Levy and Singer–Small renditions. Some attention has already been devoted to this case in Chapter 7. However, there are as many as six states (Austria/Austria–Hungary, the Ottoman Empire, Sweden, Prussia, Italy, and China) that appear in the Levy/Singer–Small inventories that are missing from the long cycle list. There are also some differences of opinion on the status of Britain and France in the post-1945 era. While at least one of these cases (the Ottoman Empire) has received attention from time to time in earlier chapters, some review of the pertinent data for states that failed to meet the minimum thresholds would seem to be in order. What these non-global powers have in common is that, in the relevant cycles, they all were active as regional seapowers.

In addition to former global powers that have lost their élite status, there have been two other types of states that failed to satisfy the global power criteria: regional Mediterranean powers of the fifteenth–sixteenth centuries that failed to adjust, or could not adjust, to the politico-economic transition away from the Mediterranean and, subsequently, European great powers that were militarily important in their regional context yet which failed to develop the requisite naval capabilities for global reach.

Two outstanding examples of the first type are Venice and the Ottoman Empire. Venice, whose activities make it an interesting candidate for study as a smaller-scale, pre-1500 prototype of the world power role, was for a time one of the leading seapowers of the Mediterranean world. But with a galley-based navy, its range was restricted to its immediate region. As noted in Table 10.2, this galley

Table 10.2   Estimations of Venetian and Ottoman numbers of warships, 1423–1859

	Venice
1423	45 light and heavy galleys (Lane, 1973)
1498	[13] war galleys (Lane, 1934)
1499	48 light galleys; 17 heavy galleys; 33 armed roundships (Sanuto, 1879)
1570	152 war galleys (Lane, 1934)
1581	146 galleys (Scammell, 1981)
1649	19 galleons (Pemsel, 1977)

1651	58 ships (Pemsel, 1977)
1656	29 sail and 38 galleys (Pemsel, 1977)
1716	26 ships (Reynolds, 1974; Pemsel, 1977)
1717	33 (Pemsel, 1977)
1744	33 ships-of-the-line (Reynolds, 1974)
1789	10 w/50–64 guns (Vecchj, 1895)
1790	'20' (von Pivka, 1980)

Ottoman Empire

1470	3–400 sail including 100 galleys (Lane, 1934)
1495	[250] (Hale, 1957)
1499	260 sail including 60 light galleys, 3 galleons, 20 large ships (Sanuto, 1879)
1571	300 ships (Braudel, 1976)
1571–2	200 ships (Braudel, 1976)
1618	15–80 galleys (Cipolla, 1965)
1649	93 ships (Pemsel, 1977)
1651	100 ships (Pemsel, 1977)
1654	76 ships (Pemsel, 1977)
1655	100 ships (Pemsel, 1977)
1656	28 sail and 70 galleys (Pemsel, 1977)
1701	28 w/60 + (Kurat, 1970)
1716	24 w/25 + (Kurat, 1970); 50 sail (Reynolds, 1974); c.54 (Pemsel, 1977)
1717	50 sail (Reynolds, 1974)
1770	14 ships-of-the-line (Woodward, 1965); 20 ships-of-the-line (Pemsel, 1977)
1784	22 ships-of-the-line (Shaw, 1976)
1787	22 ships-of-the-line (Pemsel, 1977)
1788	17 ships-of-the-line (Woodward, 1965)
1789	30 w/58–74 guns (Vecchj, 1895)
1790	30 w/50–74 guns (von Pivka, 1980)
1796	27 (von Pivka, 1980)
1804	28 (Schnitzler, 1829)
1806	15 (Mitchell, 1974)
1807	10 (Pemsel, 1977)
1810	14 (Brenton, 1823–5)
1812	14 (Brenton, 1823–5)
1821	17 (Vecchj, 1895)
1827	3 (Pemsel, 1977)
1828	6 ships-of-the-line (Woodward, 1965)
1829	8 (Mitchell, 1974)
1840	19 (Graham, 1965)
1853	c. 12 (Mitchell, 1974)
1859	7 (Pemsel, 1977)

320   *Country Data*

orientation persisted well into the seventeenth century – at a time when two other Mediterranean seapowers (France and Spain) still retained galley fleets as well but had clearly made some commitment toward ocean-going sailing vessels.

Earlier mention has been made, in Chapters 3 and 7, of the naval role of the Ottoman Empire and there is little need to repeat that material in this chapter. As in the case of its frequent opponent, Venice, the Ottoman Empire entered the modern, post-1500 period as a major, galley-based Mediterranean seapower. Unlike Venice, however, several galley fleets were sent to the Indian Ocean in the sixteenth century for service against the Portuguese. But these expeditions were neither sustained efforts nor were they particularly successful given the strategic limitations of galleys operating in oceanic waters. Galley fleets could be quite useful for coastal raiding purposes and in operations against similar fleets (cf. Guilmartin, 1974) but, in oceanic combat, galleys were simply unable to compete with the superior guns, speed, stability, and manoeuvrability of the sixteenth-century galleon and, in fact rarely attempted to do so.

Some time after the decisive defeat at Lepanto (1571, a battle for regional naval supremacy which the Ottomans lost) and well into the seventeenth century, the Ottoman Empire began to make a gradual transition to sailing fleets. Nevertheless, the numbers indicated in Table 10.2 (roughly ten to thirty ships-of-the-line between 1656 and 1859) are suggestive of a small, regional navy that was primarily active in the Eastern Mediterranean and the Black Sea – and one that was often defeated in one-sided encounters with European fleets (usually Russian) as epitomised in exaggerated fashion by the 1827 disaster at Navarino Bay.

In Table 10.3, the geographic focus is shifted to another regional naval theatre, the Baltic. There can be little doubt that military successes on land in the sixteenth and seventeenth centuries won Sweden the status of an important power in Northern Europe during this period. Sweden was also an important naval power in the Baltic and, on the basis of numbers of warships alone, would have satisfied the minimal threshold of global power naval capabilities in the seventeenth century. However, the numbers in Table 10.3 indicate a gradual decline in seapower after its defeat in the Northern Wars of the early eighteenth century. In any event, the fact remains that the operational scope of the Swedish navy was consistently limited to the Baltic area in competition with other Baltic seapowers such as the Danes and the Russians, and the successive intrusions of the non-

321

Table 10.3   Estimations of Swedish and Danish numbers of warships, 1566–1859

	Sweden
1566	70 (Bridge, 1899)
1611	151 (Reynolds, 1974)
1612	[12] (Bridge, 1899)
1628	27 (Anderson, 1969)
1630	70 w/20 + guns (Charnock, 1800–3)
1631	27 (Reynolds, 1974)
1644	33 (Charnock, 1800–3); c. 40 (Pemsel, 1977); 34 (Anderson, 1969)
1654	31 (Anderson, 1969)
1656	[45] (Pontalis, 1885)
1658	35 (Pemsel, 1977)
1668	36 w/40 + guns (Anderson, 1969);
1675	24 (Bridge, 1899); 44 ship-of-the-line (Charnock, 1800–3)
1677	25 (Pemsel, 1977)
1679	22 w/40 + guns (Anderson, 1969); 16 (Richmond, 1953; Bridge, 1899)
1689	30 w/40 + (Anderson, 1969)
1697	35 (Richmond, 1953); 34 w/46 + guns (Bridge, 1899)
1698	36 (Bridge, 1899)
1699	37 (Bridge, 1899); c. 40 (Bromley and Ryan, 1971)
1700	38 w/40 + (Anderson, 1969); 42 (Pemsel, 1977)
1702	39 (Bridge, 1899)
1703	50 sail (Bromley and Ryan, 1971)
1704	40 (Bridge, 1899)
1705	42 (Bridge, 1899)
1706	43 (Bridge, 1899)
1708	46 (Bridge, 1899)
1709	37 (Bromley and Ryan, 1971); [41] (Anderson, 1969); 47 (Bridge, 1899)
1710	[43] (Anderson, 1969; Mitchell, 1974)
1714	30 (Southworth, 1968)
1715	33 w/40 + (Richmond, 1953)
1720	[24] (Anderson, 1969; Mitchell, 1974)
1722	[21] (Anderson, 1969)
1734	[22] (Anderson, 1969)
1735	[23] (Anderson, 1969)
1738	[22] (Anderson, 1969)
1739	[27] (Vecchj, 1895)
1741	12 (Mitchell, 1974); 15 (Woodward, 1965)
1743	16 (Mitchell, 1974; Woodward, 1965)
1756	[26] (Anderson, 1969; Mitchell, 1974; Woodward, 1965)
1760	15–16 (Charnock, 1800–3)
1779	[10] (Anderson, 1969)
1780	15 (Lloyd, 1965a); 15 w/60 + (Charnock, 1800–3); [4] (Anderson, 1969)

322

Table 10.3 Estimations of Swedish and Danish numbers of warships, 1566–1859

	Sweden – continued
1781	[10] (Anderson, 1969)
1782	[1] (Anderson, 1969)
1785	[0] (Anderson, 1969)
1786	[0] (Anderson, 1969)
1787	'26'/[0] (Anderson, 1969); 20 (Woodward, 1965)
1788	20 (Mitchell, 1974); 17 (von Pivka, 1980); 15 (Pemsel, 1977); [15] (Anderson, 1969; Southworth, 1968)
1789	'25'/[21] (Anderson, 1969); 27 (Vecchj, 1895); 21 (Woodward, 1965); [21] (Pemsel, 1977)
1790	27 (Lloyd, 1965a); 25 (Woodward, 1965); [25] (Anderson, 1969; Mitchell, 1974); 21 (Pemsel, 1977); [19] (Southworth, 1968)
1791	[16] (Anderson, 1969)
1792	18 (James, 1886)
1799	27 (Charnock, 1800–3)
1800	18 (Vecchj, 1895)
1801	11 (Robison and Robison, 1942); [11] (James, 1886)
1804	12 (Schnitzler, 1829)
1807	12 (Mitchell, 1974); 11–12 (James, 1886)
1808	12 (von Pivka, 1980)
1809	11 (Richmond, 1946); [3] (Mitchell, 1974)
1810	12 (Brenton, 1823–5)
1812	11 (Brenton, 1823–5)
1815–16	13 (Anderson, 1969; Mitchell, 1974)
1817–23	12 (Anderson 1969; Mitchell, 1974)
1824	13 (Anderson, 1969; Mitchell, 1974)
1825–7	8 (Anderson, 1969; Mitchell, 1974)
1829	9 (Anderson, 1969; Mitchell, 1974); 10 (Moreau de Jonnes, 1835)
1830–1	8 (Anderson, 1969; Mitchell, 1974)
1832–6	9 (Anderson, 1969; Mitchell, 1974)
1837–8	9 (Anderson, 1969)
1839	8 (Anderson, 1969)
1840	9 (Anderson, 1969); 30 (*Almanach de Gotha*)
1859	7 (Busk, 1859; Pemsel, 1977)

	Denmark
1600	40 sail (Charnock, 1800–3)
1611	30 + (Anderson, 1969); 60 warships (Reynolds, 1974)
1628	30 (Anderson, 1969)
1630	36 warships (Charnock, 1800–3)
1643	nearly 50 warships (Charnock, 1800–3)
1644	36 warships (Charnock, 1800–3); 30 (Anderson, 1969); 30/[17] (Southworth, 1968)
1653	10 w/40 + /20 w/30 + /23 w/12 + (Anderson, 1969)
1656	9 (Rowen, 1978)
1668	21 w/40 + (Anderson, 1969)

323

Table 10.3   Estimations of Swedish and Danish numbers of warships, 1566–1859

	Denmark – continued
1675	19 small ships-of-the-line (Pemsel, 1977)
1677	19 (Pemsel, 1977)
1679	30 w/40+ (Anderson, 1969)
1689	24 w/40+ (Anderson, 1969)
1692	29 w/34+ (Bromley and Ryan, 1971)
1699	37 w/34+ (Bromley and Ryan, 1971)
1700	29 w/20+ (Anderson, 1969); 33 (Pemsel, 1977)
1703	c. 50 sail (Bromley and Ryan, 1971)
1709	[41] (Anderson, 1969)
1710	[41] (Anderson, 1969; Mitchell, 1974)
1714	24 (Southworth, 1968)
1715	38 w/40+ (Richmond, 1953)
1720	25 (Mitchell, 1974)
1721	[25] (Anderson, 1969)
1742	[18] (Anderson, 1969)
1756	[27] (Anderson, 1969; Mitchell, 1974; Woodward, 1965)
1760	c. 18 (Charnock, 1800–3)
1762	[14] (Anderson, 1969)
1779	[10] (Anderson, 1969)
1780	14 (Lloyd, 1965a); 12 w/60+/14 w/50+ (Charnock, 1800–3); [9] (Anderson, 1969)
1781	[9] (Anderson, 1964)
1782	[5] (Anderson, 1964)
1784	20 (Brenton, 1823–5); [4] (Anderson, 1969)
1785	[0] (Anderson, 1969)
1786	[0] (Anderson, 1969)
1787	[0] (Anderson, 1969)
1788	[7] (Anderson, 1969)
1789	38 (Vecchj, 1895)
1790	40 (Lloyd, 1965a); 38 w/50–90 (von Pivka, 1980)
1791	[33] (Anderson, 1969)
1792	24 (James, 1886)
1793	[31] (Anderson, 1969)
1799	nearly 40 (Charnock, 1800–3)
1800	23 (Vecchj, 1895)
1801	[10] (James, 1886)
1804	14 (Schnitzler, 1829)
1807	16 (Pemsel, 1977)
1808	2 (James, 1886)
1809	16 (Richmond, 1946); 0 (Derry, 1965)
1810	1 (Brenton, 1823–5)
1812	1 (Brenton, 1823–5)
1815	1 (Mitchell, 1974)
1826	4 (Moreau de Jonnes, 1835)
1840	31 (*Almanach de Gotha*); 6 (Anderson, 1969)

324 *Country Data*

Table 10.3 Estimations of Swedish and Danish numbers of warships, 1566–1859

	Denmark – continued
1841	6 (Anderson, 1969)
1842	6 (Anderson, 1969)
1843	6 (Anderson, 1969)
1844	6 (Anderson, 1969)
1845	6 (Anderson, 1969)
1846	6 (Anderson, 1969)
1847	6 (Anderson, 1969)
1848	6 (Anderson, 1969)
1859	4 (Pemsel, 1977)

Note: See Notes for Table 8.2.

local seapowers (first the Dutch and later the British). Apart from brief forays to Madagascar and North America, Sweden's naval history failed to satisfy the extracoastal/regional sea dimension of global power.

Although much less militarily prominent than Sweden, on land, the verdict on the Danish naval effort is fundamentally similar. Capable of fielding a respectable, if intermittent, Baltic naval presence during the early eighteenth century (as testified in part by the recurrent British concern with destroying the Danish fleet in the French Revolutionary/Napoleonic Wars), Denmark was most formidable at sea when it was allied with the Dutch in the mid-seventeenth century. Nevertheless, the scope of Danish seapower was restricted to the waters within its immediate region. Of the three principal Baltic naval powers (Sweden, Denmark, and Russia) only the slowest to develop, Russia, eventually emerged as a seapower on a greater-than-Baltic scale.

Turning to other European candidates for consideration, the discussion in Chapter 7 of Portuguese naval power is entirely focused on the sixteenth century. Portugal, absorbed by Spain in 1580, did manage to regain its independence in 1640. Although it had lost a substantial proportion of its colonial empire during this subordinated period, Portugal retained control of scattered territories in Africa, Latin America, and Asia, thereby presumably needing at least some minimal naval capability. Unlike most of the other states reviewed in this chapter, Portuguese naval activity would have been likely to satisfy the oceanic-scope criterion of global seapower. The question

Non-global Powers

then is whether the size of the Portuguese navy exceeded the élite membership minimum of 10 per cent. Although references to the size of the Portuguese navy in this era are not all that common (a telling indicator in its own right), Table 10.4 indicates that the answer is negative. After 1640, Portugal maintained a very modest naval capability which probably never exceeded a dozen ships-of-the-line.

Table 10.4   Estimations of Portuguese numbers of ships-of-the-line, 1640–1849

Portugal	
1640–1763	Never exceeded 8–10 ships-of-the-line (Charnock, 1800–3)
1649	13 (Boxer, 1972)
1652	60 ships (Pontalis, 1885)
1789	10 w/58–80 guns (Vecchj, 1895)
1792	6 (Dupuy and Dupuy, 1977)
1793	6 (Wilson, 1904; Mahan, 1892)
1795	11 (von Pivka, 1980)
1810	10 (Brenton, 1823–5)
1812	10 (Brenton, 1823–5)
1823	3 (Moreau de Jonnes, 1835)
1849	2 (*Almanach de Gotha*)

Another European state often accorded great power status because of its military significance in European territorial wars is Austria. Once again, this is a case of a state that was important on land but a continuously negligible factor at sea. In the era of sail, the Austrian navy was virtually non-existent anywhere other than the Adriatic and hardly prominent there as well, as demonstrated in Table 10.5. In 1738, a committee to evaluate the state of the Austrian navy concluded that it 'had little usefulness, caused great expense, and stood in danger of being defeated in case of attack' (quoted in Sokol, 1968, p. 6). The only time before 1860 that the size of the Austrian navy approaches anything resembling significance for our purposes is at the end of the Napoleonic Wars. Yet the five to ten ships attributed to Austria in 1814 were primarily spoils of war taken from the defeated French and, as indicated by the table, were not maintained in any meaningful way after their transfer to the Austrian navy. According to von Pivka (1980, p. 148), six ships-of-the-line under construction

326   *Country Data*

Table 10.5   Estimations of Austrian numbers of ships-of-the-line, 1725–1859

Austria

1725	3 in Adriatic (Reynolds, 1974)
1731–8	3 (Sokol, 1968)
1739	0 (Sokol, 1968)
1799	3 (Sokol, 1968)
1800	0 (Sokol, 1968)
1814	5 (Sokol, 1968); 10 (Schmalenbach, 1970; Khuepach and Bayer, 1966)
1815	0 (Sokol, 1968)
1827	2 (Moreau de Jonnes, 1835)
1830	8 (*Almanach de Gotha*)
1849	0 (*Almanach de Gotha*)
1859	1 (Pemsel, 1977); 0 (Busk, 1859)

were dismantled, two in service were destroyed by fire, and two others were converted to frigates.

Table 10.6 suggests that the Austrian naval status changed very little in the battleship era. Using the same rules and sources developed for counting the distribution of battleships in Chapter 4, Austria–Hungary was very slow to develop competitive battleships and those that were eventually built in the early twentieth century tended to be the smallest battleships afloat at that time. This tendency can be attributed to a general reluctance to allocate resources for naval purposes and to do so only in the context of its local rivalry with Italy. Despite a very small and uncharacteristic Austro-Hungarian naval participation in the 1900 suppression of the Boxer Rebellion by the great powers, Austria–Hungary was at best a local or subregional naval power up to 1918. In the last month of the First World War, Austria–Hungary transferred its entire surviving navy to the new state of Yugoslavia, only to have it almost immediately seized by Italy.

Italy, on the other hand, represents a more ambitious naval actor. At times, primarily in the latter half of the nineteenth century as shown in Table 10.6, the size of its battleship fleet surpassed the minimal 10 per cent or three-ship criterion for membership in the global power élite. Italian shipbuilders were also regarded as innovative trendsetters in the pre-Dreadnought period, establishing new standards especially for speed and fire-power in the 1880s. Moreover, the Italian navy proved to be a factor in the Mediterranean naval combat of both the twentieth century's two global wars. However,

Non-global Powers

327

unless one views naval operations in the Red Sea as a significant exception, the Italian navy's mission was restricted exclusively to the Mediterranean Sea. As a consequence, the extra-regional/oceanic activity criterion was not satisfied in the Italian case. There is no denying that Italy was reasonably active, particularly in the first half of the twentieth century, in its own region, but it did not exercise its perhaps limited potential for global power and therefore cannot be

Table 10.6   Italian and Austro-Hungarian battleships, 1861–1945

Year	Global powers	Italy	Austria-Hungary	Total
1861	3	0		3
1862	11	0		11
1863	13	0		13
1864	19	5		24
1865	32	5		37
1866	40	5		45
1867	47	5		52
1868	53	5		58
1869	55	6		61
1870	68	7		75
1871	73	7		80
1872	74	8		81
1873	76	8		84
1874	78	9		87
1875	80	9		89
1876	84	9		93
1877	92	9		101
1878	97	9		106
1879	95	9		104
1880	11	1		12
1881	13	1		14
1882	13	1		14
1883	16	2		18
1884	16	3		19
1885	17	3		20
1886	23	3		26
1887	29	4		33
1888	30	6		36
1889	34	6		40
1890	36	7		43
1891	39	8		47
1892	41	8		49
1893	46	8		54

Table 10.6 Italian and Austro-Hungarian battleships, 1861–1945

Year	Global powers	Italy	Austria-Hungary	Total
1894	41	8		49
1895	40	8		48
1896	44	8		52
1897	52	8		60
1898	60	8	–	68
1899	42	3	–	45
1900	54	3	–	57
1901	61	3	–	64
1902	70	5	1	76
1903	79	2	2	83
1904	90	4	3	97
1905	94	4	3	101
1906	103	4	4	111
1907	120	5	6	131
1908	102	4	6	112
1909	106	5	6	117
1910	19	0	0	19
1911	29	0	0	29
1912	46	0	1	47
1913	58	1	2	61
1914	78	3	3	84
1915	90	5	4	99
1916	99	5	4	108
1917	106	5	4	115
1918	107	5	2	114
1919	82	5		87
1920	78	5		83
1921	78	5		83
1922	62	5		67
1923	64	5		69
1924	58	5		63
1925	58	5		63
1926	55	5		60
1927	57	5		62
1928	57	4		61
1929	56	4		60
1930	56	4		60
1931	49	4		53
1932	47	4		51
1933	48	4		52
1934	49	4		53
1935	49	4		53
1936	50	4		54

Non-global Powers

Table 10.6   Italian and Austro-Hungarian battleships, 1861–1945

Year	Global powers	Italy	Austria-Hungary	Total
1937	50	4		54
1938	53	4		57
1939	54	4		58
1940	55	6		61
1941	46	6		52
1942	50	7		57
1943	51	5		56
1944	49			49
1945	40			40

Note: Austro-Hungarian pre-Dreadnought battleships tended to be smaller than their counterparts in other navies. As a consequence, most sources, especially the ones upon which we have most relied (Chesnau and Kolesnik, 1979, and Brassey) do not treat them as fully comparable with the ships of the major sea powers. The absence of any pre-1902 entries for Austria-Hungary can therefore be viewed as a somewhat conservative 'estimate', but it is one that has ample support in the pertinent literature. The Italian series is based on the same procedures used for the global powers as described in Chapter 4.

regarded as a fully-fledged, or even peripheral global power. It should also be kept in mind that Italy was regarded as the most marginal of European great powers.

Turning to the most recent period, there is little doubt that Germany and Japan ceased to be global competitors in the military/ naval sense after their defeats in 1945. The status of Britain and France is somewhat more controversial. In terms of the naval capabilities discussed in Chapter 4, both states fail to satisfy the post-1945 minimal criteria for the global power designation, but less obviously so than in the German and Japanese cases. For instance, both Britain and France remain navally active on an extra-regional scale. Support for this assertion is not difficult to find. Cable's (1981, pp. 223–53) illustrative chronology of the 'non-war use or threat of limited naval force' lists 104 cases that took place between 1946 and 1979 in non-local waters (from the perspective of at least one of the actors involved in each case). Cable's chronology is admittedly not exhaustive but it is interesting to note that eight states (Canada, Japan, the Netherlands, Turkey, Portugal, Spain, New Zealand and

330   *Country Data*

Australia) were responsible for slightly less than 10 per cent of the cases. Fifty-seven or about 55 per cent involved the United States or the Soviet Union. Britain and France accounted for the remaining 35 per cent. Further support is provided by the recent Falklands/ Malvinas War (1982). Nevertheless, extra-regional activity does not compensate for limited global-reach capabilities. Given the greater complexity of the indicators relied upon after 1945, however, it is useful to consider the British and French positions in terms of each type of naval capability.

Great Britain, a pioneer in naval aviation, emerged from the Second World War with roughly a third as many heavy, attack aircraft-carriers as the United States. The absolute number of British carriers declined fairly rapidly (although less rapidly from a proportional perspective) in the late 1940s and early 1950s, and stabilised at about 15 per cent of the British, French and United States total in the 1950s and 1960s, before they ceased to maintain any of the larger types of carriers in the second half of the 1970s. The one French carrier prior to 1962 was obtained from the American fleet. Two moderately small carriers were built in the early 1960s, but since that time have been subject to varying evaluations in the defence annuals (e.g. *The Military Balance*) as to the class of aircraft-carrier to which they really belong. In different years, they have been described as 'heavy attack' or 'medium attack' types but since 1978, the vessels have been regarded as light attack and are therefore no longer comparable with the other carriers enumerated in Table 10.7. One could in fact make the argument that the incomparability has been present all along.

Tables 10.8 and 10.9 respectively enumerate nuclear-attack submarines and submarines carrying nuclear ballistic-missile systems. The British nuclear-attack submarine force has steadily expanded since 1966 but as recently as 1983, their proportional share was still below 6 per cent. In the same year, France had only just begun to acquire a nuclear-attack-submarine capability. By 1993, both Britain and France will have expanded their attack-submarine fleets but neither state will match the minimum proportion required for global-power status.

Table 10.9 presents information on nuclear SLBM submarines in a format different from the one discussed in Chapter 4. The reason for this departure is that, ironically, it is more difficult to find performance characteristics (CEP data in particular) on the French sea-based-weapons systems, than on the Soviet missile systems. The

331

Table 10.7   Distribution of aircraft-carriers, 1917–93

Year	Great Britain	United States	France	Japan	Soviet Union	Total
1917	1					1
1918	3					3
1919	3					3
1920	4					4
1921	4					4
1922	4	1		1		6
1923	4	1		1		6
1924	3	1		1		5
1925	4	1		1		6
1926	4	1		1		6
1927	4	3	1	2		10
1928	5	3	1	2		11
1929	5	3	1	2		11
1930	6	3	1	3		13
1931	6	3	1	3		13
1932	6	3	1	3		13
1933	6	3	1	3		13
1934	6	4	1	3		14
1935	6	4	1	3		14
1936	6	4	1	4		15
1937	6	4	1	5		16
1938	7	5	1	6		19
1939	6	5	1	7		19
1940	7	6	1	7		21
1941	8	7	1	9		25
1942	6	4	1	5		16
1943	6	10	1	5		22
1944	8	15	1	2		26
1945	8	23	0	2		32
1946	8	25	1			34
1947	7	25	1			33
1948	7	25	1			33
1949	6	25	1			32
1950	6	27	1			34
1951	7	27	1			35
1952	7	27	1			35
1953	6	22	1			29
1954	6	19	1			26
1955	5	19	1			25
1956	3	18	1			22
1957	3	18	1			22
1958	3	16	1			20
1959	3	14	1			18
1960	3	13	1			17

Table 10.7 Distribution of aircraft-carriers, 1917–93

Year	Great Britain	United States	France	Japan	Soviet Union	Total
1961	3	16	1			20
1962	3	14	2			19
1963	3	14	3			20
1964	3	14	3			20
1965	3	15	3			21
1966	3	15	3			21
1967	3	15	3			21
1968	2	16	2			20
1969	2	15	2			19
1970	2	15	2			19
1971	2	14	2			18
1972	1	14	2			17
1973	1	14	2			17
1974	1	14	2			17
1975	1	15	2			18
1976	1	14	2			17
1977		13	2			15
1978		13				13
1979		13				13
1980		13				13
1981		13				13
1982		13				13
1983		13				13
1984		13				13
1985		13				13
1986		13				13
1987		14				14
1988		14				14
1989		14				14
1990		15				15
1991		14			1	15
1992		15			1	16
1993		14			2	16

Table 10.8   Distribution of nuclear-attack submarines, 1954–93

Year	United States	Soviet Union	Great Britain	France	Total
1954	1				1
1955	1				1
1956	1				1
1957	3				3
1958	5	4			9
1959	7	10			17
1960	8	15			23
1961	14	18			32
1962	17	18			35
1963	17	23			40
1964	21	27			48
1965	22	28			50
1966	25	33	1		59
1967	31	39	2		72
1968	36	42	2		80
1969	43	48	2		93
1970	46	55	3		104
1971	53	63	5		121
1972	57	67	5		129
1973	59	68	6		133
1974	62	73	7		142
1975	64	76	7		147
1976	64	81	8		153
1977	67	83	8		158
1978	72	89	9		170
1979	71	91	10		172
1980	74	96	10		180
1981	83	101	11		195
1982	88	108	11		207
1983	89	111	12	1	213
1984	86	114	13	2	215
1985	88	117	14	2	221
1986	87	119	14	2	222
1987	87	114	15	3	219
1988	89	109	15	3	216
1989	85	106	16	4	211
1990	88	105	17	4	214
1991	89	104	17	5	215
1992	90	103	16	5	214
1993	91	97	15	5	208

334 *Country Data*

Table 10.9 Distribution of nuclear SLBM British and French submarines, 1960–93

Year	United States	Soviet Union	Great Britain	France	Total
1960	3	6			9
1961	6	13			19
1962	9	30			39
1963	16	31			47
1964	29	40			69
1965	33	43			76
1966	40	43			83
1967	41	39	1		81
1968	41	42	3		86
1969	41	48	4		93
1970	41	46	4		91
1971	41	50	4	1	96
1972	41	58	4	1	104
1973	41	65	4	2	112
1974	41	68	4	3	116
1975	41	73	4	3	121
1976	41	79	4	4	128
1977	41	85	4	4	134
1978	41	88	4	4	137
1979	41	89	4	4	138
1980	36	87	4	5	132
1981	33	81	4	5	123
1982	33	80	4	5	122
1983	34	78	4	5	121
1984	35	75	4	5	119
1985	37	75	4	6	122
1986	36	75	4	6	121
1987	36	75	4	6	121
1988	33	75	4	6	118
1989	31	75	4	6	116
1990	28	64	4	6	102
1991	25	64	4	6	99
1992	27	64	4	6	101
1993	27	64	4	6	101

comparative number of submarines – 9 of 121 (7.4 per cent) in 1983, for example – is of course indicative in its own right but less than satisfying in view of the previous emphasis on lethality (CMP and EMT), as opposed to the mere number of launch platforms. Since the British SLBM submarines have carried Polaris A-3 missiles with sixteen tubes per submarine (MIRVed with three warheads since

Non-global Powers 335

1979), it is possible to make a more direct comparison. Adding British CMP/EMT values to those for the United States (see Tables 8.10 and 8.11) and the Soviet Union (see Tables 9.11 and 9.12), the British proportion in 1970 is 0.037 (CMP) and 0.064 (EMT), and 0.028 (CMP and 0.006 (EMT) in 1980. Thus, on average, the British relative SLBM capability position in 1970 was approximately 5.5 per cent and declined marginally to about 4.7 per cent in the early 1980s.[1]

The relative capability weight of the French SLBM force presumably appears to be roughly similar to that of the British. Prior to 1976, each of the French submarines deployed 16 MSBS M-1 missiles with 500 kiloton warheads. After 1976, emphasis was shifted to MSBS M-2 missiles with possibly heavier warheads (one half to one megaton range) but information on the rate or extent of conversion is not readily available. Finally, in 1982, one submarine was launched (but not commissioned until 1985) carrying the MIRVed MSBS M-4 with six 150 kiloton warheads per missile. Inasmuch as the Polaris A-3 warhead is smaller than the MSBS M-1 or M-2 warheads, the French EMT score would undoubtedly be higher than the parallel British score. Yet even though information on the French CEP dimension is missing, there is no reason to assume that the French missiles are more accurate than the Anglo-American versions. If they are less accurate, it is quite possible that the higher (in comparison with the British) French EMT score would be linked to a correspondingly lower CMP score.

In sum, the only post-1945 global capability in which the British or the French could satisfy a 10 per cent minimum threshold is the aircraft-carrier category. Britain's navy met such a criterion, but only prior to 1971. Whether France qualified in the 1960s and 1970s depends on how one chooses to evaluate the small Clemenceau class aircraft-carrier. In the other three categories, the relative capability scores appear to hover around the 5 per cent mark (with the exception of the weak French position *vis-à-vis* nuclear-attack submarines). Hence, even though the data are not entirely unambiguous, the exclusion of Britain and France from the global power subset after 1945 seems justified by the marginal and, in some respects declining, relative capability position. Nor is there any evidence, given the large expenditures that would be involved, that would lead one to anticipate a future radical change in this state of affairs.[2]

Finally, the last candidate for global-power consideration, China, also deserves some discussion. As Swanson (1982, p. 28) among others (see also Needham *et al.*, 1971, pp. 503–35, for an extensive comparison of the Chinese, and later, Portuguese, activities) observes,

336 *Country Data*

China's seven naval expeditions to the Indian Ocean (1405–33), that we have also noted earlier, qualified it as the first external power with an Indian Ocean presence.

What is more, these expeditions remind us that in the half-millenium prior to the modern era, China's maritime and naval operations added up to an impressive total. The beginning of ocean-going operations dates from the Sung dynasty (Lo, 1955). Under Mongol rule, an invasion of Japan was launched with some 4400 ships in 1281, and a fleet of 1000 ships sailed for Java in 1293. The Ming navy, at its zenith, consisted of some 3800 vessels, including 400 large warships that bore favourable comparison with the Mediterranean light galleys of Venice and Portugal, and over 250 'treasure' ships (government-owned ships for long-distance expeditions to the Indian Ocean and elsewhere) that might be likened to Venice's heavy galleys or the *naus* of Portugal.

Referring to Table 10.10 we indeed find the naval strength of China on the eve of the age of discoveries comparing most favourably with that of Venice, the leading naval power in the Mediterranean at that time, and also that of Portugal, an up-and-coming oceanic seapower.

Table 10.10   Comparative naval strength about 1420
(China, Venice, Portugal)

China (Ming Dynasty) about 1420 (Lo, 1955; Needham, 1971, p. 484).
Some 3800 naval vessels in all:
  400 large warships: main fleet stationed near Nanking;
  more than 250 long-distance 'treasure' ships (*pao chuan*);
  1350 patrol vessels;
  1350 combat ships attached to guard stations or bases;
  400 grain transport freighters;
Also, 3000 merchantmen ready as auxiliaries, and small craft.

Venice 1423 (Farewell Address of Doge Mocenigo; cf. Lane, 1973, p. 327).
  45 light and heavy galleys at sea, with 11 000 seamen; trained crews to
    man 100 more galleys;
  300 *navi* (roundships) with 8000 seamen;
  3000 smaller vessels (from 10 to 200 amphorae), with 17 000 seamen.

Portugal 1415 (amphibious assault on Ceuta, involving some 20 000 men;
  cf. Godinho, 1945, vol. 2, p. 148; Diffie and Winius, 1977, pp. 53–4).
  22 galleys;
  15 *fustas* (small galleys);
  70 *naus* and *barcas*;
  135 foreign (hired) vessels.

Non-global Powers 337

The large number of patrol and guard vessels in China's inventory must be accounted for by her long coastline and large rivers that needed protection from Japanese pirates. The government grain-transport fleet would be reduced in size as grain shipments from the south to the capital at Peking were just about to be routed via the Grand Canal. But the main fleet looks substantial and we know that the 'treasure' ships were of dimensions larger than those then found in the West. These were all sailing vessels, as the Chinese had no galleys, and all warships were equipped with artillery.

Overall, it is clear that at the dawn of the modern age China did have the potential for global reach. But, for a variety of reasons, this potential failed to be realised. As the capital moved to Peking, the power shifted toward the neo-Confucian mandarins and extra-regional naval activities came to an abrupt halt. After 1419, there was an almost complete cessation of maritime building. As the effective life of the larger junks may have been no more than five years, this meant a rapid erosion of fleet strength. By 1474, only 140 warships of the main fleet of 400 were left (Needham *et al.*, 1971, pp. 480, 526). In 1523, the imperial fleet bested the Portuguese in a sharp engagement off the southern coast of China, sinking two of the six Portuguese ships it encountered. But by then it had already assumed the character of a coastal defence force.

This situation has not altered much in the past 550 years, during which time China can only be described as a consistently weak, coastal-defence maritime actor. The weaknesses were well illustrated by decisive nineteenth-century naval defeats at the successive hands of the British (1840–2), the French (1884), and the Japanese (1894–5). Attempts to reform, rebuild, and modernise Chinese naval defences against the penetration of the maritime powers were not unknown but at the same time they were never particularly successful.

After 1949, naval modernisation gradually became a more meaningful goal but the strategic emphasis continued, and continues, to be placed predominantly on coastal defence. The Chinese navy currently consists of an impressive number of combat ships, including a large submarine fleet, but the vessels are almost exclusively conventionally powered and strongly biased toward smaller-class types. Again, in view of the expenditures and, in this case, the technological problems that would be involved, it seems most unlikely that China will be in a position to transform its regional navy into a more global force, at least in the immediate future.[3]

Appendix A: Naval Expenditures

We began this project with the expectation that more or less equal attention would be devoted to the seapower indicators of capital warships and naval expenditures. While some level of success was achieved in enumerating the distribution of ships among the global powers, substantially less proved to be feasible for codifying monies allocated to naval purposes. We do make use of the information that is relatively available for the period 1816–1945, as discussed in Chapter 4. Table A.1 corresponds to Table 4.4 by identifying the annual naval expenditures of the six post-Napoleonic era global powers in their original currencies and according to the sources indicated at the end of the table. To transform these expenditures into the constant 1913 British pounds listed in Table 4.4, we first attempted to correct for inflationary pressures within the national economy and currency unit by dividing each of the current naval estimates by the respective country's wholesale price index (1913 = 100). These wholesale price indexes are listed in Table A.2. Once converted to their 1913 equivalent, each annual observation was then translated into the common British pound unit utilising the 1913 exchange rate.

However, our inability to generate a sufficiently lengthy Russian wholesale price index for the period 1816–1945 (and little in the way of Soviet naval expenditure information after the First World War) forced us to employ an alternative strategy for the conversion of Russian naval spending. In this case, we first transformed each year's current ruble estimates into British pounds at that year's average exchange rate. Our exchange rate data was made available to us through the courtesy of the University of Michigan's Professor J. David Singer from the files of the Correlates of War Project. Although it is obviously not the most desirable approach, the next step in creating a constant unit involved the application of the British price index to the Russian series, expressed in current British pounds at this point.

Although we have described these data for 1816–1945 as relatively available, they cannot be considered problem-free. The series for Great Britain and the United States are the least troublesome and the most accessible. Most of the Russian series is derived from a single source (Mitchell, 1974). In contrast, a variety of sources are available for various phases of the French series. Unfortunately, many of these sources do not agree at points of overlap even though the magnitude of disagreement is not always great. More problematic in the French case are the confusions created by the use of ordinary versus extraordinary budget accounts and the conceptual problem of funding colonial administration through the Marine ministry for some portion of the nineteenth century. We think we have been able to combine both ordinary and extraordinary expenditure in most years but there is little that can be done to distil the purely naval from the strictly colonial expenses

339

Table A.1   Naval expenditures, 1816–1945
(original currencies in millions)

Year	Great Britain	France	United States	Russia/ Soviet Union	Germany	Japan
1816	10.20	48.00	3.91	19.59		
1817	6.62	44.00	3.32	23.22		
1818	6.64	42.50	2.95	23.15		
1819	6.40	45.00	3.85	26.19		
1820	6.65	50.00	4.39	25.84		
1821	6.27	52.28	3.32	27.28		
1822	5.19	60.82	2.22	25.22		
1823	5.61	73.54	2.50	26.72		
1824	6.16	63.46	2.90	23.01		
1825	5.85	63.35	3.05	20.70		
1826	6.54	58.90	4.22	21.90		
1827	6.42	62.31	4.26	24.10		
1828	5.67	81.18	3.92	27.50		
1829	5.90	73.63	3.99	31.30		
1830	5.31	90.31	3.24	31.60		
1831	5.69	71.36	3.86	30.90		
1832	4.88	64.16	4.95	30.70*		
1833	4.36	63.76	4.27	30.50		
1834	4.50	61.78	4.61	30.20		
1835	4.10	62.67	4.21	37.50		
1836	4.21	68.52	6.25	35.90		
1837	4.75	66.42	6.65	36.40		
1838	4.52	71.80	6.13	35.60		
1839	5.49	79.47	6.18	37.70		
1840	5.60	99.10	6.11	11.60		
1841	6.49	124.91	6.00	11.60		
1842	6.64	133.11	8.40	12.30		
1843	6.61	119.69	3.73	11.00		
1844	5.86	122.13	6.50	10.70		
1845	6.81	120.01	6.30	14.50		
1846	7.80	135.99	6.46	10.70		
1847	8.01	153.01	7.90	11.30		
1848	7.92	148.94	9.41	11.40		
1849	6.94	124.79	9.79	15.40		
1850	6.44	104.88	7.90	12.40		
1851	5.85	101.03	8.88	14.60		
1852	6.63	108.02	8.92	17.90		
1853	8.65	121.11	11.07	20.70		
1854	14.49	202.45	10.79	14.40		
1855	19.66	241.44	13.32	19.10		
1856	13.46	225.72	14.07	18.20		
1857	10.59	126.76	12.65	19.00		

340

Table A.1   Naval expenditures, 1816–1945
(original currencies in millions)

Year	Great Britain	France	United States	Russia/ Soviet Union	Germany	Japan
1858	9.22	133.43	14.05	18.70		
1859	11.82	293.03	14.69	18.30		
1860	13.33	241.95	11.51	21.40		
1861	12.60	206.87	12.39	21.40		
1862	11.37	218.91	42.64	19.60		
1863	10.82	137.64	63.26	18.03		
1864	10.90	193.06	85.70	20.10		
1865	10.26	192.07	122.62	21.10		
1866	10.68	179.29	43.29	24.10		
1867	10.84	159.67	31.03	17.50		
1868	11.14	155.58	25.78	18.10		
1869	9.43	163.28	20.00	18.80		
1870	8.97	195.95	21.78	20.10		
1871	9.46	167.04	19.43	21.16		
1872	9.28	143.51	21.25	22.30	31.08	
1873	10.06	151.43	23.53	22.80	25.97	
1874	10.46	152.68	30.93	25.40	38.73	
1875	10.80	155.53	21.50	25.80	49.21	2.83
1876	11.01	170.08	18.96	27.10	41.01	3.42
1877	10.79	192.69	14.96	32.40	60.33	3.17
1878	11.79	197.47	17.37	32.70	61.71	2.82
1879	10.23	194.37	15.13	31.00	43.66	3.14
1880	10.51	193.68	13.54	29.40	39.73	3.42
1881	10.56	207.10	15.69	30.70	38.00	3.26
1882	10.26	222.05	15.03	30.70	36.38	3.41
1883	10.73	259.11	15.28	34.00	39.81	6.16
1884	11.43	298.44	17.29	34.20	48.43	6.26
1885	12.66	309.44	16.02	38.50	52.06	5.33
1886	13.27	272.21	13.91	44.60	50.47	8.91
1887	12.33	199.84	15.14	40.00	52.36	9.84
1888	13.00	180.99	16.93	40.90	51.05	9.85
1889	15.27	199.03	21.38	40.80	54.90	9.36
1890	15.55	201.39	22.01	40.90	71.73	10.22
1891	15.58	229.99	26.11	45.50	85.40	9.60
1892	15.73	251.98	29.17	48.20	90.44	9.25
1893	15.48	253.30	30.14	50.40	81.24	8.27
1894	17.55	274.19	31.70	51.20	78.53	10.45
1895	19.72	268.10	28.80	54.90	85.89	13.70
1896	22.17	265.93	27.15	58.00	92.07	18.84
1897	20.85	260.78	34.56	59.90	114.02	50.00
1898	24.07	289.66	58.82	67.10	131.25	59.00
1899	26.00	322.45	63.94	83.10	153.91	62.00

341

Table A.1   Naval expenditures, 1816–1945
(original currencies in millions)

Year	Great Britain	France	United States	Russia/ Soviet Union	Germany	Japan
1900	29.52	372.95	55.95	86.60	167.14	58.00
1901	31.04	344.36	60.51	95.60	205.64	44.00
1902	31.18	298.58	67.80	98.30	217.40	36.00
1903	35.48	304.69	82.62	12.35**	224.98	36.00
1904	36.83	292.96	102.96	11.95**	228.57	21.00
1905	33.30	316.01	117.55	12.39**	248.18	23.00
1906	31.43	305.90	110.47	12.49**	175.36	62.00
1907	31.14	315.70	97.13	8.85**	303.36	72.00
1908	32.19	330.70	118.04	10.22**	347.45	72.00
1909	35.28	347.69	115.55	9.65**	419.93	71.00
1910	40.38	303.63	123.17	9.72**	434.34	84.00
1911	42.86	518.89	119.94	11.69**	451.86	100.00
1912	44.37	496.69	135.59	17.68**	462.99	95.00
1913	48.83	553.00	133.26	24.48**	480.25	96.00
1914	103.30	651.32	139.68		334.79	83.00
1915	205.73	581.57	141.84			84.00
1916	209.88	821.28	153.85			117.00
1917	227.39	1059.65	239.63			162.00
1918	334.09	1163.98	1278.84			216.00
1919	156.50	1507.62	2002.31			316.00
1920	88.40	900.52	736.02			403.00
1921	80.80	1090.67	650.37			484.00
1922	56.20	1230.33	476.78			374.00
1923	52.60	1102.00	333.20			275.00
1924	55.60	1479.74	332.25		104.30	248.00
1925	59.70	1311.85	346.14		155.10	229.00
1926	57.60	1608.30	312.74		203.30	327.00
1927	58.10	2396.16	318.91		223.40	274.00
1928	56.90	2571.07	331.34		214.70	268.00
1929	55.80	3410.63	364.56		200.50	268.00
1930	52.60	3061.17	374.16		198.00	242.00
1931	51.10	3311.34	353.77		191.90	227.00
1932	50.00	2256.96	357.52		187.40	313.00
1933	53.50	2782.90	349.37		311.80	410.00
1934	56.60	2724.61	296.93		496.50	483.00
1935	64.80	2804.12	436.27		695.10	536.00
1936	81.10	3563.09	528.88		1160.70	567.00
1937	102.00	4617.00	556.67		1478.50	645.00
1938	127.30	6142.00	596.13		1756.30	679.00
1939		21256.00	672.72		2389.90	804.00
1940			891.49			1034.00
1941			2313.06			1497.00

342

Table A.1   Naval expenditures, 1816–1945
(original currencies in millions)

Year	Great Britain	France	United States	Russia/ Soviet Union	Germany	Japan
1942			8579.59			
1943			20888.35			
1944			26537.63			
1945			30047.15			

*extrapolated
**expressed in British pounds

Sources:
Great Britain: 1816–1913 (Page, 1968) 1914–18, *Brassey's Naval Annual*, (multiple volumes); 1919–38 (Mitchell and Deane, 1962).
France: 1816–20 (DeNervo, 1865); 1821–9 (Chasseriau, 1845); 1830–67 (Block, 1875); 1868–1937 (Ministère du Travail, *Annuaire Statistique*, multiple volumes); 1938–9 (Ministère des Finances, 1946).
United States: 1816–1945 (US Bureau of the Census, 1975).
Russia: 1816–24 (Blioch, 1892); 1825–31 (Mitchell, 1974); 1832 (extrapolated); 1833–62 (Mitchell, 1974); 1863 (Wolowski, 1864); 1864–70 (Mitchell, 1974); 1871 (*Statesman's Year Book*); 1872–1902 (Mitchell, 1974); 1903 (Cobden Club, 1905); 1904–13 (Mitchell, 1974).
Germany:1872–96 (Cohn, 1972); 1897–1913 (*Statistisches Jahrbuch fur des Deutsche Reich*, multiple volumes); 1924–39 (Dulffer, 1973).
Japan: 1875–96 (Ono, 1922); 1897–1941 (*Japan Statistical Yearbook*, 1949).

without access to more detailed budgetary information on an annual basis for the pre-1886 era. The ordinary–extraordinary problem applies as well to the Japanese case but we are much less confident that we have been able to capture the full amount of Japanese naval spending. Finally, the German series is characterised by multiple budgetary accounts of relevance prior to the First World War (a problem that seems to be manageable with available sources) and a general scarcity of reliable information after 1913. The problems associated with the German series are compounded further by the unusual inflation in the early 1920s and the budgetary secrecy of the Nazi era.

In general then, the 1816–1945 naval expenditures must be viewed as rough estimates subject to problems of missing data (i.e. Soviet naval expenditures), crude manipulations on our part (the dependence on wholesale price indexes), confusing budgetary practices, and multiple and often conflicting sources necessitating the recourse to an inordinate amount of serial splicing. All these problems are particularly acute during periods of global war. Indeed, what information is available for naval spending in both the First and Second

Table A.2   Price indexes for naval expenditures, 1816–1945 (1913 = 100)

Year	Great Britain	France	United States	Germany	Japan
1816	136	164	148		
1817	152	176	148		
1818	151	168	144		
1819	139	143	123		
1820	125	132	104		
1821	114	128	100		
1822	109	119	105		
1823	113	128	101		
1824	115	115	96		
1825	125	126	101		
1826	110	117	97		
1827	110	116	96		
1828	106	111	95		
1829	104	112	94		
1830	103	112	89		
1831	106	107	92		
1832	103	108	93		
1833	101	109	93		
1834	106	110	88		
1835	106	114	98		
1836	116	116	112		
1837	111	109	113		
1838	112	113	108		
1839	123	112	110		
1840	121	116	93		
1841	114	116	90		
1842	105	113	80		
1843	99	104	73		
1844	102	102	75		
1845	104	104	81		
1846	103	111	81		
1847	108	117	88		
1848	94	97	80		
1849	90	96	80		
1850	90	96	82		
1851	86	95	81		
1852	89	103	86		
1853	106	120	95		
1854	118	128	106		
1855	118	133	108		
1856	117	135	103		
1857	120	130	109		
1858	105	118	91		
1859	108	118	93		

Table A.2   Price indexes for naval expenditures, 1816–1945 (1913 = 100)

Year	Great Britain	France	United States	Germany	Japan
1860	113	124	91		
1861	108	122	81		
1862	113	122	102		
1863	114	123	130		
1864	112	122	189		
1865	110	114	181		
1866	113	116	171		
1867	111	113	159		
1868	108	114	155		31
1869	101	112	148		38
1870	104	115	132	92	39
1871	108	119	127	100	39
1872	121	124	133	114	43
1873	120	124	130	120	43
1874	114	114	123	112	44
1875	110	111	116	100	45
1876	108	112	108	95	47
1877	104	113	104	91	43
1878	95	103	89	83	44
1879	92	101	88	81	45
1880	96	103	98	87	47
1881	93	101	101	85	48
1882	95	98	106	81	45
1883	95	95	99	80	42
1884	90	87	91	78	39
1885	83	85	84	75	41
1886	78	82	80	72	42
1887	76	79	83	73	44
1888	79	83	84	75	45
1889	79	86	79	82	46
1890	82	86	80	87	48
1891	81	85	80	86	47
1892	77	82	75	80	49
1893	77	81	76	77	52
1894	70	75	69	73	54
1895	68	73	70	72	55
1896	69	71	66	72	60
1897	70	72	67	76	67
1898	74	74	69	79	71
1899	79	80	75	83	72
1900	86	85	80	90	75
1901	81	82	79	83	71
1902	81	81	84	81	74
1903	81	83	85	82	81
1904	78	81	86	82	85

Table A.2   Price indexes for naval expenditures, 1816–1945 (1913 = 100)

Year	Great Britain	France	United States	Germany	Japan
1905	81	85	86	86	88
1906	88	90	89	92	90
1907	92	94	93	97	98
1908	82	87	90	90	94
1909	86	87	97	91	90
1910	92	93	101	93	90
1911	96	97	93	94	94
1912	98	102	99	102	100
1913	100	100	100	100	100
1914	100	102	90	105	96
1915	123	138	100	140	96
1916	160	185	122	150	116
1917	208	257	168	177	147
1918	230	335	188	216	192
1919	254	347	198	413	235
1920	316	497	221	1476	257
1921	202	341	140	1899	200
1922	163	323	138		194
1923	163	413	144		198
1924	171	479	141	122	206
1925	164	538	148	129	200
1926	152	688	143	131	178
1927	146	604	137	136	169
1928	145	610	139	140	169
1929	140	598	136	142	165
1930	123	520	124	129	137
1931	108	443	104	115	114
1932	105	389	93	99	129
1933	105	371	94	96	147
1934	109	353	107	102	149
1935	109	335	115	105	153
1936	116	389	116	108	159
1937	135	538	124	109	194
1938	125	616	113	109	204
1939	126	646	110	111	229
1940	168	849	113	114	253
1941	188	1041	125	116	271
1942	196	1214	141	118	296
1943	201	1412	148	121	316
1944	205	1591	149	124	359
1945	209	2249	152		544

Sources: The primary price index sources are Mitchell (1975) for Great Britain, France, and Germany; US Bureau of the Census (1975) for the United States; and Emi (1963) for Japan.

346 *Appendix A*

World Wars is of such dubious reliability that we prefer to rely strictly on the warship distribution data for 1914–18 and 1939–45 in constructing the long cycle concentration index (see Tables A-1 and A-2).

However manageable the problems of comparing naval expenditures in the era 1816–1945, the problems proved to be far more intractable in the pre-Napoleonic period. Although some useful information is available on exchange rates (McCusker, 1978), it is extremely difficult to create price indexes for the non-British cases. While this alone would constitute a serious handicap to comparison, the basic information that is available on naval spending becomes less and less reliable the farther back in time one attempts to travel. English/British information on naval spending is available as far back as the Elizabethan period but the data after 1692 are far more reliable and useful than the spotty pre-1692 data. Sixteenth-century information on Portugal appears to be virtually non-existent, as a result of the damage done by an eighteenth-century earthquake to Portuguese royal records. Spanish information on naval spending does not appear to be readily accessible in anything resembling a serial form prior to the second half of the eighteenth century. The naval accounts for the United Provinces of the Netherlands also appear to be difficult to locate so far, short of some determined archival digging. In marked contrast, a great deal of French information exists, particularly between roughly 1662 and 1788. Unfortunately, the bookkeeping practices of the Old Regime were not designed for the purposes of public scrutiny. None of the authorities on this period seem to be particularly confident that any of the various, and of course conflicting, series that have survived are either authentic or accurate (cf. Legoherel, 1965). The revolutionary regimes of the last decade of the eighteenth century failed to improve the information retrieval situation. Only after the advent of Napoleon is it possible to reconstruct French naval spending in serial fashion.

Table A.3 summarises the information we were able to acquire on naval spending. To economise on space we cite only the appropriate source and the year for which naval spending information is available in some fashion. Usually, the information that is found consists of an expenditure figure applicable for some year. In some cases, it is clear that the information represents only part of that year's actual spending or, alternatively, constitutes some type of rough average for several years (indicated by parentheses in Table A.3). Obviously, we are in no position to comment on the specific quality of the bulk of these numbers. But we do strongly suspect that Table A.3 does not exhaust all the information that exists in some form. It represents only the information that we encountered in our largely non-archival search.

Table A.3 Additional information on naval spending

Spain

Braudel (1976) 1534–72
Parker (1970b) 1571–6, 1588
Dominguez Ortiz (1971) 1590s
Elliott (1970) 1608
Israel (1977) 1620s
Elliott (1963) 1620–1
Canaga Arguelles (1826) 1640, 1741, 1758, 1772, 1799
Ibanez de Ibero (1943) 1653
Kamen (1969) 1705–7, 1713–16, 1717–18
Muhmann (1975) 1723, 1740, 1749–78, 1786–1805
Moreau de Jonnes (1835) 1758, 1772, 1799, 1833, 1835
Merino Navarro (1981) 1759, 1768–1868
Coxe (1815) 1778
Desdevises Du Dezert (1899) 1786–1806, 1798, 1805

Netherlands

Ten Raa and De Bas (1911) 1600–07, 1626–35, 1637–48, 1667
Dirks (1890) 1623, 1626–7, 1632
Rowen (1978) 1653, 1665, 1670–1
Pontalis (1885) 1666, 1671–2
Temple (1972) 1670
Wijn (1964) 1710

England/Great Britain

Dietz (1932) 1556, 1558, 1559–61, 1564–6, 1571–80, 1585–90, 1592, 1594,
    1596–7, 1599–1603, 1606–7
Oppenheim (1961) 1561, 1563–1600, 1602–47, 1651–9
Charnock (1800–03) 1578–88
Richmond (1953) 1590, 1594, 1605
Clowes (1897–1903) 1652, 1656–8, 1715–1900
Chandaman (1975) 1660–88
Sinclair (1790) 1689–1710, 1714–88
Cooper (1751) 1689–92
Derrick (1806) 1694
Mitchell and Deane (1962) 1692–1915, 1920–39
Vecchj (1895) 1793–6, 1835–60
Page (1968) 1815–1914
Hirst and Allen (1926) 1817, 1837, 1857, 1867, 1887
Cobden (1862) 1835–59
Wright (1942/1965) 1850, 1870, 1880, 1890, 1900, 1910, 1914, 1920, 1929,
    1937
Buxton (1888) 1858–86
Brassey (multiple volumes) 1861–87, 1892–1928
Taylor (1954) 1870, 1880, 1890, 1900, 1910, 1914
Hurd (1902) 1874–1902

348

Table A.3   Additional information on naval spending

England/Great Britain – continued

House of Commons (1914) 1896–1914
Hislam (1908) 1884–1908
Enock (1923, 1951) 1900–45
Hyde (1976) 1920–38

France

Tramond (1947) 1547, 1607, 1609
Mallet (1789) 1600–56, 1662–78, 1679–95
Burckhardt (1965) 1609
Lacour-Gayet (1911) 1624, 1642, 1655–6
Cole (1964) 1624, 1626, 1660, 1662
Legoherel (1965) 1631–5, 1637, 1707–89
Perkins (1971) 1641, 1656
Memain (1936) 1642, 1856
The State of France (1760) 1642, 1712, 1722, 1734, 1739–42
Vecchj (1895) 1662–7, 1835–59, 1892
Neuville (1977) 1662–1709, 1724–5, 1744–5
Ranum and Ranum (1972) 1671
Symcox (1974) 1683–1700
Dumarsais (1958) 1704
Deschamps (1902) 1707
Carré (1911) 1715–16, 1739–40, 1744
Margry (1879a) 1716
Wilson (1936) 1722, 1739–41, 1744–8
Loir (1893) 1726, 1734, 1740, 1748
Dorn (1963) 1728, 1742, 1745
Margry (1879b) 1744–54
Lacour-Gayet (1905) 1759, 1776–7, 1776–80, 1782
Jouan (1950) 1770
Lloyd (1965a) 1778–88
Hampson (1959) 1789–91
Marion (1914) 1792, 1798, 1801–5, 1814–15
Montesquiou (1797) 1797
Thomazi (1950) 1802
France (1803–14) 1803–14
Mollien (1895) 1806–13
DeNervo (1865) 1815–20
Mallez (1927) 1815–30
Porter (1838) 1814–36
Block (1875) 1816, 1819, 1821–2, 1830–75
Chasseriau (1845) 1820–45
Kaufmann, de (1884) 1830–81
Cobden (1862) 1835–59
Bartlett (1963) 1847, 1852

349

Table A.3   Additional information on naval spending

France – continued

Ministère de la Marine et des Colonies (multiple volumes) 1860–67, 1869–75
Wright (1942/1965) 1850, 1870, 1880, 1890, 1900, 1910, 1914, 1920, 1929, 1937
Ministère du Travail (multiple volumes) 1867–1937
Fisk (1922) 1867, 1872, 1883, 1893, 1902, 1912, 1919
Brassey (multiple volumes) 1876–86
Abeille (1906) 1890, 1892–4, 1896–1905
Cobden Club (1905) 1892–1904
House of Commons (1914) 1896–1914
Enock (1923, 1951) 1900–38, 1944
Ministère des Finances (1946) 1919–39
League of Nations (multiple volumes) 1920–39
Tiffen (1937) 1928–38

Russia/Soviet Union

Blioch (1892) 1701, 1706, 1710, 1725, 1804–25
Kluchevsky (1960) 1724–5
Slany (1958) 1725–32
Mitchell (1974) 1806, 1815, 1818, 1822, 1825–31, 1833–62, 1864–70, 1872–1902, 1904–13
Schnitzler (1829) 1818
Violette (1971) 1855–70
Wolowski (1964) 1863
Grierson (1886) 1875–85, 1887
Taylor (1954) 1870, 1880, 1890, 1910, 1914
Wright (1942/1965) 1870, 1880, 1890, 1900, 1910, 1914, 1921, 1929, 1937
Clarke (1898) 1880, 1884, 1890–8
Cobden Club (1905) 1889–1904
House of Commons (1914) 1896–1914
League of Nations (multiple volumes) 1918–21, 1923–4

Germany

Cohn (1972) 1872–99
Abeille (1906) 1872–3, 1883, 1886, 1889–90, 1892–4, 1896–1905
Taylor (1954) 1870, 1880, 1890, 1900, 1910, 1914
Wright (1942/1965) 1870, 1880, 1890, 1900, 1910, 1914, 1929, 1937
Hurd and Castle (1913/1971) 1874, 1889, 1901–13
Hislam (1908) 1884–1908
Cobden Club (1905) 1884–92, 1897–1904
House of Commons (1914) 1896–1914
Statistisches Jahrbuch fur des Deutsche Reich (multiple volumes) 1897–1919
Enock (1923, 1951) 1900–20, 1924–43

350

Table A.3   Additional information on naval spending

Germany – continued

Bogart (1919) 1913
Dulffer (1973) 1924–39
League of Nations (multiple volumes) 1924–9
Homze (1976) 1932–9

Japan

Ono (1922) 1875–1913
Andreades (1932) 1875, 1903, 1906
Abeille (1906) 1882, 1884, 1888
Wright (1942/1965) 1880, 1890, 1900, 1910, 1914, 1920, 1929, 1937
Japan Statistical Yearbook (1949) 1897–1944
Enock (1923, 1951) 1900–45
House of Commons (1914) 1905–14
Brassey (multiple volumes) 1906–20
League of Nations (multiple volumes) 1920–39

Appendix B

Table B.1 Long cycle concentration values (alternative index)

Year		Year		Year		Year	
1494	0.360	1534	0.501	1574	0.275	1614	0.473
1495	0.200	1535	0.417	1575	0.254	1615	0.474
1496	0.200	1536	0.432	1576	0.248	1616	0.461
1497	0.175	1537	0.458	1577	0.236	1617	0.451
1498	0.175	1538	0.473	1578	0.252	1618	0.462
1499	0.175	1539	0.456	1579	0.263	1619	0.436
1500	0.092	1540	0.437	1580	0.275	1620	0.387
1501	0.175	1541	0.421	1581	0.306	1621	0.368
1502	0.420	1542	0.429	1582	0.297	1622	0.339
1503	0.395	1543	0.421	1583	0.320	1623	0.343
1504	0.393	1544	0.386	1584	0.331	1624	0.368
1505	0.458	1545	0.334	1585	0.343	1625	0.367
1506	0.531	1546	0.318	1586	0.351	1626	0.361
1507	0.551	1547	0.296	1587	0.386	1627	0.330
1508	0.561	1548	0.279	1588	0.403	1628	0.318
1509	0.585	1549	0.253	1589	0.338	1629	0.314
1510	0.576	1550	0.236	1590	0.359	1630	0.332
1511	0.562	1551	0.303	1591	0.387	1631	0.332
1512	0.489	1552	0.290	1592	0.396	1632	0.338
1513	0.471	1553	0.293	1593	0.403	1633	0.340
1514	0.483	1554	0.340	1594	0.411	1634	0.331
1515	0.487	1555	0.323	1595	0.421	1635	0.342
1516	0.470	1556	0.330	1596	0.422	1636	0.342
1517	0.388	1557	0.330	1597	0.430	1637	0.330
1518	0.388	1558	0.302	1598	0.386	1638	0.321
1519	0.390	1559	0.307	1599	0.368	1639	0.315
1520	0.340	1560	0.260	1600	0.350	1640	0.489
1521	0.423	1561	0.245	1601	0.309	1641	0.430
1522	0.410	1562	0.258	1602	0.336	1642	0.375
1523	0.407	1563	0.267	1603	0.343	1643	0.329
1524	0.393	1564	0.249	1604	0.352	1644	0.301
1525	0.436	1565	0.208	1605	0.358	1645	0.257
1526	0.443	1566	0.234	1606	0.363	1646	0.210
1527	0.463	1567	0.265	1607	0.369	1647	0.188
1528	0.444	1568	0.254	1608	0.431	1648	0.164
1529	0.417	1569	0.236	1609	0.446	1649	0.185
1530	0.440	1570	0.183	1610	0.466	1650	0.221
1531	0.459	1571	0.264	1611	0.473	1651	0.272
1532	0.417	1572	0.258	1612	0.473	1652	0.365
1533	0.479	1573	0.239	1613	0.473	1653	0.367

352

Table B.1 Long cycle concentration values (alternative index)

Year		Year		Year		Year	
1654	0.378	1699	0.253	1744	0.317	1789	0.200
1655	0.332	1700	0.247	1745	0.322	1790	0.203
1656	0.316	1701	0.259	1746	0.323	1791	0.202
1657	0.309	1702	0.269	1747	0.360	1792	0.224
1658	0.301	1703	0.273	1748	0.357	1793	0.235
1659	0.298	1704	0.287	1749	0.322	1794	0.214
1660	0.293	1705	0.301	1750	0.317	1795	0.240
1661	0.326	1706	0.309	1751	0.316	1796	0.250
1662	0.314	1707	0.319	1752	0.311	1797	0.290
1663	0.313	1708	0.338	1753	0.320	1798	0.299
1664	0.318	1709	0.353	1754	0.320	1799	0.276
1665	0.302	1710	0.360	1755	0.324	1800	0.264
1666	0.269	1711	0.365	1756	0.310	1801	0.263
1667	0.240	1712	0.375	1757	0.265	1802	0.267
1668	0.230	1713	0.384	1758	0.288	1803	0.269
1669	0.234	1714	0.416	1759	0.313	1804	0.269
1670	0.240	1715	0.378	1760	0.311	1805	0.298
1671	0.243	1716	0.379	1761	0.318	1806	0.310
1672	0.246	1717	0.375	1762	0.330	1807	0.335
1673	0.240	1718	0.361	1763	0.355	1808	0.340
1674	0.240	1719	0.446	1764	0.362	1809	0.448
1675	0.248	1720	0.434	1765	0.359	1810	0.450
1676	0.256	1721	0.432	1766	0.356	1811	0.491
1677	0.251	1722	0.412	1767	0.358	1812	0.503
1678	0.239	1723	0.401	1768	0.364	1813	0.507
1679	0.251	1724	0.382	1769	0.365	1814	0.523
1680	0.261	1725	0.362	1770	0.366	1815	0.579
1681	0.263	1726	0.354	1771	0.353	1816	0.559
1682	0.254	1727	0.345	1772	0.348	1817	0.497
1683	0.261	1728	0.342	1773	0.335	1818	0.504
1684	0.262	1729	0.342	1774	0.335	1819	0.471
1685	0.261	1730	0.337	1775	0.335	1820	0.453
1686	0.274	1731	0.332	1776	0.332	1821	0.469
1687	0.267	1732	0.337	1777	0.316	1822	0.470
1688	0.253	1733	0.335	1778	0.303	1823	0.459
1689	0.251	1734	0.346	1779	0.299	1824	0.458
1690	0.263	1735	0.357	1780	0.295	1825	0.433
1691	0.290	1736	0.362	1781	0.280	1826	0.461
1692	0.285	1737	0.357	1782	0.292	1827	0.453
1693	0.281	1738	0.355	1783	0.253	1828	0.419
1694	0.262	1739	0.343	1784	0.223	1829	0.428
1695	0.267	1740	0.345	1785	0.225	1830	0.403
1696	0.265	1741	0.372	1786	0.225	1831	0.412
1697	0.260	1742	0.350	1787	0.222	1832	0.382
1698	0.265	1743	0.345	1788	0.232	1833	0.379

353

Table B.1   Long cycle concentration values (alternative index)

Year		Year		Year		Year	
1834	0.362	1874	0.350	1914	0.390	1954	1.000
1835	0.356	1875	0.367	1915	0.353	1955	1.000
1836	0.334	1876	0.363	1916	0.353	1956	1.000
1837	0.354	1877	0.364	1917	0.339	1957	1.000
1838	0.339	1878	0.357	1918	0.339	1958	1.000
1839	0.303	1879	0.361	1919	0.476	1959	1.000
1840	0.337	1880	0.484	1920	0.365	1960	0.460
1841	0.340	1881	0.481	1921	0.423	1961	0.490
1842	0.319	1882	0.478	1922	0.401	1962	0.482
1843	0.372	1883	0.475	1923	0.405	1963	0.529
1844	0.318	1884	0.474	1924	0.380	1964	0.544
1845	0.332	1885	0.479	1925	0.384	1965	0.540
1846	0.371	1886	0.453	1926	0.366	1966	0.540
1847	0.338	1887	0.442	1927	0.352	1967	0.529
1848	0.330	1888	0.451	1928	0.343	1968	0.518
1849	0.311	1889	0.479	1929	0.321	1969	0.434
1850	0.329	1890	0.467	1930	0.324	1970	0.415
1851	0.310	1891	0.418	1931	0.321	1971	0.410
1852	0.324	1892	0.411	1932	0.359	1972	0.405
1853	0.330	1893	0.383	1933	0.314	1973	0.410
1854	0.379	1894	0.368	1934	0.273	1974	0.387
1855	0.427	1895	0.383	1935	0.276	1975	0.379
1856	0.375	1896	0.390	1936	0.264	1976	0.358
1857	0.364	1897	0.340	1937	0.260	1977	0.352
1858	0.348	1898	0.332	1938	0.255	1978	0.316
1859	0.372	1899	0.285	1939	0.202	1979	0.283
1860	0.393	1900	0.286	1940	0.226	1980	0.268
1861	0.489	1901	0.283	1941	0.329	1981	0.261
1862	0.354	1902	0.296	1942	0.372	1982	0.268
1863	0.297	1903	0.297	1943	0.392	1983	0.283
1864	0.356	1904	0.319	1944	0.478	1984	0.280
1865	0.242	1905	0.319	1945	0.507	1985	0.290
1866	0.335	1906	0.290	1946	1.000	1986	0.287
1867	0.371	1907	0.253	1947	1.000	1987	0.252
1868	0.388	1908	0.277	1948	1.000	1988	0.240
1869	0.385	1909	0.286	1949	1.000	1989	0.242
1870	0.350	1910	0.389	1950	1.000	1990	0.244
1871	0.372	1911	0.350	1951	1.000	1991	0.218
1872	0.361	1912	0.318	1952	1.000	1992	0.232
1873	0.376	1913	0.304	1953	1.000	1993	0.210

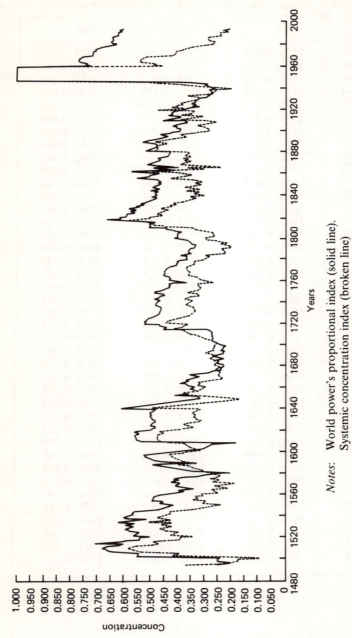

Notes: World power's proportional index (solid line).
Systemic concentration index (broken line)

Figure B.1 Two indexes of seapower concentration, 1494–1993

Notes

1   Sea Power and Global Politics

1. The risk theory is discussed further in Chapter 9, in the treatment of the development of the German navy.

2   Sea Power and Its Measurement

1. At a very early phase in the naval expenditure data collection for this project a number of European yearbooks (i.e. *Almanach de France, Almanach de Gotha, Diplomatisches Jahrbuch, Gothaischer Kalendar,* and *Statesman's Yearbook*) were examined. Generally, the quality of the data outcome did not really justify the resources expended in this search.
2. The states that met our qualifications for global power status, and the years in which they qualified, are identified in Chapter 5 (Table 5.1). A number of states that failed to qualify are discussed in Chapter 10.
3. As discussed in Chapter 4, we will restrict our employment of naval expenditures as a partial indicator of global capability to the period 1816–1945. See appendix A for a brief treatment of the problems encountered, and sources used, in working with naval expenditure data.

3   Rules for Counting Warships, 1494–1860

1. The nature of sixteenth-century ships is discussed at greater length in Chapter 7.
2. Most of the English royal fleet was sold after the death of Henry V to pay for his debts (Oppenheim, 1961, p. 18).

4   Rules for Counting Warships, 1861–1993

1. Price indexes and the native currency expenditure data are reported in appendix A (Tables A.1 and A.2).
2. Specific attribute details on ballistic-missile weapon systems are made available in Chapters 8 (the United States) and 9 (the Soviet Union).

5   The Long Cycle of World Leadership

1. Chapter 10 provides some treatment of states that failed to qualify as global powers. The post-1945 cases of Britain and France are also discussed.

6   The Future of Sea Power

1. Two great power lists (Levy, 1983, and Singer and Small, 1972) are compared, in Chapter 10, with the global power list generated by the long cycle's emphasis on global-reach capabilities.

355

356 *Notes*

8 The World Powers: The Netherlands, Great Britain and the United States

1. Britain's naval status after the Second World War is reviewed in Chapter 10.

9 The Other Global Powers: France, Spain, Russia/the Soviet Union, Germany and Japan

1. Post World War II France's naval status is considered in Chapter 10.
2. Japanese naval development after the Second World War is examined in Auer (1973).

10 Non-global Powers

1. New MIRVed warheads of 60 kiloton magnitude were fitted in three of the British SSBN between 1982 and 1986.
2. France anticipates a seventh SSBN in 1994 (see Hyland, 1985 for a discussion of the future French developments). Britain expects to deploy four new submarines with Trident II missiles in the mid-1990s.
3. The latest *Jane's Fighting Ships* (1985–6) credits China with one Soviet Golf class (diesel) and two Xia class submarines (operational in 1985 and 1986 respectively). The nuclear Xia class carries fourteen tubes for the CSS-NX3 missile. Four more are planned. In addition, China has possessed three nuclear-attack submarines since the late 1970s. Three more are being built.

Bibliography

ABEILLE, LEONCE (1960) *Marine Française et Marines Etrangères,* Paris: Libraire Armand Colin.

ALBION, ROBERT G. (1926) *Forests and Sea Power: The Timber Problem of the Royal Navy, 1652–1862,* Cambridge: Harvard University Press.

Almanach de France (multiple volumes) Paris: Société Nationale.

Almanach de Gotha (multiple volumes) Gotha: Justus Perthes.

ALMEIDA, FORTUNATO DE (1929) *Historia de Portugal,* Vol. 6. Coimbra: Impresa de Universitade.

L'Ancienne France: La Marine et Les Colonies (1888) Paris: Libraire de Firmin-Didot.

ANDERSON, MATTHEW S. (1961) *Europe in the Eighteenth Century, 1713–1783,* London: Longmans, Green & Co.

———— (1972) *The Ascendancy of Europe: Aspects of European History, 1815–1914,* London: Longman.

ANDERSON, ROGER C. (1935) *Lists of Men-of-War, 1650–1700: Part I, English Ships, 1649–1702,* Society for Nautical Research Occasional Publication, no. 5, Cambridge: Cambridge University Press.

———— (1969) *Naval Wars in the Baltic, 1522–1850,* London: Francis Edwards.

ANDREADES, ANDRÉ (1932) *Les Finances de l'Empire Japonais et Leur Evolution, 1868–1931,* Paris: Libraire Félix Alcan.

ANDREWS, KENNETH R. (1984) *Trade, Plunder and Settlement: Maritime Enterprise and the Genesis of the British Empire, 1480–1630,* Cambridge: Cambridge University Press.

ARCHIBALD, EDWARD H. H. (1968) *The Wooden Fighting Ship in the Royal Navy, AD 897–1860,* Poole: Blandford Press.

AUER, JAMES E. (1973) *The Postwar Rearmament of Japanese Maritime Forces, 1945–71,* New York: Praeger.

BAIN, NISBET R. (1908) 'Peter the Great and His Pupils (1689–1730)', pp. 518–57 in A. W. Ward, G. W. Prothero, S. Leathes (eds) *Cambridge Modern History: The Age of Louis XIV,* vo. 5, Cambridge: Cambridge University Press.

BALLARD, G. A. (1927) *Rulers of the Indian Ocean,* London: Duckworth.

BALLESTEROS Y BERETTA, ANTONIO (1932) *Historia De España Y Su Influencia en la Historia Universal,* vol. 9, Barcelona: Salvat Editores.

BARFLEUR (1907) *Naval Policy: A Plea for the Study of War,* Edinburgh: Blackwood.

BARKER, J. ELLIS (1906) *The Rise and Decline of the Netherlands,* London: Smith & Elder.

BARTLETT, CHRISTOPHER J. (1963) *Great Britain and Sea Power, 1815–1853,* Oxford: Clarendon.

BAUER, JACK K. (1969) *Ships of the Navy, 1775–1969, Volume 1: Combat Vessels,* Troy, NY: Rensselaer Polytechnic Institute.

BAUGH, DANIEL A. (1965) *British Naval Administration in the Age of Walpole,* Princeton: Princeton University Press.

358 *Bibliography*

———— (1977) *Naval Administration, 1715–1750*, London: Naval Records Society.

BEKKER, CAJUS (1974) *Hitler's Naval War*, New York: Kensington.

BENIANS, E. A. (1940) 'The Beginnings of the New Empire, 1783–1793', pp. 1–35 in J. Holland Rose, A. P. Newton, E. A. Benians (eds) *The Cambridge History of the British Empire: The Growth of the New Empire, 1783–1870*, vol. 2, Cambridge: Cambridge University Press.

BERMAN, ROBERT (1975) 'Soviet Naval Strength and Deployment', pp. 419–423 in Michael MccGwire, Ken Booth, John McDonnel (eds) *Soviet Naval Policy: Objectives and Constraints*, New York: Praeger.

BIRD, KEITH W. (1977) *Weimar, The German Naval Officer Corps and the Rise of National Socialism*, Amsterdam: B. R. Gruner.

BLECHMAN, BARRY M. (1975) 'The Evolution of the Soviet Navy', pp. 65–97 in George H. Quester (ed.) *Sea Power in the 1970s*, New York: Dunellen.

BLIOCH, JAN GOTLIB (1892) *ØHHAHCЫ POCCIU XIX CTO ETI*, 3 vols, Moscow.

BLOCK, MAURICE (1875) *Statistique de la France*, vol. 1, Paris: Buillaumin.

BLOK, PETRUS J. (1900) *A History of the People of the Netherlands*, 4 vols, trans. Ruth Putnam and Oscar A. Bierstadt, New York: Putnam.

———— (1975) *The Life of Admiral De Ruyter*, trans. G. J. Renier, Westport, Conn.: Greenwood Press.

BOGART, ERNEST L. (1919) *Direct and Indirect Costs of the Great World War*, New York: Oxford University Press.

BORJESON, H. J. (1936) *Lists of Men-of-War, 1650–1700: Part III, Swedish Ships*, Greenwich: Society for Nautical Research, Occasional Publications.

BOUCHARD, LEON (1971) *Système Financier de l'Ancienne Monarchie*, New York: Burt Franklin.

BOURET DE CRESSE, A. J. B. (1824) *Histoire de la Marine de Tous Les Peuples*, vol. 2, Paris: Chez Aimé André.

BOURNE, RUTH (1939) *Queen Anne's Navy in the West Indies*, New Haven: Yale University Press.

BOXER, CHARLES R. (1965) *The Dutch Seaborne Empire, 1600–1800*, New York: Knopf.

———— (1969) *The Portuguese Seaborne Empire, 1415–1825*, New York: Knopf.

———— (1972) *Four Centuries of Portuguese Expansion, 1415–1825*, Berkeley: University of California Press.

BRADFORD, JAMES C. (1984) 'The Navies of the American Revolution', pp. 3–26 in Kenneth J. Hagan (ed.) *In Peace and War: Interpretations of American Naval History, 1775–1984*, Westport, Conn.: Greenwood Press.

BRASSEY'S NAVAL ANNUAL (multiple volumes) Portsmouth: J. Griffin and Co.

BRAUDEL, FERNAND (1976) *The Mediterranean and the Mediterranean World in the Age of Philip II*, 2 vols., trans. Sian Reynolds, New York: Harper & Row.

BREEMER, JAN S. (1983) *US Naval Developments*, Annapolis: The Nautical and Aviation Publishing Company of America.

Bibliography 359

BRENTON, EDWARD P. (1823–5) *The Naval History of Great Britain*, 5 vols. London: C. Rice.

BREYER, SIEGRIED (1973) *Battleships and Battle Cruisers, 1905–1970*, trans. Alfred Kurti, Garden City, NY: Doubleday.

———— and POLMAR, NORMAN (1977) *Guide to the Soviet Navy*, 2nd edn, Annapolis: Naval Institute Press.

BRIDGE, CYPRIAN A. G. (ed) (1899) *The Russian Fleet Under Peter the Great*, London: Naval Records Society.

BRODEUR, NIGEL (1975) 'Comparative Capabilities of Soviet and Western Weapon Systems', pp. 452–568 in Michael MccGwire, Ken Booth, and John McDonnel (eds) *Soviet Naval Policy: Objectives and Constraints*, New York: Praeger.

BRODIE, BERNARD (1941) *Sea Power in the Machine Age*, Princeton: Princeton University Press.

BROMLEY, J. S. and RYAN, A. N. (1971) 'Navies', pp. 790–833 in J. S. Bromley (ed.) *New Cambridge Modern History: The Rise of Great Britain and Russia, 1688–1715/25*, vol. 6, Cambridge: Cambridge University Press.

BRUIJN, J. R. (1970) *De Admiraliteit Van Amsterdam in Rustige Jaren, 1713–1751*, Amsterdam: Scheltema & Holkema.

BRUUN, GEOFFREY (1963) *Europe and the French Imperium, 1799–1814*, New York: Harper & Row.

BUHL, LANCE C. (1978) 'Maintaining "An American Navy", 1865–1889', pp. 145–173 in Kenneth J. Hagan (ed.) *In Peace and War: Interpretations of American Naval History, 1775–1978*, Westport, Conn.: Greenwood.

BURCKHARDT, CARL J. (1965) *Richelieu and His Age: Assertion of Power and Cold War*, vol. 1, New York: Harcourt Brace & World.

BUSK, HANS (1859) *The Navies of the World*, London: Routledge, Warnes & Routledge.

BUXTON, SIDNEY (1888) *Finance and Politics: An Historical Study, 1783–1885*, vol. 2, London: John Murray.

CABLE, JAMES (1981) *Gunboat Diplomacy: Political Applications of Limited National Force*, 2nd edn, New York: St Martin's Press.

CALLENDER, GEOFFREY (1924) *The Naval Side of British History*, London: Christophers.

CANAGA ARGUELLES, JOSÉ (1826) *Diccionario de Hacienda, vol. 1*, London: Imprenta Espanola de M. Calero.

CARRÉ, H. (1911) *Histoire de France: Louis XV (1715–1774)*. vol. 8, Second Part, Paris: Hachette.

CHALMERS, GEORGE (1794) *An Estimate of the Comparative Strength of Great Britain*, London: Stockdale.

CHANDAMAN, C. D. (1975) *The English Public Revenue, 1660–1688*, Oxford: Oxford University Press.

CHANG, TIEN-TSE (1934) *Sino-Portuguese Trade from 1514 to 1644: A Synthesis of Portuguese and Chinese Sources*, Leyden: Brill.

CHARNOCK, JOHN (1800–03) *A History of Marine Architecture*, 3 vols, London.

CHASSERIAU, F. (1845) *Précis Historique de la Marine Française: Son Organisation et Ses Lois*, vol. 1. Paris: Imprimerie Royale.

360 *Bibliography*

CHAUNU, PIERRE AND CHAUNU, HUGUETTE (1955–6) *Seville et Atlantique*, 8 vols, Paris.

CHESNEAU, ROGER and KOLESNIK, EUGENE M. (eds) (1979) *Conway's All the World's Fighting Ships, 1860–1905*, New York: Mayflower Books.

CIPOLLA, CARLO M. (1965) *Guns and Sails in the Early Phase of European Expansion, 1400–1700*, London: Collins.

CLARIGNY, CUCHEVAL (1861) *The Army and Navy Budgets of France and England*, London: Ward.

CLARK, GEORGE (1970a) 'The Nine Years War, 1688–1697', pp. 223–53 in J. S. Bromley (ed.) *New Cambridge Modern History: The Rise of Great Britain and Russia, 1688–1725*, vol. 6, Cambridge: Cambridge University Press.

————— (1970b) 'From the Nine Years War to the War of the Spanish Succession', pp. 381–409 in J. S. Bromley (ed.) *New Cambridge Modern History: The Rise of Great Britain and Russia, 1688–1725*, vol. 6, Cambridge: Cambridge University Press.

CLARKE, GEORGE S. (1898) *Russia's Sea Power: Past and Present or the Rise of the Russian Navy*, London: John Murray.

CLOWES, WILLIAM L. (1897–1903) *The Royal Navy*, 7 vols, London: Sampson, Low, Marston.

COBDEN, RICHARD (1862) *The Three Panics: An Historical Episode*, 4th edn, London: Ward.

COBDEN CLUB (1905) *The Burden of Armaments: A Plea for Retrenchment*, London: T. Fisher Unwin.

COHN, S. (1972) *Die Finanzen des Deutschen Reiches Seit Seiner Begrunding*, Glashutten im Taunus: Verlag Detter Auvermann K.G.

COLE, CHARLES W. (1964) *Colbert and a Century of French Mercantilism*, 2 vols, Hamden, Conn.: Archon Books.

COLLEDGE, J. J. (1969) *Ships of the Royal Navy: An Historical Index: Major Ships*, vol. 1, New York: Augustus M. Kelley.

COLLINS, JOHN M. (1980) *US–Soviet Military Balance: Concepts and Capabilities, 1960–1980*, New York: McGraw-Hill.

————— (1985) *US–Soviet Military Balance, 1980–1985*, Washington, DC: Pergamon-Brassey's.

COLOMB, JOHN CHARLES R. (1867) *The Protection of our Commerce and Distribution of Our Naval Forces Considered*, London: Harrison.

Congressional Record (1977) 5 August, 27606.

COOMBS, DOUGLAS (1958) *The Conduct of the Dutch: British Opinion and the Dutch Alliance During the War of the Spanish Succession*, Hague: Martinus Nijhoff.

COOPER, J. P. (1970) 'Sea Power', pp. 226–38 in J. P. Cooper (ed.) *New Cambridge Modern History: The Decline of Spain and the Thirty Years War, 1609–48/59*, vol. 4, Cambridge: Cambridge University Press.

COOPER, M. (1751) *The History of Our National Debts and Taxes, 1688–1751*, vol. 1, London.

CORBETT, JULIAN S. (1898) *Papers Relating to the Navy During the Spanish War, 1585–1587*, London: Navy Records Society.

————— (1900) *The Successors of Drake*, New York: Burt Franklin.

Bibliography

——————— (1911) *Principles of Naval Strategy*, London: Longmans, Green.

COWBURN, PHILIP (1965) *The Warship in History*, New York: Macmillan.

COXE, WILLIAM (1815) *Memoirs of the Kings of Spain of the House of Bourbon, 1700–1788*, vol. 5, 2nd edn, London: Longman *et al.*

CREIGHTON, M. (1897) *History of the Papacy*, New York.

DANVERS, FREDERICK, C. (1966) *The Portuguese in India*, 2 vols, New York: Octagon Books. Originally published in 1894.

DENERVO, G. (1865) *Les Finances Françaises sous La Restoration, 1814–1830*, vol. 1, Paris: Michel Levy Frères.

DERRICK, CHARLES (1806) *Memoirs of the Rise and Progress of the Royal Navy*, London.

DERRY, T. K. (1965) 'Scandinavia', pp. 480–94 in C. W. Crawley (ed.) *New Cambridge Modern History: War and Peace in an Age of Upheaval, 1793–1830*, vol. 9, Cambridge: Cambridge University Press.

DESCHAMPS, PHILIPPE (1902) *Les Finances D'Autrefois et Celles D'Aujourd'Hui: Les Budgets de La France, 1870–1902*, Paris: A. Lemerre.

DESDEVISES DU DEZERT, G. (1899) *L'Espagne de L'Ancien Régime: Les Institutions*, Paris: Société Française D'Imprimerie et de Librairie.

DICKSON, P. G. M. and SPERLING, JOHN (1970) 'War Finance, 1689–1714', pp. 284–315 in J. S. Bromley (ed.) *New Cambridge Modern History: The Rise of Great Britain and Russia, 1688–1725*, vol. 6, Cambridge: Cambridge University Press.

DIETZ, FREDERICK C. (1932) *English Public Finance, 1558–1641*, New York: The Century Co.

DIFFIE, BAILEY W. and WINIUS, GEORGE D. (1977) *Foundations of the Portuguese Empire, 1415–1580*, Minneapolis: University of Minnesota Press.

Diplomatisches Jahrbuch (multiple volumes) Gotha: Justus Perthes.

DIRKS, JACOBUS J. BACKER (1890) *De Nederlandsche Zeemacht in Hare Verschillende Tijdperken Geschetst*, 2 vols, S'Gravenhage: De Gebroeders Van Cleef.

DISMUKES, BRADFORD and MCCONNELL, JAMES M. (eds) (1979) *Soviet Naval Diplomacy*, New York: Pergamon Press.

DMYTRYSHYN, BASIL (1977) *A History of Russia*, Englewood Cliffs, NJ: Prentice Hall.

DOMINGUEZ ORTIZ, ANTONIO (1960) *Politica Y Hacienda De Felipe IV*, Madrid: Editorial de Derecho Financiero.

——————— (1971) *The Golden Age of Spain, 1515–1659*, trans. James Casey, New York: Basic Books.

DORN, WALTER L. (1963) *Competition for Empire, 1740–1763*, New York: Harper & Row.

DUFFY, JAMES (1955) *Shipwreck and Empire: Being An Account of Portuguese Maritime Disasters in a Century of Decline*, Cambridge: Harvard University Press.

DULFFER, JUST (1973) *Weimar, Hitler und die Marine; Reichspolitik und Flottenbau, 1920–1939*, Dusseldorf: Droste Verlag.

DUMARSAIS, DUPUIS (1858) *Histoire de la Marine Française Sous Louis XIV*, vol. 5, 2nd ed. (Paris).

362 *Bibliography*

DUPUY, R. ERNEST and DUPUY, TREVOR N. (1977) *The Encyclopedia of Military History*, revised edn, New York: Harper & Row.

DUTOT (1739) *Political Reflections on the Finances and Commerce of France*, London: A. Millar, reprinted Clifton, NJ: Augustus M. Kelley, 1974.

DYSON, FREEMAN (1984) *Weapons and Hope*, New York: Harper & Row.

EDLER, FRIEDRICH (1911) *The Dutch Republic and the American Revolution*, Baltimore: Johns Hopkins Press.

EDMUNDSON, GEORGE (1922) *History of Holland*, Cambridge, Cambridge University Press.

EHRMAN, JOHN (1953) *The Navy in the War of William III, 1689–1697*, Cambridge: Cambridge University Press.

ELLIOTT, J. H. (1963) *Imperial Spain, 1469–1716*, New York: St Martin's Press.

———— (1970) 'The Spanish Peninsula, 1598–1648', pp. 435–73 in J. P. Cooper (ed.) *New Cambridge Modern History: The Decline of Spain and the Thirty Years War, 1609–48/59*, vol. 4, Cambridge: Cambridge University Press.

EMI, KOICHI (1963) *Government Fiscal Activity and Economic Growth in Japan, 1868–1960*, Tokyo: Kinokuniya.

ENGELS, FRIEDRICH (1956) *Selected Military Works*, Moscow: Voenizdat (in Russian).

ENOCK, ARTHUR G. (1923) *The Problem of Armaments*, New York: Macmillan.

———— (1951) *This War Business*, London: Bodley Head.

FERNANDEZ DURO, CESAREO (1972–3) *Armada Española desde La Union de Los Reines de Castilla y de Aragon*, 9 vols, Madrid: Museo Naval.

FISK, HARVEY E. (1922) *French Public Finance in the Great War and Today*, New York: Bankers Trust Company.

FONSECA, HENRIQUE QUIRINO DA (1926) *Os Portugueses No Mar: Ementa Historica das Naus Portuguesas*, vol. 1, Lisboa: Tipografia do Comercio.

FRANCE (1803–1814) *Administration des Finances de la République Française*, Paris: L'Imprimerie de la République.

FRANKS, HORACE G. (1942) *Holland Afloat*, London: Netherland Publishing Company.

FRÈRE-COOK, GERVIS and MACKSEY, KENNETH (1975) *The Guinness History of Sea Warfare*, Enfield: Guinness Superlatives.

FULLER, JOHN F. C. (1955) *Military History of the Western World*, New York: Funk & Wagnall.

GATLAND, KENNETH W. (1977) 'Soviet Missiles', pp. 212–31 in Ray Bonds (ed.) *The Soviet War Machine: An Encyclopedia of Russian Military Equipment and Strategy*, revised edn, London: Hamlyn.

GAXOTTE, PIERRE (1970) *The Age of Louis XIV*, trans. Michael Shaw, New York: Macmillan.

GODINHO, VITTORINO MAGALHAES (1945) *Documentos Sobre a Expansão Portuguesa*, vol. 2, Lisboa: Editorial Gleba.

———— (1969) *L'Economie De L'Empire Portugais Aux XVe et XVIe Siècles*, Paris: SEVPEN.

Bibliography

363

———— (1982) *Os Discobrimentos e a Economia Mundial*, Lisboa: Editorial Presenca.

GORSHKOV, S. G. (1979) *The Sea Power of the State*, Annapolis: Naval Institute Press.

Gothaischer Genealogisches Taschenbuch Nebft Diplomatisch-Statischen Jahrbuch (multiple volumes) Gotha: Justus Perthes.

Gothaischer Kalendar (multiple volumes) Gotha: Justus Perthes.

GRAHAM, GERALD S. (1965) *The Politics of Naval Supremacy: Studies in British Maritime Ascendancy*, Cambridge: Cambridge University Press.

GRAHAM, WINSTON (1972) *The Spanish Armadas*, London: Collins.

GRANT, A. J. (1908) 'The Government of Louis XIV (1661–1715)', pp. 1–31 in A. W. Ward, G. W. Prothero, S. Leathes (eds) *Cambridge Modern History: The Age of Louis XIV*, Cambridge: Cambridge University Press.

GRAVIÈRE, JURIEN, DE LA (1879) *Les Marins Du XV et Du XVI Siècle*, 2 Vols, Paris: E. Plon.

GRIERSON, J. M. (1886) *The Armed Strength of Russia*, London: Intelligence Branch of the War Office.

GUILMARTIN, JOHN F., Jr (1974) *Gunpowder and Galleys: Changing Technology and Mediterranean Warfare at Sea in the Sixteenth Century*, Cambridge: Cambridge University Press.

GUNSTON, BILL (1977) 'Soviet Warships', pp. 128–53 in Ray Bonds (ed.) *The Soviet War Machine: An Encyclopedia of Russian Military Equipment and Strategy*, revised edn, London: Hamlyn.

HA, YOUNG-SUN (1983) *Nuclear Proliferation, World Order and Korea*, Seoul: Seoul National University Press.

HAIG, ROBERT M. (1929) *The Public Finances of Post-War France*, New York: Columbia University Press.

HALE, J. R. (1957) 'International Relations in the West: Diplomacy and War', pp. 259–91 in G. R. Potter (ed.) *New Cambridge Modern History: The Renaissance, 1493–1520*, vo. 1, Cambridge: Cambridge University Press.

HALL, D. G. E. (1955) *A History of South-East Asia*, London: Macmillan.

HAMPSON, NORMAN (1959) *La Marine de l'An II: Mobilisation de la Flotte de l'Ocean, 1793–1794*, Paris: Libraire Marcel Rivère.

HANNAY, DAVID (1909) *A Short History of the Royal Navy, 1689–1815*, vol. 2, London: Methuen.

HANOTAUX, GABRIEL (1932) *Histoire du Cardinal De Richelieu: La Polique Intérieure Du Cardinal*, vol. 4, Paris: Libraire Plon.

HARCOURT-SMITH, SIMON (1943) *Alberoni or the Spanish Conspiracy*, London: Faber & Faber.

HARING, CLARENCE H. (1918) *Trade and Navigation Between Spain and the Indies in the Time of the Hapsburgs*, Cambridge: Harvard University Press.

HEADLAM, CECIL (1921) 'International Relations in the Colonial Sphere, 1763–1783', pp. 685–716, in J. H. Rose, A. P. Newton, E. A. Benians (eds) *Cambridge History of the British Empire: The Old Empire*, vol. 1, Cambridge: Cambridge University Press.

364 *Bibliography*

HERODOTUS (1954) *The Histories*, trans. de Selincourt, New York: Penguin Books.

HERWIG, HOLGAR H. (1980) *'Luxury' Fleet: The Imperial German Navy, 1888–1918*, London: Allen & Unwin.

HESS, ANDREW C. (1970) 'The Evolution of the Ottoman Seaborne Empire in the Age of the Oceanic Discoveries, 1453–1525', *American Historical Review* 75 (December) pp. 1892–1919.

HEZLET, ARTHUR (1967) *The Submarine and Sea Power*, New York: Stein & Day.

HIRST, FRANCIS W. and ALLEN, J. E. (1926) *British War Budgets*, Oxford: Oxford University Press.

HISLAM, P. A. (1908) *The Admiralty of the Atlantic*, London: Longmans, Green.

HOEBER, FRANCIS P. (1977) 'Strategic Forces', pp. 18–53 in Francis P. Hoeber and William Schneider, Jr (eds) *Arms, Men and Military Budgets: Issues for Fiscal Year 1978*, New York: Crane, Russak.

HOLCK, P. (1936) *Lists of Men-of-War, 1650–1700: Part III, Danish–Norwegian Ships*, Greenwich: Society for Nautical Research, Occasional Publications.

HOMZE, EDWARD L. (1976) *Arming the Luftwaffe: The Reich Air Ministry and the German Aircraft Industry, 1919–39*, Lincoln: University of Nebraska Press.

HOUSE OF COMMONS, UNITED KINGDOM (1914) *Naval Expenditure (Principal Naval Powers)*, London: HMSO.

HOVGAARD, WILLIAM (1920) *Modern History of Warships*, London: E. & F. N. Spon.

HOWARTH, DAVID (1974) *Sovereign of the Sea Power*, London: Quartet Books.

HOWARTH, STEPHEN (1983) *The Fighting Ships of the Rising Sun*, New York: Atheneum.

HUDSON, GEORGE (1976) 'Soviet Naval Doctrine and Soviet Politics, 1953–1975', *World Politics* 29 (October) pp. 90–113.

HUME, MARTIN (1927) *The Court of Philip IV: Spain in Decadency*, New York: Brentano's.

HURD, ARCHIBALD S. (1902) *Naval Efficiency*, London: Chapman & Hall.

———— and CASTLE, HENRY (1971) *German Sea-Power: Its Rise, Progress, and Economic Basis*, Westport, Conn.: Greenwood Press (original in 1913).

HYDE, H. MONTGOMERY (1976) *British Air Policy Between the Wars, 1918–1939*, London: Heinemann.

HYLAND, JOHN J. (1985) 'French Nuclear Forces', *Naval War College Review*, 38 (May–June) pp. 65–82.

IBANEZ DE IBERO, CARLOS (1943) *Historia de la Marina de Guerra Española desde el Siglo XIII Hasta Nuestros Dias*, 2nd edn, Madrid: Espasa-Calpe.

IBN KHALDUN (1967) *The Muqaddimah*, trans. Franz Rosenthal, vol. 2, Princeton: Princeton University Press.

IISS (multiple volumes) *The Military Balance*, London: International Institute for Strategic Studies.

Bibliography 365

INNES, ARTHUR D. (1931) *The Maritime and Colonial Expansion of England Under the Stuarts (1603–1714)*, London: Sampson Low, Marston.

ISRAEL, JONATHAN I. (1977) 'A Conflict of Empires: Spain and the Netherlands, 1618–1648', *Past and Present*, 76 (August), pp. 34–74.

————— (1982) *The Dutch Republic and the Hispanic World, 1606–1661*, Oxford: Clarendon.

JAMES, WILLIAM (1886) *The Naval History of Great Britain*, 6 vols, London: Richard Bently.

Jane's Fighting Ships (multiple volumes) London: Sampson Low, Marston.

Japan Statistical Yearbook (1949) Tokyo: Nihon Statistical Association, edited by Executive Office of the Statistics Commission and Statistics Bureau of the Prime Minister's Office.

JENKINS, E. H. (1973) *A History of the French Navy*, London: Macdonald & Jane's.

JENTSCHURA, HANSGEORG, DIETER JUNG, and PETER MICKEL (1977) *Warships of the Imperial Japanese Navy, 1869–1945*, trans. Anthony Preston and J. D. Brown. Annapolis: Naval Institute Press.

JONES, DAVID R. (ed.) (1981) *The Military–Naval Encyclopedia of Russia and the Soviet Union*, vol. 3, Gulf Breeze, Fl.: Academic International Press.

JONGE, J. C. DE (1869) *Geschiedenis van het Nederlandsche Zeewezen*, 6 vols, Zwolle: Van Hoogstraten & Gorter.

JOUAN, RENÉ (1950) *Histoire de la Marine Française*, Paris: Payot.

KAMEN, HENRY A. F. (1969) *The War of Succession in Spain, 1700–15*, London: Weidenfeld & Nicolson.

KAUFMANN, RICHARD DE (1884) *Les Finances de la France*, Paris: Guillaumin.

KENNEDY, PAUL M. (1976) *The Rise and Fall of British Naval Mastery*, New York: Charles Scribner.

————— (1983) *Strategy and Diplomacy, 1870–1945*, London: Allen & Unwin.

KHUEPACH, ARTHUR and BAYER, HEINRICH (1966) *Geschichte der KUK Kriegsmarine*, Grax-koln: Verlag Hermann Bohlaus Nachf.

KLUCHEVSKY, VASILY O. (1960) *A History of Russia*, vol. 4, trans. C. G. Hogarth, New York: Russell & Russell.

KORB, LAWRENCE J. (1984) 'The Erosion of American Naval Preeminence, 1962–1978', pp. 327–46 in Kenneth J. Hagan (ed.) *In Peace and War: Interpretations of American Naval History, 1775–1984*, Westport, Conn.: Greenwood Press.

KURAT, A. N. (1970) 'The Retreat of the Turks, 1683–1730', pp. 608–647 in J. S. Bromley (ed.) *New Cambridge Modern History: The Rise of Great Britain and Russia, 1688–1925*, vol. 6, Cambridge: Cambridge University Press.

LACOUR-GAYET, GEORGES (1902) *La Marine Militaire de la France sous le Règne De Louis XV*, Paris: Honoré Champion.

————— (1905) *La Marine Militaire de la France sous Le Règne De Louis XVI*, Paris: Honoré Champion.

————— (1911) *La Marine Militaire de la France sous Les Régimes de Louis XIII et de Louis XIV: Richelieu, Mazarin, 1624–1661*, vol. 1, Paris: Honoré Champion.

366 *Bibliography*

LAMBELET, JOHN C. (1974) 'The Anglo-German Dreadnought Race, 1905–1914', *Peace Science Society (International) Papers*, 22: 1–45.

———— (1975) 'A Numerical Model of the Anglo-German Dreadnought Race', *Peace Science Society (International) Papers*, 24: 29–48.

———— (1976) 'A Complementary Analysis of the Anglo-German Dreadnought Race, 1905–1916', *Peace Science Society (International) Papers*, 26, pp. 49–66.

LAMBI, IVO N. (1984) *The Navy and German Power Politics, 1861–1914*, Boston: Allen & Unwin.

LAMONTAGNE, ROLAND (1966) *Ministère de la Marine: Amérique et Canada*, Montreal: Les Editions Lemeac.

LANE, FREDERICK C. (1934) *Venetian Ships and Shipbuilders of the Renaissance*, Baltimore: Johns Hopkins University Press.

———— (1973) *Venice: A Maritime Republic*, Baltimore: Johns Hopkins University Press.

LAUGHTON, JOHN K. (ed.) (1892) *The Naval Miscellany*, vol. 2, London: Navy Records Society.

LAVISSE, ERNEST (1911) *Histoire De France: Louis XIV, de 1643 a 1685*, vol. 7, Second Part, Paris: Hachette.

LEAGUE OF NATIONS (1922) *Budget Expenditure on National Defense, 1913 and 1920–22*, Geneva.

———— (1923) *Statistical Enquiry into National Armaments, Part II; Budget Expenditure on National Defense, 1921–1923*, Geneva.

———— (1925–6) *Armaments Year-book*, Geneva.

LE CONTE, PIERRE, (1932) *Repertoires des Navires de Guerre Français*, Caen: A. Mouville.

———— (1935) *Lists of Men-of-War, 1650–1700: Part II, French Ships, 1648–1700*, Society for Nautical Research Occasional Publications, no. 5, Cambridge: Cambridge University Press.

LEGOHEREL, HENRI (1965) *Les Trésoriers Généraux de la Marine (1517–1788)*, Paris: Editions Cujas.

LEVY, JACK S. (1983) *War in the Modern Great Power System, 1495–1975*, Lexington: University of Kentucky Press.

LEWIS, MICHAEL (1948) *The Navy of Britain: A Historical Portrait*, London: Allen & Unwin.

LLOYD, CHRISTOPHER (1961) *The Nation and the Navy*, London: Cresset Press.

———— (1965a) 'Navies', pp. 174–90 in A. Goodwin (ed.) *New Cambridge Modern History: The American and French Revolutions, 1763–1793*, vol. 8, Cambridge: Cambridge University Press.

———— (1965b) 'Navies', pp. 76–90 in C. W. Crawley (ed.) *New Cambridge Modern History: War and Peace in an Age of Upheaval, 1793–1830*, vol. 9, Cambridge: Cambridge University Press.

———— (1975) *Atlas of Maritime History*, New York: Arco Publishing.

LO, YUNG-PANG (1955) 'The Emergence of China as a Sea Power During the Late Sung and Early Yuan Period', *Far Eastern Quarterly*, 14, pp. 489–503.

LOIR, MAURICE (1893) *La Marine Française*, Paris: Libraire Hachette.

Bibliography

LUBLINSKAYA, ALEXANDRA D. (1968) *French Absolutism: The Crucial Phase, 1620–1629*, trans. Brian Pearce, Cambridge: Cambridge University Press.

LYNCH, JOHN (1969) *Spain Under the Hapsburgs: Spain and America, 1598–1700*, vol. 2, New York: Oxford University Press.

———— (1984) *Spain Under the Hapsburgs*, 2nd edn., 2 vols, New York: New York University Press.

MAHAN, ALFRED T. (1890) *The Influence of Sea Power upon History, 1660–1783*, New York: Wang Hill.

———— (1892) *The Influence of Sea Power Upon the French Revolution and Empire, 1793–1812*, 2 vols, London: Sampson, Low, Marston.

MALLET, JEAN R. (1789) *Comptes Rendus de l'Administration des Finances du Royaume de France, sous Henri IV, Louis XIV*, Paris: Buisson.

MALLEZ, PAUL (1927) *La Restauration des Finances Françaises après 1814*, Paris: Libraire Dalloz.

MARCH Y LABORES, JOSÉ (1854) *Historia de la Marina Real Española*, vol. 2, Madrid: José Maria Ducazcal.

MARCUS, GEOFFREY J. (1961) *A Naval History of England: The Formative Centuries*, London: Longman.

MARGRY, PIERRE (1879a) 'Une Famille dans la Marine au XVIII Siècle: Première Partie', *Revue Maritime et Coloniale*, 62 (September) pp. 640–73.

———— (1879b) 'Une Famille dans la Marine au XVIII Siècle: Première Partie', *Revue Maritime et Coloniale*, 63 (October) pp. 205–36.

MARIEJOL, J. H. (1911) *Histoire De France: Henri IV et Louis XIII, (1598–1693)*, vol. 6, Part 2, Paris: Hachette.

MARION, MARCEL (1914) *Histoire Financière de la France depuis 1715*, 6 vols, Paris: Arthur Rousseau.

MASSON, PIERRE and MURACCIOLE, JOSÉ (1968) *Napoléon et la Marine*, Paris: J. Peyronnet.

MATTINGLY, GARRETT (1959) *The Armada*, Boston: Houghton Mifflin.

———— (1963) *The 'Invincible' Armada and Elizabethan England*, Ithaca: Cornell University Press.

MccGWIRE, MICHAEL (1973a) 'Comparative Warship Building Programs'. pp. 144–150 in Michael MccGwire (ed.) *Soviet Naval Developments: Capability and Context*, New York: Praeger.

———— (1973b) 'The Structure of the Soviet Navy', pp. 151–162 in Michael MccGwire (ed.) *Soviet Naval Developments: Capability and Context*, New York: Praeger.

———— (1973c) 'The Turning Points in Soviet Naval Policy', pp. 176–209 in Michael MccGwire (ed.) *Soviet Naval Developments: Capability and Context*, New York: Praeger.

———— (1973d) 'Soviet Naval Policy: Prospects for the Seventies', pp. 491–519 in Michael MccGwire (ed.) *Soviet Naval Developments: Capability and Context*, New York: Praeger.

———— (1975a) 'Current Soviet Warship Constructions and Naval Weapons Development', pp. 424–451 in Michael MccGwire, Ken Booth, and John McDonnel (eds) *Soviet Naval Policy: Objectives and Constraints*, New York: Praeger.

368 *Bibliography*

————— (1975b) 'Soviet Strategic Weapons Policy, 1955–70', pp. 486–502 in Michael MccGwire, Ken Booth, and John McDonnel (eds) *Soviet Naval Policy: Objectives and Constraints*, New York: Praeger.

————— (1975c) 'Command of the Sea in Soviet Naval Strategy', pp. 623–36 in Michael MccGwire, Ken Booth, and John McDonnel (eds) *Soviet Naval Policy: Objectives and Constraints*, New York: Praeger.

————— (1980) 'A New Trend in Soviet Naval Developments', *Naval War College Review*, 33 (July–August): 3–12.

McCUSKER, JOHN J. (1978) *Money and Exchange in Europe and America, 1600–1775: A Handbook*, Chapel Hill: University of North Carolina Press.

McGRUTHER, KENNETH R. (1978) *The Evolving Soviet Navy*, Newport, RI: Naval War College Press.

McKEE, ALEXANDER (1963) *From Merciless Invaders*, London: Souvenir Press.

McMAHON, WILLIAM E. (1978) *Dreadnought Battleships and Battle Cruisers*, Washington, DC: University Press of America.

MEIGGS, RUSSELL (1972) *The Athenian Empire*, Oxford: Clarendon.

MEMAIN, R. (1936) *Le Matériel de la Marine de Guerre sous Louis XIV*, Paris: Librarie Hachette.

MENDONCA, HENRIQUE LOPES DE (1892) *Estudos sobre Navios Portugueses nos Seculos XV e XVI*, Lisboa: Tipographia da Academia Real das Sienças.

MERINO NAVARRO, JOSÉ P. (1981) *La Armada Española En El Siglo XVIII*, Madrid: Fundacion Universitaria Española.

la Marine, Paris: Imprimerie Impériale.

Prudent, vol. 4, New York: Macmillan.

MIDDLETON, DREW (1976) *Submarine*, Chicago: Playboy Press.

MINISTÈRE DE LA MARINE, FRANCE (1838) *Rapport sur le Matériel de la Marine*, Paris: Imprimerie Impériale.

MINISTERE DES FINANCES, FRANCE (1946) *Inventaire de la Situation Financière (1913–1946)*, Paris: Imprimerie Nationale.

MINISTÈRE DE LA MARINE ET DES COLONIES, FRANCE (multiple volumes) *Compte Définitif des Despenses de L'Exercise/Comptes Généraux des Despenses Ordinaires et Extraordinaires*, Paris: Imprimerie Impériale.

MINISTÈRE DU TRAVAIL, FRANCE (multiple volumes) *Annuaire Statistique*, Paris: Imprimerie Nationale.

MITCHELL, BRIAN R. (1975) *European Historical Statistics, 1750–1970*, London: Macmillan.

————— and DEANE, PHYLLIS (1962) *Abstract of British Historical Statistics*, Cambridge: Cambridge University Press.

MITCHELL, BRIAN R. and JONES, H. G. (1971) *Second Abstract of British Historical Statistics*, Cambridge: Cambridge University Press.

MITCHELL, DONALD W. (1974) *A History of Russian and Soviet Sea Power*, New York: Macmillan.

MITCHELL, MAIRIN (1949) *The Maritime History of Russia, 1848–1948*, London: Sidgwick & Jackson.

MODELSKI, GEORGE (1972) *Principles of World Politics*, New York: Free Press.

Bibliography 369

———— (1974) *World Power Concentration*, Morristown, N.J.: General Learning Press.

———— (1978) 'The Long Cycle of Global Politics and the Nation State', *Comparative Studies in Society and History*, 20 (April) pp. 214–35.

———— (1983) 'Long Cycles of World Leadership: An Annotated Bibliography', *International Studies Notes*, 10 (Fall) pp. 1–5.

———— (1986) *Long Cycles in World Politics*, Seattle: University of Washington Press; and London: Macmillan.

MOLLIEN, FRANÇOIS (1895) *Mémoires d'un Ministère du Trésor Public, 1780–1815*, 4 vols, Paris: H. Fournier.

MONTESQUIOU, A. P. (1797) *Du Gouvernement des Finances de France*, Paris.

MOORE, J. E. (1977) 'The Soviet Navy', pp. 112–27 in Ray Bonds (ed.) *The Soviet War Machine: An Encyclopedia of Russian Military Equipment and Strategy*, revised edn, London: Hamlyn.

MOREAU DE JONNES, ALEXANDRE (1835) *Estadistica De Espana*, trans. Pascual Madoz e Ibanez, Barcelona: M. Rivadeneyra Y Compania.

MORRIS, ERIC (1977) *The Russian Navy: Myth and Reality*, New York: Stein & Day.

MOTLEY, JOHN L. (1900) *History of the United Netherlands*, 6 vols, New York: Harper & Brothers.

MUHMANN, ROLF (1975) *Die Reorganization der Spanischen Kriegsmarine, im 18, Jahrhundert*, Koln: Bohlau-Verlag.

NEEDHAM, JOSEPH (1969) *The Great Titration: Science and Society in East and West*, Toronto: Toronto University Press.

———— with the collaboration of LING WANG and GWEI-DJEN, LU (1971) *Science and Civilization in China*, vol. 4, part 3, Cambridge: Cambridge University Press.

NEUVILLE, M. D. (1977) *Etat Sommaire des Archives de la Marine Anterieures a la Revolution*, Nendeln, Liechtenstein: Kraus Reprint (original in 1898).

NICOLAS, LOUIS (1949) *Histoire de la Marine Française*, Paris: Presse Universitaire de France.

———— (1958) *La Puissance Navale Dans L'Histoire: Du Moyen Age à 1815*, Paris: Editions Maritimes et Coloniales.

———— (1973) *Histoire de la Marine Française*, 3rd edn, Paris: Presses Universitaires de France.

OLAGUE, IGNACIO (1950–1). *La Decadencia Española*, vol. 1, San Sebastian: Libreria Internacional.

OLESA MUNIDO, FRANCISCO FELIPE (1968) *La Organizacion Naval de Los Estados Mediterranees Y en especial de España Duarte Los Siglos XVI Y XVIII*, vol. 1, Madrid: Editorial Naval.

OLIVEIRA MARQUES, ANTONIO H. DE (1976) *History of Portugal*, 2nd edn, New York: Columbia University Press.

ONO, GIICHI (1922) *War and Armament Expenditures of Japan*, New York: Oxford University Press.

OPPENHEIM, MICHAEL (1961) *A History of the Administration of the Royal Navy and of Merchant Shipping in Relation to the Navy from MDIX to MDCLX*, Ann Arbor: Shoestring Press.

370 *Bibliography*

OUDENDIJK, JOHANNA K. (1944) *Johan De Witt en De Zeemacht*, Amsterdam: N.V. Noord-Hollandsche Vitgevers Maastschappÿ.

OWEN, JOHN H. (1938) *War at Sea Under Queen Anne, 1702–1708*, Cambridge: Cambridge University Press.

PADFIELD, PETER (1972) *The Battleship Era*, London: Rupert Hart-Davis.

———— (1973) *Guns at Sea*, London: Hugh Evelyn.

———— (1979) *Tide of Empires: Decisive Naval Campaigns in the Rise of the West, Volume 1: 1481–1654*, London: Routledge & Kegan Paul.

PAGE, WILLIAM (1968) *Commerce and Industry*, New York: Augustus M. Kelley (original published in 1919).

PARKER, GEOFFREY N. (1970a) 'The Emergence of Modern Finance in Europe, 1500–1730', pp. 527–94 in C. M. Cippola (ed.) *The Fontana Economic History of Europe*, London: Collins.

———— (1970b) 'Spain, Her Enemies and the Revolt of the Netherlands, 1559–1648', *Past and Present*, 49 (November) pp. 72–95.

———— (1972) *The Army of Flanders and the Spanish Road, 1567–1659: The Logistics of Spanish Victory and Defeat in the Low Countries Wars*, Cambridge: Cambridge University Press.

———— (1977) *The Dutch Revolt*, Ithaca: Cornell University Press.

———— (1979) 'Warfare', pp. 201–19 in Peter Burke (ed.) *The New Cambridge Modern History: Companion Volume*, vol. 13, Cambridge: Cambridge University Press.

PARKES, OSCAR (1966) *British Battleships*, rev. edn, London: Seeley Service.

PARRY, J. H. (1963) *The Age of Reconnaisance*, New York: New American Library.

———— (1966a) *The Establishment of the European Hegemony: 1415–1715*, 3rd edn, revised, New York: Harper & Row.

———— (1966b) *The Spanish Seaborne Empire*, New York: Alfred A. Knopf.

———— (1971) *Trade and Dominion: The European Overseas Empires in the Eighteenth Centuries*, New York: Praeger.

PARSONS, TALCOTT (1969) *Politics and Social Structure*, New York: Free Press.

PAULLIN, CHARLES O. (1968) *Paullin's History of Naval Administration, 1775–1911*, Annapolis: US Naval Institute Press.

PELLIOT, PAUL (1931) 'Les Grands Voyages Maritimes Chinois au Début du 15e Siècle', *T'oung Pao*, 30, pp. 236–448.

PEMSEL, HELMUT (1977) *A History of War At Sea*, trans. I. G. D. G. Smith, Annapolis: Naval Institute Press.

PENN, C. D. (1913) *The Navy Under the Early Stuarts*, Manchester: Faith Press.

PERKINS, JAMES B. (1971) *Richelieu and the Growth of French Power*, Freeport, NY: Book for Libraries Press.

PERRY, CHARLES M. (1974) 'Major US–Soviet Strategic Nuclear Delivery Vehicles, 1946–1973', pp. 275–83 in Geoffrey Kemp, Robert L. Pfaltzgraff, Jr, and Uri Ra'anan (eds) *The Superpowers in a Multinuclear World*, Lexington, Mass.: D. C. Heath.

Bibliography

PEYSTER, HENRI DE (1905) *Les Troubles De Hollande: A la Veille de la Révolution Française (1780–1795)*, Paris: Alphonse Picard et Fils.

PIVKA, OTTO VON (1980) *Navies of the Napoleonic Era*, Newton Abbot: David & Charles.

POLMAR, NORMAN (1969) *Aircraft Carriers*, Garden City, NY: Doubleday.

————— (1974) *Soviet Naval Power: Challenge for the 1970s*, New York: Crane, Russak.

————— (1978) *The Ships and Aircraft of the US Fleet*, 11th edn, Annapolis: Naval Institute Press.

————— (1984) *The Ships and Aircraft of the US Fleet*, 13th edn, Annapolis: Naval Institute Press.

PONTALIS, ANTONIN LEFÈVRE (1885) *John De Witt*, 2 vols, trans. S. E. and A. Stephenson, London: Longmans, Green.

PORTER, G. R. (1838) *The Progress of the Nation: Interchange, and Revenue, and Expenditure*, London: Charles Knight.

POWELL, J. R. (1962) *The Navy in the English Civil War*, Hamden, Conn.: Archon Books.

PRESTAGE, EDGAR (1929) *Afonso de Albuquerque: Governor of India*, Watford: Voss & Michael.

RANUM, OREST and RANUM, PATRICIA (eds) (1972) *The Century of Louis XIV*, New York: Walker.

RAPKIN, DAVID P., THOMPSON, WILLIAM R. and CHRISTOPHERSON, JON A. (1979) 'Bipolarity and Bipolarization in the Cold War Era: Conceptualization, Measurement, and Validation', *Journal of Conflict Resolution*, 23 (June) pp. 261–95.

RASLER, KAREN A. and THOMPSON, WILLIAM R. (1983) 'Global Wars, Public Debts, and the Long Cycle', *World Politics*, 35 (July) pp. 489–516.

RAY, JAMES L. and SINGER, J. DAVID (1973) 'Measuring the Concentration of Power in the International System'. *Sociological Methods and Research* 1 (May): pp. 403–437.

RENAUT, FRANCIS P. (1932) (1973) *Le Crépuscule d'une Puissance Navale: La Marine Hollandaise de 1776 à 1783*, Paris: Editions Maritime et D'Outre-Mer.

REUSSNER, ANDRÉ and NICHOLAS, L. (1963) *La Puissance Navale Dans L'Histoire: De 1815 à 1914*, vol. 2, Paris: Editions Maritimes et D'outre-Mer.

REYNOLDS, CLARK G. (1974) *Command of the Sea: The History and Strategy of Maritime Empires*, New York: William Morrow.

RICHMOND, HERBERT W. (1946) *Statesmen and Sea Power*, Oxford: Oxford University Press.

————— (1953) *The Navy as an Instrument of Policy, 1558–1727*, edited by E. A. Hughes, Cambridge: Cambridge University Press.

ROBISON, S. S. and ROBISON, MARY L. (1942) *A History of Naval Tactics from 1530 to 1930*, Annapolis: US Naval Institute Press.

ROHWER, JURGEN (1975) *Superpower Confrontation on the Seas: Naval Development and Strategy Since 1945*, The Washington Papers, vol. 3, no. 26, Beverly Hills: Sage.

372 Bibliography

RONCIÈRE, CHARLES DE LA (1909–32) *Histoire de la Marine Française*, 6 vols, Paris: Libraire Plon.

ROSE, J. HOLLAND (1921a) 'National Security and Expansion 1580–1660', pp. 14–135 in J. H. Rose, A. P. Newton, E. A. Benians (eds) *Cambridge History of the British Empire: The Old Empire*, vol. 1, Cambridge: Cambridge University Press.

———— (1921b) 'Sea Power and Expansion, 1660–1763', pp. 507–37 in J. H. Rose, A. P. Newton, E. A. Benians (eds) *Cambridge History of the British Empire: The Old Empire*, vol. 1, Cambridge: Cambridge University Press.

———— (1940a) 'The Conflict with Revolutionary France, 1793–1802', pp. 36–82 in J. Holland Rose, A. P. Newton, E. A. Benians (eds) *The Cambridge History of the British Empire: The Growth of the New Empire, 1783–1870*, vol. 2, Cambridge: Cambridge University Press.

———— (1940b) 'The Struggle with Napoleon, 1803–1815', pp. 83–128 in J. Holland Rose, A. P. Newton, E. A. Benians (eds) *The Cambridge History of the British Empire: The Growth of the New Empire, 1783–1870*, vol. 2, Cambridge: Cambridge University Press.

ROSINSKI, HERBERT (1957) *The Development of Naval Thought*, edited by B. Mitchell Simpson, Newport: Naval War College Press.

ROWEN, HERBERT H. (1978) *John de Witt, Grand Pensionary of Holland, 1625–1672*, Princeton, NJ: Princeton University Press.

SADAO, ASADA (1973) 'The Japanese Navy and the United States', pp. 225–59 in Dorothy Berg and Shumpei Okamoto with the assistance of Dale K. A. Finlayson (eds) *Pearl Harbor as History, Japanese–American Relations, 1931–1941*, New York: Columbia University Press.

SANDLER, STANLEY (1979) *The Emergence of the Modern Capital Ship*, Newark: University of Delaware Press.

SANUTO, MARINO (1879) *I Diarii*, vol. 4, Venezia: Nicolo Barozzi.

SCAMMELL, G. V. (1981) *The World Encompassed: The First European Maritime Empires, c. 800–1650*, Berkeley: University of California Press.

SCHERER, JOHN L. (1977) *USSR: Facts and Figures Annual*, vol. 1, Gulfbreeze, Florida: Academic International Press.

———— (1978) *USSR: Facts and Figures Annual*, vol. 2. Gulfbreeze, Florida: Academic International Press.

SCHMALENBACH, PAUL (1970) *Kurze Geschichte der KUK Marine*, Herford: Hoehlers Verlagsgesellschaft.

SCHNITZLER, J. H. (1829) *Essai d'une Statistique Générale de l'Empire de Russie*, Paris: F. G. Levrault.

SELVAGEM, CARLOS (1931) *Compendio de Historia Militar e Naval de Portugal*, Lisbon: Impresa Nacional.

SERJEANT, R. B. (1963) *The Portuguese off the South Arabian Coast*, Oxford: Oxford University Press.

SHAW, STANFORD (1976) *History of the Ottoman Empire and Modern Turkey: Empire of the Gazis, The Rise and Decline of the Ottoman Empire, 1280–1808*, Cambridge: Cambridge University Press.

SHERWIN, RONALD G. and LAURENCE, EDWARD J. (1979) 'Arms Transfers and Military Capability: Measuring and Evaluating Conventional Arms Transfers', *International Studies Quarterly*, 23 (September) pp. 360–89.

Bibliography 373

SILBURN, P. A. (1912) *The Evolution of Sea-Power*, London: Longmans, Green.

SINCLAIR, JOHN (1790) *The History of the Public Revenue of the British Empire, Part III*, London: T. Cadell.

SINGER, J. DAVID and SMALL, MELVIN (1972) *The Wages of War, 1816–1965*, New York: John Wiley.

SIPRI (multiple volumes) *World Armaments and Disarmaments*, Stockholm: Stockholm International Peace Research Institute.

SLANY, WILLIAM (1958) *Russian Central Governmental Institutions, 1725–1741*, unpublished Ph.D. dissertation, Cornell University.

SOKOL, ANTHONY (1968) *The Imperial and Royal Austro-Hungarian Navy*, Annapolis: United States Naval Institute.

SOUTHWORTH, JOHN VAN DUYN (1968) *The Age of Sails: The Story of Naval Warfare Under Sail, 1213 A.D.–1853 A.D.*, New York: Twayne.

SPROUT, M. T. (1941) 'Mahan', pp. 415–45 in E. M. Earle (ed.) *Makers of Modern Strategy*, Princeton: Princeton University Press.

The State of France (1760) (no author) London: I. Pottinger.

Statesman's Yearbook (multiple volumes), New York: Macmillan.

Statistisches Jahrbuch für das Deutsche Reich (multiple volumes), Berlin: Verlag fur Politik und Wirtschaft.

STEINBERG, JONATHAN (1965) *Yesterday's Deterrent*, New York: Macmillan.

STEUBEL, HEINRICH (1951) 'Die Finanzierung der Aufrüstung im Dritten Reich', *Europa Archiv*, 6, pp. 4128–4136.

STEVENS, WILLIAM O. and WESTCOTT, ALLAN F. (1943) *A History of Sea Power*, New York: Doubleday.

STRADLING, R. A. (1981) *Europe and the Decline of Spain: A Study of the Spanish System, 1580–1720*, London: Allen & Unwin.

SUE, EUGENE (1835) *Histoire de la Marine Française*, Paris: Félix Bonnaire.

SWANSON, BRUCE (1982) *Eighth Voyage of the Dragon: A History of China's Quest for Seapower*, Annapolis: Naval Institute.

SYMCOX, GEOFFREY (1974) *The Crisis of French Sea Power, 1688–1697*, Hague: Martinus Nijhoff.

SYMONDS, CRAIG L. (1980) *Navalists and Antinavalists: The Naval Policy Debate in the United States, 1785–1827*, Newark: University of Delaware Press.

TAPIE, VICTOR-LUCIEN (1975) *France in the Age of Louis XIII and Richelieu*, trans. D. McN. Lockie, New York: Praeger.

TAYLOR, ALAN J. P. (1954) *The Struggle for Mastery in Europe, 1848–1918*, Oxford: Oxford University Press.

TEITLER, G. (1977) *The Genesis of the Professional Officer's Corps*, Beverly Hills: Sage.

TEMPLE, WILLIAM (1972) *Observations Upon the United Provinces of the Netherlands*, edited by George Clarke, Oxford: Oxford University Press. Originally published 1673.

TEN RAA, J. J. G. and DE BAS, F. (1911) *Het Staatsche Leger, 1568–1795*, 8 vols, Breda: De Koninklijke Militaire Academie.

THOMAZI, AUGUSTE (1950) *Napoléon et Ses Marins*, Paris: Editions Berger-Levrault.

374 Bibliography

THOMPSON, I. A. A. (1976) *War and Government in Hapsburg Spain, 1560–1620*, London: Athlone Press.

THOMPSON, WILLIAM R. (ed.) (1983) *Contending Approaches to World System Analysis*, Beverly Hills: Sage.

THUCYDIDES (1954) *The Peloponnesian War*, translated by Rex Warner. Harmondsworth: Penguin.

TIFFEN, CHARLES (1937) *La Course Aux Armaments et Les Finances Publiques*, doctoral thesis, Paris: Libraire Générale de Droit et de Jurisprudence.

TILL, GEOFFREY (1984) *Maritime Strategy and the Nuclear Age*, New York: St Martin's.

TRACY, NICHOLAS (1975) 'British Assessments of French and Spanish Naval Reconstruction, 1763–1768', *The Mariner's Mirror*, 61 (February) pp. 73–85.

TRAMOND, JOANNES (1947) *Manuel d'Histoire Maritime de la France des Origines à 1815*, Paris: Challamel.

TRASK, D. and TRASK, F. (1984) 'The American Navy in a World at War, 1914–1919', pp. 205–20 in Kenneth J. Hagan (ed.) *In Peace and War: Interpretations of American Naval History, 1775–1984*, Westport, Conn.: Greenwood Press.

TREASURE, GEOFFREY R. R. (1966) *Seventeenth Century France*, New York: Barnes & Noble.

TUTE, WARREN (1983) *The True Glory*, New York: Harper & Row.

US BUREAU OF THE CENSUS (1975) *Historical Statistics of the United States: Colonial Times to Present*. Washington, DC: Government Printing Office.

US DEPARTMENT OF THE NAVY (1969) *American Ships of the Line*, Washington, DC: Navy History Division.

VECCHJ, AUGUSTO VITTORIO (1895) *Storia Generale Della Marina Militare*, 2nd edn, 3 vols, Livorno: Raffaello Giusti.

VELARDE, F. ARRANZ (1940) *Compendeo de Historia Maritima de España*, Santander: Martinez.

VIOLETTE, AURELE J. (1971) *Russian Naval Reform, 1855–1870*, unpublished Ph.D. dissertation, Ohio State University.

VOGEL, W. and SZYMANSKI, H. (1936) *Lists of Men-of-War, 1650–1700: Part III, German Ships*, Greenwich: Society for Nautical Research, Occasional Publications.

VOVARD, ANDRÉ (1948) *La Marine Française*, Paris: J. DeGigord.

VREUGDENHIL, A. (1938) *Lists of Men-of-War, 1650–1700: Part IV, Ships of the United Netherlands, 1648–1702*, Society for Nautical Research, Occasional Publications, no. 5, Cambridge: Cambridge University Press.

WALKER, B. W. (1860) 'Statement of the Number of Ships, Under Their Different Ratings, in the Naval Service from 1763 to 1859', *British Sessional Papers, 1860*, vol. 42, pp. 545–57.

WALLERSTEIN, IMMANUEL (1974) *The Modern World System: Capitalist Agriculture and the Origins of the European World Economy in the Sixteenth Century*, New York: Academic Press.

——— (1980) *The Modern World-System II: Mercantilism and the Consolidation of the European World-Economy, 1600–1750*, New York: Academic Press.

Bibliography

WARD, MICHAEL D. (1984) 'Differential Paths to Parity: A Study of the Contemporary Arms Race', *American Political Science Review*, 78 (December) pp. 287–317.

WATSON, BRUCE M. (1982) *Red Navy at Sea: Soviet Naval Operations on the High Seas, 1956–1980*, Boulder, Col.: Westview Press.

WEIGLEY, RUSSELL F. (1973) *The American Way of War: A History of United States Military Strategy and Policy*, Bloomington: Indiana University Press.

WEINLAND, ROBERT G. (1973) 'The Changing Mission Structure of the Soviet Navy', pp. 292–305 in Michael MccGwire (ed.) *Soviet Naval Developments: Capability and Context*, New York: Praeger.

————— (1975) 'Soviet Naval Operations: 10 Years of Change', pp. 375–86 in Michael MccGwire, Ken Booth, John McDonnell (eds) *Soviet Naval Policy: Objectives and Constraints*, New York: Praeger.

WEINSTEIN, DONALD (1960) *Ambassador from Venice: Pietro Pasqualino in Lisbon 1501*, Minneapolis: University of Minnesota Press.

WHITESTONE, NICHOLAS (1973) *The Submarine: The Ultimate Weapon*, London: Davis-Poynter.

WHITEWAY, RICHARD S. (1967) *The Rise of Portuguese Power in India, 1497–1550*, 2nd edn, London: Susil Gupta.

WIJN, J. W. (1964) *Het Staatsche Leger: Part III, 1711–1715*, vol. 8, S'Gravenhage: Martinus Nijhoff.

WILCOX, L. A. (1966) *Mr Pepy's Navy*, London: G. Bell.

WILLIAM, HENRY (1979) *The Tudor Regime*, Oxford: Oxford University Press.

WILLMOTT, H. P. (1982) *Empires in the Balance: Japanese and Allied Pacific Strategies to April 1942*, Annapolis: Naval Institute Press.

WILMOTT, NED and PIMLOTT, JOHN (1979) *Strategy and Tactics of War*, Seacaucus, New Jersey: Chartwell Books.

WILSON, A. M. (1904) 'The Naval War', pp. 447–86 in A. M. Ward, G. W. Prothero, and Stanley Leathes, (eds) *Cambridge Modern History: The French Revolution*, vol. 8, Cambridge: Cambridge University Press.

WILSON, CHARLES H. (1957) *Profit and Power: A Study of England and the Dutch Wars*, London: Longmans, Green.

WILSON, H. M. (1936) *French Foreign Policy During the Administration of Cardinal Fleury, 1726–1743*, Cambridge: Harvard University Press.

WOLOWSKI, M. C. (1864) *Les Finances de la Russie*, Paris: Librairie de Guillaumin.

WOODWARD, DAVID (1965) *The Russians at Sea*, London: William Kimber.

WOODWARD, ERNEST L. (1935) *Great Britain and the German Navy*, Oxford: Oxford University Press.

WRIGHT, QUINCY (1942/1965) *A Study of War*, 2nd edn, Chicago: University of Chicago Press.

Index

Actium, *see* Sea battles
Albuquerque, Afonso de, 168, 171
Alcaçovas, Treaty of (1479), 152
Alfred, 202
Almeida, Fortunato de, 168
Almeida, Francisco de, 7, 21, 168, 171
Anderson, Roger C., 160
Andrews, Kenneth R., 204, 205
Anglo-German Naval Treaty (1935), 308
Aragon as seapower, 158, 267
Armada, *see* Sea battles
Armadas
da Malabar, 171
da Portugal, 170
de Flandes, 190, 271
de la mar del sur, 271
de las Islas de Barlovento, 269
de mar oceano, 268, 269, 271
del Norte, 171
para la guardia de costa y navíos de Indies, 153, 268
Athens as seapower, 5–6
Austria as seapower, 325–6
Austria–Hungary as seapower, 326–9

Bacon, Francis, 7, 20–1, 144
Ballard, G. A., 55
Barker, J. Ellis, 188
Bartlett, Christopher J., 209
Beachy Head, *see* Sea battles
Bekker, Cajus, 308
Bird, Keith W., 308
Bonaparte, Napoleon, 273
Boxer, Charles R., 40, 55, 166, 189, 192
Bradford, James C., 232,
Brandenburg as seapower, 304
Braudel, Fernand, 43, 56, 155, 156, 157, 175, 268
Breemer, Jan S., 236
Breyer, Siegfried, 77

Britain as seapower, *see* England
Bruijn, J. R., 192
Buhl, Lance C., 74, 233

Cable, James, 239
Cabot, John, 153
Cabral, Pedro, 171
Campillo y Cossio, José del, 272
Cape Passaro, *see* Sea battles
Capital warships, 50ff
aircraft carriers, 83–7, 141–2
armed sailing ships, 51–61
battleships, 35, 73–5, 79
nuclear submarines, 83–90, 142–4
ships-of-the-line, 34–6, 61–7
Caravel, *see* Ship types
Carrack, *see* Ship types
Carreira da India, 171, 172
Cartier, Jacques, 155
Castille as seapower, 158, 267
Castle, Henry, 304, 306
Catherine II, 285
Charles I, 205
Charles V, 154, 155
Charnock, John, 55
Chaunu, Huguette, and Pierre, 57, 58, 161, 166, 170
Chesme, *see* Sea battles
Chesneau, Roger, 74
China as seapower, 6, 140, 155–6, 335–7
Choiseul-Amboise, Etienne François, Duc de, 249
Christopherson, Jon, 41
Chung Ho, 155
Churchill, Winston, 23
Cinque ports, 203
Cipolla, Carlo M., 27, 28, 40, 51, 158, 159, 160
Clowes, William, 32, 159, 165, 166, 171
CMP (Counter Military Potential), 88, 91, 293
Cobden, Richard, 28

376

Index

Cochin, 161, 168
Colbert, Jean-Baptiste, 207, 248
Colledge, J. J., 54, 61
Coligny Gaspard de, 247
Colomb, John, 8
Colomb, P. H., 8, 11
Columbus, Christopher, 152, 153
Coral Sea, 243
Coral Sea, *see* Sea battles
Corbett, Julian, 10, 51
Correlates of War Project, 338
Cortes, Hernando, 153
Coxe, William, 272
Creighton, M., 7
Cromwell, Oliver, 205, 206
Cunha, Nono da, 174

Danvers, Frederick C., 55
Deane, Phyllis, 32
Denmark as seapower, 324–5
Diffie, Bailey W., 55, 161, 171
Dismukes, Bradford, 287
Diu, *see* Sea battles
Dominguez Ortiz, Antonio, 268
Downs, *see* Sea battles
Drake, Francis, 154
Dreadnought, *see* Ship types
Duffy, James, 55, 159, 166, 167
Dyson, Freeman, 144, 145

Edward VI, 204
Ehrman John, 34
Elizabeth I, 204
Elliott, J. H., 153, 271
EMT (equivalent megatonnage), 89, 91
Engels, Friedrich 8
England as seapower, 10, 53, 106–7, 113, 127, 129–31, 138, 165, 166, 193, 202–12, 329–30, 334–5
Ensenada, Zenon de Somodevilla, 272
Erasmus, 7

Falkland Islands, *see* Sea battles
'Fighting Instructions', 25, 206
Fonseca, Enrique Quirino da, 56, 61, 161
France as seapower, 53, 57, 59, 129–30, 138, 154–5, 246–50, 266, 329–30, 334
Francis I, 154–5
Franks, Horace G., 191
Frederick the Great, 304
Frere-Cook, Garvis, 270
Frobisher, Martin, 154

Galleon, *see* Ship types
Galley, *see* Ship types
Germany as seapower, 9–10, 304–10
Global powers, 18, 41–5, 97ff, 134–40, 149
criteria, 44–5
prospects for additions, 137ff
Global wars, 18–23, 127–32
length of, 112
next, 84–5, 141–6
role of sea battles, 8–9, 20–2
substitute for, 146–7
triggers, 19, 20
Gloire, La, 250
Godinho, Vittorino Magalhaes, 43–4, 55, 167, 168
Gorshkov, S. G., 8, 10–11, 85, 142
Graham, Gerald S., 10, 38
Great Harry, 159
Great Michael, 159
Grotius, Hugo, 188
Guerre de Course (commerce raiding), 9, 190, 205, 248, 250, 308
Guilmartin, John F. Jr., 55, 320
Gujerat as seapower, 156

Ha, Young-sun, 95
Hall, D. G. E., 154
Haring, Clarence H., 268
Hawkins, John, 154
Hearst, W. R., Jr., 144
Hecateus, 5
Henry VII, 153, 160, 165, 203
Henry VIII, 160, 165, 203–4
Herodotus, 5
Hess, Andrew C., 43, 55
Hitler, Adolf, 308
Hobbes, Thomas, 7
Hogue, La, *see* Sea battles
Howarth, David, 204

378   *Index*

Howarth, Stephen, 313
Hudson, George, 11
Hurd, Archibald, 304, 306
Hyland, John J., 356

Ibn Khaldun, 6
India as seapower, 139–40
Israel, Jonathan I., 190
Italy as seapower, 326–9
Ivan the Terrible, 284

James I, 205
Japan as seapower, 139, 310–14, 329
João II, 159
João III, 170
Jones, John Paul, 232
Jonge, J. D. de, 59
Jutland, *see* Sea battles

Kamen, Henry A. F., 272
Kennedy, Paul M., 206, 207, 211, 307
Khrushchev, Nikita, 287
Kolesnik, Eugene M., 74
Korb, Lawrence, 236

Lambelet, John C., 77
Lambi, Ivo N., 307
Laurance, Edward J., 33
Le Conte, Pierre, 54, 59, 61
Legoherel, Henri, 346
Lepanto, *see* Sea battles
Levy, Jack S., 317, 318
Lewis, Michael, 206
Leyte Gulf, *see* Sea battles
Lo, Yung-Pang, 336
Long cycle theory, 14–26, 42, 44, 87, 93, 134, 148, 316
Long cycles of world leadership, 97ff
  and global wars, 14–16
  and seapower, 14–16
Louis XIV, 248
Lynch, John, 268

McConnell, James M., 287
McCusker, John J., 346
McGwire, Michael, 303
McMahon, William E., 77

Macksey, Kenneth, 270
Magellan, Ferdinand, 153
Mahan, Alfred T., 4, 8–11, 15, 18, 22, 28, 273
Mameluke Egypt as seapower, 36, 156
Manila Bay, *see* Sea battles
Manuel, 170
Mattingly, Garrett, 40, 153, 161, 171
Meiggs, Russell, 6
Midway, *see* Sea battles
Minos, 5
Mitchell, Brian, 32
Mitchell, Donald W., 285, 338
Mitchell, William (General), 83
Mitterrand, François, 144
Modelski, George, 15, 41
Monck, George, 206
More, Thomas, 8
Motley, John L., 7, 59–60

Nau/nao, *see* Ship types
Naval expenditures, 28–33, 44, 48–9, 75, 338–47
Naval personnel, 29
Navarino Bay, *see* Sea battles
Navigation Act (1651), 206
Needham, Joseph, 6, 155, 156, 335–7
Nicholas II, 7
Noord, Oliver van, 154

Old Oligarch, 5
Oliveira Marques, Antonio H. de, 55, 167
Oppenheim, Michael, 203
Ottoman Empire as seapower, 43–4, 156–7, 318–20

Padfield, Peter, 27, 40, 74, 160, 206
Parry, J. H., 153, 155, 160, 168, 270
Parsons, Talcott, 13
Patino, José, 272
Paullin, Charles O., 234
Pelliot, Paul, 156
Pemsel, Helmut, 210, 211, 235
Pepys, Samuel, 206
Pericles, 5
Peter the Great, 284
Piedade, 161

Index

379

Pimlott, John, 85
Pius II, 7
Pivka, Otto von, 209, 272, 325
Pizarro, Francisco, 153
Polycrates, 5
Portugal as seapower, 7, 53, 56, 106, 113, 124, 151–85, 324–5, 329, 336, 337
Powell, J. R., 271
Power projection, 10, 12
Prestage, Edgar, 168
Preveza, *see* Sea battles
Prussia as seapower, 304–5

Quiberon Bay, *see* Sea battles

Raleigh, Walter, 7, 8, 144
Rapkin, David P., 41
Rasler, Karen, 208
Ray, James L., 100
Reagan, Ronald, 236
Regional powers, 18, 43–4, 134, 144, 149, 284, 318
Resende, Garcia de, 158, 159
Reynolds, Clark G., 7, 170, 171
Richelieu, Cardinal, 247, 248
Richmond, Herbert W., 268
Risk theory, 9–10, 232, 306–7
Roosevelt, Franklin D., 23
Rosinski, Herbert, 9–10
Rota do Capo, 171
Rowen, Herbert H., 190
Russia/USSR as seapower, 10–11, 283–7, 293, 302–4, 330

Sadao, Assada, 313
SALT I, 303, 304
SALT II, 243
Sandler, Stanley, 36
Scharnhorst, 310
Schepen van force, *see* Ship types
Sea battles
  Actium, 20
  Armada, 21, 22, 36, 154, 158, 172, 189, 205, 269
  Beachy Head, 207
  Cape Passaro, 272
  Chesme, 285

Coral Sea, 235, 313
Diu, 21, 156
Downs, 190–1, 271
Falkland Islands, 307
Gibraltar, 59–60
La Hogue, 21, 22, 207, 248
Jutland, 21, 210, 307
Lepanto, 21, 52, 156, 320
Leyte Gulf, 21, 314
Manila Bay, 234
Midway, 21, 235, 313
Navarino Bay, 320
Nile, 21
Oran, 266
Pearl Harbor, 21, 313
Preveza, 156
Quiberon Bay, 207
Sinope, 79, 285
Sluys, 203
Terceira, 21, 155, 247
Texel, 192
Trafalgar, 12, 21, 22, 208, 249, 272, 273
Tsushima, 286, 312
Zuider Sea, 21
Sea Beggars, 21, 59, 188
Sea control, 10, 11
Seapower
  characteristics, 11–13
  concentration indexes, 95, 100–4
  definitions, 3–4
  Greek concepts, 4–6
  indicators, 28ff
  Mahanian thesis, 8ff, 133
  role in long cycle approach, 14ff
  world order functions, 3, 11–13, 26, 140–1
Seapower and
  command of the sea, 7, 11, 17, 19
  global warfare, 18–23, 140–6
  innovation, 23–5, 61, 66, 73, 75, 144, 146, 159
  ocean power, 4
  space power, 13, 137
  world powers, 16–18, 44, –5, 137
Seapower as power medium, 13–14
Serjeant, R. B., 156, 160
Shaw, Stanford, 43
Sherwin, Ronald E., 33

380   *Index*

Ship-of-the-line, *see* Capital warships
Ship types
  caravel, 57, 58, 158, 174
  carrack, 158–9,
  Dreadnought, 75, 210, 234, 250, 307
  galleon, 57, 58, 160–5, 173, 174, 269
  galley, 27, 56, 157 (heavy, 158, 336; light, 158, 336)
  nau (Great Ship), 159, 160, 164, 166–7, 172–3, 174, 336
  Schepen van force, 190
  ship-of-the-line, *see* Capital warships
  treasure ships, 156, 336–7
  zabra, 269
Silvius, Aeneas, 7
Singer, J. David, 100, 317, 318, 338
Sinope, *see* Sea battles
Sluys, *see* Sea battles
Small, Melvin, 317, 318
Sokol, Anthony, 325
Soviet Union as sea power, *see* Russia
Space systems, 144–7
Spain as seapower, 53, 54–9, 106, 128, 152–4, 174–5, 267–73
Sprout, M. T., 91
Stalin, Joseph, 286
Steinberg, Jonathan, 9
Strozzi, Filippo, 155, 247
Swanson, Bruce, 335
Sweden as seapower, 320–4
Symcox, Jeffrey, 34–5, 192
Symonds, Craig L., 232, 233

Teitler, G., 188, 192, 248
Temple, William, 188
Terceira, *see* Sea battles
Texel, *see* Sea battles
Thalassocracy, 5
Thompson, I. A. A., 268
Thompson, William R., 15, 41, 208
Thucydides, 5, 7, 8
Tirpitz, 310
Tirpitz, Alfred von, 9, 232, 306–7

Tordesillas, Treaty of (1494), legitimacy of, 154–5
Trafalgar, *see* Sea battles
Tramond, Joannes, 155
Trask, David, 234
Trident II, 87, 143, 243
Tsushima, *see* Sea battles
Tute, Warren, 208

Union of Utrecht (1579), 98, 187
United Provinces of the Netherlands as seapower, 7, 59–61, 106, 113, 124, 132, 187–93
United States as seapower, 10, 107, 113, 130–2, 230, 330

Valla, Lorenzo, 7
Vecchj, Augusto V., 55
Venice as seapower, 6, 21, 156, 318–20, 336

Walker, B. W., 209
Wallerstein, Immanuel, 52
Ward, Michael D., 95
Washington Treaties of Naval Limitation (1922–3), 10, 211, 235, 250, 312–13
Watson, Bruce M., 287
Weigley, Russell F., 235
Wainland, Robert G., 287
Weinstein, Donald, 159, 168
Wellington, Duke of, 22
Western Europe as sea power, 138–9
Whitestone, Nicholas, 85
Whiteway, Richard S., 55
Wilhelm II, 9, 305
Wilmott, H. P., 313
Wilmott, Ned, 85
Wilson, Woodrow, 234
Winius, George D., 55, 161, 171
Woodward, David, 285
World powers, 135–6, 149
  and nation-states, 136

Yung Lo, 155

Zaragoza, Treaty of (1529), 153
Zuider Sea, *see* Sea battles